5th Day

THE LORD IS WATCHING ALL OUR MOVES TRUST ME! HE IS GOOD TO THE GOOD AND WRATHFUL TO THE BAD!!!

For your sake, God Will destroy the power of the wicked and bring their reign of terror to a sudden end in Jesus' Name. However, you must obey His Commandments and live in the fear of God and in holiness and righteousness to get the best out of God! Then you can take up a taunt against your oppressors in Jesus' Name. Amen! So, let this be our portion who hope in You securely in Jesus' Name. Amen!!! Isaiah 14:3-6 NIV

When your ways are pleasing unto the Lord He Will Take Good Care of you as in the Scripture above and in addition, He Will Cause your enemies to be at peace with you! Is this not worth working towards as a lifetime objective? Well, Lord Grant unto us the willingness to do Your Will in Jesus' Name. Amen!!! Proverbs 3:23,24 NASB

The Day of Judgement is coming folks. Do not let anybody deceive you with fine sounding words and arguments! Meditate carefully on the above Scriptures! This is the Word of God! Love God passionately with your all and love your brethren as yourself. In fact, you are encouraged to love your enemies too! Hmmmm! May God Help us to love as Jesus Christ Commanded us so as to please the Lord our God in Jesus' Name. Amen. We shall not partake of the lake of fire in Jesus' Name. But this should not just be a prayer offered; we must follow it up rigorously with the fear of God and holy and righteous living in Jesus' Name. Amen!!! Matthew 25:41-46 (NIVUK)'

Beware of false prophets! They will also perform wonders and signs but these will not be of the Lord's making at all! Pray for the spirit of discernment! Do not believe for a minute that all these signs and wonders that we're witnessing today are all from the Lord! Avoid all evil and appearances of evil at all costs. Thus, you will save your soul and those of your hearers in Jesus' Name. Amen! Father, Help us to see when You are testing us so not to yield to evil in Jesus' Name. Amen!!! Deuteronomy 13:1-5

6th Day

GOD IS ABLE TO DEAL WITH ALL OUR ENEMIES, ANXIETIES AND WORRIES! GOOD TREES DON'T BEAR BAD FRUITS BUT GOOD!!!

Most of our worries are hardly only to do with personal tragedies; but rather worries, anxieties and persecution from enemies and their likes! This Scripture assures us that God is Able to fully deal in His Wrath with all of these. All we need to do is believe and have faith and act accordingly. Lord, Help us who believe, trust and hope in You to demonstrate our faith in You fully to the very end in Jesus' Name. Amen!!! Isaiah 41:11,12 NASB

I'm not pretending that it's easy for man to love and pray for their enemies, persecutors, foes and adversaries! It's neither easy nor practical as far as man's thinking is concerned. However, when we have faith in the Lord Jesus Christ, we ought to take on the Mindset of Jesus Christ and act accordingly. There is a place for praying against one's enemies and their actions; but the better place is to practice what is clearly advocated for in this Scripture. This is very pleasing unto God who says to us that when we do so, it's like heaping burning coals on the heads of our enemies! This is huge; and more effective in dealing with our enemies. Please God, Help us to be wise; and to apply Your Wisdom always in Jesus' Name. Amen!!! Matthew 5:43-47 NLT

What Just Judgement of and from the King ultimately, at the end of all things! What is the rational/basis of the judgement? It's made very clear! Love one another! This is the ultimate Commandment of the Lord! You can only be faithful to this Commandment if you love the Father with all you've got! Based on your treatment of others is how you're going to be Judged at the end of the day! So, be very careful indeed how you entertain anyone at all including and especially strangers. You will be entertaining the Lord Jesus Christ and not know it! It's made absolutely and abundantly clear in the above Scriptures! O Lord, Help me, my family and all who truly love and follow You, to obey Your Commandment in Jesus' Name. Amen!!! Matthew 25:34-40 (NIVUK)

Know that good fruits will never grow on bad trees and bad fruits will never grow on good trees. No matter how you graft them, they will never function contrary to that way. That is the natural order of things. Only God in Jesus' Holy Name CAN Make the difference! God is Able to make a bad tree good and vice versa should He Choose so to do! The only way a good tree can be made bad is if the tree ceases to produce good fruits and begins to produce bad ones (which can happen). Then it will be cut down and uprooted! However, a good tree will be trimmed and pruned to be even more fruitful by cultivation and looking after! Jesus, Have Your Way in my life and family and in all who follow You sincerely; for only You Know who they are who follow You sincerely in Jesus' Name. Amen!!! Matthew 7:16-18 NKJV

7th Day

OUR GOD HELPS US TO DEAL WITH ALL OUR ENEMIES AND PERSECUTORS! OFFER RIGHT AND JUST SACRIFICES!!!

When you are persecuted for the sake of righteousness, you are Blessed; so rejoice and be glad because you share in the lot of the prophets who have gone before you and you partake of our Lord Jesus Christ's sufferings! Father, please Grant us to bear up when faced with persecution and hold on to You in Jesus' Name. Amen!!! Matthew 5:10-12 NIV

Strive to please God in all your ways and God Will Cause even your enemies to live at peace with you. If you have very little, but in righteousness; it's better than having much, guilty of injustice! The Blessings of God makes one rich without adding sorrows to it. Lord, Help me. Bless us in Your Own special way in Jesus' Name. Amen!!!

Strive after the righteousness of the Lord; for the Lord Will then be your Strength in times of trouble and your salvation will be from and of Him. He Will Help, Save, Deliver and Keep you from the wicked! He Will Bless you this way because you trust and hope in Him alone. Help us o Lord to never leave You; but rather to hold firmly and tightly onto You all of our days in Jesus' Name. Amen!!! Proverbs 16:7,8 NIV

We want to remain as Your sheep o Lord; Help us not to be as goats. When the great separation shall take place, Father, count us worthy to be with the sheep on Your Right in Jesus' Name. Amen!!!

What sacrifices are you offering up unto the Lord God Almighty? Do you really care about what pleases Him? You want to be like Cain or Abel? Remember Abel was murdered by his brother, Cain because Abel's sacrifice was accepted by God and Cain's rejected! If you remain in wickedness and evil, no matter how "good" your sacrifice is, do you think it will please God? No, not at all; better to clean up your act and enter into the righteousness of God and obey His Word! Then you will please Him and He Will accept your sacrifices! Help us o Lord to offer what is right, just and befitting unto You in Jesus' Name. Amen!!! Isaiah 1:11-17

8th Day

FEAR ONLY GOD! ANY OTHER FEAR IS NOT OF GOD! GOD IS NOT UNJUSTUNLIKE MAN! NEEDED, REJECTED AND BRUISED!!!

When you yield your life unto the Lord, He Will Cover you fully; and He is very faithful. That very faithfulness will be for you a defence! No evil shall befall you and you need fear nothing at all except Him! Lord, please Cover my family, myself and all who trust and hope in You in Jesus' Name. Amen!!! Psalm 91:4-6 NIV

Here, God is reminding us to get it into our heads and very beings that in a way, we dishonour Him and prove Him to be a liar and unfaithful (which He Can never be) when we fear mankind who will die instead of Him who lives forever! Lord, Help us who love and fear You to keep our focus on You and fear no other in Jesus' Name. Amen!!! Isaiah 51:12 KJV

Whatever we experience in life, no matter how challenging, we have victory! All things work for the good of all who love the Lord and are Called according to His purposes in Jesus Christ. Amen! Nothing shall separate us from the Love of God in Jesus Christ. NOTHING! Just believe, hope and trust in Him! Lord, my family and I, as well as all who look up to You need You to Help us to believe Your Word in Jesus' Name. Amen!!! Romans 8:37-39 NASB

We have a firm and confirmed assurance in God Almighty through Jesus Christ that we shall be fully protected from all evil and harm all through our lives! Does it mean that we shall not go through adversity? No! But through it all we must trust in the One who Lives forever and never ever dies! He Will Keep His Covenant of Love with us and Enable us to have a covenant of peace with our environment in Jesus' Name. Amen! O Lord, I believe in Your Word; Help me, my family and all who fear Your Name, to communicate this faith to others in my world and generation in Jesus' Name. Amen!!! Job 5:19-23

I have a Light and Salvation in the Lord my God that is Greater and Bigger than any threats that I may face in life! I shall fear no evil! The Lord Strengthens my heart and even in the face of war or any form of adversity, I remain firm, steadfast and unshaken, strong in Jesus' Name. Amen! So, let this be our portion o Lord, for we trust and hope only in You. Amen!!! Psalm 27:1-3 NKJV

God's Ways and Thoughts, hence Judgements are different than man's! God is Just and not like man! However, God's Judgements may not make sense to man; because we are not the same and do not think alike. To man, it makes no sense to take from the little someone has and give to the one that has so to increase that of the one that has! That is the God I serve! He is Jehovah my Lord God Saviour and King. His Name is Jesus Christ! Help us who hope in You to understand Your Ways o Lord and to receive Your Truth into our lives so we can be truly free in Jesus' Name. Amen!!! Matthew 25:24-30 (NIVUK)

A prophetic picture of what happened and what will happen! The very One that we need, we reject, brutalise, bruise and hurt! First, you must believe in His Holy Sacrifice and sufferings and totality of His Story as Revealed Truth! Then, you must commit your life unto Him to enjoy the benefits of His Covenant of Love and Blessings in Jesus' Name. Amen! Faith is a Gift from God that I need o Lord; and my whole family with me and all who put their hope and trust in You o Lord my Father. So please as You Have Granted unto us, do not let us lose our faith in Jesus' Name. Amen!!! John 19:37

9th Day

FAITH COMES BY HEARING; HEARING BY THE WORD OF THE LORD GOD! GET FAITH; BE FAITHFUL! THIS PLEASES GOD!!!

Again I stress that faith is not seeing is believing at all; that's what the world teaches! Faith is substantiating what you hope for as if you have received it; even as in believing you have evidence of things you have not seen nor received, even though you don't! Therefore, faith is believing even though you have not seen nor received what you hope and pray for yet. Believe you have it in hand already even though you don't. That is faith. So, faith will be seen as foolishness to and by the world! Strive to please God; for without faith no man can please God! Do this regardless of what the world thinks, says or does! Help us o Lord to have faith in Jesus' Name. Amen!!! Hebrews 11:1-3 KJV

Do you want to be rooted and established in love and receive the power of the saints to grasp the width, length, height and depth of the love of Jesus Christ? A love that surpasses human knowledge and or understanding; that fills the believer up to the measure of the fullness of God! By being so rooted and established, you will have Jesus Christ dwelling in your heart by faith! This I want for my family and I and all who love and fear Your Name o Lord. Grant unto us in Jesus' Name. Amen!!! Ephesians 3:17-19 NIV

Since, I asked Jesus Christ to take over my life and gave Him my all, it is Jesus Christ that is living through me in the life that I now live by faith in the Son of God! I have been crucified with Jesus Christ, who Gave Himself for me! My life is not the same anymore; no longer mine to live as I please! Thank You Lord Jesus! Help me to live more and more for You daily and please continue to live through me and mine and all yours in Jesus' Name. Amen!!! Galatians 2:20 NASB

Whatever you may be going through in terms of adversity, troubles, unpleasantries etc. is momentary! They will NEVER last forever! As long as they're not the result of your sinfulness and or wrongdoing, they will be helping to produce for you an eternal weight of glory beyond all comparison! What are you looking at? Circumstances that you see?

Hmmmm! What you see is temporal; it is what you do not see that is eternal. The unseen Spirit Controls the tangible which you can see! Just put your hope and trust in the Lord God Almighty in Jesus Christ! All will be well in Jesus' Name. Amen. Just believe!!! Corinthians 4:17,18 NASB

Faithfulness is always rewarded in good measure according to the measure of faith expended! If you are faithful with a little, you will be blessed with more; if you are faithful with much, you will be blessed with much more! That is to say, you will be entrusted with more and much more respectively, according to your faithfulness! Remember that the Lord Will take from those who have little and give to those who have much! This makes no sense to mankind; but to God alone be all the glory, for He alone Knows and Can Do all things in Jesus' Name. Amen! Remember also, that unto whom much is given, much is desired! Live as wise and not unwise. May the Good Lord Help us all to live for Him and thus fulfill our destinies in Jesus' Name. Amen!!! Matthew 25:19-23 (NIVUK)

Many are praying for the Lord to pass them over in times of the execution of God's Wrath! However, this is never for nothing or for free. God's Love is fully conditional! The Passover comes with an instruction that must be fulfilled! The Lord Has Spoken! If you obey the Word of the Lord and take heed of His Commandments, then the angels of the Lord will put signs upon you and your household and home! When the Lord's Wrath is striking the lands, it will pass you over in Jesus' Name. So, obey the Word of the Lord! Help me Lord to understand Your Word and to appreciate that You o Lord Paid a heavy price for my salvation! Help me and mine to do our bit in the journey of faith, so to receive the promises of God in Jesus' Name. Amen!!! Exodus 12:3-14 NKJV

10th Day

JOY THAT IS FROM GOD IS BEYOND COMPREHENSION! JESUS' KINGDOM IS ENDLESS! MAKE THE MOST OF THINGS!!!

No matter what I'm faced with; whether things are fine and favourable or not, I will rejoice in the Lord, God of my salvation. He's my Strength and will Favour me and all mine Divinely always in Jesus' Name. Amen!!! Habakkuk 3:17-19 KJV

See faith at work in the above Scripture! A special powerful joy deriving from a God that I have never seen before; yet I am not crazy! This comes to me as the goal of my faith and the salvation of my soul. Jesus Christ is my Lord God Saviour and King! Amen!!! 1 Peter 1:8,9 NIV

Those who are Saved by and in the Lord will return with great joyful thanksgiving to His Holy Hill, Mount Zion. They will obtain gladness and joy with everlasting joy on their heads; no more sorrow and sighing in Jesus' Name. O what a time that will be. Thank You Jesus that You Will Help my family and I to see this time in Divine Favour though Jesus Christ my Lord. Amen!!! Isaiah 51:11 NASB

When I look at my life and see all that the Lord Has Done for me, I am overwhelmed with the Joy of the Lord my God! For He Has adorned me like a bridegroom or a bride in their glorious attires! The Lord Will Judge the nations justly and every knee shall bow and every tongue confess that He is the Lord! His Righteousness shall be revealed and the whole world will see Him in His Glory; sadly, not all will be able to go with Him to His Destination! Lord, please count my family and I worthy of this Glory in Jesus' Name. Amen!!! Isaiah 61:10,11 NLT

And in the sixth month the angel Gabriel was sent from God unto a city of Galilee, named Nazareth, to a virgin espoused to a man whose name was Joseph, of the house of David; and the virgin's name was Mary. And the angel came in unto her, and said, Hail, thou that art highly favoured, the Lord is with thee: blessed art thou among women. And when she saw him, she was troubled at his saying, and cast in her mind what manner of salutation this should be. And the angel said unto her, Fear not, Mary: for thou hast found favour with God. And, behold, thou shalt conceive in thy womb, and bring forth a son, and shalt call his name JESUS. He shall be great, and shall be called the Son of the Highest: and the Lord God shall give unto him the throne of his father David: And he shall reign over the house of Jacob for ever; and of his kingdom there shall be no end. Luke 1:26-33 KJV

The prophetic "Good News" of the advent of our Lord Jesus Christ was received with great fear by Mary. She was however assured by the angel of the Lord that all is well as powerful words were spoken of the Lord that would blow anyone's mind away with fear! Who gives birth to God? Meditate on the Words and it is very clear what the message is! Glory be unto the Lord God Almighty in Jesus Christ for He is truly the Lord God Almighty who came to mankind to show us the way! Thank You Jesus!!!

Who said you can live anyhow you like? You have been deceived again. You better be wise! Yes, make the most/best of every chance you get; because the days are evil and you may never get another chance in your lifetime! Be alert always and act wisely! May God Give us all the wisdom we need to wisen up and act accordingly every time in Jesus' Name. Amen!!! Ephesians 5:15-16 NIV

11th Day

YOUR CONSCIENCE IS YOUR HEART'S MONITOR! WHAT'S THE CONDITION OF YOURS?!!

Often we judge others at points of our own guilt. Check yourself; judge yourself, lest you be judged. Let mercy prevail over judgement. Jesus Christ is about love and mercy; not however as a license to sin! Father, Help my family and I to allow mercy and love to prevail over judgement; in Jesus' Name. Amen!!! John 8:7,9 KJV

Purity begets purity unto those who are pure and purity inclined; whilst to the unbeliever and defiled, nothing is pure - even as their minds and consciences are defiled. As a believer, you must strive always for purity of heart, mind and all ways in Jesus' Name. Amen!!!

As a believer, you must act and behave in a manner that wins respect! Be sincere, not over indulging in wine or other intoxicants nor chasing after dishonest gain. Such attitudes and manners as would bring the Faith and or the Name of the Lord into disrepute must be loathed and avoided at all costs! Lord, please Help me to be worthy of You, my Calling and the Faith at all times in Jesus' Name. Amen!!! 1 Timothy 3:8,9 NIV

We are all prone to be hypocritical rather often for a variety of reasons; and would often quote the Scriptures to justify such behaviour! Can you imagine Jesus Christ being accused of acting against The Law for Healing a man on the Sabbath! In our faith and religion, can it be wrong to do good at any time? Should it ever be wrong to act in Love? Lord, please Help us to do and judge rightly all the time in Jesus' Name. Amen!!! Matthew 12:9-14 NKJV

12th Day

LIGHTEN UP THE EYES OF MY HEART O LORD! I AM SAVED BY GRACE! I HAVE THE PEACE OF GOD! TRUST ME O LORD; AND GUIDE MY HEART! HELP ME TO DISCERN THE TIMES!!!

Open the eyes of my heart o Lord and lighten them up so that I might see all that You Want for me to see of You and around me. I want to know Jesus Christ and the great Power of His Resurrection! The Power that is like the working of His Mighty Strength! Lord, Help my family and I and all who believe, fear, love and trust You, to know You o Lord in Jesus' Name. Amen!!! Ephesians 1:18,19 NIV

I love the peace that You give o Lord because it surpasses human understanding! I want more of this peace for I have tasted and seen that like the Lord is Good and His Mercies endure forevermore; this peace is good for humankind! Give me this peace that will keep my heart and mind in Jesus Christ my Lord, Halleluyah Amen Thank You Jesus!!! Philippians 4:7 KJV

Help me, my family and all who believe in You, o Lord; that we might understand that we are saved by Grace through faith - a gift from God not of our own strength nor accord; and certainly not of works! Then we shall not boast as if it were not so! Give us understanding and wisdom from Heaven above to live life on this earth for and in the Name of Jesus Christ our Lord God and Saviour King. Amen!!! Ephesians 2:7-9 NASB

Everybody has something entrusted into their hands by God from Heaven above. Do you know what you have been entrusted with? We all ought to know what gifts and talents God Has Given us in living through life! Many spend a whole lifetime looking for what has been there all along and yet never find it or them! Some have been Given by God to help others locate their God Given gifts and talents! I pray today for you reading this that your helper locates you and helps you discover not just your gifts and talents, but your purpose in life. God Leads us in diverse ways! God Shows some of us directly; but for some, He Sends others to reveal these things to us. I pray that in any which way, that God Will Reveal yours to you in Jesus' Name so you will not live your life in vain in Jesus' Name. Amen!!! Matthew 25:14-18 (NIVUK)

I want to believe God without need for any evidence; except that which comes when preaching His Word with signs and wonders following in Jesus' Name. Amen! I don't want to be like Thomas! I just want to believe God all the days of my life and pass this faith on to my children and their children so they likewise pass it on accordingly in Jesus' Name. So, help me o Lord God Almighty in Jesus' Name. Amen!!! Matthew 16:1-4 NKJV

13th Day

THE LORD ANSWERS PRAYERS OF RIGHTEOUSNESS; IT IS SIN THAT BLOCKS THAT ACCESS! DO NOT DECEIVE YOURSELF! BE PREPARED; MAKE UP YOUR MIND; AND BE FIT FOR PURPOSE!!!

If you love life and wish to see good days, then watch your tongue and lips against evil, lies and deceit! Do good; seek and pursue peace. Refrain from all evil and its appearances! Live holy and righteous lives so to be heard by the Lord when you pray; for the Lord's Face is against the workers of iniquity! Lord, Help my family, myself and all who fear Your Name to do good and refrain from evil and all it's appearances in Jesus' Name. Amen!!! 1 Peter 3:10-12 NIV

Is God's Hand too short to save or His Ears too heavy to hear? NO! The problem is you and your sins which separate you from God and blocks your access to the Throne of Mercy and Grace; thus, His Face is kept hidden from you, such that He Will not hear your prayers! Refrain from sin and do good and God Will hear and answer your prayers in Jesus' Name. Amen! Anyone listening?!! Isaiah 59:1,2 KJV

Confess your sins one unto another and pray for each other so that you may be healed. Please be very very careful not to expose yourself willy nilly to just any Tom Dick and Harry! You don't want to get bitten in the butt! Live a righteous and holy life and enjoy God's Favour with your prayers and life in Jesus' Name. Amen! Be very wise in the decisions you take having to do with your life! Lord, Give us wisdom to seek help in the right places in Jesus' Name. Amen!!! James 5:16 RSV

Many say they are good people and I've heard it many times. Wow! How people come to that conclusion about themselves still beats me. Anyway, I know am not perfect and am struggling with being good; may God Help me in Jesus' Name. Amen! I'm a sinner; the worst of all sinners! Forgive me o Lord; Cleanse me and I'll be whiter than snow! Teach me Your Ways o Lord and Help me to stick with Your Ways in Jesus' Name; and my family with me. Amen!!! John 1:8-9 NASB

Lord Jesus Christ, Help my family, myself and all who love and fear you to be ready, prepared and get our timings right so we're not late on the Day of Reckoning in Jesus' Name. Help us to be like the virgins who were ready for the banquet and went in with the Bridegroom! O Lord, Help us in Jesus' Name. Amen!!! Matthew 25:10-13 (NIV UK)

To be a disciple of Jesus Christ, you must hate all else and love Him without compromise! You must bear your cross and follow Jesus Christ without looking back. Following Jesus Christ is not fun and is not a business for making profit! Many have got it all wrong and need to repent before it's too late; for where they are headed is hell fire as things stand. Lord Help us who love and fear You in spirit and in truth to know Your Way and stick with You all through to the very end in Jesus' Name. Amen!!! Luke 14:25-30

If you truly and sincerely want to follow Jesus Christ, you have to prioritise Him above everything else in your life and not question His Authority ever! Do not be like one who puts his hand to the plough and looks back. You must be fit for the purposes of the Kingdom of God! Father, Help Prepare me, my household and all believers as appropriate; to be fit for the purposes of the Kingdom of God in Jesus' Name. Amen!!! Luke 9:57-62

14th Day

YOU MUST UNDERSTAND WHAT FAITH IS BEFORE YOU CAN EFFECTIVELY APPLY FAITH OR HAVE FAITH! WHAT IS FAITH?!! holy

Faith is being sure of what you hope for and certain of what you have not seen. If only people understand this fact and apply it in their lives, a lot would be achievable that appears impossible! The spirit speaks to the tangible reality in the Name of the Lord and there is a cause and effect. Spirit Word then comes tangible reality! Help me and my family o Lord to dare to believe in Jesus' Name. Amen!!! Hebrews 11:1-3 KJV

Do you know that Jesus Christ can Dwell in your heart by faith? I have Him in my heart and I am so Blessed because He Lifts me up, Turns me around and Plants my feet on solid ground. God is a Good God; yes, He IS! Continue to fill my family and I increasingly in our hearts through Jesus Christ our Lord! Amen! Help me and my family o Lord to grasp the width, length, height and depth of Your Love that surpasses all knowledge and understanding! Fill me and my family with me likewise to the measure of all the fullness of God in Jesus' Name. Amen!!! Ephesians 3:17-19 NIV

When Jesus Christ came into my life, I ceased to live carnally; but Jesus Christ lives in me! My life right now, I live by faith in Jesus Christ, who loved me so much that He Gave His Life for me! So, by faith, it is possible to live in and for Jesus Christ and that He lives in and through me. With man this may appear impossible; but with God all things are possible. What can the Lord not do? Father, thank You for making the impossible possible in my life all the time by faith in Jesus' Name. Amen!!! Galatians 2:20 NASB

Believer! Your troubles are all temporary NOT forever! Do not look at circumstances, which are seen and temporary; but rather at the unseen, which are eternal! The unseen control the seen; even as the unseen Spirit controls all things seen and unseen! Do not give in to anxiety nor fear; for the Lord our God is Able to ensure that all is well with you and yours in Jesus' Name. Trust and hope in Him unshakably in Christ Jesus. Amen!!! 2 Corinthians 4:17,18 NASB

By faith, it is not enough to do what is right; timing is very crucial! Sometimes timing could mean life or death even. Please God allow us to do what is right by You and to do so in good time and at the right time! Bless me and my family o Lord and all believers at the right time when Your Glory will be revealed in our lives and experiences in Jesus' Name. At a time when even our enemies will marvel and want to know our God o Lord Bless us in Jesus' Name. Amen!!! Matthew 25:1-9 (NIVUK)

Trust God with every sowing. Sow good seeds though very carefully and not bad seeds. In due season, you will reap a bountiful harvest of goodness and mercy from God Almighty! Be a blessing to others; for you do not know how but God Will Surely Repay your kindness and love sown into other people's lives! If you keep a careful watch on the time, you will not do any work at all. Tick says the clock; do what you have to do quickly. Time is very critical in life. You are Given time to live on earth; don't waste time! Nobody lives life without any sorrows at all; be prepared. Live your life but remember it will not all be light. There will be some dark times. Through it all put your faith and trust and hope in the Lord Jesus Christ; the Author and Finisher of our faith! Amen!!! Ecclesiastes 11:1-10 NKJV

15th Day

WHEN THE EYES OF THE LORD ARE WATCHING OVER YOU, YOU ARE FULLY PROTECTED! PERFECTION COMES ONLY IN JESUS' NAME!!!

Hmmmm! The Eyes of the Lord are not automatically on everybody; and He doesn't automatically answer everyone's prayers! His Eyes are on the righteous; but His Face is against the wicked and evil ones! If you're evil, better repent or forget it. If you suffer for doing good, the Lord is pleased with you. No harm will befall you. If the Lord is with and for you, who can be against you? Fear God and obey His Commandments and do not fear man or his terrors! Help me to have full confidence in You o Lord; so as not to fear man in Jesus' Name. Amen!!! 1 Peter 3:12-14 KJV

Praising God for delivering you from the terrors of man is akin to taunting the terrorists; as opposed to rejoicing at the downfall of the enemy. So, feel free to give Him praise whenever He Gives you victory against your enemies. Give me a heart and mouth of praise o Lord in the face of victories against my enemies in Jesus' Name. Amen!!! Isaiah 14:3-6 NIV

O for man to obey the Word of the Lord; that it may go well with man! Do you want to walk securely in your way without your foot stumbling; nor fearing to lay down and have sweet sleep? Then fear God and obey His Commandments and live for Him! Lord, Help me to live for You in Jesus' Name. Amen!!! Proverbs 3:23,24 NASB

What is the Lord's charge to you? Are you faithful to that which the Lord Has Given you to do? You had better be! If you are faithful to God, you will be Blessed bountifully! Otherwise, your reward shall be negative accordingly; you will be assigned to a place together with the hypocrites and wicked where there will be weeping and gnashing of teeth in everlasting shame, contempt and pain! Lord, I want to be in the place with the righteous! Help me to make it there in Jesus' Name; and my family with me. Amen!!! Matthew 24:45-51 NIVUK

The law cannot make us perfect for Jesus Christ. Otherwise the advent of Christ would be of no effect! Thank God for Jesus Christ who came to give us a taste of God in the flesh and to show us the Way, Truth and Life unto Perfection in the Father's Name, through the Son, who holds all Power and Dominion in Jesus' Name. Amen!!! Hebrews 10:1 NKJV

16th Day

FINDING YOUR PURPOSE HERE ON EARTH? I PROPHESY THAT YOU RECEIVE THE GIFT OF FAITH IN JESUS CHRIST RIGHT NOW AND PREACH THE GOSPEL! YOU SHALL BE FULFILLED!!!

The angels are ministering spirits of God that God Sends around the world with whatever messages He Has for all humanity! Angels are like spirits moving all around delivering God's messages everywhere! Their primary message is the Gospel! Fear God, obey His Commandments, worship Him the Creator of all humanity and the whole universe including the Heavens and the earth! May God Open our eyes, ears and minds to receive a revelation of the True Gospel and Give us the Power and Authority to proclaim it in Jesus' Name. Amen!!! Revelation 14:6,7 NIV

NOW I make known to you, brethren, the gospel which I preached to you, which also you received, in which also you stand, by which also you are saved, if you hold fast the word which I preached to you, unless you believed in vain. For I delivered to you as of first importance what I also received, that Christ died for our sins according to the Scriptures, and that He was buried, and that He was raised on the third day according to the Scriptures. 1 Corinthians 15:1-4 NASB

Many are called but few are chosen; of the chosen are some of the most stubborn! Please do not be headstrong with God or with the Word of God. Learn from the children of Israel! Sift through and discern whatever you receive to be sure that everything is aligned with the Word of the Living God! When you have received the Truth, the Lord Will Confirm this with your spirit and you will know and you will be set free in Jesus' Name. Meditate on the above Scripture very seriously so as to get from it the Will of the Lord for you, your family and your lives in Jesus' Name. Amen! Lord please prepare us to receive Your Word undiluted by the Power of the Holy Spirit in Jesus' Name. Amen!!!

God's love for humanity, like Himself is very dynamic and carries great potential! It's like a blank cheque! If you write out what you need from the bank on it, it must be very accurate; otherwise, it's null and void! With the Love of God, the condition is to believe and accept Jesus Christ as Lord God and Saviour; believing in the truth and sanctity of His Sacrifice and associated events! Then you receive baptism afterwards as a kind of seal. Otherwise, you shall be condemned! This is the Word of God! The Word of God NEVER said everybody shall be saved and is loved equally and unconditionally! Those are the words of men and women who think they know more than God! The Word of God is very clear. Lord, please Teach us the Truth of Your Word and Help us to obey in Jesus' Name. Amen!!! Mark 16:15,16 NASB

Get ready; be prepared in and out of season! Take heed; for the Lord Jesus Christ is coming back again at a time when no one knows - and those who are not ready and therefore unprepared will lose out eternally! I plead Your Blood over my life and family o Lord to Help us be well prepared for Your Coming so that we do not lose out on Eternity in Jesus' Name. Amen!!! Matthew 24:43-44 (NIVUK)

O Lord please put a sign of Your Holy Blood Shed for us on Calvary on our lives so that when You Send Your Wrath upon the lands, we are protected and shall not partake of this impending doom! Famine of the Word of God is doom unto mankind because we need the Word of God for life. The Word of God is the Word of Life! Jesus Christ is the Way Truth and Life! Lord I need You always in my life and family. Please don't ever leave nor forsake me in fulfillment of Your Promise to all who have faith in You in Jesus' Name. Amen!!! Amos 8:11-14 NKJV

17th Day

EAGERLY CRAVE THE MILK OF THE WORD OF GOD! GIVE THANKS AND KEEP YOUR WAY PURE! PREPARE FOR THE DAY OF THE LORD!!!

The way a new born baby craves after the breast milk of the mother, the believer must earnestly and sincerely crave after the Truth of the Word of God! Especially having tasted and seen that the Lord is Loving, Good and Gracious! Lord, please help my family and I to crave after the pure and sincere milk of Your Word in Jesus' Name! Amen!!! 1 Peter 2:2-3 KJV

Can you honestly say that the Word of God is sweeter than honey to your mouth and that you carry the Aroma of Jesus Christ around you wherever you go? Do you hate falsehood and lies? Where do you get your understanding from? Do you rely on your own understanding or on that which derives from God and His Word? Your answers to these questions will help define and measure your position with regard to the Word of God and the things of God! Help my family And I o Lord; that Your Word be a Lamp unto my feet and a Light to my paths! I want to be able to swear, confirm and profess that I shall keep Your Word, Commands and righteous ordinances in Jesus' Name. Amen!!! Psalm 119:103-106 NASB

The only way to keep one's ways pure is to live according to the Word of God! This applies to both the young and old. Help my family and I o Lord to seek after Your Heart with my whole heart, treasure Your Word, not wander from Your Commandments nor sin against You o Lord in Jesus' Name! Amen!!! Psalm 119:9-11 NASB

Thanksgiving due to God from all of humanity for the Advent of Jesus Christ beautifully expressed above! This is in fulfillment of the prophetic Word of God in Christ Jesus! Touch my heart o Lord that I might be grateful for who You Are in Jesus' Name!!! Luke 1:68-75 KJV

On that Great Day of the Lord o Lord my Father God Saviour and King, help me and my family to be able to stand and be Saved in Jesus' Name! Amen!!!

18th Day

WAIT FOR GOD'S GRACE IS BETTER THAN GOING YOUR OWN WAY! HE TAKES CARE OF HIS OWN! CAN YOU BELIEVE HIM?!!

God never leaves His people nor forsakes them in times of need! As His people, you must proclaim His Power, Might and Works! It pleases God so to do. The Lord our God is Awesome in His Sanctuary! Give Him Praise somebody! Praise the Lord! Halleluyah! Help me o Lord not to keep the knowledge of You to myself; Help me to proclaim You all over the world in Jesus' Name. Amen!!! Psalm 68:34,35 NIV

When the Lord Defends His children, He Strengthens them supernaturally! The weak amongst them suddenly become emboldened and strong and bold as lions. The Power of the Lord is made manifest in them and the Angel of the Lord Stands with them into whatever situations they find themselves in. They never lose a battle! Lord, I invite You into all my life and circumstances forever and ever in Jesus' Name. Amen!!! Zechariah 12:8 KJV

All things work for the good of them who love the Lord and are Called according to His Purposes! Are you on the Lord's side? Then this applies to you. Otherwise, don't even go there at all! God Blesses His people and expects thanksgiving to flow in and out of season no matter what you're going through! To God be all the Glory in Jesus' Name. Amen! Lord, let this be my family's portion and mine too in Jesus' Name. Amen!!! 2 Corinthians 4:15 NASB

Those who belong to the Lord must act increasingly like Him in every way; in faith in love and daily living! As the Lord Encourages us, we must encourage one another; even as iron sharpens iron! Vengeance is mine says the Lord, I Will Repay! God Will surely Deliver us and repay our enemies according to what they mete out to us in Jesus' Name. Amen! I will trust & hope in the Lord my God!!! Isaiah 35:3,4 NASB

Who cares to fear the Lord today? Not to fear God did not start today; but it has its consequences! Teach me to fear You o Lord; that my life may be made right before You in Jesus' Name and my family with me in Jesus' Name. Amen!!! Romans 3:18

19th Day

THANKSGIVING, BEING GRATEFUL PLEASES GOD! IF YOU KNOW GOD, GLORIFY HIM! BE SLAVES UNTO RIGHTEOUSNESS! WATCH AND PRAY! OBEY THE COMMANDMENTS OF THE LORD!!!

Who is the Master of the multiplier effect? Clearly Master Jesus Christ! What did He do first? He Gave thanks! He thus fed a multitude of people with just five loaves and two fishes! What a miracle based on thankful faith working through Love! There was a lot leftover! Who is like Him? Nobody else like Him! Lord Teach me and my family to be like You in Jesus' Name. Amen!!! Matthew 14:19,20 NIV

The Goodness and Greatness of God is very visible to every human being; except we deliberately fail to acknowledge! Yet many fail and give excuses and do not glorify Him as God; nor give Him due Honour and Respect! They dwell in vanity in thoughts, deeds and actions from their darkened hearts! In their "wisdom" their foolishness became evident! The consequences are dire! For nobody toys with God or His Word without dire consequences! Please God, Help my family and I to appreciate You and give You due Glory and Honour in Jesus' Name. Amen!!! Romans 1:20-22 KJV

You are either a slave unto sin leading to death or to obedience to the Word of God leading to righteousness and life! There are no grey areas really! You are either living in sin or not! May God Help my family, self and all who love and fear Him to be enslaved only unto Him and His Word to obey with just rewards accordingly in Jesus' Name. Amen!!! Romans 6:16-18 NASB

Salvation is very personal! No husband will be saved necessarily because of his wife and vice versa! When the Lord Comes a second time and the elect are caught up with Him in the air, some will be taken up and others left behind. We all need to be prepared in and out of season because nobody knows the Time this will take place. But be assured that the Lord is Coming! Father, please prepare my family and I for this Time in Jesus' Name. Amen!!! Matthew 24:40-42 (NIVUK)

Love does no harm to its neighbour! If you dishonour your parents, sleep with another man's wife or woman's husband, covet other people's things, then you are doing them harm! We would do well to keep the Commandments of God; not for God's sake, but for our own sake and for the sake of other human beings like us! So, ultimately, obeying God's Commandments is in our own best interests and our present and future generation's wellbeing! Father, Help my family and I to honour You and Your Words and Commandments in Jesus' Name. Amen!!! Exodus 20:17

20th Day

BE VERY GRATEFUL! DO YOU NOW FEEL YOU OWE GOD GRATITUDE? WE WHO BELIEVE ARE THE AROMA OF JESUS CHRIST! PUT YOUR FAITH TO WORK THROUGH LOVE!!!

Do you understand that our God in Jesus Christ always Leads us in Victory? That means you and I will never lose a battle! Do you think because Jesus Christ was crucified and John the Baptist beheaded, they lost the battle? Think again! Greater gain unto them both. Jesus Christ is the Lord God Almighty! John the Baptist is in Heaven! Being the aroma of Jesus Christ means you carry His Spirit with you wherever you go; you are His ambassador! Likewise, your family has an aroma as do you! However, the aroma of Christ supersedes all others. So, I opt for the aroma of Christ every time in my life. Help me o Lord to carry the aroma of Jesus Christ; bringing life to others according to the LIFE that I carry around with me in Jesus' Name. Amen!!! 2 Corinthians 2:14-15 NIV

There must be no sexual immorality amongst believers at all! Anything that connotes sexual immorality; be it in dressing, behaviour or attitude must be shunned and avoided completely. Such is not the aroma of Christ Jesus; but rather of the evil one! Foolish talking; even in jest/joking likewise must not be condoned nor engaged in at all! Greed and all filthiness is considered idolatry in God's Eyes and such as perpetuate any of such behaviour cannot have a place in the Kingdom of Christ and of God! Father, Help me to remove anything and everything that would not allow me to gain access into the Kingdom of Christ and of God in Jesus' Name. Amen!!! Ephesians 5:3-5 KJV

Believers ought always to encourage each other in the Word of God; with psalms, hymns, spiritual songs etc.; singing and making melody inwardly and outwardly unto the Lord Jesus Christ always, with thanksgiving! This is appropriate with due fear unto the Lord God in Jesus Christ! Lord, Help me to do so increasingly in my life day by day in Jesus' Name. Amen!!! Ephesians 5:19-21 NASB

The Day of the Lord is coming when the Lord Jesus Christ Shall Come again! Nobody knows the time though except God alone! Normal activities will continue as it was in the days of Noah when the floods came suddenly upon the people and swept them all away; apart from Noah, his wife and his three sons and their wives! Be prepared in and out of season; for the Lord our God in Jesus Christ shall surely come as promised! Father, please prepare me to be ready for the second coming of our Lord Jesus Christ. Amen!!! Matthew 24:36-39 (NIVUK)

What is "it"? It is FAITH! May God allow my family's faith and my faith to lead to good testimonies like in the cases of our forefathers in the Faith in Jesus' Name. Amen! May God Give us a revelation of what faith truly is and Enable us to have true faith that moves mountains. For the only thing that matters in life is Faith that works through Love! Help me to have Faith and Love in increasingly good measures according to my Father's Riches in Glory in Jesus' Name. Amen!!! Hebrews 11:2

21st Day

THERE SHALL BE JUDGMENT FOR ALL! FOR SOME IT SHALL LEAD TO EVERLASTING THANKSGIVING; OTHERS DAMNATION!!!

This is a glimpse of what happens in Heaven. One can only imagine what happens in Heaven apart from what we have in terms of the Inspired Word of the Living God! For sure we know that our God is Holy; was, is and is to come! He is Eternal! Yesterday, today and forever Jesus Christ is the Lord God Almighty and is Eternal! Heaven is aglow and alight with Joy, Love, and Thanksgiving in ever overflowing beauty and magnificence in Jesus' Name. Amen! O Lord, I want to go to Heaven when I die; Help me to make it with my family in Jesus' Name. Amen!!! Revelation 4:8-10 NIV

We ought to ascribe greatness and thanksgiving unto the Lord our God for who He is, what He has done and all He Promises to do! Nations rage against You o Lord and we can see with our own eyes the animosity towards You. They forsake the fact that You Possess the Power to Judge all and Give to all their due rewards. Some to suffer Your Wrath and others Blessed by Your Grace in Jesus' Name. Amen! Father, consider me worthy to receive Your Mercy and Grace on that Day o Lord in Jesus' Name. Amen!!! Revelation 11:17-18 KJV

And all the angels were standing around the throne and around the elders and the four living creatures; and they fell on their faces before the throne and worshiped God, saying, "Amen, blessing and glory and wisdom and thanksgiving and honour and power and might, be to our God forever and ever. Amen." Revelation 7:11-12 NASB

Again, a glimpse into what happens in Heaven! God is greatly praised, worshiped, adored and glorified! When we all get to Heaven, what a time of rejoicing that will be! When we all see Jesus, we'll sing and shout in victory! O Lord, Help me to be with the saints when they are marching into Heaven in Jesus' Name. Amen!!!

May God Enable us to be Blessed to discern the sign of the times! Only by so doing can we know how to respond to the circumstances we find ourselves in at any given time! The Word of God is Eternal! Heaven and earth will pass away; the Words of God will never! Father, Help us to appreciate and understand You, Your Ways and Your Words in Jesus' Name. Amen!!! Ephesians 5:8

I was born and bred in darkness until I came to know Jesus Christ as my personal Lord God and Saviour King! Now I am in the Light. Should I return to darkness having known the Light? Hmmmm! This is what many of us do. We somehow tend to show preference for darkness as against Light. May God Help us to choose Light over darkness always in our lives in Jesus' Name. Amen!!!

22nd Day

THANKS BE UNTO THE LORD JESUS CHRIST THAT WE HAVE THIS HOPE OF ETERNAL LIFE! WHEN HE COMES THE ELECT SHALL BE GATHERED UP UNTO HIM FROM EARTH'S FOUR CORNERS!!!

When I meditate on the Lord Jesus Christ; all He Stands for and what He Has Done for me, I am deeply humbled because my filthiness and unworthiness is revealed unto me. Also, I see clearer, His Holiness, Godliness, Countenance etc.; and I am drawn closer to Him every day! I am enslaved unto His Laws and His Person in my mind and all! However, in my sinful nature, I am enslaved to the law of sin and death. Jesus Christ set me free; and Gave me an opportunity to be done away with the law of sin and death, to embrace the law of Love and Life with freedom in Jesus Christ. For this and much more o Lord, I am forever grateful! Thank You Lord Jesus for such love that exists nowhere else but in You!!! Romans 7:24-26 NIV

When we break the Bread and drink the Cup, we do so in thanksgiving for the Supreme Sacrifice; the Giving of the Body and Blood of Jesus Christ on the Cross at Calvary! Although we who believe are many, we partake of one Loaf of Bread and One Cup; the Body and Blood of Jesus Christ! He's enough for us; the Man of Galilee is enough for us! Behold, how good and pleasant it is when brothers dwell together in unity! Lord, please Help unite us in You in Jesus' Name. Amen!!! 1 Corinthians 10:16-17 NIV

We have true victory only in Jesus Christ! Better to trust/hope in Him! For if you trust in the law for your victory and justice, you forget that the law is actually the power of sin. When you keep sinning, you are dying; killing yourself slowly. The sting of death is sin! Will you continue to allow death to sting you? We all have that choice to make! Help me o Lord to make the right choice and stop sinning! Then I have true victory; for only Jesus Christ Can Make this possible! The alternative is to focus on doing the work of the Lord unshakably! For in the Lord only, is our labour not in vain! So, Help me and my family o Lord in Jesus' Name. Amen!!! Corinthians 15:56-58 KJV

One day is coming when the Lord Jesus Christ shall return to earth with great noise, pomp and glory! On that day, inhabitants of the earth shall mourn; the elect of God shall be gathered from the whole earth, to be caught up with the Lord in the air! Will you be there? It's easy to say nobody knows; but we have been Given a Standard by which to measure ourselves before the final Judgement! Help me o Lord and my family with me; that we be counted worthy to be in that great gathering on that Day in Jesus' Name. Amen!!! Matthew 24:30-31 (NIVUK)

Father God, please do not allow my labour and that of my family to be in vain o Lord in Jesus' Name. I know that for us to bear good fruit that will last, we need Your Breath! Grant us bountifully o Lord, so that our sowing will not be upon unfertile soil but rather on very fertile soil so as to yield for us a bountiful harvest ultimately in Jesus' Holy Name. Amen! I have seen the Lord's Goodness, His Mercy and Compassion; I have seen the Lord's Goodness, Halleluyah! Praise the Lord! For o Lord You Have Been so good, You Have Been so good to me. O Lord You Are Excellent in my life every day! Amen! Halleluyah!! Thank You Lord Jesus!!! !" Matthew 13:4-9

23rd Day

THANKSGIVING UNTO GOD CAN NEVER BE OVER EMPHASIZED!
THE SUN SHALL SHINE NO MORE! FEAR IS NOT FROM GOD!!!

It is good to praise and thank the Lord! Halleluyah! Tell of all He Has Done; sing unto Him in exaltation! Praise draws God's Presence unto His own people! Lord, Help us to appreciate You in Jesus' Name. Amen!!!

If you take a look at your life reflectively and meditatively, you will find that you have enjoyed God's Mercy at one time or the other; or indeed many many times without number! God is therefore always due our thanksgiving which comes out of a heart of love and faithfulness! Father, Give me a heart to love You and show gratitude for all that You Do for me in my life in Jesus' Name. Amen!!!

You who forget God and or claim there is no God at all; consider your position very well or risk being torn in pieces without anyone to deliver you! For those who appreciate God in their lives and show it in thanksgiving and in ordering your ways according to His Word; you honour God and He Will Show You His Salvation in Jesus' Name. Amen! Lord, Grant that my family and I be part of the latter in Jesus' Name. Amen!!!

This is a message for a sign of the end times. On that day, the Sun shall not shine anymore; for it shall be darkened! The moon shall turn to blood and will not give its light. The Heavens and earth shall be shaken and the Lord Shall Appear in the midst of sinners. The saints shall be caught up with Him in the air; not sinners! Where will you be? Hmmmm! Now is the time to repent; it will be too late on that day or when you are already dead! Lord, Help my family and I not to lose out on that day in Jesus' Name. Amen!!!

Fear is not Given to mankind by God. Even the fearful will not make it into the Kingdom of Heaven. Perfect love drives away all fear according to the Scriptures. God Gives not the spirit of fear; but rather of love, power and a sound mind! Fill my family and I o Lord with Your Love, Power and a sound mind in Jesus' Name. Amen!!!

24th Day

THE SIGNIFICANCE OF GRATITUDE IN ALL THINGS IN LIFE EMPHASIZED! DENY SELF, TAKE UP CROSS, FOLLOW JESUS!!!

Receiving Jesus Christ is not the end of your faith in Him; it's the beginning! To be rooted in Jesus Christ, there is a lot of work for the believer to do! Gratitude most essential; but you must follow the Biblical teachings obediently. Don't listen to those who teach you that once saved, always saved; salvation can be lost, just like the Holy Spirit may be withdrawn from a person living contrary to the Word of God as experienced by many already. Be careful. Father Help my family and I to have a grateful heart and to take up our Cross and follow Jesus Christ obediently in Jesus' Name. Amen!!!

Without Love, all else is meaningless; with all else, put on Love. Love is the bond of perfection. Be ye holy and perfect as God is is all about the application of Love, which does no harm to neighbours! Your holy living affects not God but fellow human beings like yourself, animals, birds and your environment really! But significantly spiritually reckoned as per dealings with human beings! Gratitude is an essential part of love for a heart that appreciates God and Goodness. Love encourages others too; all in the Name of the Lord Jesus Christ and for His sake. So, Help my family and I please o Lord in Jesus' Name. Amen!!!

We are to show gratitude to God even for our very Faith which is in itself a Gift from God; many do not have this gift sadly! With our gratitude, the fear of God must be evident and made manifest. Remember that our God is an all-consuming Fire! Lord Help my family and I to fear You in addition to being grateful in Jesus' Name. Amen!!!

Let all the world in every corner sing unto the Lord in gratitude that He Has Created us and not we by ourselves! We are supposed to be the sheep of His Pasture. We ought to enter His Gates with thanksgiving and His Courts with praise and Bless His Holy Name! For the Lord our God is Good and His Mercy endures forever! What excuse have you got not to be grateful to God? If a slave can think deeply, even he or she will be grateful! In Yoruba: b'eru ba mo'nu ro; a dupe! Lord, Help me to be grateful for all You Do and Have Done for me in my life and family in Jesus' Name. Amen!!!

Following Jesus Christ is not about doing nothing except accepting Him as Lord God and Saviour and making the relevant confessions! There is much more! You must deny yourself, take up your cross and follow Him daily! You must forsake your life and all else for Him and then you will gain true Life! May God Grant my family and I the wisdom to walk with Him in the Light of His Love in Jesus' Name. Amen!!!

25th Day

FOR THE BELIEVER, THE LORD IS SAVIOUR, KEEPER, REFUGE, COMFORTER, DELIVERER AND! FORSAKE WORLDLY LUSTS!!!

You cannot deceive nor mock God; He Surely Knows those who are His, who rely on Him - separate from pretenders and hypocrites! For them He's a veritable Stronghold in times of trouble!!!

For the genuinely oppressed (not those who are rebellious) - God Knows the difference - God is their refuge in troubled times. Those who seek Him and Know His Name to do so, He NEVER puts to shame; He never leaves nor forsakes them. God is Just!!!

Delight yourself in the Lord and He Will Strengthen your resolve to live life to the fullest and Bless you! Once the Lord delights in your way, He Will firm up your steps; that though you stumble He Will uphold you with His Hand and not let you fall. Thank You Lord that You Count me worthy in Jesus' Name. Amen!!!

He keeps the feet of His godly ones, but the wicked ones are silenced in darkness; For not by might shall a man prevail. 1 Samuel 2:9 NASB

The Godly ones are Kept standing by God; but the wicked who think that they can prevail only by their might and despise the Lord, are silenced in darkness! The Godly are Kept in the Light of God; for their hope/trust and all are in the Name of the Lord. Help me o Lord to remain on Your Side in Jesus' Name. Amen!!!

When you wait upon the Lord faithfully believing that only He Can Save you, He Will not disappoint you. That's why He turns to you and hears you cry. The Lord Will lift you out of the pit of despair, from the mud and mire of life; He Will Plant your feet on solid ground and firm up and steady your steps as you walk along in Jesus' Name. The Lord is Good all the time; all the time the Lord is Good. Thank You Jesus for Your Faithfulness! Amen!!!

It is the Grace of God that Enables a man by the Power of the Holy Spirit to forsake worldly lusts and live a sober, Godly life in today's world! The believer must keep his focus on our God and Saviour Jesus Christ, who Poured Himself out with great love on the Cross to purify us believers for Himself and for His Works of Goodness and Mercy. Teach these things authoritatively; and He our Lord God and Saviour Will Back you up with His Holy Spirit. Do not let anyone despise you; they will do, but never let them get to you in Jesus' Name. So, Help us o Lord to do Your Will in Jesus' Name. Amen!!!

26th Day

LOVE ONE ANOTHER SINCERELY FROM THE HEART; HATE EVIL; AND PROVE YOUR LOVE IN OBEYING THE WORD OF GOD!!!

How can you call what is not sincere love? How can you claim to love when you do not hate evil, but rather act as though you love evil? Do you know that you can train yourself to embrace love and goodness with righteousness? Bodily exercise profits a little bit but spiritual exercise profits in all things! Practice love and hospitality. Put brotherly love into action; honour others about yourself. Yes! You can do this. Start now! It's never too late to love. Father, come into my life and rule over me always forever with and in LOVE. Thank You Lord Jesus. I pray in Jesus' Name. Amen!!!

God's "new" commandment has been since beginning of creation! Love! We are urged to love each other as God Loves us. This is how others will know that we are His disciples. This command is not for everybody willy nilly. This is for believers specifically and should not be misapplied! We who believe must be characterised and hence identified by LOVE! Lord, Help us to love one another sincerely and earnestly from deep in our hearts in Jesus' Name. Amen!!!

Did you ever consider that obedience to the Truth and God's Word purifies your soul? Well, now you know! Our confidence in God is through Jesus Christ because He is in every way God! In loving one another, we are also purifying our souls. We should love each other purely and sincerely from our heart! May God Help us to do this increasingly all our lives in Jesus' Name. Amen!!!

The purpose of God's Instructions and Commandments to us is that we all who believe should be filled with pure love from pure hearts, a clear conscience and a sincere faith! Everything about us must be driven by a deep sincere faith that works through love! Can you swing that? Will you at least have a go? It seems impossible because of the many intrigues of mankind but it's not impossible for those who believe! Father, please make the impossible possible in my life and the lives of all who trust and hope in You sincerely in Jesus' Name. Amen!!!

For those of you and us who have been Taught the way of Love by God Himself and are putting this to practice always, let us love increasingly as we have been Taught! Loving is sowing seeds and we shall ultimately reap a bountiful harvest of love with faith and righteousness in Jesus' Name. Amen. Lord, Help us to increase in love always in thoughts, words and deeds in Jesus' Name. Amen!!!

When the Lord Blesses you, strive to be a blessing to the servants of God in your life who serve you in spirit and in truth! Such servants will present such in the Presence of God; in short, to God and you will be increasingly Blessed! The believer should put this to practice always in Jesus' Name. Amen! May God Bless us to do this more and more in Jesus' Name. Amen!!!

27th Day

OUR GOD IS FAITHFUL; HIS PROMISES ARE YES AND AMEN IN CHRIST JESUS! OBEY HIM AND ENJOY DIVINE FAVOUR ALWAYS! FORCEFUL VIOLENT FAITH WORKS AND PLEASES GOD!!!

You o Lord are worthy to be praised, exalted and adored for You are Perfectly Faithful; proved by Your Marvelous Deeds prophesied long ago. Help me o Lord to give thanks, exalt, praise and magnify You and Your Name in Jesus' Name. Amen!!!

When You walk according to the Ways of the Lord in obedience to His Word, He Will Grant you rest, peace, protection and all goodness to enjoy! He Will Keep your heart inclined unto Himself; to walk in His Ways in keeping with His Commandments, Statutes and Judgments, as Instructed in the days of old to be kept forever! Lord, please draw us unto Yourself; that we may do right by You and thus enjoy Your best in every way in Jesus' Name. Amen!!!

"For the mountains may be removed and the hills may shake, But My loving kindness will not be removed from you, And My covenant of peace will not be shaken," Says the LORD who has compassion on you. O afflicted one, storm-tossed, and not comforted, Behold, I will set your stones in antimony, And your foundations I will lay in sapphires. "Moreover, I will make your battlements of rubies, And your gates of crystal, And your entire wall of precious stones. All your sons will be taught of the LORD; And the well-being of your sons will be great. In righteousness you will be established; You will be far from oppression, for you will not fear; And from terror, for it will not come near you. Isaiah 54:10-14 NASB

Even though the mountains and hills may shake or be removed, the Lord's Loving kindness and Covenant of peace will not shake. This is for those that fear Him and prove their love to Him with their obedience to His Word! No matter what you face, He Will Protect, Defend, Uphold and Root you to His Word. He Will Bless you and your children with and after you. You will not live in fear and or oppression; you shall be established in righteousness! Is it not so good to be in the Lord Jesus Christ? Father, please Root me to Your Word and let me be forever established in Your Righteousness in Jesus' Name. Amen!!!

Every Promise made to you by the Lord God shall come to pass as in the case of Israel in Jesus' Name. Amen. However, have you heard from Him? Do you know how to seek His Face? Do you know how to wait on the Lord? Do you dig into His Word to find out His Will for your life? You need to train yourself; submit yourself for training by the Holy Spirit in the Ways of the Lord. If you do, you will forever be satisfied with good things according to His Promises in Jesus' Name. Amen! Who is ready to follow the Lord Jesus Christ? I have decided to follow Jesus; will you join me? Seriously?!!

You who by your actions enjoy whitewashing darkness in your lives and ways; so as to deceive the world and yourselves, take heed, or you cannot deceive God, who Sees all things! Your very actions shall stand as evidence against you on the Day of Judgment! Repent and seek forgiveness for all your sins and hypocrisy; perhaps the Lord Will be Merciful to Forgive you and Heal you and Bless you in Jesus' Name. Amen! Do not be deceived; God is not mocked. A man will reap what he has sown! Amen! Mercy o Lord, I plead in Jesus' Name. Amen!!!

You need violent forceful faith to be effective and fruitful not just in taking and entering into the Kingdom of God, but also to bear good fruits therein! This has been the case with the forefathers in the Faith from time immemorial. It will not change. You need to be bold, courageous and fearless in the Faith. Are you in the Faith? Is your faith violent, forceful, bold, courageous and fearless? If not, ASK and God Will Grant unto you in Jesus' Name. Amen! Lord, Grant me this type of effective faith in Jesus' Name. Amen!!!

28th Day

SHOW ME WHO AMONGST US IS CLEAN AND WITHOUT SIN AND I'LL SHOW YOU JESUS CHRIST MY LORD GOD SAVIOUR AND KING! STRIVE AGAINST HYPOCRISY AND LIES (SATANIC PLOY)!!!

Many deceivers abound; pretenders who talk as if they are God and without sin. They sound like they're holy and righteous but with their cupboards loaded with skeletons. Arrogant and without humility; and yes loved by the people and mostly very popular! Watch out; lest you be caught out and lose out on the Kingdom of Heaven. They do not want anything to do with the Kingdom of God and always serve to block those who want to enter! Their judgements await! As for those who humble themselves willingly and are willing to bow to the Lord and who want to be Saved, I offer to you, Jesus Christ, Son of the Living God; God who came to humanity in the flesh - Wonderful, Counselor, Everlasting Father! All you need to do is believe His Story and Sacrifice and prove your faith with deeds commensurate with your profession and confession! Father, Help our unbelief and Teach/Lead us in the Way of Holiness and Righteousness through Jesus Christ our Lord God and Saviour in Jesus' Name. Amen!!!

There is a great hypocrisy and falsehood in the teachings of some so-called ministers of the Gospel; so much so that you must scrutinise whatever you are taught by studying the Holy Bible for yourself and asking the Holy Spirit for Revelation and Discernment to be sure you are being fed the correct spiritual food. Many simply trust in these "servants" of God not knowing that they are servants of satan their master, the liar and father of all lies and liars! They preach to you standards that they themselves do not live by or use! Whatever right that you need to do is discouraged as long as it's not in their personal interest and or for the benefit of their stomachs and or pockets! Flee from them. God Will Reveal their hearts to you if you seek after the Truth of God! Father, please Deliver us from false prophets and their teachings; Lead us aright in Jesus' Name. Amen!!!

Falsehood and lies cannot and should not be the portion of believers in the Lord Jesus Christ! Being born again, you must strive against and resist the devil! Your mind must be submitted with your life and your everything to the Truth of Jesus Christ. You shall know the Truth and the Truth shall set you free is what the Word of God says. But nobody will force you to root yourself in the Truth. That is your responsibility! Be renewed in your mindset and knowledge according to the Image of Him who created you, Jesus Christ our Lord! Father, draw us unto Yourself in Jesus' Name. Only You Can Help us o Lord; please Help us in Jesus' Name. Amen!!!

29th Day

FRUIT OF THE WOMB IS GOD'S REWARD TO MANKIND, A BLESSING; SO CRUCIAL TO FAITH IN JESUS CHRIST!!!

The Word of God says that sons are a heritage from the Lord and children His reward. I believe the Word of God. Indeed as arrows are in the hands of a mighty warrior are sons born in one's youth. Because, by the time they grow up to be responsible adults, their father (parents) are still young and fit. They will be able to take care of the family business and defend the family against intruders etc. So, it is a special Blessing from God to have a son; however it is a great reward to have children, male or female. Many make the mistake of assuming and always trying to equalise the male and female children. God did not make us equal! Both men and women have their roles carved out by God. This is now a very controversial issue in today's world; however, I'm compelled only to speak the Word of God as Revealed to me! Father, Help us to decipher Your Word in Jesus' Name. Amen!!!

Who does not know that parents are very proud of their children in general; especially when the children are doing well and living right? The significance of fatherhood to children has been heavily politicised and underplayed in today's world where many now say men are not that relevant in the family scheme! However, even to the female children, their father is often more important to them than their mother or indeed anyone else in the world apart from their husbands when they marry! The best thing for a family is for both parents to be present to care for the children and raise them together God Willing! Lord Help us to preserve our families in Jesus' Name. Amen!!!

God Shows Mercy to the barren women and Blesses them with their own children so they can make a home. Is a home complete without children? Even in the Sight of God the Giver, a Home is made up of a Husband,

Wife and Children! Never mind all the evil political correctness pervading the environment of today! When God Blessed Abraham to make him a multitude of people. He started with one son only, the rest is history! God is GREAT! Enlarge my coast o Lord I pray in Jesus' Name. Amen!!!

Jesus Christ never rebuked the little children nor did He ever side-line them. He brought the children into the mainstream of His Ministry and Spoke the Word that all who come into the Kingdom of God must come only as little children. What a holy recognition for the little children! Wow! Help me o Lord to be as a little child always in Your Presence in Jesus' Name. Amen!!!

How many of our ministers today fly all over the world claiming to be winning souls to whom they preach corrupted messages which in turn prevent the people's access into the Kingdom of God. You must scrutinise what you're being taught carefully to be sure that it is the Word of God so you do not get led astray! God Help us to learn the truth of Your Word so we are not led astray in Jesus' Name. Amen!!!

Which nation on earth is not guilty of this charge laid by the Lord? May God Help to cleanse our lands and heal us so we do not all perish in Jesus' Name. Amen!!!

Straying from the Way of God is harlotry according to the Word of God and that enslaves the heart like new wine. Once the heart is enslaved, it becomes a servant to the master (enslaver)! Do you not know that you are a slave to the one who has mastery over you and your life? Be careful folks; lest you bow to masters other than the Lord God of hosts! Help us o Lord to have Your Yoke firmly around our necks so we serve only You in Jesus' Name. Amen!!!

30th Day

OUR GOD IS AN AWESOME, SOLID, MERCIFUL, RELIABLE GOD! YOU CAN TRUST/HOPE IN HIM FULLY IN ALL THINGS!!!

They that love and fear the Lord can be sure of safety, blessings and well-being; because God Takes Special note and cares for them adequately and effectively. God Will NEVER leave nor forsake them! O Lord, my Father, please let me continue to abide in You and You in me, through Jesus Christ my Lord, God and Saviour. Amen!!!

This God is very trustworthy; He never lets His own down. No shaking for the righteous with Him in Jesus' Name. Lord, Grant me to have confidence in You and in Your Presence in Jesus' Name. Amen!!!

The Word of God is the greatest source of comfort for the believer; and there is a reason why we have the Word of God! In this world of sin and evil, there will always be troubles coming our way; but we must not fear, for we have the Word of God for assurance that all will be well in Jesus' Name. Jesus Christ, our Lord has overcome the world and when we trust/hope in Him, we have no need for fear! He Will Take good care of us and our interests. Help me o Lord, that all my interests and I are fully catered for in You in Jesus' Name. Amen!!!

Jesus Christ never leaves His own in confusion and turmoil; but rather in peace, tranquility and harmony! No need for any anxiety of heart, nor fears, just believe Him and in His Word. All shall be well with you in Jesus' Name. Amen! Lord, Help my unbelief! Make my heart to be right with You and that I may have right standing with You, my Lord, God and King in Jesus' Name. Amen!!!

We have a lot of hypocrites who profess faith in Jesus Christ for a show! They are very vane and love vanity! They teach for the benefit of their own stomachs. The believer must be very careful not to be like them; desiring official tags and or positions is their lot and not yours the believers'!

Whoever wants to be great amongst you must be your servant. It is those who humble themselves that will be exalted by God and those who exalt themselves shall be put down! Be wise! Father, Teach us to be wise and to discern, know and do Your Will in Jesus' Name. Amen!!!

Before the advent of Jesus Christ, the modicum of justice differed; then it was an eye for an eye and a tooth for a tooth, although vengeance is Mine says the Lord! However, with the advent of Jesus Christ, you do not any longer need to defend nor fight for yourself! The battle is the Lord's; He Will fight your battles for you and avenge you upon your enemies in Jesus' Name. Amen!!!

31st Day

PRAY FOR LEADERS! BELIEVERS IN LEADERSHIP; SERVE WILLINGLY NOT AS A MUST! LIVE BY THE WORD OF GOD!!!

Religion and politics? Somebody asked! Let humans learn to be fair and sincere for a change! Everyone talks about and is involved in politics in one way or the other! But the moment a servant of God comments on political issues, he/she gets labeled! Let us examine God's Word as above and reflect on it! If God does not want servants of God to be involved in politics, why would He ask us to pray for leaders? When things happen in politics and servants of God say nothing, they still get blamed and labeled; so it's a no win situation. Just be focused on Your Commander as a servant of God; He is the One you must please not any man. Learn to ignore the ignorance of men and women who think they alone possess wisdom! God, continue please to Direct the steps of Your servants in Jesus' Name. Amen!!!

When you serve as an elder believer, you should do it willingly; not as though compelled as a must! God Knows the role money can play in the life of human beings. Money can turn a saint into a monster in the twinkle of an eye! Do not be greedy; and don't lord it over those under your care. Lead by example. Servant leadership as Jesus Christ modeled perfectly is the best option in the Eyes of God! Lord, Help us to obey Your Word; so we can live successfully and effectively for Your Name's sake in Jesus' Name I pray. Amen!!!

Imitate the faith of the faithful who preach the Word of God to you. So, you cannot afford to follow anyone blindly; you must watch their lives very closely and be sure they practice what they're preaching to you! You will see and experience the results of their conduct; then if positively spiritual in Jesus' Light, then imitate! Otherwise, don't even bother! It's very dangerous to imitate the ways of a person that is fake or makes claims of following Jesus unmatched with their lifestyle and daily living! Lord, Help us to make the right choices and decisions in the Faith in Jesus' Name. Amen!!!

God is not a God of the dead but rather of the living! My pastor preached this to me many years ago. I saw him several years later and he changed his message to God's a God of both the living and the dead. I disagreed politely! We get into "superior" wisdom when we do not remain humble in our disposition to the Word of God! We are overpowered with intellect; this works against the very core essence of faith! Be careful what you believe! Do not add to or take away from the Word of the Living God or you pay dearly! Help us o Lord; that we might live according to Your Holy Word daily in Jesus' Name. Amen!!!

Satan always attacks the believer's mind! You have to be bold, strong, focused and courageous in your faith; otherwise you may lose it! Your mindset will be challenged and attacked; sometimes relentlessly! You must stand firm and remain standing in the Faith in the teachings of Jesus Christ. Many live for their stomachs; and will do anything it takes to fill their stomach - no matter how good or bad! The believer must live in, for and by the Word of the Living God alone at all times! Jesus Conquered satan with and in the Word of the Living God! Remember also that satan knows the Word of God and will try hard to use it against you as well! Father, Grant us wisdom in Jesus Christ to overcome the wiles of the devil in Jesus' Name. Amen!!!

32nd Day

WHEN YOU COMMIT YOUR ALL INTO GOD'S HAND, HE WILL GUARD, GUIDE, DIRECT AND PROTECT ALL YOUR AFFAIRS! STRIVE TO PLEASE HIM ALWAYS AND BE BLESSED!!!

Is this God your God permanently or you have only given Him temporary access in your life? Do you want God to be your temporary or permanent Guide, Guard, Protection and Director of your life? Do something about it NOW! May God Give you the wisdom to act before it's too late in Jesus' Name. Amen!!!

And thine ears shall hear a word behind thee, saying, This is the way, walk ye in it, when ye turn to the right hand, and when ye turn to the left. Isaiah 30:21 KJV

Listen out for the Voice of the Lord and He Will Direct your paths in life. Learn to listen to His Voice and obey! May God sensitize you to His Voice and give you the heart to obey so to be Blessed in Jesus' Name. Amen!!!

God is Love and is Kind! He Will Lead and Guide the blind aright even through paths they do not know. If you make out that you can see and are not blind, you lose out of the Blessings of God. If however you humble yourself and accept that you are blind, you will see by His Grace in Jesus' Name. Amen!!!

No matter how bad your situation is, if you put your trust/hope in the Lord, you will not ever be put to shame. He Will always Light up your paths no matter how dark; He Has the Power - for to Him even darkness is as Light! You need not fear any evil; for you have the Lord on your side always. Help me to stay on Your side o Lord in Jesus' Name. Amen!!!

Do the Lord's Will and work in His vineyard, doing what He puts your way; and He Will Bless you in all your ways! He Will Bless you and your children with you. Your whole household will be Blessed. He Will Help you always to rebuild your walls and you will be as a well-watered fountain and never lack any good things in Jesus' Name. Stay in the Lord's Will therefore in Jesus' Name. Amen!!!

Wherefore, my beloved brethren, let every man be swift to hear, slow to speak, slow to wrath: For the wrath of man worketh not the righteousness of God. Wherefore lay apart all filthiness and superfluity of naughtiness, and receive with meekness the engrafted word, which is able to save your souls. But be ye doers of the word, and not hearers only, deceiving your own selves. For if any be a hearer of the word, and not a doer, he is like unto a man beholding his natural face in a glass: For he beholdeth himself, and goeth his way, and straightway forgetteth what manner of man he was. But whoso looketh into the perfect law of liberty, and continueth therein, he being not a forgetful hearer, but a doer of the work, this man shall be blessed in his deed. James 1:19-25 (King James Version)

Be slow to speak or anger and quick to hear. Anger does not bear good fruit nor does it lead to righteousness in the Lord! Avoid all appearances of evil and stay away from all evil. It is in your best interests to obey the Word of God as stated so you will be Blessed in every way. May God Help us all to live for Him in Jesus' Name. Amen!!!

The Lord Will not automatically be with you or anyone! You must seek good and not evil so you will live and God Will be with you! You must hate all evil and love the good! You must act justly always so the Lord God Almighty will be good and gracious to you always in Jesus' Name. Amen! Take heed the Word of God!!!

33rd Day

**YOU HAVE TO SERVE SOMEBODY; THE DEVIL OR THE LORD!
I HAVE DECIDED TO FOLLOW AND SERVE JESUS MY LORD!!!**

A pop musician sang long ago: you gonna have to serve somebody... whether it be the devil... whether it be the Lord... you gonna have to serve somebody! No two ways about it! If not the Lord, it has to be the devil! There's no in between! As for me and my household, we will serve the Lord! That is the bottom line for me. May God Help you my reader to make the right choice as I have done. No one can force you; this is a choice you must make yourself.

We who believe are to serve the Lord with fear, trembling and rejoicing; striving to please the Lord, lest he be angry. I want to be blessed because I take refuge in Him. Help me o Lord to remain dwelling in the secret place of the Most High God in Jesus' Name. Amen!!!

It is written! Every one knees and all, tongues and all, must bow to Him and confess His Lordship in Jesus' Name. Amen! Father, please let my confession be only to You and my knee bow only to You in Jesus' Name. Amen!!!

My heart is fixed, O God, my heart is fixed: I will sing and give praise.

I have my heart fixed on You o my Lord! I have decided to follow Jesus! No turning by, no turning back! Help my heart o Lord to remain fixed on You in Jesus' Name. Amen!!!

Never use God as an excuse to sin; because God does not tempt anyone! When and if you sin, stop blaming it on God please! Take responsibility! Please God, Help me to live for you and not to engage wilfully in sin! Sin is so sweet and very tempting. O Lord please protect me in Jesus' Name. Amen!!!

34th Day

THE JUDGE (JESUS CHRIST) IS STANDING AT THE DOOR! PRODUCE FRUIT OR LOSE THE KINGDOM OF GOD! HEAVEN'S FOOD; FEED ME O LORD IN JESUS' NAME. AMEN!!!

Do not judge people arbitrarily at all; and if you must judge, do so rightly and for good reason. God is all in all and He would sometimes use us to rebuke, admonish, correct and judge each other. However, it's much better that we judge ourselves, lest we be judged! With regard to the Faith, judge yourself to see that you are still in the faith! Is there any point in judging people based on their preferences for one day over another in the Faith? I would say no point. But let each person be fully convinced in what they believe by faith; for anything not done in faith is better not done at all and without faith anyway, no one can please God! Lord Help us not to judge other people; and we must, to do so with good intentions and to judge justly and rightly in Jesus' Name. Amen!!!

God Has Called us to humility and gentleness! Be completely humble and gentle in all your dealings with each other and with other people. This will please the Lord our God! Father, Give us Your Holy Spirit to Enable us to humble ourselves and be gentle always in Jesus' Name. Amen!!!

In the Faith, lots of patience is required; and stand firm because the Lord is Coming back again; and He Will Judge all! Grumbling is not pleasing to God; even against each other, let alone against God Almighty! Father, Help us not to grumble; we live in a world full with evil. Help us o Lord, in Jesus' Name. Amen!!!

Produce fruits in keeping with righteousness for the Kingdom of God; otherwise, you will not enter in or if you are already in, you will be removed! Our Lord God is an all-consuming FIRE! When you are full with the Truth and you are not afraid nor ashamed to preach and teach the Truth, the authorities will come against you! Such authorities include and will usually begin with the authorities within the so-called household(s) of faith! Hmmmm! Jesus Christ will Judge; and He Will be fully Just! Lord, Help us to fulfill our Calling and to produce fruits in keeping with righteousness in Jesus' Name. Amen!!!

When in the Lord's service and under His Guidance and Direction, you will often find that there will be times when you will not be able to eat normally and you will not even be hungry. At such times, you will be Fed from Heaven above with food that mankind do not ordinarily know about! There is nothing like the food of the Holy Spirit! Jesus Knew this food always because of His being the Holy Deity! Feed us Heavenly Father, Feed me, with the food that man does not know about in Jesus' Name. Amen!!!

35th Day

OFFER SACRIFICES OF PRAISE AND THANKSGIVING ALWAYS;
BEWARE FALSE MIRACLES; REJECTED YET EXALTED LORD!!!

For in the day of trouble he will keep me safe in his dwelling; he will hide me in the shelter of his tabernacle and set me high upon a rock. Then my head will be exalted above the enemies who surround me; at his tabernacle will I sacrifice with shouts of joy; I will sing and make music to the LORD. Hear my voice when I call, O LORD; be merciful to me and answer me. Psalm 27:5-7 NIV

I will give thanks and praise to the Lord, my Rock, Salvation, Redeemer, Deliverer, Fortress and my all in all! He Will deliver me from my enemies around me and exalt my head above them. For this reason, I will shout with joy, sing and make music to the Lord my God; who Hears my voice when I call and shows me mercy even in answering me! O Lord, please continue to hear and answer me when I call unto You in Jesus' Name. Amen!!!

But I have trusted in Your mercy; My heart shall rejoice in Your salvation. I will sing to the LORD, Because He has dealt bountifully with me. Psalm 13:5,6 NKJV

They that trust in the Name of the Lord shall renew their strength; they shall run and not be weary; they shall walk and not faint! My hope and trust is in You o Lord! You always deal mercifully and bountifully with me; I will praise you in song and with musical instruments. My heart shall continue to rejoice in Your Salvation o Lord. Help me to not forget nor forsake Your Blessings upon my life and family o Lord; give me a heart of thanksgiving in Jesus' Name. Amen!!!

He sent His word and healed them, And delivered them from their destructions. Let them give thanks to the LORD for His loving kindness, And for His wonders to the sons of men! Let them also offer sacrifices of thanksgiving, And tell of His works with joyful singing. Psalm 107:20-22 NASB

Tell out my soul the greatness of the Lord; including all that He has done for me and for us! Shout out His praises from the mountain tops and declare His Goodness and Mercy! He Sent His Word to heal our diseases and delivered us from all evil; for this and more, we shall thank Him! Help us to acknowledge Your Kindnesses to us in Jesus' Name. Amen!!!

Jesus said to them, 'Have you never read in the Scriptures: "The stone the builders rejected has become the cornerstone; the Lord has done this, and it is marvellous in our eyes"? Matthew 21:42 (NIVUK)

Even though you may be rejected; remember that He was rejected first! What then happened to Him, He is Lord! Rejected, yes; but now exalted above all! That same way, if you walk with the Lord and in His Ways obediently, you will be rejected and suffer persecution! However, you will ultimately be exalted in Jesus' Name. Amen! Lord, Help us to endure when faced with persecution in Jesus' Name. Amen!!!

Today, there's a huge drive and following for miracles and the relevant pastors. Be wary folks. Be very wary children of God. Follow God not man nor miracles! You had better receive the Love of the Truth into your lives so that you will be saved. Only the Love of the Truth can set you free and save you! Otherwise, you will be under the strong delusion sent from the Lord to those who are perishing because they have not received the love of the Truth! Help us o Lord to love the Truth. Open our hearts to receive the Truth in Jesus' Name. Amen!!!

36th Day

WORK IN THE NAME OF THE LORD IS NEVER IN VAIN; STRIVE TO BE DRIVEN BY LOVE TO WORK IN HIS NAME ALWAYS!!!

God is Just! Remember this always. Whatever comes your way, God Knows about it; whether you choose to believe that or not! Our God is in full control! The diligence you show to God in showing love to His anointed and beloved servants and your own brethren shall not go in vain! Do not stop. Stopping would jeopardise your ultimate hope and goal; so keep doing the good to ensure your lot in Jesus Christ through your patient faithful perseverance. So, Help us please o Lord in Jesus' Name. Amen!!!

The effectiveness of the Gospel preached will produce such fruits as evidenced by the willingness of the recipients to engage in doing good works in the Name of the Lord unto His saints and the brethren believers continuously. All of this is achieved with the Help of the Word delivered with "power" in the Holy Spirit and with deep conviction. If you do not believe deeply in what you are preaching, there is no point; for anything not done in faith is best not done at all. Help us o Lord to be driven by a faith that works through love; because this is the only thing that matters in Jesus' Name. Amen!!!

We all can learn a lot from the ant and its ways! You need to study the ways of the ant or learn from what others have studied about the ant. Do not emulate the sluggard who revels in making trouble and getting tired unproductively and extremely lazy; always sleeping and tired and heavy! The ways of the sluggard is an open invitation to poverty and want! Emulate the ways of wisdom like the ant's every way. The ant is so organised and effective although without an official leader! Ants collaborate to achieve great feats daily. Lord, Help us to learn from the ant and be as the ant! Hmmm! Who would have thought that one of the tiniest creations of God has anything to teach us or that we can learn from? Teach us in Jesus' Name. Amen o Lord!!!

In short and simple words. The stubborn ones that initially refuse to believe the Word of God and later do so obediently putting their learning to practice are better than those who accept willingly but refuse to obey! Hence, the despised ones we call unbelievers and sinners who turn and appreciate the Word of God with humility and change their ways are far better than those of us who claim to be born again and continue in utter disobedience! Help us to take the right decision and stick to it right through to the end!!!

The Lord is wanting to gain access into your heart today! He Will and Does not ever force His Way into anyone's heart! Listen! Do you hear His Voice and or His Knocking? Will you let Jesus Christ in today? He wants to have fellowship and Holy Communion with you! Oh what a joy unspeakable awaits you if you will just let Him in! Come into my life/ heart (3ce) Lord Jesus! Come in today, come in to stay; come into my life/ heart, Lord Jesus. Amen!!!

37th Day

GOD'S KINGDOM: NOT ABOUT WORDS BUT POWER! ARE WE MAKING DISCIPLES? LIVE FROM PREACHING THE GOSPEL!!!

In following Jesus Christ effectively, you need the Holy Spirit for "Power"; as you preach the Word of God, His Power manifests! That's the way it was right from the beginning, so it is now and so it shall forever be, world without end. Amen! We need "Power" o Lord; Give us "Power" o Lord to do Your Will in Jesus' Name. Amen!!!

Some believers just do not grow, basically out of pure carelessness and a lack of zeal for the undiluted Word of God! They need milk, not solid food; they are still infants, unacquainted with teachings about righteousness! Whilst those that trained themselves through constant use of the Word of God, are able to distinguish good from evil! They can handle solid food! Father, Help me grow in the Word of God, so I am able to teach and not remain in infancy, in Jesus' Name. Amen!!!

We have the Command from the Lord to do the work of the ministry: to teach all nations, baptizing them in the Name of God, the Father, Son and Holy Spirit. We ought to teach others to obey the Commandments of God (Jesus Christ)! In so doing, He Will be with us to the very end (always; not sometimes)! Amen! Are we doing this? Hmmm! Check yourself; you who claim to be in the Faith! Are you still in the Faith? May God Help us not to stray from His Ancient Paths in Jesus' Name. Amen!!!

For the disobedient, the Word of the Lord will be perceived as orders upon orders all lined up to be obeyed; and a little here and a little there! Hence, they shall stumble backwards repeatedly, be broken, snared and taken captive. They shall remain perpetually in sin; as if there is no way out! To obey is better than sacrifice! Help us o Lord; for without Your Help, we are finished. Help us in Jesus' Name. Amen!!!

Jesus Christ was wise in responding to challenges and queries regarding His Authority/Power Whilst they were trying to catch Him out, He ended up catching them out in their craftiness! Boxed up; they couldn't answer Him and He in turn refuse to give into their craftiness! Lord Teach us to be wise like You in Jesus' Name. Amen!!!

This Scripture legitimises reaping from sowing the Word of the Living God! However, it does not authorise the schemings of mankind - of those who preach the Gospel purely for gain! God is not mocked; we shall all reap whatsoever we sow! Help true servants of God who minister to you; meet their needs and God Will Bless you in Jesus' Name. Half a word is enough for the wise! Lord, only You can "Touch" hearts to give to Bless Your servants! So let it be o Lord, in Jesus' Name. Amen!!!

38th Day

RESPONSIBILITIES TO GOD WITH TRUTH AND MERCY?
GOD'S OR MAN'S GLORY? WHO BOWS TO WHO? FAITH
CAN DO!!!

A true believer must understand that all Glory belongs to God; even though God Gave some glory to mankind! The glory of young men is in their strength; grey hair, the splendour of the old; woman's hair, her glory! May God Enable us all to know and understand that no one lives in this life for ever; and to be wise to take stock in Jesus' Name. Amen! Also, that we might know that all of man's glory is vanity at best; so therefore, before the Lord or in His Presence or in prayer, man's glory must bow, be humbled and or covered in humility (as counseled by the Word of God in the case of head-covering for women, when praying or prophesying)! May God Help us to be wise to obey His Word and not lean upon our own understanding In Jesus' Name. Amen!!!

Everybody has their responsibilities to God, expressed through behaviour and attitudes towards fellow human beings! When you serve mankind and or look after the creation of God, you are serving God; especially in serving mankind! The responsibilities of the old is laid out as above; meditate dutifully on the Word of God! Do we still care in this world about our responsibilities? As young men, women, parents, children, people in authority etc., do we know or take our responsibilities seriously? Hmmmm! Let us all remember that an account is taken of everything we are doing on earth, including every foul word that we speak! Help us please o Lord God, to do what is right in Your Sight in Jesus' Name. Amen!!!

The Power of God, like His Love is very much present and available to all; but who has faith to tap into this Power? To the faithful, the Power of the Lord is manifested. There is no limit to what the Lord Can Do through our faith! Faith can achieve much; and in fact can do all things through Jesus Christ who Gives us strength! Speak the Word! Think, speak and do by faith in Jesus' Name; and you will see the Hand of God Almighty! Father Give us a faith that moves mountains in Jesus' Name. Amen!!!

What does the Lord require of us according to the Word of God? To love God and act justly and with mercy! We do have a part to play! We have a duty and responsibility to God! We do not just receive the Love, Grace and or Blessing of God in vain! If the Love, Grace and Blessing of God were unconditional, we would have absolutely no responsibility to God at all. There would be nothing required of us! But, all through the Word of God, God makes all these clear to mankind. Be wise to know that you need to allow your faith to manifest and work through love to please God and for Him to continue His Love towards you and Bless you in Jesus' Name. Amen! This is what I see all through the Word of God! Help us o Lord to be wise to know and act upon the Word of the Living God in Jesus' Name. Amen!!!

39th Day

TO FOLLOW JESUS, SELF DENIAL IS CRITICAL! FORSAKING WORLDLY LUSTS, WALK IN THE HOLY SPIRIT (YOUR MASTER)! WHAT YOU SOW, YOU SHALL REAP! LISTEN TO GOD'S VOICE!!!

This is for the proponents of God's so-called unconditional love! Why is there a need for Jesus to say this to us if His Love to us is absolutely unconditional? Saved by Grace and all? Where then does the self-denial fit in or come to play? At what stage of the unconditional love do we have to do anything at all to have or continue to receive the Love of Jesus Christ who is God?! I shudder to think what would happen if God dealt with mankind according to our devious, fleshly and emotional way!? Hmmmm! Please Help us o Lord to discern Your Word, correctly teach and apply the Word in our lives in Jesus' Name. Amen!!!

We are clearly required to deny ourselves and live holy, godly lives; forsaking fleshly lusts and worldliness! At the same time, we must not lose focus of our Blessed hope; the Second Coming of our Lord Jesus Christ, the Great God, our Saviour! Yet, some argue that Jesus Christ is not God! Is this Scripture not clear for example?!!

When you say you belong to Christ, it cannot be simply by your words alone; it must be through your action! Faith living is not words-led; it's action-driven! If for Christ, then live by Christ's Standards and Word! God, Father, please Help us to live for You in Jesus' Name. Give us Your Holy Spirit to Help us in Jesus' Name. Amen!!!

We are slaves to whosoever or whatsoever we obey or has mastered us! What or who is your master? More critically, who or what do you want to be your master? Jesus! I want you! I want and need you to be my Master! It is You, Lord Jesus, that I want to obey! Keep me away from evil and sin; Help me to commit fully to Your Word and Standard in Jesus' Name. Amen!!!

You have the choice to keep deceiving yourself or to shape up and obey and trust in God and live for Him! If you live for evil and sin, you are sowing evil fleshly seeds and you will reap accordingly! Likewise, if you live holy and godly, you are sowing seeds of good by the Holy Spirit and will reap accordingly too! Do not be tired of sowing good seeds; for ultimately you shall reap accordingly! In doing good, prioritise the faithful, the believer! May God Grant us wisdom to discern good from evil and to focus on good in Jesus' Name. Amen!!!

Hear my cry o Lord. Let me be like You. May I be like You. I love You more than anything and anyone o Lord! Keep me from strife, evil, etc.! I have no power of my own; Holy Spirit, I look up to You, I know, I have no power of my own! Help me o Lord; I need Your Help every breath I take. I shall not dwell on circumstances. Keep me well focused and rooted in You I pray in Jesus' Name. Amen!!!

40th Day

GODLINESS WITH CONTENTMENT IS GREAT GAIN!
THE LOVE OF MONEY IS THE ROOT OF ALL EVIL! LEARN
CONTENTMENT!!!

When you are at peace in your heart, soul and mind, you will not succumb to the spirit of greed, covetousness and avarice! If you believe that God is with you and for you, He Will Provide all your needs. Put your whole trust in Him. Then the love of money will be far from you. Then the root of evil will not be established in your life. Otherwise, you are in trouble! Father Lord, please keep us free from the love of money which is the root of all evil in Jesus' Name. Amen!!!

If we have our basic needs met, there is no need for succumbing to the love of money, which leads to other associated loves! Be contented with what the Lord Provides for you and save yourself from unnecessary heartaches! After all, we brought nothing into this world and take nothing with us when we leave! Father, Grant us wisdom to obey Your Word and be free from the love of money; so that the root of evil shall not be established in our lives in Jesus' Name. Amen!!!

Do not fret when evil doers prosper! Do not envy them! You cannot be like them; if you fret and envy them, you will be tempted to be like them to your own peril! Just fear God and obey His Commandments! There is a hope and a future for the man of peace; for the righteous man who fears the Lord! Bless us o Lord; that we may fear You and obey Your Commandments in Jesus' Name. Amen!!!

The believer will have opportunity to experience diverse stages in life for their own learning and benefit; so they can trust God and be contented whilst living holy, godly lives! You can live through any circumstances because the believer can do all things through Jesus Christ who Gives them strength! Thank You Lord that You Give us strength to be able to do all things; because with You, nothing shall be impossible! Amen!!!

The Lord is Able to Bless but also possesses the Power to curse! May we not fall under the wrath of the Lord nor His curse in Jesus' Name like the fig tree! Please Help us o Lord in Jesus' Name. Amen!!!

41st Day

IF YOU PUT YOUR TRUST/HOPE IN THE LORD JESUS CHRIST, HE WILL PROTECT, GUIDE, DEFEND, DISCIPLINE AND BLESS YOU!!!

The Name of the Lord is a formidable Shield, Buckler, Fortress, and Defence for the believer! He is very reliable and trust worthy indeed, in every possible way - including ways that you cannot think of! Blessed be the Name of the Lord! Thank You Lord Jesus!!!

The Lord Will Keep you when you put all your hope/trust in Him. You will come to no harm (even though you may be tested fiercely)! You will be protected and preserved from all evil in both your going out and coming in forever in Jesus' Name. I will call upon the Lord, who is worthy to be praised; so shall I be saved from my enemies! The Lord Reigneth! Blessed be the Lord; may the Rock of my salvation be exalted! The Lord Reigneth! Blessed be the Lord; may the Rock of my salvation be exalted! Amen and Amen!!!

The redeemed of the Lord are known to the Lord and called by name; they are His! No matter what they go through in life, they will come to no harm; nor in their own strength, but just because they belong to the Holy One of Israel! Thank You o Lord for Your Protection and Support always in my life and in the lives of all who believe in Your Holy Name. Amen!!!

If you allow yourself to be humble enough to dwell in the shelter of the Most High God, you will abide in the Shadow of the Almighty! Then you can have confidence to witness and testify to the fact that the Lord is indeed your refuge and fortress! You no longer have need for fear! Just trust in God and be always conscious of His Divine Protection and trust fully in Him! Regardless of what happens even around you, you will be Kept Safe by His Mighty Presence around you. I submit myself fully to You o Lord; please be my family's shelter from all evil in this world in Jesus' Name. Amen!!!

The wrath of the Lord came upon those desecrating the Temple! Do not think that because God is Love and forgives etc. that He Will not punish sin and rebellion! Many take the Name of the Lord for granted. Let us remember how He disciplined Israel! Although the Father punishes the son that He Loves, it is futile and very dangerous to keep trying God willfully; for He is an Awesome God, an all-consuming Fire! Lord, I pray that You do not let Your wrath come upon me in Jesus' Name. Amen!!!

Check yourselves believers and test yourselves that you are still in the faith; so that your hearts are not deceived to turn aside to serve and worship other gods! You can have the Lord's Protection and all; but you have a responsibility to check yourself and strive to stay on the Lord's side and not bend towards the worldly ways and paths. Father, please, keep my heart and family so as not to stray away from Your Ways in Jesus' Name. Amen!!!

42nd Day

GOD IS FAITHFUL; CALLS TO FELLOWSHIP WITH JESUS! HE IS A COVENANT-KEEPING GOD! AVOID THOSE DIVIDING YOU!!!

Covenant-keeping God; there is no one like You! Alpha Omega, there is no one like You! Halleluyah! He is a jealous God! He keeps His Covenant of Love with a thousand generations of those who love Him and keep His Commandments! O Lord, please Help us to do Your Will so that we can enjoy Your Covenant-keeping nature in Jesus' Name. Amen!!!

Our Lord God visits the sins of the fathers upon their children right up to the third and fourth generations of those who hate Him (if you do not obey God, it is considered that you hate Him; no grey areas in this)! If you are not on His side, you are against Him and hence you are under His Judgement here on earth; even before the Judgement to come! Help us o Lord to be obedient to Your Word; so we are not under Your Judgement!!!

O Lord my Father, please Help me to be faithful to You as You are to me; that I may stand firm to the end with my confession of hope in You without wavering! I know that You are a Covenant-keeping God; and You have Called me into fellowship with Your Son, Jesus Christ. Help me to be faithful to Your Call upon my life to the very end in Jesus' Name I pray with thanksgiving in my heart. Amen! Halleluyah!!!

Be alert and observant! If you are not alert, how can you be observant? For example, you do need to be aware of those causing divisions amongst the brethren, so to avoid them like a plague; for they do not serve our Lord Jesus Christ! They use flattery to deceive many, for the sake of their own belly, to satisfy their greed and avarice! In your obedience, be wise unto good and simple unto evil with the knowledge that God Will certainly crush satan under your feet in due season. I pray that the Grace of our Lord Jesus Christ fall permanently upon us who hope in Him sincerely and truthfully in Jesus' Name. Amen!!!

43rd Day

GOD'S CHILDREN HAVE A GREATER HOPE IN RIGHTEOUS LIVING; HUMBLY TRUST GOD; DON'T BE LAZY NOR CONCEITED; JUDGEMENT SECURED FOR SATAN!!!

Eyes have not seen, nor ears heard, nor the heart conceived, what the Lord has in store for those who love Him! We who believe hope for the second coming of our Lord Jesus Christ and that when He appears we shall be changed in the twinkle of an eye from mortality to immortality and be like Him! In such hope, we are purified, even as He is pure! Father, please do not allow our hope to be dashed or come to nothing in Jesus' Name. Amen!!!

The Grace of God unto salvation has been availed unto all mankind; for all to choose to believe Him or not! We must choose to live sober, righteous, godly lives in this evil world; awaiting the glorious second coming of our GREAT GOD (please note those who say Jesus Christ is not God) and our Saviour, Jesus Christ! The One who gave Himself for us; that we might be redeemed and purified unto Himself, a chosen generation, a royal priesthood, a peculiar people, zealous for doing good deed! O Lord, Enable us to fulfill destiny in Jesus Christ. Amen!!!

Wealth, like success engenders a measure of conceit. The minister of the Gospel must instruct the rich not to be conceited nor put their trust and hope in their riches; but rather on God, who richly supplies all things unto us for our enjoyment! Father, Enable us to put our full trust and hope in You and in nothing else in Jesus' Name. Amen!!!

Regarding true believers, we who believe must continue to hope for the best according to the gift and grace of salvation although we may admonish and be very disciplined and unwavering in our approach! Know this! That God will never forget your labour of love and such will never go in vain; especially as meted out to the saints! God's Promises are yes and amen in

Christ Jesus; even according to His Promise made to Abraham which He fulfilled in due season and unfailingly! The believer must not be slothful; but follow after the example of diligence unto the attaining of the ultimate goal of faith in Jesus Christ. Help us o Lord in Jesus' Name. Amen!!!

The judgement of God upon satan is secure! Just like the false prophet and the beast have already received their judgement and it shall come to pass that they shall be cast into the fiery lake where they will be tormented from everlasting to everlasting in Jesus' Name. So, let no one make any mistake about it; there is no peace for the wicked! Satan is doomed forever in Jesus' Name. O Lord, please spare Your children; so we do not partake of the judgement of the devil in Jesus' Name. Amen!!!

44th Day

WHO IS THIS JESUS CHRIST OUR REDEEMER THAT LIVES FOREVER IF NOT THE ALMIGHTY GOD? HE IS JUST!!!

As for me, I know that my Redeemer lives, And at the last He will take

His stand on the earth. Even after my skin is destroyed, Yet from my flesh I shall see God; Whom I myself shall behold, And whom my eyes will see and not another. My heart faints within me! Job 19:25-27 NASB

Because He Lives, I can face tomorrow; because He Lives, all fear is gone! Because I know, He Holds the future, my life is worth the living just because He Lives! Because my Redeemer Lord lives, I know that I shall live too in Jesus' Name! I shall see Him face to face on that Day! My hope is not crushed nor dead/defeated! My hope is alive in Jesus' Name. Amen!!!

Who is my Rock and Redeemer, my Commanding Officer, who I desire to please with the words of my mouth and the meditation in my heart? Is He not God? Who is called Biblically, Wonderful, Counselor, Prince of Peace, Everlasting Father, Mighty God? Who is God except our Lord; who is the Lord except our God? How can we miss such a revelation of Truth? The Way Truth and Life (JESUS CHRIST) is the Lord God of Abraham, Isaac and Jacob! Blessed be His Glorious Name. Halleluyah! Amen!! Thank You Jesus!!!

Who is this Redeeming Angel that saves from all evil? He is referred to as an Angel of the Lord or of God! He is called many names; yet one and same God! Also, what is this blessing except the one God Himself pronounced upon Abraham! Why are humans so hardened and fail to believe that Jesus Christ is LORD? Nobody else can do what He has done and does! Yes, He referred to "His Father" often in Scriptures; but that is for our own good and learning! At the same time, He made statements like: "when you see Me, you have seen the Father!" Is it not partly why He was crucified? Because He called Himself God and Son of God etc.? O Lord, I thank You for this revelation; do not let this world take this away from me in Jesus' Name. Amen!!!

Again "our Redeemer" from of old! Abraham nor Israel may not acknowledge us; but there is ONE who Knows us! Our Redeemer! His Name is Jesus, Higher than any other name. The sweetest name of all! The Strong Tower; to whom the righteous run and are Saved! At the Name of Jesus, every knee shall bow and every tongue confess that Jesus Christ is Lord! What does He is Lord mean if not He is God? Tell me you who are claiming to be wise! O Lord, do not let me shake in the knowledge of who You Are in Jesus' Name I pray. Amen!!!

Jealousy and envy no matter how much it may appear to be justifiable is never a good thing. It always leads to negativity! Be contented with whatever you have. That will help you avoid greed and avarice; and keep your eyes focused aright, as against the focus on what somebody else has that you earnestly crave! Many evil ideas are laid to rest at the feet of contentment! Many wars are never started because of contentment! God is Just! He Can And Will do whatever pleases Him; who can challenge Him? There is wisdom in the story of the owner of the vineyard choosing to pay everybody one denarii regardless of when they started their daily work for him! Father, Grant unto me Godliness with contentment; that I might have great gain in Jesus' Name. Amen!!!

Abraham's faithfulness is rewarded because it is sincere! Faithfulness is likened unto Truth; and incurs a Blessing from the Lord always. As long as the faithfulness is not unto evil; because satan loves to mimic good! Abraham's Blessings are mine! I am Blessed in the morning, afternoon, evening and all! My whole body is Blessed and wherever I go or am, Blessings flow in Jesus' Name. O Father, Bless me increasingly and forever as You Blessed Abraham our father in the faith in Jesus' Name. Amen!!!

45th Day

JESUS CHRIST, LORD GOD IS OMNIPOTENT, OMNISCIENT, OMNIBENEVOLENT, OMNIPRESENT, OMNILOVING!!!

Once in the Lord Jesus Christ, NOTHING can separate us from God's Love in Christ Jesus our Lord; nothing! He is All-Powerful to redeem, protect, deliver us from every threat, danger, negative force that may come against us to try and snatch us from His Love! Father Lord God, I know You Will NEVER leave nor forsake us; nor let anything separate us from Your Love. Thank You Lord in Jesus' Name. Amen!!!

I recall these same words spoken of the Lord Jesus Christ in the New Testament so many years later! If almost or exactly the same words are used to address and or describe two powers, does it make no sense then to accept that both powers are one and the same? Well, Biblically, it is made explicit that Jesus Christ is the Lord God Almighty! Only God Can do any and everything; unto whom all hearts are open and all desires are known. He is Omniscient, All-Knowledgeable!!!

The Lord our God is All-Powerful, Omnipotent! From His Works, we can see the evidence of His Great Power and His Outstretched Hands - in His creation! Nothing is too difficult for Him! Be Thou exalted and glorified o Lord in my life, family and in all who trust You truthfully In Jesus' Name. Amen!!!

Who is like unto Thee o Lord? What nation or individual is likeable unto the Spirit of God? Who can perform His kind of feats? There is none Holy as the Lord; there is none besides Thee; neither is there any Rock like our God, there is none Holy as the Lord! The whole world is absolutely nothing; incomparable with the Lord God Almighty! How Great is our God, His Name and Renown. He Performed and Performs Great feats like no other! Help us o Lord that we might appreciate and give You due reverence in Jesus' Name. Amen!!!

If the owner of a vineyard has power to give remuneration to his workers as he deems fit and is just in doing so, how much more Just is our God in giving us our dues in life and in the life to come! Jesus Christ be praised for ever more; from everlasting to everlasting! Like those workers complaining, we can complain all we want, God is Just in dealing with everybody in this world; who can charge Him? Father, I ask in Jesus' Holy Name that You Show me Your Mercy and Grace in Jesus' Name in all that I engage in in my life. Amen!!!

Draw near to God and He Will Draw near to you; the Bible says! Yet, no one can come near to Jesus Christ unless the Father (He) Draws him! Only Jesus Can Enable anyone to draw near to Him; and He possesses the Power to raise all whom He Chooses up at the last Day! O Father, in Jesus' Name, Help me to be amongst those that You Will raise up at the last Day in Jesus' Name. Amen!!!

46th Day

THE REDEEMED HAVE TRUE SABBATH REST IN CHRIST JESUS! HE RESCUED US FROM THE FUTILE LIVES WE LIVED BEFORE!!!

Even in the coming to us in the flesh in Jesus Christ, God set us a perfect example of life in Him; likewise, He Showed us the way in resting, encouraging us to do the same. Strive to enter into that rest therefore; so you do not fall like the children of disobedience! Lord God our Father, Help us to enter into Your rest, secured in Your Love!!!

Our Lord Jesus Christ markets and celebrates doing good; calling upon those who are suffering and under heavy yokes of bondage to come to Him for rest assured! He Counsels all to be yoked in Him and learn from His humility and meekness; hence, to find rest for their souls. He assures all that His yoke is bearable, as is His burden. However, only the humble will come to Him; for to come to Him is to accept your weakness and inability to resolve your own problems and that you do need help. However, for all who come humbly like little children, they will find rest and peace for their souls in Jesus' Name. Amen. Lord, Help us to come to You; so to find rest for our souls in Jesus' Name. Amen!!!

In the creation effort, even God rested on the seventh day and Blessed that day and sanctified it; what an exemplary leadership directly from the Lord for mankind to follow! Do we understand, let alone follow the Lord's Counsel though? Hmmm. May God Help us to understand, appreciate and obey His Counsel; for His Will is the best option for us in life in Jesus' Name. Amen!!!

Our redemption and the ransom for our futile lives lived prior to Jesus Christ coming into our lives did not come through perishable things like the cravings of mankind for silver, gold, etc.! Oh no! Rather, we were saved by the Precious Blood of Jesus Christ; as destined before the foundation of the world, manifested in the end times for our sake. Oh thank You Lord Jesus for the Saving Grace extended unto myself, family and all who choose to believe in Jesus' Name. Amen!!!

What shall wash my sins away? Nothing but the Blood of Jesus! What can make me whole again? Nothing but the Blood of Jesus! O Precious Blood of God, that washed me white as snow; no other blood I know, nothing but the Blood of Jesus! What else shall I render unto the Lord for my sinfulness and filth that will please Him? For the salvation extended unto me free of charge by the Blood of the Lamb, what is required of me? Simply to act justly, love mercy, walk humbly with my God and to Love! Father, Help me to show appreciation for Your Supreme Grace to Save my soul by Loving You and proving that love by obeying Your Word in Jesus' Name. Amen!!!

47th Day

OUR HOPE LIVES IN CHRIST JESUS; AN ANCHOR THAT KEEPS OUR SOUL! LOVE WILL NOT LET HOPE DISAPPOINT US! WHO TRULY SEEKS THE LORD? FOR A CLEAN HEART I PRAY LORD!!!

When you become born again, you have a new birth into this living hope through the Rising of Jesus Christ from the dead into an inheritance that can never perish or fade. This inheritance is kept in Heaven for all who are shielded by the Power of God until the coming of the Final Salvation to be ultimately revealed!!!

The love of God being poured out into the believer's heart through the Holy Spirit renews our hope continuously so that hope does not disappoint us. If your hope is truly in Christ Jesus, you will never be disappointed; especially in as much as you live your life in obedience to His Word and Will. Thank You Lord Jesus for Your Faithfulness!!!

God has set a hope before us who believe and have chosen to take refuge in Him, as strongly encouraged by His Holy Spirit; and our God does not and cannot lie! This hope is the anchor that keeps our soul steadfast and sure in Jesus Christ; giving us access into the veil, even the Holy of holies. Of course, Jesus Christ has gone ahead of us as a Priest forever in the order of Melchizedek! Lord, Help us to follow You in Jesus' Name. Amen!!!

I am unclean o Lord; thoroughly unclean and without hope, except in YOU alone! Renew my heart o Lord! Create in me a new heart; a clean heart, with a right spirit. Please Lord, do not reject me or cast me away from Your Presence, nor take Your Holy Spirit from me. For then I would be finished; and this wicked, evil world will take me over! Let me know again the joy of Your Salvation and uphold me with Your free Holy Spirit; then I will teach Your Ways Taught to me to transgressors like me and they will be renewed like You do me! Deliver me from all evil and its appearances. I will praise You o Lord from everlasting to everlasting in Jesus' Name. Amen!!!

Who is clean and with understanding and knowledge of the Holy One? Who truly seeks after Him faithfully as required by His Word? All have sinned and fallen short of His Glory! O Father, forgive us and draw us unto Yourself; that we might be true worshipers! Let Your Presence come and flood our hearts until all we see is You throughout our lives in Jesus' Name. Amen!!!

48th Day

WHO IS YOUR MASTER THAT YOU SERVE? WHO DO YOU HONOUR WITH YOUR WEALTH? PERSECUTION INEVITABLE!!!

Who is your master? You better know that you are a slave to whomsoever you serve or whatsoever has mastered you! Think of your lives folks. Whether you like it or not, you do have a master and some of you may have masters; and I am not meaning degrees, I mean things or people in your life that you have become a slave to! One thing I know is that you cannot serve God and money or any other master. Your loyalty to one will suffer! I urge you to submit only to God! Lord, Help my family, myself and all who love you sincerely to submit only to You; so that You alone will be and remain our Master in Jesus' Name. Amen!!!

If the Lord Blesses you materially, it is in your best interests to remember the Lord first in thanksgiving! Therefore, honour the Lord with your wealth and the first fruits of all you have been blessed with. Thus, you will overflow continuously in His Blessings in Jesus' Name. This requires wisdom; especially in this age when many servants of God use human intellect to take your money and prevent you from blessing those who God Wants you to bless! Father, Give us wisdom to give according to Your Will in Jesus' Name. Amen!!!

Make provision for the Lord's servant as God Leads you to purpose in your heart or as He Directs you to do and you will be forever replenished in Jesus' Name. Also, remember the needy; that you may bless them and be Blessed in return from Heaven above in Jesus' Name. God Will always Bless you as you give to the needy and the servants of the Lord! Open our eyes o Lord; that we may give those You Want us to give in Jesus' Name. Amen!!!

As long as you are a follower of Jesus Christ, you will experience persecution in one way or the other! How you react to persecution matters to God and for the sake of your faith! Many are the afflictions of the righteous but the Lord Delivers them from them all! Look at the example above. Isn't God Good? No matter how the enemies may gather, just stick with the Lord and keep calling His Name, you will have victory and be vindicated. Thank You Lord Jesus because I have You! I shall fear no evil in Jesus' Name. Amen!!!

49th Day

WITH THE GOSPEL OF JESUS CHRIST, REMINDERS ARE MOST ESSENTIAL! FOR ETERNAL LIFE, THE PERISHABLE MUST GIVE WAY TO THE IMPERISHABLE! JESUS WAS BORN IN A MANGER!!!

When you receive the Gospel of our Lord Jesus Christ, it's essential that you do not forget it! So, you need to put to practice what you learnt and keep reading the Word of God to feed your spirit continuously! The Saving Grace is dynamic; not static. The love of God does not end! Position yourself such that you are in good stead; ready to receive the Blessings of God in abundance in Jesus' Name. Amen. Father, please keep me well oiled and rooted in the Gospel of my Lord Jesus Christ in Jesus' Name. Amen!!!

For this perishable body must put on the imperishable, and this mortal body must put on immortality. When the perishable puts on the imperishable, and the mortal puts on immortality, then shall come to pass the saying that is written: "Death is swallowed up in victory."

Power must change hands! Death will not have victory over any saint of God (true believer). If in Christ Jesus, even though you may die, yet shall you live again. One day, soon and very soon, the perishable body shall arise and take on a new imperishable body (glorious body) to be with the Lord forevermore! Please meditate on the follow words - the sting of death is sin and the law is the power of sin! Keep yourself busy doing the Lord's work because that is the only work for which that the labour will never be in vain! Help us o Lord and Lead us o Father to be busy and led by You in our lives every day in Jesus' Name. Amen!!!

To get Eternal Life Jesus Christ told the man to keep the Commandments! Why do some of your teachers tell you that the Old Testament is irrelevant because of the advent of the same Jesus Christ who gave the above answer when asked directly? Hmmmm! You better read the Word of God for yourself lest you be found wanting on that Day! In addition, give up the world and build up treasures in Heaven; this is very explicit. The young man, very wealthy was very sad because he was very wealthy! The thought of giving up all his wealth saddened him. Where do you think his treasure was? In Jesus Christ or in his wealth? Think my people! Think! Help us o Lord to order our priorities right. Order our steps o Lord in Jesus' Name I pray thankfully. Amen!!!

God's reckoning is not by human worldly standards! Jesus Christ could have been born with a silver spoon in his mouth! But no; He was born in a humble place, a manger! How excellent our God is! Can you imagine! The Lord of lords and King of all kings; Wonderful, Counselor, Everlasting Father, Eternal God, the Rock of Ages was born in a manger! God is great. This is a great lesson in itself to behold! So, why does it matter so much to you where you live and how you live; that you must always excel above all your peers or else you will never have joy? Hmmm! Teach us Your Wisdom o Lord; this is the only way we shall be free from worldliness. In Jesus' Name. Amen!!!

50th Day

SO YOU THINK YOU HAVE A LIFE? DO YOU HAVE "THE LIFE"
THOUGH? GOD IS THE WAY, TRUTH AND LIFE! ETERNAL
LIFE!!!

And the testimony is this, that God has given us eternal life, and this life
is in His Son. He who has the Son has the life; he who does not have the
Son of God does not have the life. 1 John 5:11-12 NASB

If you have Jesus Christ, then you have Eternal Life! Jesus Christ Himself
is the Eternal Life of God! He is the Lord God Almighty Himself who
came to humanity in the flesh to show us the way. He is the Way, Truth
and Life! If you do not have Jesus Christ, you do not have life really. Only
in Jesus' Christ do you have life abundantly, even Eternal Life!!!

Many fail to accept the truth of this Scripture above which proves beyond
any doubts whatsoever that Jesus Christ is the Lord God Almighty! If the
Word was with God in the beginning and we know for certain that the
Word was God, surely the Word must be God! We also know that Jesus
Christ is the Word of the Living God; the Power and Wisdom of God
and the exact representation of His Being. Also, He is the Wonderful
Counselor, the Prince of Peace and the Everlasting Father! Can anyone
else besides God bear such identities? Hmmmm! Better for you to believe
and accept Him!!!

Jesus Christ, like every true servant of God was tested all the time by the
enemies of God! The enemies are not usually those you expect; they are
those you least expect oftentimes. The Pharisees had the undiluted Word
of God; but what did they make of it except a mockery! Jesus gave them
God's Heart about marriage but clearly man always finds a way to do his
own will. May God allow us to do His Will in Jesus' Name. Amen!!!

It is not the things that go into a man that defile the man; but rather the
things that come from the man! This is basically because the things that
come from the man come from his heart; all sorts of deviousness laden with
diverse sins and iniquities. How true. So, God's Name be praised and God

is Truth and satan is a liar and the father of all lies and liars. Believe God and resist the devil. God our Father, please Help deliver us from satan and his wiles and Help us to follow Jesus Christ's Truth, His Word and Spirit always in Jesus' Name. Amen!!!

51st Day

THE VIRTUES OF CRUCIFIXION, HUMILITY, THANKSGIVING AND THE CERTAINTY OF GOD'S JUDGMENT IN CHRIST JESUS!!!

I do not need to boast except in what the Cross that Jesus Christ died on and the total experience of His Crucifixion means and has achieved for me in my life! Crucially, that I have been crucified to the world and vice-versa! Lord Help me to reject every worldly/fleshly temptation to the very end in Jesus' Name. Amen!!!

The servant of the Lord must not be prideful nor arrogant! Feeling that you are superior to others because you feel so Blessed is not from God; especially in talking about and or testifying/witnessing to the truth of the Gospel in spirit and in truth with the Help of Jesus Christ's Holy Spirit! Essentially, the goal is to know Christ Jesus, Him Crucified; and the Power of His Resurrection! Lord please Keep me free from pride and arrogance in the discharge of my Christian duties and my walk with Jesus Christ. Amen!!

Yes, we are supposedly under Grace and need more Grace for our walk with the Lord and in the Lord! We received much Grace after we received forgiveness for our sins! Is therefore this potential for increased Grace in our lives a license to sin? Is the freedom that comes with coming into Jesus Christ our license to sin? Can we continue in sin and expect God's Grace to continue to increase in our lives under our self-proclaimed "unconditional love" of Jesus Christ? Hmmmm! Be very careful what and how you believe folks! The death and resurrection of Jesus Christ for us really ought to mean a baptism into His death (our death to the flesh/sin) and our being called to live a new life in Jesus Christ. Help us o Lord to live for Jesus Christ. Amen!!!

When you minister Jesus Christ and the reconciliation that attends this ministry unto people, you must remember to keep them uplifted in prayer with thanksgiving for them too! Where possible, it is good to maintain some form of communication with them both in spirit and in the physical; to keep encouraging them to stand fast in the Word of God and in the traditions taught them in Jesus' Name. Also, pray that they may continually be established in faith that works through love via every good work. This is pleasing to God and beneficial to man (including you the messenger)! O Jesus, please Help us to do right by you in Jesus' Name. Amen!!!

The above Scripture reminds of us the certainty of God's judgement coming upon all sin and ungodliness committed and spoken against the Lord, His Word and His Holy Spirit! Grumbling, complaining whilst walking lustfully in sin is condemned and we are urged not to engage in such or other evil. We who believe are neither to use flattery to gain advantage, nor mockery and divisiveness with the promotion of sensuality, which leads people astray and evidences a lack of the Holy Spirit! Father, please Keep us safe from the ways of this world and flesh; that we may serve You as righteousness requires in Spirit and in Truth in Jesus' Name. Amen!!!

52nd Day

THE LORD IS HIGH AND MIGHTY; YET HE LOOKS UPON THE LOWLY, DEFENDS THEM AGAINST THEIR ENEMIES!!!

Great is the Lord and worthy to be praised and adored! Although our God is High and Mighty, He takes note of the lowly/humble and He Blesses them and defends their cause against their enemies! He Shows enduring love to the humble and wise who fear His Name!!!

Whom shall I give my thanksgiving and praise except the Lord of Hosts? Who is Mighty like Him? Who Has Power like Him? He is Able, abundantly Able to deliver and to save all who trust in Him. I will trust You o my Lord and praise You from everlasting to everlasting! You have done great things; therefore, I will forever Bless Your Holy Name! Your Name o Lord is a Strong Tower to which the righteous run and are saved! I will trust in Your Name and run always to Your Holy Name; for I know that there I will be very safe and secure in Jesus' Name. Amen!!!

All Glory, Power, Honour and Adoration be unto the Lord Most High God! You are the only One who is Able to Establish my gospel preached by Your Spirit; the revelation of an age long hidden mystery. A mystery revealed by Your written Word through prophetic guidance; for all nations to believe and obey. Only You o Lord are Wise. Blessed be Your Glorious Name Eternally in Jesus' Name. Amen!!!

I pray that the Lord God would Bless my family, myself, all believers and those who will believe His Word on hearing the witnessing of the saints in life, in Jesus' Name. Amen! In Jesus Christ, believers have all sufficiency in all things and in all ways and abundant provision is made in Jesus Christ for them to do every good work in Jesus' Name. Amen!!!

53rd Day

BE MERCIFUL AND EMBRACE GODLY WISDOM TO THRIVE AND PROSPER IN LIFE!!!

When you have received God's Favour, that must be mercy received for you and set you up in good stead to show mercy to fellow humans; just like you received forgiveness! However, if you receive mercy and refuse to show mercy, then you will be treated like the above servant; and it will be your own fault! Unto whom much is given, much is desired! This Scripture above is telling us that God Will treat us likewise if we fail to forgive our brethren! Hmmm! So, do you forgive or not! Be warned; you risk the wrath of God if you do not forgive - and that is apart from the risk to your own health and well being! Lord, Help us to forgive even as we have been forgiven in Jesus' Name. Amen!!!

Wisdom is calling out to her children! Laying out the value of wisdom for us all who care to listen and hear to obey and be Blessed to receive! Letting you know that if you will seek out and find wisdom, you will understand the fear of God and find the knowledge of God. God Gives wisdom and knowledge and understanding comes from the Mouth of the Lord! The fear of God is the beginning of wisdom! Do you want wisdom? Well then! Please o Lord, Teach us the way of wisdom, Your wisdom is my heart's desire o Lord; that I may learn the fear of the Lord and be deeply enriched by it in Jesus' Name. Amen!!!

54th Day

THE GOSPEL IS ACTUALLY THE SAVING POWER OF GOD FOR ALL WHO BELIEVE! I AM NOT ASHAMED!! REVIVE ME O LORD!!!

A young man threw a challenge to all believers today. He said they should read their Bibles and go out and share the gospel! The truth is many are ashamed of what people will say and afraid of persecution; so they don't want to ruffle any feathers. You hear things like: "your faith is personal"; "I don't go round throwing my faith in people's faces"; "I don't do Bible bashing"; etc. This is akin to being ashamed (not proud) of the Gospel really! Ever since the time of John the Baptist, the Kingdom of God has suffered violence and the violent take it by force! The Kingdom of God is not for the fearful or timid; it's for the bold and courageous! O Lord, Give me the boldness and courage to preach the Gospel of Truth in Jesus' Name. Amen!!!

Jesus Christ made clear that if you are ashamed of Him and His words in this our evil contaminated generation, He Will also be ashamed of you when He returns in His Fathers Glory with the holy angels of God Almighty! Check yourself! Are you in the faith? Are you not ashamed of the Gospel of Jesus Christ? If you are not, what are you doing about it? Help my family and I o Lord to do what is right with the Gospel of Light in Jesus' Name. Amen!!!

Many are not only ashamed of the Lord and His Gospel; but also of his servants who suffer daily in His Name! It is by the Power of God that His servants suffer for the Holy Name; having been Saved and Called unto a holy calling! This not due to works, but rather according to His purpose and grace; given in Jesus Christ before the beginning of the ages. This has been manifested through the revelation of Jesus Christ in the flesh; who came to abolish death and offered humanity life and immortality through the holy Gospel for which people like me were appointed heralds, preachers, apostles and teachers, with accompanying sufferings and persecutions! Blessed be His Holy Name. Halleluyah! Amen!! Thank You Jesus!!!

Touch us o Lord! Change our hearts! You are the God of our salvation! Do not remain angry with us. Let Your anger towards us cease o Lord I plead on behalf of my brethren! Do not let Your anger reach unto all our generations o Lord! Revive us o Lord even if You've done it before; revive us again o Lord in Jesus' Name. That we may rejoice in Thee; show us Your mercy o Lord and Grant us Your salvation! Please Lord, I beseech You in Jesus' Name. Amen!!!

Folks, learn to honour the Name of the Lord! We often wittingly or unwittingly take the Name of the Lord in vain! This is a sin unto the Lord! You will not be guiltless when you do this! Strive always to please God! You will not please God when you take His Name in vain! Faith that works through love; o yes! However, do not take the Name of the Lord in vain. May the Lord Give us wisdom and understanding of reverence for His Name and His Word, so we do not take His Name in vain; through Jesus Christ our Lord God and Saviour, Amen!!!

55th Day

I AM SORTED. THE LORD RULES ULTIMATELY! I WILL COME OUT AS PURE GOLD FROM TESTING! SACRIFICE YOUR BODY!!!

I have trusted and will forever trust you o Lord; for I know that You Can and Will sort me out, heart and all! For this reason, I will arise and praise You with all I've got at my disposal, including musical instruments! Great is Your Mercy, Truth, Faithfulness and Love in all ways. Be exalted o Lord above the Heaven and earth o Lord. Come, take Your place! Help my heart o Lord; that I might know You and the Power of Your Resurrection increasingly in Jesus' Name. Amen!!!

Advice and instruction are good for man to accept for wisdom; of course having been sifted through the discernment of the Holy Spirit! Man proposes and God disposes; at the end of all, the Lord's purposes prevail over man's! God Rules! Jesus Christ Rules over the affairs of men ultimately! Reign in me o Sovereign Lord in my life and family o Lord; come Reign in us in Jesus' Name. Amen!!!

Awimayehun (The One who speaks and does not change His Mind); Asoromatase (The One who speaks and His Word never goes astray but rather is very accurate)! He is the Lord! When He speaks, His Word Stands firm and fast! His Counsel is likewise, supreme! He brings to nothingness all of the counsel of the heathen and nullifies all their devices and makes them of no effect! The Lord's Counsel stands forever. The nation is blessed that makes the Lord it's God; and the people He has Chosen for His inheritance! Selah! Count my family and I worthy o Lord to be part of such a nation that You have Chosen for Your inheritance o Lord in Jesus' Name. Amen!!!

I will love to be tried by the Lord and found not wanting; but rather come out pure as gold! For only He Can Do this for me. Draw me to Yourself that I might be a worshipper and true; let Your Presence come and flood my heart till all I see is You! Help me to hold fast to Your steps and keep Your ways and not turn aside o Lord. Help me not to depart from Your Commandments and to treasure the Words of Your Mouth in Jesus' Name far more than my portion of food etc. Amen and Amen!!!

This ordinance is from and of the Lord God Almighty in Jesus Christ! That we who believe present our bodies wholly, holy and pure as a living sacrifice; acceptable to the Lord, which is our spiritual act of sacrifice! We must not conform to the likeness of this evil wicked world; but rather be transformed through the renewal of our minds. This way, we shall prove the good, acceptable and perfect Will of God! Lord, who can do this except with Your Help? The world is very strongly tugging at us all the time o Lord. Save us! Help us to present our bodies as stated for and unto Your Glory in Jesus' Name. Amen!!!

56th Day

THERE IS A STANDARD WITH FAITH IN JESUS CHRIST; FOLLOW IT! THE SERVANT OF ALL IS GREATEST! OBEY THE WORD!!!

God is very great; and He created all things for His good pleasure! That is, His creation is to please Him! You can only please the one whom you prioritise, think of and about, learn of and about, meditate upon, revere and love! When you love someone, you learn what pleases and displeases them; you do the former and avoid the latter! Apply this to the Lord God Almighty and with His Help you can learn about and of Him and strive to please Him. If God is pleased with you, you will enjoy the best of your creator! However, you do need faith; for without faith, no man can please God! Help me o Lord; lead me so that I may please You in all that I think, speak or do in Jesus' Name. Amen!!!

This is the Lord's prayer! This is the guidance we have in the Name of the Lord for praying to God! Prayer of course can take different forms and such are inexhaustible; however, we do have this for a guide! Praise God, seek after His Kingdom and Will to be done; ask for needs to be met and seek for forgiveness even as you forgive! Pray against temptations because they abound and seek for deliverance from evil! Recognise, declare and proclaim your acknowledgement that all power, glory and the Kingdom belong to the Almighty God in Jesus Christ. Amen!!!

It is human thinking to want to know who is the greatest etc.! This is often asked from the wrong motives rooted in selfishness and delusions of grandiose regarding how important people are! But there is a wisdom that is from above in Jesus Christ! When the question was put to Jesus Christ, please study His response! Jesus' response is more about who is the chief servant of all? He is the leader and the greatest! Hmmm! Food for thought! Lord Teach us how to serve and lead in our generations in Jesus' Name. Amen!!!

There is a standard in the Word of God! This standard is a body of rules and regulations for the faith walk! If followed, how blessed humanity would truly be! For God rewards obedience always! Whether young or old, male or female, slave or master, king, queen or subjects and servants, there is a word for you to live by! Learn this standard and apply to your lives daily to win God's approval and be Blessed in Jesus' Name. Amen!!!

57th Day

JESUS CHRIST: ETERNAL KINGDOM IS HIS! BE DILIGENT IN CHRIST JESUS! PAY YOUR TAXES! BE YE PERFECT AND HOLY!!!

Jesus Christ rules over all! His Kingdom is everlasting. If you fall, believe that you shall rise again. If bowed down, believe that you shall be raised. Look up onto God for all your needs and they will be met in Jesus' Name. God does not ever fail those who look up to Him for all things and in all ways! Jesus Christ rules! God rules! Do you believe? Will you believe? Can you believe?!!

If you have been Called, you will know; and then it is up to you to be diligent in your calling! You need to do all it takes to make your calling and election sure and effective in Christ Jesus! If you obey the Word of God, you will never fail; and you will be Led through an "entrance" into the Kingdom of God - the Everlasting Kingdom of Jesus Christ, our Lord God and Saviour! Please God, Lead my family and I into Your Eternal Kingdom through Jesus Christ. Amen!!!

Living life has never and will never be fair! However, for the best possible chance of successful living, we all need Jesus Christ in our lives. He Makes all things better and work together for our good; when we love Him and are Called according to His purposes! The tax administrators hassle others for tax but not themselves and their immediate families and or children. This simply implies that taxes are never exacted from everybody in the same way. There is discrimination in the process. However, Jesus Christ led by example in making adequate provision for the tax! Lord, Teach us Your Wisdom and Understanding to live life with faith in Your Name. Amen!!!

Noah was a special man with Godly privileges all round! He was singled out for life; with his three sons, their mother and their wives! He was adjudged by God as righteous in a generation clearly evil and obscene! Please God, this could not have been possible without You. Be with me like Noah; and Help me to live for You as Noah did, with my family in Jesus' Name. Amen!!!

58th Day

THE BELIEVER IS BURIED WITH CHRIST IN BAPTISM AND SHOULD WALK LIFE ANEW AS JESUS ROSE FROM THE DEAD!!!

Therefore we have been buried with Him through baptism into death, so that as Christ was raised from the dead through the glory of the Father, so we too might walk in newness of life. Romans 6:4 NASB

To go through Jesus for the cleansing power and be washed in His precious Blood, you must go through being crucified and buried with Him in baptism. Then raised with Him, you must enter into a new phase in life, living your life anew and afresh in Jesus Christ! You must allow your mind to be renewed by submission in full to the Word of the Living God in Jesus Christ! Lord we do not say that this is easy to do but by Your Grace and shed Blood nothing shall be impossible for us in Jesus' Name. Amen!!!

In the futility of man's thinking and wickedness of his heart, Jesus Christ was condemned to die through the popular demand and wish of a people to whom He was Sent for their own deliverance! Wow! God is Great! The people hated Him for his righteousness and never once thought that they were acting out a definitive script God had Written and Spoken of long before! However, God's plan came to fruition against the plan of man! Jesus Christ was raised from the dead and He Lives forever. He is the Lord; our Great and Living God! O Halleluyah Amen Thank You Jesus! May we not be caught in our own craftiness and wickedness of heart. May God deliver us from death into life in Jesus' Name. Amen!!!

Are you born again? If you are in Christ Jesus, then you are born again! Are you a new creation? If you are in Christ Jesus, then you will know that you are renewed in all ways and you will testify to the difference as will people around you and those you meet! You cannot be renewed and "hidden". The ministry of reconciliation is not a silent passive one! When you have been "Touched", you cannot keep it to yourself! Lord, Help us to fulfill our destiny in Jesus Christ for our lives and for Your Name's sake. Amen!!!

We are all created (whether we like it or not; acknowledge it or not) in Jesus Christ for good works prepared beforehand for us to walk in! That is our primary destiny! For us to fulfill our destiny, we must enter into Jesus Christ through faith! He is our peace; having broken down and abolished (through giving Himself, His Flesh) every wall and enmity between us and God! He did not come to abolish the Law; but to fulfill it - thereby creating a "new" man through this remarkable feat. Hence, making peace; He is our Peace! Thank You Jesus for who You Are and what You Did! Halleluyah! Amen!!!

The heart of man is deceitful and desperately wicked! Not just today; but from the beginning according to the Word of the Living God! So much so that God regretted making man and decided to wipe out man and all the other creatures He Made for and with man! Hence, the floods! But God is so merciful! He found Noah, a righteous man pleasing to Him and spared Noah, his three sons and their mother and wives! God is so so so merciful; however, take Him for granted at your own peril. He is merciful but also a consuming fire! O Lord, let me see Your mercy in my life and not Your Wrath in Jesus' Name I pray for my family, myself and all who sincerely look up to You for deliverance and salvation in Jesus' Name. Amen!!!

59th Day

AS A BELIEVER, ENSURE THAT ALL THAT YOU DO GLORIFIES THE LORD JESUS CHRIST!!!

To live a believing life walking in the faith, strive always to ensure that everything you engage in brings God glory. It's one thing to pray for God to be glorified in your daily living; it's another to strive for letting God be glorified in all that you do as a believer! You have to be God conscious all the time for this to happen. May God Grant us to let Him be the focus of all that we think, speak and do in Jesus' Name. Amen!!!

Whatever gift or ability given you by God as believers must be used in the service of one and all in Jesus' Name. If speaking, all must speak as an oracle of the Lord, being used by God. Do everything with the enabling of Jesus Christ and to the glory of God always. This is not easy in this evil world; however, may God Help us in Jesus' Name to do what is right in the Name of the Lord. Amen!!!

Who is like our God? Who is wise like Him? Who can fully understand His Ways? Who knows His Mind and is able to offer God counsel? All things are indeed for Him, through Him and unto Him; including all glory for ever and ever Amen. He Has done great things; blessed be His Holy and Glorious Name. Halleluyah! Amen!!!

What tremendous faith! Telling the Lord that if He is willing, He can make him clean was a way of letting the Lord know that he believes in His Power to heal and deliver! Of course the Lord was pleased to "touch" the leper and he was healed! When the Lord comes again, will He find faith on the face of the earth? Do you have faith? Judge yourself indeed and see if you are still in the faith?!

60th Day

THOUGH REDEEMED; GOD WILL HAVE HIS WAY! HIS WORD IS FULLY AND FIRMLY ESTABLISHED IN HEAVEN AND ON EARTH!!!

Are you redeemed? If not, look above and see what you will miss?! What will you do when you see me with everlasting joy on my head and you see that I found gladness with joy without sorrow and sighing? Hmmm! You better come running to Jesus today or tomorrow may be too late; nobody knows when death will come calling. After death, it will be too late to receive Jesus Christ!!!

Gratitude shall fill the hearts of the redeemed and they will come and express themselves in the Presence of the Lord their God! They shall have great peace as a well-watered garden and prosper like trees planted beside a stream of flowing water; whose leaves are evergreen, bearing fruits all year round. No more sorrow for such people. Do you want to be amongst them? Then you must give your life to Jesus Christ today and let Him be Master over your soul!!!

The reward of the redeemed is also such that they will never hunger nor thirst ever again. They will not suffer from the heat of the sun and need no light; for the Lamb of God will be their Shepherd and their Light round the clock. They will be led to the Springs of Living Water and their God shall wipe away every tear from their eyes forever. No more sorrow no more pain for them! Glory! Halleluyah!!!

God Spoke a Word over the woman from the sin in the Garden of Eden as above! Is it not the case today still? God is Good right? Why has He not forgiven this particular transgression? That's how dangerous it is to disobey God's Word or take Him for granted! The choice is entirely yours! Everything is permissible but not everything is beneficial. Be careful how you take God's Word!!!

61st Day

GOD IS IN CONTROL; ALL THINGS WORK FOR THE BELIEVERS' GOOD! DO RIGHT ALWAYS! THERE IS POWER IN JESUS' NAME!!!

The One who searches hearts knows the Mind of the Spirit. He is the Lord God Almighty and His Name is Higher than any other name. His Name is Jesus! His Name is Lord! He intercedes for the saints (believers) according to the Will of God! May His Will always manifest in our lives and experiences in Jesus' Name. Amen. Accordingly, every evil hand that comes against us as believers will be cut off in the Name of the Lord Jesus Christ and every evil machination targeted against us shall be frustrated in the Holy Name of Jesus Christ! They may gather against us for evil, but God Almighty will turn it for our good; because the heart of the king is in the Hand of the Lord God and He Turns it whichever way He chooses! The Good Acceptable and Perfect Will of God for us is always good and in our best interests; so be it o Lord, in Jesus' Name. Amen!!!

When you are in a position to act against an injustice, act wisely, rightly and quickly; do not delay! You do not know whether your hesitation and or inaction would cause such a backfire that would also consume you and your household with you! Perhaps you have been brought into such a position by God, for just that reason for you to act. May God Grant us the wisdom to act and do what is right all the time in whatever position we find ourselves in Jesus' Name. Amen!!!

Who says prayer does not work especially on behalf of those who cannot fight for themselves; the distressed, underprivileged, widows, orphans, poor, impoverished, oppressed, etc. God is very close to them! When you cry out against their enemies and oppressors, God is very close to you to act in their best interests. Cry out on behalf of even your nation, like mine, Nigeria without giving up nor being discouraged! Let us not be weary in doing good, the Bible says; for in due season, we would reap a harvest accordingly in Jesus' Name. Amen!!!

They that know their God shall do exploits! They that know and use the Name of the Lord our God shall experience His Miraculous Hand and Power in Jesus' Name. Believe, speak in Jesus' Name. Command in Jesus' Name. Act in Jesus' Name; and you will experience the supernatural Hand of God Almighty in Jesus' Name. Amen!!!

62nd Day

YESTERDAY, TODAY, FOREVER, JESUS IS THE SAME! ALL MAY CHANGE, BUT JESUS, NEVER! GOD'S PROMISES ARE YES AND AMEN IN JESUS CHRIST!!!

No matter how many promises God makes to us as believers, they are Yes and Amen in Jesus Christ! It is God that Blesses us so much and gives us His Holy Spirit as a guarantee of the best yet to come! His Word is firm and secure once given in Jesus' Name. Just believe!!!

Jesus Christ is the Word of the Living God! Heaven and earth will pass away, but the Word of God remains unshakeable forever! God in Jesus Christ strengthens our hearts by His Grace; and this is good! Do not be led astray by diverse and strange teachings; they are false!!!

May we not fall short in the gifts of the Holy Spirit; even as we await the second coming of our Lord Jesus Christ! He is able to keep us to the very end and present us blameless in His Sight. He's a Faithful God. We have been called into holy fellowship with Jesus Christ, Son of the Living God! Remain in the vine; abide in Him and you shall not fall nor fail in Jesus' Name. This is our portion as we hold fast unto His Mighty Right Hand in Jesus' Name. Amen!!!

The Anointing of God is the Holy Spirit that leads us into all truth and all righteousness! He's not automatically given; you must exercise faith sacrificially to receive the Anointing of God! It's not unconditionally given at all! However, it's given by Grace. You cannot live a deliberately sinful life and expect the Anointing to remain with you even if you had received Him before! The Anointing is for real not fake like satan mimics. Be diligent and you will be rewarded in your faith walk in Jesus' Name. Amen!!!

The Word of God is better and more effective when received by faith not by intellect! Intellect led the disciples to think Jesus was talking about bread! Whereas He was talking about the teachings of the Pharisees and

Sadducees! However, Jesus Christ mercifully put them straight; then they understood. The Word of God requires discernment of the Holy Spirit! May God fill us abundantly with His Holy Spirit for the faith walk in Jesus' Name. Amen!!!

By faith Abraham pleased God and it was accounted unto him as righteousness! By faith Enoch was taken and did not see death. God took him. God took Moses' body also by faith and no one ever saw his dead body. God took care of him too. Without faith it is impossible to please God! Believing in a God that you do not see is faith and this pleases God greatly and you will be blessed for this faith in Jesus' Name. Amen!!!

63rd Day

BELIEVER'S WATCHWORD: JUSTICE AND RIGHTEOUSNESS! TAKE CARE OF THE NEEDY! PRESS ON IN THE FAITH!!!

Thus says the LORD: "Keep justice, and do righteousness, For My salvation is about to come, And My righteousness to be revealed.

Surely the love of God must include His Blessings! If we have the love of God; we must enjoy His Blessings as a result! If the Blessings and Love of God was unconditional, why would God need for us to keep justice and do righteousness? Why would God say whosoever obeys this instruction or counsel is Blessed? Please let us be wise! For if a non-believer obeys the Word of God, they would be treated as appropriate in the Eyes of God contrary to what believers are taught in their churches etc.! The Judge is standing at the door! Jesus Christ is the Judge, Lord of all!!!

The Lord gave us word to protect, defend, take care of and speak up for the weak, oppressed, aliens, orphans, widows, etc. and not shed innocent blood! Then if we obey this word, blessings shall abound unto us in our comings and goings in Jesus' Name. So again, to be blessed by God, you have to obey His Word; to be loved by God you have to please Him essentially. Therefore, there are sure and certain conditions attached to the Love and blessings of God all through the Holy Scriptures! Let us be wise and submit to God!!!

God's Thoughts are different than man's thoroughly! This is evidenced in the above scripture again! The disciples were thinking carnally, whilst the Lord was Spiritual in orientation! The yeast of the Pharisees and Sadducees is about their teachings that has the potential to spread like gangrene and quickly pollute the minds of people! We all are to guard against such in Jesus' Name and not take the sound word of God for granted!!!

In Christ Jesus, by faith, we must press on towards the ultimate goal of Salvation unto Eternal Life and not look back. Once you believe, satan will keep trying to turn you back to your old ways in diverse guises. Resist the devil and he will flee from you. So, be on guard and guard your spirit!!!

64th Day

JESUS CHRIST IS MY STRENGTH! I BEAR HIS FULL ARMOUR ON ME! HE IS IN FULL CONTROL AND I SUBMIT TO HIS WILL!!!

As a soldier of Christ Jesus, what armour do you bear? It is in your best interests to bear only the full armour of God; that is all you need for all your battles. When you have this on, all you need to do is stand your ground in His Name; for the battle is the Lord's and the victory is ours in Jesus' Name. Stand firm. Help us o Lord to stand firm with Your Armour fully in place on us in Jesus' Name. Amen!!!

Even as we stand as explained above, we must do so without any fear! Boldly and courageously, we must stand very firmly against all enemy attacks. LOVE must be our watchword! We must do everything in and with love to be maximally effective in Jesus' Name. Amen. Help us to love effectively in Jesus' Name o Lord. Amen!!!

I will cry out unto You o Lord whenever I am overwhelmed with this world's cares; because I know that Your Holy Spirit will lead me to the Rock that is Higher than I! You have never and will never fail me as my shelter; You are a Strong Tower from the enemy. That is Your Name! My hope and all is in You. You are enough for me o Lord! Thank You for this privilege to have You on my side! Halleluyah!!!

Are we not to learn and increase in the faith from the testimonies and witness of our forefathers in the Faith? Is this not so that we can faithfully pass on the message to ours and future generations? I say yes to both questions. Help us to do so with integrity and God's Love and to endure the hardship that accompanies this in Jesus' Name as a good soldier of the Lord. Amen!!!

Man's limitations is the beginning of the manifestation of God's Power! What did the disciples have to offer? Nothing except the little they were able to garner from the crowds. What did Jesus do? He gave thanks, breathed upon the little they produced and that little was supernaturally multiplied to feed so many people with more than enough left over. That is my God. That is the God that is true. That is the God that I serve. O what joy! Thank You Lord for who You are!!!

God Himself Exalted Jesus Christ to His Place; a place where only He Occupies! Why? This is because God Knows that He, Jesus and the Holy Spirit are ONE and the same! This is so hard for mankind to take and accept; except unto whom it is REVEALED! For this belief/faith, many are willing to kill the believer and die for contrary faiths and opinions! Why? This is because of pride and ignorance! Submit today to the Supreme and Sovereign Will of God in Jesus' Name. Amen!!!

65th Day

JESUS CHRIST, MESSIAH CAME FOR A PURPOSE: "MESSIAH"! SAVIOUR KING LORD GOD; THAT'S WHO/WHAT HE IS; MESSIAH!!!

Why did Jesus Christ come? Why was He Sent? Is it not obvious in the Word of God that Jesus Christ was Sent to Save? Even in the Old Testament, we have the written Word about Jesus Christ being the Messiah, Saviour, Everlasting Father, Prince of Peace etc. that was to come?! We have evidence in the New Testament that He Came truly; and through a virgin as prophesied in the Old Testament! If Jesus Christ lives in you, then the "seed" of God lives in you and thus you do not and cannot sin, for you are born of God! Praise God! Halleluyah!! Amen!!!

God is Love! Love is made complete in giving and receiving! Although love is perfect; when given, it is not complete until received! True, God Loves all with the potential of completeness; so He gave! However, the choice to receive rests squarely with the receiver. You believe faithfully and then receive for the love to be manifested in the receiver! God's love reached out to us first; we prove our love for Him in return in faithfully receiving and obeying His Word! Wow! It takes God's Love, Grace and Mercy to receive His Love! Help us to receive Your Love o Lord; for no one can come to You except You Draw one to Yourself. Help us in Jesus' Name. Amen!!!

Potentially, God's love for all is given! God would love to love everyone; but is it really possible for God to love the wicked? I read in the Word of God that God hates the wicked (Psalm 11:5 - The Lord examines the righteous, but the wicked, those who love violence, he hates with a passion). That is why God Told me that until love is received by the one to whom love is sent, it is incomplete! Although love in itself is complete! We cannot be saved by His Life if we do not receive and accept His Sacrifice, Name and Word! We have a Great and Mighty God!!!

No plant/tree that was not planted by the Lord will stand; they will be uprooted in Jesus' Name. Amen! When you see evil appearing to prosper in the lands, do not be disturbed. They and theirs are headed for destruction;

and their wealth is all laid in store for the righteous! God is Good and Just! He Will Repay!!!

As long as you have Jesus Christ, there is relative equality; for in the Spirit into which you are thus baptised, there is equality and oneness like in the world of angels! However, this does not mean that man equals to woman nor husband equal to wife etc.! God's Word is full and complete, orderly, and not confusing! We still must obey the Word of God and not use the excuse of this Scripture to fulfill our own whims etc.! Obedience leads to life and prosperity; disobedience incurs a curse unto death and destruction! Be warned!!!

66th Day

WHEN IN TROUBLE, CALL ON GOD WITHOUT CEASING; HE'S NEARBY! AVOID PRIDE; EMBRACE HUMILITY ALWAYS!!!

We often don't make a big deal of slandering each other; yet it's offensive to God! When you slander your brethren in wrongful judgment, you come against the law in judgment; thereby not keeping the law but judging it! How can God be pleased with you then? Hmmm! Be careful how you relate to your brethren so you will not offend God! Help us o Lord in Jesus' Name. Amen!!!

It appears that God is hiding when we're facing hard times and it seems like forever; however, don't stop calling out to God for help at such times, because God is around the corner, closer than you can imagine. He'll come through for you in Jesus' Name. Amen! The wicked act boastfully and contrary to God's Ways to their shame and impending judgment!!!

The upright shun evil, even as they guard their ways and as such guard their lives! The end result of pride is destruction and a fall. It's better to be humble and low in spirit but amongst the oppressed than to partake of the largess gathered by the proud! God opposes the proud and gives grace to the humble!!!

Anger and hot temper bring forth no good. Pride never exalts a man; but rather diminishes mankind. However, honour awaits a man with lowly spirit and humble. God is just; He favours the humble and lowly in spirit over and above the proud who can never please God!!!

So you want to be high and lifted up? Then humble yourself and God Will remember you in due season to lift you up! Take heed of the word of God! Suffering is not necessarily a bad thing like some people preach; for it leads to much strengthening! Sobriety is good for your faith; make the best of being sober! Put all your troubles before the Lord; He Cares and Will Deliver you from all your troubles if you will trust and hope in Him. Lord keep us trusting in you in Jesus' Name. Amen!!!

God adds to His own Himself; man does not need to help God in this regard. Concentrate on doing and obeying the Will of God! Only God can cause people to receive Him and His Word gladly. No man can save another man. Only Jesus Christ can save! Take note! Take heed of the Word of God in Christ Jesus. Amen!!!

67th Day

FAITH, KNOWLEDGE RESTING ON THE HOPE OF ETERNAL LIFE; GOD'S PROMISE BEFORE TIME BEGAN! SURE AND SECURE!!!

God is not a man that He should lie; nor a son of man that He would change His Mind! Before the beginning of time made a promise to His own who choose to love, believe and follow Him; the promise is one of faith and knowledge, resting on the hope of Eternal Life! As a follower and believer in God, you qualify for having faith and knowledge. I believe wisdom comes with that too. All of these rest on the hope of Eternal Life! O Lord my God, I wonder awesomely at You! How great Thou Art!!!

To qualify for His Promise, you have to know His Voice; otherwise how could you hear Him? You must have an identity with Jesus Christ; He must know you! You must be able to hear His Voice! Eternal Life is the bottom line of God's Promise to mankind. How is it that it is Jesus Christ that gives this Eternal Life? How is it that this Eternal Life Himself is Jesus Christ? Sadly, not everybody can see nor believe or accept that this same Jesus Christ is the Lord God Almighty! Jesus Christ is the Lord God Almighty! Although Jesus Christ humbles Himself in not directly equating Himself with God, He makes it abundantly clear in more than enough words that He and the Father are ONE and when you meet/see Jesus Christ, then you have seen/met the Father! Just believe!!!

There shall be a sure and certain judgment for all; depends on which side you fall into with your life weighed on the scales of God! The one leading unto Eternal Life; and the other unto Eternal wrath and indignation! With God, there is and will be no partiality the way man knows it! God is Just and will judge Justly! O Lord, Help me and mine and all who are truly Yours to make Eternal Life in Jesus' Name. Amen!!!

This is the key to Eternal Life; believing and accepting the word as delivered above! Failure to accept this word is automatic condemnation! It is expedient for all and in the general best interests of all who chose to accept and believe the word and act on it in Jesus' Name. Amen!!!

68th Day

WITH GOD FIGHTING YOUR BATTLES, VICTORY ALL THE WAY! GIVE HIM HIS DUES AND GOD WILL BLESS AND HELP YOU!!!

God always Leads us victoriously. He causes us to ooze His sweet aroma always wherever we are! To those being saved we are the sweet aroma; whereas to those perishing, we are a stench! No wonder they will hate us as they hated our Lord Jesus Christ first! However, God Will Vindicate us and uphold our cause in Jesus' Name. Amen!!!

Offer to God His dues wherever you call upon His Name and He Will be there to bless you. Remember that God is Present in the midst of His people; so let us bow before Him. For He Heals the broken hearted; He has turned our darkness into light and our night into day! This is God's Touch for His faithful ones. Where do you stand?!!

Who has known the Mind of the Lord or been His instructor or counselor? Who can challenge His judgments? The riches of God's Wisdom and Knowledge is very deep! I find that it is worthy for humankind to strive to get close to God in order to get to know His and His Ways! May God be merciful to reveal to us His Ways; for they are profitable unto us!!!

Be careful what you ask of the Lord because you might just get it! Be sure you are ready for it! Peter thought he was ready and had the faith to do the Will of the Lord Jesus Christ to walk on the water! However, he started but couldn't finish because he became afraid and cried out to the Lord. The Lord saved him but rebuked him for doubting! Fear is powered by doubt! Faith powers the impossible to be transformed and made possible! Lord Help us to have faith in Jesus' Name. Amen!!!

Jacob's mother was very much in on his deception. So, both were unclean. Yet, God so loved Jacob and hated Esau! Who can challenge God? Would you then rate God as unjust? Do you know His Mindset to judge Him? Better for you to bow to God's Will and hold your peace than to do the opposite and pay a dire price! Wisdom knows and is known by her children. Lord please Teach us Your Wisdom in Jesus' Name. Amen!!!

69th Day

LOVED, CALLED BY GOD? BELIEVE! HE ALWAYS WORKS IN YOUR BEST INTERESTS! FEAR NOT; YOU ARE BLESSED!!!

Hold fast to the confession you made by faith from the start; God is Faithful! Live your life in loving and doing good; also encourage your brethren to do likewise. This would be very pleasing to God; the Holy One who has Called you for His Own Purpose. Help me in so doing o Lord in Jesus' Name. Amen!!!

Be fully assured in the Blessed assurance that the God who called you into fellowship with His Son, Jesus Christ is Faithful to do you good if you obey His Commandments to love and always do good! He Will never leave nor forsake you in Jesus' Name. Amen!!!

Do you know and believe that in everything you experience in life, God who you love and the One who Called you for His Own Purpose, works for your good and in your best interests? Can you and will you trust, hope, believe in Him accordingly? This is a Blessed assurance and it will be in the believers' best interests to live in this confidence in Jesus' Name. Amen. Lord, please Give me reasons increasingly to be encouraged to live full of confidence in You in every way in Jesus' Name I pray with thanksgiving. Amen!!!

My God who walks on water! Yes! That's my God! For Him, nothing shall be impossible! I put my hope, faith, trust and all in Him and so for me nothing shall be impossible; because I know that I can do all things through Jesus Christ who Gives me Strength! Amen!! Halleluyah, thank You Jesus!!!

I claim this prophetic word of Blessing for my family and myself and speak the same into the life of everybody taking this message on board needfully according to faith in Jesus Christ! In Jesus' Name. Amen! Father, You Spoke into my life that I am of Abraham's heritage and therefore Abraham's Blessings are mine! So, I encourage you all to bless me; for if you do, you will be blessed! Don't ever even try to curse me; for if you do, you stand accursed! Selah! Thank You Lord Jesus! I am BLESSED!!!

70th Day

IS THE HOLY SPIRIT/TRUTH IN YOU? DO NOT LET SHAME ROB YOU OF YOUR BLESSING/REST! DO NOT LOVE THE WORLD!!!

As a believer, if you have enjoyed the Blessing and Mercy of Almighty God in Jesus Christ, you have a duty to testify. If you do not, just as when living a disobedient lifestyle, you cannot be at peace. Likewise, if you shy away from suffering for the sake of the Gospel and Name of Jesus Christ, how could you be at peace? Your conscience will continue to prick you; telling you that you are doing something wrong. Your Calling is not of your own accord; but a Call through the Grace of God, given even before time began, to serve the Lord God Almighty in Christ Jesus! Lord, embolden me and mine to live for You without shame and to stand up and be a witness to Your Power and Glory at any and every time in Jesus' Name. Amen!!!

A popular pastor once told me that he couldn't deal with an issue presented to him because he was not in the Spirit! He had to wait to be in the Spirit! Let us reason this out to see if it is in accordance with the Word of God! The Bible says if the Spirit of God dwells in you, you are not in the flesh! It does not say that at times you will be in the Spirit and at other times not. The Holy Spirit is very consistent; He dwells in you, then He is in you permanently! He Can however be withdrawn is why David said "take not Your Holy Spirit from me"! The world cannot receive Him because it does not see nor know Him. But the believer in whom He Dwells knows Him for He Dwells in him! O Lord, please pour Your Holy Spirit into me abundantly in Jesus' Name. Amen!!!

There must be a Sabbath Rest for God's servants/children! Jesus often took time out to rest and be alone in prayer and meditation. This is exemplified in the above Scripture. He dismissed the crowds, having met their needs (both spiritual and physical)! It is very important for us to do good though; because if you do evil, your heart cannot rest. This is why most people suffer untold hardships unnecessarily! Please Help us o Lord to do good in Jesus' Name. Amen. Give us rest o Lord in Jesus' Name. Amen!!!

The Bible makes very clear that we should not love worldliness! As long as we love the things in the world that the world rely on and come to rely on such things, are we not worldly? Some of us preach this but are very unliked and unpopular; but we bear the "shame" of constant ridicule because we are considered and called all manners of names including hypocrites because we are not perfect! Well, I would rather "suffer" this way than not preach the truth of God's Word; for I desire to please God and not man. God Knows that I am not perfect and He is fully aware of all my imperfections. Like Abraham, Isaac, Jacob (Israel), David, etc., God Loves me and Covers my all in Jesus' Name. I rejoice always. Amen!!!

71st Day

DO NOT BEFRIEND THE WORLD AND BE AN ENEMY OF GOD! GOD SAYS DO NOT WORRY! TRUST WHOLLY IN THE LORD!!!

If only we would actually reflect on the counsel in the Word of God as delivered above in all truth and sincerity, we stand to learn and thus gain much. We worry too much and it does us no good but harm all the time and yet we do not stop worrying; even though the Word of God says that we should not worry! Please God, Help us to learn of Your Holy Ways and not worry so we can benefit from the Blessings in the Word of God!!!

It is very easy to envy sinners when we see them prospering in the lands. It is very easy to wish we were like them and in their shoes because our focus is like that of the world; to succeed! Our focus is clearly stated in the Word of God; fear God and obey His Commandments. Then, our expectations and hope shall not be cut off! O Lord, please Help us to keep our focus aright upon the fear of God and obedience to His Commandments; that it may go well with us all the days of our lives in Jesus' Name. Amen!!!

God jealously desires the Spirit He put into us! We must keep our focus all the time on pleasing Him and doing His bidding. We can only do this by living in the fear of Him; there is no other way. When our focus is shifted off God, we dwell on the world and the apparent successes of the worldly/ sinners; hence, we get enticed. When enticed, we do our best to befriend the world (even as believers) so as to be accepted by and acceptable to them. Thus, we become enemies of God wittingly or unwittingly. Beware! God is not mocked; we shall reap whatever we sow!!!

Jesus ministered to the crowds of people and was very sensitive to their needs because He Knew that a lot of them came from far and wide and would be hungry after a while. Here we are about to "experience" the generosity of spirit exuded by Jesus Christ always in His Ministry. He was Powerful yet very Compassionate! The disciples were also sensitive to the needs of the crowds and wanted Jesus Christ to send them away to go and feed themselves. Jesus had something else in mind; He wanted to Provide for their needs! O what a God we have! He steered the disciples in precisely that direction in telling them to give the people something to eat!!!

The Lord Knew that the worshiping of idols is very attractive to the ordinary mind of mankind. Hence, He warned and counseled against the children of God getting enticed and ensnared by idol worshiping! God also Knew that idol worship is abominable and He wanted to Protect the children of God from abomination that would work against their best interests with God. However, the attraction is always way too strong. Please God, Help us to stay on Your side and not follow after the ways of idolatry in Jesus' Name. Amen!!!

Let us follow after the ways of God even in worshiping Him if we want to please Him; because God is not impressed nor pleased with the things that impress and please mankind! We love to please and commend each other! Alas! We do this at the expense of pleasing God! Help us o Lord; that our hearts be flooded with Your Presence and Your Holy Spirit that we desire only to do Your Will in Jesus' Name. Amen!!!

72nd Day

FEAR AND SERVE THE LORD REGARDLESS OF REPROACH; GOD WILL BLESS/REWARD YOUR FAITHFULNESS!!!

Blessed are ye, when men shall revile you, and persecute you, and shall say all manner of evil against you falsely, for my sake. Rejoice, and be exceeding glad: for great is your reward in heaven: for so persecuted they the prophets which were before you. Matthew 5:11,12 KJV

When you believe and follow Jesus Christ, people will revile, persecute and say evil against you falsely for the sake of Jesus Christ! Rejoice! Great is your reward in Heaven. This is not at all easy in practice; we need God's Help and Staying Power to live with such levels of discord! YOU will wonder with you've done to deserve such etc. God is Telling you not to worry; rejoice!!!

For us who follow the Lord in Spirit and in Truth, like I've said above, be prepared for persecution and false accusations/allegations etc.! However, don't fear reproach from men nor be terrified by their insults. Don't even be anxious nor live in fear of such; don't waste your energy or life! But continue to hope in the Lord knowing that your faith will not go in vain and that your salvation and righteousness is forever!!!

Stop fretting because of the wicked prospering! It's a waste of your time and life! Just focus on trusting/resting in the Lord your God and He Will let your light shine and Give you judgement. Be patient to wait upon the Lord and He Will Deliver you and Bless you in Jesus' Name. Amen!!!

Do not be arrogant or prideful trusting in your wealth etc. because you can lose it all in one fell swoop! Do you make light of the fact that a lot of wealthy people are so wretched, miserable, poor, blind and naked and desperate! Even if you're wealthy, use your wealth to bless God Almighty and take care of the needy, poor and impoverished! Hence, God Will Bless you! !!

73rd Day

WHEN GOD IS ON YOUR SIDE, YOU ALWAYS HAVE VICTORY; GOD IS FAITHFUL... OBEY HIM for YOUR OWN GOOD!!!

"Listen" in the above sense is listening, hearing and doing (full obedience) to reap the benefits listed!!!

The "curse" is hereby "lifted" in Jesus' Name! Just meditate on the Word of God and be obedient! Good Lord! Can we blame God when we're the ones continuously flouting His Laws etc.? Hmmm! Fear God! Obey His Commandments and live! Please Help my family and I o Lord to be hearers and doers of Your Word in Jesus' Name. Amen!!!

Because the Lord is my LIGHT, I cannot ever again walk in darkness! Amen! Because the Lord is my Salvation, my Rock, my Fortress, my Rampart, I have no more fear of this evil cruel world! My Lord Protects me and at the same time "sorts" out my enemies! Because the Lord is on my side, it is well with me and no weapons formed against me shall prosper in Jesus' Name. Amen!!!

That man is unfaithful does not and will never equate man with God for God's Faithfulness remains intact regardless of man's unfaithfulness! God is faithful in Blessing and in Judgment! Yes! God is Just! Halleluyah! Amen!!!

God's Word can only be Right and full with Truth! That's why He Loves Righteousness and Justice! THE Goodness of the Lord can be seen all over the world! All over the world the Spirit is Moving... all over the world as the prophets said it would be... all over the world, there's a mighty revelation... of the Glory of the Lord as the waters cover the sea! Deep down in my heart likewise in Jesus' Name. Amen!!!

When we live in disobedience, satan tempts us with something or the other and would always "give" us something "desirable"! In this case "their eyes were opened"! Yet, they were both shamed and afraid! We always have excuses and always blame someone or the other and we hardly ever take responsibility! However, whose loss is it when we disobey? Ours fully!!!

Blessings for obedience and curses for disobedience has always been God's Way and remains the same! When in obedience we walk in automatic Blessings mode but when otherwise (in sin) we walk in automatic curses (we don't have to be cursed)! Once we're outside of the Word of God, we're unprotected from the evil one period! Lord please Help me to live my life in, with and for Your Name's sake in Jesus' Name I pray with thanksgiving. Amen!!!

74th Day

LIFE and PROSPERITY; DEATH and DESTRUCTION; YOU CHOOSE! DWELL ONLY ON THE POSITIVE; OBEY and BE AN OVERCOMER for BLESSINGS!!!

The Lord Has Laid before us all what is good and which way to follow for salvation and eternal life; however, He Will not force us to follow! We all must choose our path and all will be responsible for the choices they make! Why is it that whenever God counsels us to do good, we do the opposite? He Tells us to walk in one way, we walk in the opposite way! Hmmm! Despite knowing the Blessings for obedience and curses for disobedience stance of God, we still refuse to obey! If He chooses to destroy us, can we really say He didn't warn us? Can we blame Him? Hmmm! Help my family and I o Lord to obey Your Word and be Blessed in Jesus' Name. Amen!!!

Be always positive! Think and dwell only on the beautiful things of life so as not to miss out on them! Learn what is good and godly and draw inspiration from these! Forsake negativity because there is no virtue in them! O Lord I need You to be with me all the time in Jesus' Name. Amen!!!

There's one thing hearing, knowing, reading the Word of God; it's a completely different thing DOING obeying the Word of God! When you obey the Word of God you're laying for yourself a solid foundation on solid rock and building on the rock and your house will never fall! Which would you choose? I have made my choice to follow Jesus in learning His Word and obeying the Word of God! Please Help me Lord in Jesus' Name. Amen!!!

These are the games people play in the Name of the Lord! They play eye service and tell people what they want to hear to win them over to their side and receive blessings from them only! They don't care about their welfare spiritually at all! May God spare us from such people in Jesus' Name! May we not lose out on our salvation and the blessing of God to come even Eternal Life in Jesus' Name. Amen!!!

To overcome is to do the Will of God till the very end in maximum obedience! To overcome is to have God's Favour regardless of the person! To overcome is to be Blessed by God in a diversity of ways as stated in the Scriptures above in Jesus' Name. Amen! Yes Lord! This is reserved for those that You my Lord Favour! Thank You Lord Jesus for Favouring me this way in Jesus' Name. Amen!!! Meditate deeply on the words!!!

75th Day

IT TAKES HUMILITY to SUBMIT ONE'S LIFE to GOD ALMIGHTY and LET JESUS CHRIST REIGN THEREIN; HUMBLE YOURSELF and BE LIFTED UP!!!

We who believe ought to set our sights not on the difficulties of the faith walk but on the "prize" - the never fading Crown of Life that Jesus Christ will bestow upon those He Considers are deserving! Believing God itself is an act of humility! It's pride that keeps people away from God. THE fact that God opposes the proud alone should keep people working diligently against pride in their lives however, most just don't care! THE fact that God Gives Grace to humble ought to make humility very attractive to all so as to be lifted up; alas, we see the opposite in most of our lives. We need God desperately; yet some people will not submit! Yet, Judgment is coming! Lord, I ask for Your Help that I might walk humbly in the faith so as not to lose or miss the prize in Jesus' Name. Amen!!!

Do not engage in fleshly judgment especially before time; when the Great Judge who will Judge Justly is just around the corner! Every hidden secret will be laid bare by Him who does not miss anything we all do/say in our lifetime! Wow! May God Have Mercy on us for we are all very guilty of sin and not one of us deserves that Crown of Life! This alone ought to keep us humble; yet, we boast against fellow brethren as if whatever we think we have over them was not "Given" to us! Lord, Teach us to humble ourselves and not to be jealous nor envious of our brethren and stop boasting over things that we are "given" that we perceive others not to have! Help us o Lord in Jesus' Name. Amen!!!

So also Abraham 'believed God, and it was credited to him as righteousness.' Understand, then, that those who have faith are children of Abraham. Scripture foresaw that God would justify the Gentiles by faith, and announced the gospel in advance to Abraham: 'All nations will be blessed through you.' So those who rely on faith are blessed along with Abraham, the man of faith. Galatians 3:6-9 (NIVUK)

Abraham is the father of faith and so all who have faith after him are his children and heirs according to the Promise of God to him! In Abraham,

God first announced the gospel that all nations will be blessed through him who was considered by God to be the man of faith and unto him his faith was credited as righteousness! Wow! Abraham's Blessings are mine! Whosoever shall bless me shall be blessed and whosoever shall curse me shall be cursed! Jesus Reigns and Lives in me! O Glory Halleluyah thank You Jesus!!!

Isn't this what we do in our so called churches today? We heap up sin upon sin; yet on Sundays we gather in worship and thanksgiving bringing all manners of gifts "to God" with lots of announcements of activities including offerings?! How very apt! This is what we love over and above Jesus Christ our Lord and God who is looking for true worshipers who will worship Him in Spirit and in Truth! O Lord, Have Mercy on us in Jesus' Name. Amen!!!

76th Day

ALL HAVE ACCESS to THE FATHER THROUGH JESUS CHRIST'S BLOOD and WITH THE AROMA OF HOLY CHOICE GIFTS and PRAISE! YOU CHOOSE!!!

Once upon a time, like most, I lived in abject poverty of spirit; steeped in abominable sinfulness! But through the Blood of Jesus, I became redeemed, now reconciled to God, I say thank You Lord Jesus for Saving me from imminent death and destruction and Giving me Eternal Life! Do you want Eternal Life? Come to Jesus; the Author and Finisher of the Faith! Only Jesus Can Save!!!

Wherever you find yourself, serve the Lord there; with your choicest contributions, gifts and holy things - which would be a soothing sweet aroma unto the Lord God Almighty! May the Lord accept my offerings in Jesus' Name! Your offering may be in the form of praises to God or a gift unto the less fortunate and or servant of God who the Lord Has Used to touch your life in one form or the other! May the Lord Teach you wisdom in this regard in Jesus' Name. Amen!!!

Jesus Christ Gives us confidence and boldness to reach/access His Holiness because He's such a Merciful God! Draw me to Yourself that I might be a worshiper and true; let Your Presence come and flood my heart, till all I see is You! Yes o Holy Spirit! Thank You o Lord for the opportunity Given me to access Your Holiness in Jesus' Name. Amen!!!

Many of us are still suffering from generational curses upon our generations due to our great fathers before us abandoning the Faith in the Holy God and opting for idols! THE curse remains until we choose to abandon such idols and return to the true Holy God in Jesus Christ. Then, the curse will be lifted and our destiny restored in Jesus' Name. Amen! Is that you? Do you know of feel that is you and you need help in this regard? Get in touch with me! I am willing, ready and able to help you overcome this problem in Jesus' Name. Amen! Do not hesitate!!!

77th Day

GOD TAKES NO PLEASURE IN THE DESTRUCTION OF THE WICKED; HENCE THE CAUTIONS BEFORE REPRIMAND! HUMBLE YOURSELF, REPENT!!!

If you repent of your sins and begin to obey God's Commands and do right, you will find God's Favour and live! Please God therefore; turn from sin and live! Make no mistakes however; if you do not turn, you will be destroyed and die!!!

When you turn from evil and begin to do good/right, your reward is Eternal Life! Why don't you opt for what lasts forever folks?!!

Still on the same matter of turning from your sinful ways and returning to the Ways of the Lord God Almighty and be restored! God Has His Role but you must play your part in shunning evil! God won't shun evil for you! YOU have that duty/responsibility!!!

Jerusalem of God! Children of God, desist from wickedness and evil so you may be Saved! YOU have a part to play! It's not just about Grace Grace Grace! For how long will you continue in evil/sin? If you want to be Saved, you know what to do! Just do it!!!

Turning from evil/sin involves a lot of humility! Especially you who are known as the Lord's and called as such! Humble yourself, seek His Face and turn from wickedness! Then will God Hear from Heaven and Forgive your sin and He Will HEAL your land! There is a part you must play! It's not just going to happen by this Grace we all abuse!!!

You are all guilty! We all are! We turned away from God's Ways and Commands and failed to do right! To your tents o Israel! Let us return to God so He Will Return to us! He is Faithful and will Keep His Covenant if and when we obey! Enjoying His Best (LOVE) is not unconditional at all as many think and preach! We have a duty and a responsibility!!!

When Jesus Touched my heart, I became a changed man! I began to preach, teach and spread the Gospel of Jesus Christ so much so that word went around that I, a former worldly person am now spreading the Good News of the Gospel of Jesus Christ! All this I did without the help of man or having submitted to any authority but that of Jesus Christ! God Still Does this today; and I am a living witness!!!

A fool's way is right in his/her own eyes! THE person who heeds counsel is wise though! A fool may think he/she is wise; but wisdom resides with the one who heeds Godly Counsel!!!

78th Day

ETERNAL LIFE: MY CHOICE for MY LIFE! HOW ABOUT YOU! HAVE YOU RECEIVED ETERNAL LIFE? TOMORROW MAY BE TOO LATE!!!

Eternal Life is not for everybody! If God Loved everybody unconditionally and equally, then why woudn't He Give Eternal Life to all likewise without conditions? Hmmm! Believe what you like but God Told me that He Does not Love anyone unconditionally nor equally! There is a condition attached to God's Love! YOU have a choice to obey God or not! YOU have a choice and an opportunity to receive and accept the Son of God and receive His Love and Eternal Life!!!

We were in the filth of life and the world! Jesus Christ Intervened on our behalf to Save us and wash us thoroughly through the Holy Spirit! We were cut off from the Throne of Grace and Mercy! Jesus Christ reconciled us to the Throne. Now we have our lives back and much more... even Eternal Life! Halleluyah! Amen!!!

Even though I may be suffering now, I remain unashamed because I know the One I have my faith in is Trustworthy and is Able to take good care of me and keep safe all I entrusted into His Hands... even my life! Help me o Lord to keep and hold fast to the pattern of sound doctrine I received when I came to You Lord Jesus in faith and in Love through the Holy Spirit Dwelling in me!!!

Only God is Able to keep the believer from falling and present him/her before His Glorious Throne without fault and with great joy! All Glory, Majesty, Power and Authority belongs and be unto Him, Jesus Christ our God and only Saviour before the ages, now and forevermore. Amen and Amen and Amen!!!

There is a FIRE that burns all the enemies of God but does no harm to His Children; but burns all their enemies too! That fire is Given whenever God Feels the need to do so for spiritual warfare! THE enemy knows the difference and generally stays away when this fire is burning in and or around the children of the Almighty God! Thank You Lord Jesus for Your Divine Protection over my family and I and all who wish us well!!!

79th Day

GOD IS LOVE BUT HE CUTS OFF UNFRUITFUL BRANCHES;
WHILST PRUNING THE FRUITFUL ONES! MAKE NO
MISTAKES ON THIS!!!

"I am the true vine, and my Father is the gardener. He cuts off every branch
in me that bears no fruit, while every branch that does bear fruit he prunes
so that it will be even more fruitful.

John 15:1,2 NIV

God (Jesus Christ) is the Vine and Gardener because He incarnated Himself
to come to mankind in sinful flesh! We know and call Him LOVE and often
assume wrongly that He loves everybody and equally to and that He is so
merciful, He Will not destroy! How wrong! He is an All-Consuming Fire!
He Will Destroy a majority in the unending unquenchable fire! He Cuts off
branches that are barren and prunes those that are fruitful! Even pruning is not
an easy process. So, God is not cheap! Following God is a very costly business!
It's not a take take matter! It's give and take! YOU get Blessed but you have to
sacrifice (especially your love of this evil/cruel world)!!!

Those who misquote the Scriptures tell you that the law is no longer
relevant! However when you rightly divide the Word of Truth you find
that unto whom much is Given, much is desired! In the New Testament,
Grace requires increased holiness without which no one would see the
Lord! It requires living a holy life following after the Spirit of the Living
God and not after the sinful flesh! So, God Sent His Son to Enable us to
do just that by believing in Him and following His example!!!

You who fall into sin often give in without even trying to get out of it even
though God Promised a way of escape because sin is so sweet! Satan comes
with a sweet aroma to disguise his intent to steal, kill and destroy! Resist
the devil and he will flee! If only we would obey the Word of the Living
God! There is a way of escape always and you will not be tempted beyond
that which you can bear! God is Good!!!

You must contend for and stand up for the Old Time Religion and stop following after the so called modernisation of Faith in Jesus Christ. THE only path that leads to the Ancient of Days (Jesus Christ) is the Ancient Path; no other will do! Godless men have changed the Grace that comes with Faith in Jesus Christ into a license for immorality; thereby denying our Lord Jesus Christ, the Only Sovereigh and Lord God Almighty!!!

Obeying the law in itself and following after the dictates will not justify the flesh because sin is made visible through the advent of the law; where there is no law, there is no sin! When you sin, you contravene the law though; i.e. you're lawless! However, only in Jesus Christ is human flesh justified through faith in Him! No one can force another to believe in Jesus Christ. At best you can share/witness to the Gospel; only Jesus Christ Himself through His Holy Spirit can anyone come to the Light!!!

80th Day

IF IT HAD NOT BEEN FOR THE LORD WHO HAS BEEN ON MY SIDE MY ENEMIES WOULD HAVE HAD A FIELD DAY OVER MY LIFE!!!

My hope is built on nothing less than Jesus' Blood and Righteousness; no merits of my own I claim but wholly trust in Jesus' Name!!!

Who will advocate for me against my adversaries? If not because I have Jesus as Lord, the cares of life... the worldly woes would have overwhelmed me! I'd have been long forgotten but for Jesus Christ in my life. Oh I thank You Jesus!!!

The death and resurrection of Jesus Christ so significantly gives hope to the hopeless, strength to the weak, succour and comfort to the broken hearted, peace to the troubled and more just because Jesus Christ is full with mercy, compassion and love especially for the needy! This spiritual largess comes by faith and salvation and leads to the attainment of the ultimate goal... the Crown of Life that will never fade away!!!

And if we know that He hears us in whatever we ask, we know that we have the requests which we have asked from Him. If anyone sees his brother committing a sin not leading to death, he shall ask and God will for him give life to those who commit sin not leading to death. There is a sin leading to death; I do not say that he should make request for this. All unrighteousness is sin, and there is a sin not leading to death. We know that no one who is born of God sins; but He who was born of God keeps him, and the evil one does not touch him. 1 John 5:15-18 NASB

Be merciful to one another because mercy prevails over judgment! May God Help us especially against the sin which leads to death quite apart from unrighteousness all of which is sin! There is a sin that we do not even need to pray for; that which leads to death! This is only Revealed by God Himself by faith! Blessed be His Holy Name forever and ever Amen!!!

Sometimes in the faith journey, we are left all alone (everyone deserts us)! Every true believer would most likely experience this! But pray for the deserters that it will not be held against them because God takes it very seriously when we break faith with one another especially with saints of God! May God Deliver us who believe from every deadly snare/arrow and evil attack; and may He Bring us safely home to His Heavenly Kingdom in Jesus' Name. Amen!!!

Look and consider the recommendation of godliness in faithful living! Lowliness, gentleness, long-suffering, bearing up with each other in LOVE... keeping the unity of the Spirit in the bond of Peace! Look at those of us who call ourselves Christian Faithful today! Is any of these virtues really live in our daily living even in our homes with our wives and children let alone at work, play etc. Hmmm... true... only God Knows those who are truly worshiping and serving Him in spirit and in truth!!! May God Help us all in Jesus' Name. Amen!!!

81st Day

SHARE YOUR FAITH, FOCUS YOUR MIND ON THE GOAL and PUT YOUR BODY UNDER STRICT CHECK (FULL SUBMISSION) IN JESUS CHRSIT!!!

When you come to believe in the Lord Jesus Christ, you can't keep it to yourself (at least it's not in your best interests to do so)! Better to share your faith with others; as in so doing, you gain a fuller, richer understanding of the Goodness of God in Christ Jesus! In refreshing and meeting the need of the servant of God, you encourage them and give them great joy! Do this diligently in Jesus' Name!!!

This is faith: though you do not see Jesus Christ, yet you love Him, believe in Him and have inexpressible joy, full with glory! As a benefit for your faith in Him, you have salvation for your soul! Only Jesus Can Save. No man can save you; only Jesus is the Answer! Only Jesus is the Way and the Life! Put your trust/faith in Him!!!

In my faith, I am not aimless and without purpose; I am very focused (at least I do try my best to be)! I place a great restriction of my body/flesh in order to keep me from sinning (especially willfully)! As a preacher of the Word of God; I don't want to miss the prize through disqualification even after preaching to others! This means I have work to do as well and not just say Jesus paid the price fully and it is all over and I don't need to do anything! This is a fallacy being preached by people!!!

Jesus Christ felt the need to Reveal the Power of God to specific disciples of His (not everyone of them)! Interestingly, Moses and Elijah appeared to them talking with Jesus! Peter felt the need to mark the place with the erection of tabernacles for the 3 of them. Then a Voice Spoke from Heaven confirming the Sonship of Jesus Christ and that God is Pleased with Him! Wow! If such happened today who would believe? God is Great beyond human understanding but yet fools say there is no God!!!

82nd Day

YOUR RELIGION SHOULD BE SERVICE-BASED and DRIVEN BY LOVE for EACH OTHER; NO EYE SERVICE, BE TRUTHFUL and SINCERE!!!

Basically, in your daily living, reach out to each other and do not follow after the selfish "look-after-number-one" worldly agenda of today! Humble yourself and be willing to lend a hand, serve your brethren! Keep love flowing in Jesus' Name. Amen!!!

You may be enslaved even to a Christian brother/sister; serve as though your serving Jesus Christ is what the Word of God says! Leave all matters of judgment to God regarding whether or not a Christian should have slaves or not!!!

Offer service and hospitality to each other; remembering the weak, sick, impoverished, oppressed, prisoners, orphans, widows etc.! For whatever you do for any one of these, you do for Jesus Christ and He Will Call all to account some day in this regard! Be prepared in and out of season for the Day of the Lord will surely come!!!

Endure hardship! There are spiritual benefits of going through hardships! Don't let anyone deceive you and or make you feel bad when going through hardships! Follow the Standard of God for no one receives a victor's crown except they've competed according to the rules otherwise they'd be disqualified! Diligence and hard work pay off in the long run!!!

Fear only the ONE who Sent you with the message not those you're delivering to! If they listen to you, then they're listening to ME; if they reject you, then they've rejected ME! So, it's not for you to feel bad and or discouraged when rejected. Be fully assured that it's ME they're rejecting not you! Unless of course I didn't Send you! !! Hmmm!!!

83rd Day

IF IN JESUS CHRIST, THEN WALK IN THE LIGHT! ALL WHO FELLOWSHIP WITH HIM MUST WALK IN HIS LIGHT!!!

How glorious it must have been for the disciples and all who encountered Jesus Christ "live" on earth? What a great privilege! But then did they all see it as such? But according to Hebrews 11, to walk by faith is even more glorious! Jesus Told the doubting Thomas that he had proof that He was Crucified and Rose again, but Blessed are those who believed without proof! Walk by faith in Jesus' Light so darkness does not overtake you as a believer! Remember that satan waits around prowling, wanting to devour! YOU can only be sons of Light when/if you walk in the Light. JESUS is the LIGHT!!!

There is nobody who is absolutely ignorant of their walk in darkness in my view; when you're living in sin, you know through universal ideologies/ means! If you have fellowship with Jesus Christ, you do not walk in darkness! If you walk in the light, you have fellowship with other believers and the Blood of Jesus purifies all from all sin. If you however claim to have no sin, the truth is not in you! So, you activate the Cleansing Blood of Jesus in having fellowship with other believers!!!

Jesus answered, "Are there not twelve hours in the day? If anyone walks in the day, he does not stumble, because he sees the light of this world. But if any one walks in the night, he stumbles, because the light is not in him." John 11:9-10 RSV

Those who walk in the light of day are unlikely to stumble because the light enables them to see; unlike those who walk at night who stumble because the light is not in them and it's dark! As a believer, you have the advantage of walking in the light of God because you belong to the LIGHT!!!

If you're blessed to be wealthy in this world, do not be prideful/arrogant or put your hope in your wealth because your wealthy today, tomorrow you may not be. Wealth is so unpredictable/uncertain. Rather, hope in

God in Jesus Christ who according to His Riches in Heaven makes all provisions for us to enjoy all things through Jesus Christ our Lord! Trust/hope/faith in your wealth is equivalent to self-deceit and would lead you astray because riches are fleeting like your human beauty!!!

The law with the relevant sacrifices it demands cannot perfect the man! If the law could achieve perfection for the man, there would not be a need to offer such sacrifices continuously; for there would be no more consciousness of sins once the man is purified! The blood of bulls/goats cannot take away sins; so there is a need to offer atonement continuously. However, Jesus Christ came to shed His holy unblemished Blood as a once for all Sacrifice and this is effective not just for the forgiveness of sins but also for reconciling us with the Lord God Almighty in Jesus Christ!!!

84th Day

PRIDE IS DEFINITELY NOT A FRUIT OF RIGHTEOUSNESS! IT IS WHAT BROUGHT SATAN DOWN FROM GLORY! AVOID IT!!!

Job's words only attest to the reward due to the wicked! Pride is as a necklace for the wicked and like the proverbial "necklace" in jungle justice will serve as fuel for the destruction of the wicked and will "help" bring down the prideful/arrogant!!!

Nobody knows tomorrow except God; and no man is God except He who IS both Man and God, Jesus Christ! So, mortal man, better stop boasting about tomorrow and give up on self-praise; because you do not know what tomorrow holds in store and when others praise you, it's more authentic/real/true! Be wise!!!

If you must boast at all, let it be in the Lord God Almighty; that you know Him and even as you testify of Him! YOU can commend yourself all you want; it means nothing to God! It is he who the Lord God Himself Commends that He Approves! Mankind love to approve/commend one another and applaud accordingly! Who matters to God the most is the one the Lord Himself commends, recommends... approves! Again, be wise and stop following after the foolishness of mankind!!!

We who believe are like strangers in this world; for we've been Called forth out of darkness into His Marvelous Light and He Has Saved us from this darkness and we must rejoice in His Power and Might! We're a royal priesthood, holy nation, chosen generation, peculiar, strange etc. So, no need to keep wondering why we're different; nor wishing/wanting to be like everybody else which is a very common statement believers make! Flee from fleshly/worldly lusts that war against our souls and deal so uprightly even amongst the ungodly such that even as they speak evil of you, when they observe your righteous ways, they will praise our God on that Day!!!

The anointing of God is not ever automatically transferable! It's not impossible either for such a transfer to occur! However, it happens by faith; and faith is sincere, truthful, honest and pure... childlike for it to please God! When the Anointing of Jesus Christ (God) shows up, life/health/power flows through any vessel as chosen and anointed by God Almighty in Jesus Christ!!!

85th Day

WHEN LED BY THE HOLY SPIRIT OF GOD YOU DO NOT
CONTINUE TO REVEL IN SIN; PUT FLESH to DEATH and LIVE
BY THE SPIRIT!!!

When in Jesus Christ, we have an obligation alright; but it's not to the sinful, fleshly nature to live according to its dictates because that leads to death even if it seems right to us! Our obligation however is to live according to the dictates of the Holy Spirit which leads to life by putting to death that sinful/fleshly nature and its desires! Yes you can!!

Who amongst us can do these? Be truthful to yourself! Until you can do this, you still have work to do on your faith! Many claim righteousness in vain but God Alone Ascribes righteousness unto whom He Wishes! But that does not mean we should stop preaching holiness and righteousness because we cannot do what is right all of the time! Father God please count me worthy in Jesus' Name. Amen!!!

Jesus Demands your all (absolutely everything) to focus on following Him! He Assures of absolutely no regrets! He Promises much more than whatever we give up for His sake in terms of Blessings that'll accrue unto us. He is very Faithful to His Word. I believe Him. Now do you? If you do, then come to Him right now at the expense of everything that has and that will hold you back. Come now!!!

The only goal that needs to be scored in Jesus Christ is the goal of LOVE! Love driven by sincere faith that comes of a good conscience! Is it not true that many have wandered away from the Faith into meaningless talk (in their attempt to be popular/relevant/famous and known as "super" pastors with "healing" powers)! These know very little about the Love of God nor the faith that drives this Love. May God Help us to keep away from such pride/arrogance and from falling prey into the hands of such men/women in Jesus' Name!!!

Examine this woman's faith! She remains humble even in the era where most women today are being trained never to take even from their own husbands! She displays the Sarah-like faith recommended for daughters of Abraham following Jesus Christ. They call their husbands Lord/ Master and their beauty comes from within not external in dressing with make-up and super hairdos with "human" and other type attachments and all the fake beauties!!! To God Alone be all the Glory in Jesus Christ!!! Halleluyah!!! Amen!!! Thank You Jesus!!!

86th Day

THE LORD WILL LEAD/GUIDE/TEACH/INSTRUCT YOU; DO NOT FEAR OR WORRY WHICH WAY YOUR HEADED! HAVE FAITH IN JESUS CHRIST!!!

I will instruct you and teach you in the way you should go; I will counsel you and watch over you. Do not be like the horse or the mule, which have no understanding but must be controlled by bit and bridle or they will not come to you. Psalm 32:8,9 NIV

At times when confusion attacks our minds and we're not sure which way to go or even what to do; and even at other times when we think we know - we should really seek the Lord and listen out for His Voice - He Will Speak to us and Lead us in the way He Wants for us to go! We must have faith/trust/hope in Him. He NEVER Leads His own astray and He NEVER fails! Jesus Christ is always safe for us!!!

The Lord Does not order everyone's steps willy nilly; He Orders the steps of the righteous (good people) and Delights in their ways! When the Lord is Pleased with a person's ways, He Causes even their enemies to be at peace with them!!! Hmmm... Isn't He Faithful and Sure?!

Although people make plans, at the end of the day, everything is in God's Hands! YOU may plant as an expert farmer, do you have the power to make whatever you've planted grow? No! It's all in God's Holy Hands! O Lord, please order my steps that I may never stray from Your Ways in Jesus' Name. I need You o Lord more and more with each passing day! I need Your Love, Power, Grace, Mercy and Peace in my life, for my family and ministry! Cause me to prosper Lord; enlarge my coast in Jesus' Name. Amen!!!

87th Day

THE POWER to FORGIVE SINS BELONG to GOD and HE GIVES ACCORDING to HIS WILL and DESIRE. COME, SUBMIT to HIM IF IN NEED! HE WILL DELIVER and FORGIVE YOU!!!

God has a heart to forgive sins but are we sorry for our sins or we want to just take His Loving Heart for granted? Hmmm! When God forgives, you experience a manifestation of His Blessing in your life so much so that others who hear of what He's Done for you will tremble and be in awe!!!

Forgiveness comes in the Name of Jesus Christ! His Message is of LOVE, repentance, forgiveness of sins and proving your repentance with doing good!!!

When you're in Jesus Christ you're renewed through submission of your everything to God including your mind! God Does this by reconciling us to Himself through Jesus Christ and He Gave us the ministry of reconciliation (not just given to the pastors; all believers have this)!

We have an authentic testimony of and about Jesus Christ! We have more than enough for us to believe and it's impossible to have everything about Jesus Christ written down. But God Designed for us to have enough for us to choose to believe!!!

The angel of the Lord despite all the power Given to testify remains humble as a fellow servant of all who have the testimony of Jesus! Worship God alone (not any man/woman)! The spirit of Prophecy is the Spirit of Jesus Christ! Jesus is alive and hence His Spirit cannot be a ghost!!!

88th Day

THE KINGDOM OF GOD EXISTS ONLY BY RIGHTEOUSNESS; IT'S FUTILE SEEKING AFTER THE KINGDOM OF GOD WITHOUT THE RIGHTEOUSNESS THAT GOES WITH IT!!!

Many love to talk about belonging to the Kingdom of God but want nothing to do with the righteousness that goes with it; the very thing that makes it the Kingdom of God. Be wise in living for God otherwise lose the Kingdom and all that goes with it!!!

If you're living righteously, know that it shall be well with you for you shall not labour in vain! If not, seek after righteousness and reap the benefits for it's a fruitful endeavour. Preach, teach and live as an example for others to follow in your righteousness!!!

Is it so difficult/complex to witness for Jesus? No! It's human beings that have introduced diverse brain-led, knowledge based ideologies and trick based razzmatazz orchestrated by charlatans all "in the Name of the Lord!" Beware of wolves in sheep's clothing claiming to be of the Faith!!!

The Scripture suggests that there will be a lot of deception regarding the last days and the coming of the Lord; so, believers must watch and pray fervently, ceaselessly. Many boats are berthing; don't jump on the wrong boat because not all these boats have a righteous destination; and for the children of the Promise, there is only one destination - Jesus Christ (Eternal Life)!!!

89th Day

I NEED THE PEACE OF JESUS CHRIST IN MY LIFE ALWAYS. GRANT ME O LORD IN JESUS' NAME!!!

The Peace of God (Jesus Christ) is REAL! However, it is your responsibility (as well as mine) to let it rule in our hearts because we were called to peace. Likewise, we're to let the Word of Jesus Christ Dwell in us richly, even as we teach and admonish (encourage) each other with all wisdom, psalms, hymns, spiritual songs, with grateful hearts! We're to do whatever we do in word/deed all in the Name of Jesus Christ, with thanksgiving to the Father through Jesus Christ!!!

When God Loves you, He Gives you amongst other things, Peace! God hates the wicked and the violent (Psalm 11 vs 4)... no peace for the wicked! Gbam! So, if you want to remain wicked, you will reap a just reward; but if you repent and change your ways, God Will Take you back and Bless you with His Love including Peace in Jesus' Name. Amen!!!

Have no anxiety about anything, but in everything by prayer and supplication with thanksgiving let your requests be made known to God. And the peace of God, which passes all understanding, will keep your hearts and your minds in Christ Jesus. Philippians 4:6,7 RSV

Stop worrying; God Says not to! But put your concerns into prayer and supplication with thanksgiving to God Almighty in Jesus' Name. In so doing, enjoy the peace of the Almighty God because you have FAITH!!!

When you have faith, you trust in God and your mind is secure and steadfast! When your mind is all over the place, this is symptomatic of a lack of faith, hence no peace/rest. Jesus Christ our Lord/God is our Everlasting Rock of ages!!!

Jesus exits the scene temporarily (for three days) in dramatic and spectacular form (day turns into night suddenly)! He Said He was thirsty; and they gave Him drink ridiculously! Jesus Said (Declared): "it is finished." He bowed His head and gave up His Spirit (when He was ready; not before)!!! He had Power to give it up and when ready, He Took up His Spirit again (He Rose again on the 3rd day)! Halleluyah! Amen!! Thank You Jesus!!!

This is the response to good discipline! We all must learn from this as explained in Hebrews 12! There is a sorrow that is Godly; and it is good because it produces repentance and leads to salvation unlike worldly sorrow which leads to death! God be praised forever more in Jesus' Name. Amen and Amen and Amen!!!

90th Day

PRIDE DOES NOT PAY; IT COMES BEFORE A FALL! HUMBLE YOURSELF ALWAYS!!!

Rage begets much destruction! Pride, like rage goes before destruction! Can we deduce that anger, which leads to rage is rooted in pride and all work together to wreak destruction? Hmmm... With the Godly information we have on pride and with we know about anger and rage, shouldn't we rather humble ourselves and learn to endure rather than give in to anger/rage/pride for the sake of peace and love? Hmmm! God hates pride, arrogance, evil behaviour and perverse speech (which includes cursing, swearing, hurtful words etc.). Can you say you're a Christian when you engage in perverse speech. How often do you get told to trust in your heart? THE Bible says the heart is a deceitful and desperately wicked and if you trust your heart, your a fool! Whose report do you want to go with? Those who stray from God's Commandments are under a curse; and the proud disobey His Words!!! Check yourself!!!

Why was Pilate (with all his power) afraid? Straying from truth induces fear in the heart of man. The sinner runs when no one is chasing; but the righteous are as bold as a lion! The sinner runs because of guilt (having strayed from truth). But when you walk in spirit and truth, fear has no hold over you. Try truth! Be careful with power because it can change hands at any time. The one who betrays an innocent man is guilty of a greater sin than the one who doles out judgement based on falsehood. Humans take note (liars, cheats, false accusers, and false witnesses)!!!

Balaam was as a prophet of the Lord! He had and knew the Word of God! God Spoke to him and he obeyed God! No matter the type of enticement, oh servant of God, speak only what the Lord Tells you to say and it will be well with you in Jesus' Name!!!

91st Day

WHEN YOU LEARN FROM THE MASTER; NO USE UNLESS YOU OBEY!!!

Lord God, You Are my Master/Teacher and have been since childhood! I continue to tell the world of Your Mighty Power/Works! Please God, let me get old/grey and please Keep Your Covenant of Love with me as with our forefathers in the Faith not to leave nor forsake me. Please God, let me declare You unto my generation and upcoming ones; let me fulfill my destiny in Jesus Christ before You Call me home in Jesus' Name I pray with thanksgiving. Amen!!!

Like the 4th Commandment (I believe) about honouring the parents, God is Telling us here to walk in the way that He Commanded us likewise!! That is how important it is to obey God's Commandments/Laws! Hmmmm eni a wi fun, Oba je ko gbo (i.e. the one we have told, Lord, let them hear and obey!!!

For all those lovers of positions in the body of Christ, to whom positioning has become as gods (& there are many), this Word is very apt/direct! If servant leadership of Jesus Christ is the object, people would not kill and engage each other with fetish to attain positions! Humble yourself, that you may be exalted in due season by God!!!

JESUS CHRIST IS THE KING OF THE WAY, TRUTH and THE LIFE!!! Pilate enquires of the Lord if He IS a King! Jesus Answers in very clear terms; and states that for that very reason He was born to testify to the truth and everyone on the side of Truth listens to Him (true to this day)!!!

When you pray and have not received an answer; do not be discouraged! Just believe that God Has not forsaken you! Like this widow, you will yet receive your Answers in Jesus' Name! Persevere! Will Jesus find faith on earth (in you and I) when He comes? Hmmmm... keep striving and don't give up!!!

92nd Day

WORK DILIGENTLY IN THE NAME OF THE LORD!!! BEAR LASTING FRUITS!!! YOU WILL BE REWARDED!!!

Work to help people come to know and fear the Lord and to help the brethren, especially the ones doing God's Work; help them fervently and diligently - your labour is of love and will never be in vain in Jesus' Name - you will be rewarded. Show this diligence to the end to make your hope sure and inherit the promises of God - now I'll do that. God please help me in Jesus' Name. Amen!!!

Go learn from the ant about diligence and hard work and rewards! Combine this with godliness and contentment and entry into God's Rest! Then you will not need to work like an elephant and be rewarded like an ant! Don't give in to laziness which does not bear good fruit; but rather poverty and perpetual wanting!!!

The sluggard says, "There is a lion in the road! A lion is in the open square!" As the door turns on its hinges, So does the sluggard on his bed. The sluggard buries his hand in the dish;

Empty boastfulness is the lot of the lazy! Always tired and never active; hardly ever willing to even try! Lazy in everything in life; even to eat - but is the wisest in his own eyes! Is that you? A change of heart will change your direction for good! Try; believe God and just try! Peace!!!

For those reading this who have been cheated, oppressed, held captive, I proclaim release in the Name of Jesus Christ! I decree the imminence of the promises of God for you and yours in your unique situation in Jesus' Name! Your oppressors and adversaries will be brought to book in Jesus' Name. You will have victory! Can you believe/trust God???

This prayer is for those that heard the message of the Lord and believe and it's a blessing that transfers even unto those who will choose to believe their message too! Wow, what a Saviour? What a Blessing! Thank You Lord Jesus for Loving me (us)!!! Help me to stay true to You and to the Faith in Jesus' Name. Amen!!!

93rd Day

ARE YOU BEARING FRUITS THAT WILL LAST? ARE YOU LEARNING? ARE YOU MATURING OR YOU REMAIN CHILDISH? OBEY/TRUST GOD and LEARN!!

When you "follow follow" people as my Nigerian brethren would say... when you can't stand on your own feet and follow others aimlessly, blindly, how can you ever learn? You by so doing prove that you do not learn! Hence, instead of you having learnt and sharing your learning with other people, you still need to be spoon-fed like an infant needing milk and not solid food. What a shame. Solid food is for the mature, who have trained themselves to know good from evil! Are you mature or still a child; you alone know deep down! No use deceiving yourself; God Knows all and will Reveal in due season!!!

Do you know it takes guts/confidence etc. in the Name of the Lord to learn God's Word enough to minister same to others far and near; teaching others to obey what you have learnt to obey such that you exemplify such teachings/learning and be a role model of same? There is no point in going to sit every time in a church and you remain unfruitful in your own life. The harvest is ripe and the workers few. ARE you one of those the Lord Sent to work but remain idle?? Hmmm!!

The Word of God is not all about goodies and prosperity like your pastors feed you every time! The Word of God breaks you and if you respond humbly and cry out to the Lord for Help, He'll rebuild you and fill you with His Holy Spirit for guidance all through your life. Your choice!!

Preaching God's Word is foolishness to the perishing but to the saved, it is the Power of God. What is it to you? YOU can't hide from God! God uses the humble foolish things of this world to confound the intelligence of the wise! He is a stumbling block and foolishness to many; but to those being saved, the Power of God. Jesus Christ is the Power and Wisdom of God!!

If you value the Word of God you would know to value anything about His Kingdom and do all within your power to gain access to the relevant knowledge, information etc. that would enable you to get in even through the narrow gate!! May God Help you as you humble yourself! For God opposes the proud and gives Grace to the humble!!!

94th Day

GOSSIP: IT FUELS THE FIRE OF QUARRELS, WHICH IS FUEL FOR STRIFE; AVOID BOTH AT ALL COSTS!!!

Gossip mongering promotes quarrels so don't be surprised when you're sowing the seeds of gossip and you experience endless quarrels; which in turn promotes strife! Gossip is sweet though and popular as a result but the end result of it is strife!!!

Do not be an "amebo" (rumour monger) in your family or community; fear the Lord! Likewise, do not do anything that would cause harm and or injury to your neighbour at all (be it grievous, bodily or not)! Fear the Lord your God!!!

Do not stir up evil within your family and or community (including at work); if you do so, you're worthless, as good as spoilt (anything spoilt is no longer fit for any good use). The words of an evil worthless person are like a scorching fire (do you not know some like that?); and be on the lookout for those that separate intimate friends... they bear bad news, spreading bile from one to another; spreading slander on to another until a quarrel develops and strife rages between them, thereby separating them! This is evil!!! Don't get involved; fear God!!!

95th Day

I REALLY WANT and NEED ETERNAL LIFE: JESUS IS ETERNAL LIFE!!!

Do you know that anyone that will not eat the Bread of Life cannot be a part of Him (likewise drinking of His Blood)! The Bread of Life is Eternal Life! Anything else you eat will be passed out and you will die ultimately; only the Bread of Life when you eat, you will live forever! The choice again is fully yours!!!

Death has no power over the righteous so struggle to enter into the righteousness of God in Jesus' Name for everlasting victory!! We shall be changed into the form that Jesus Christ is in... how awesome!! Some copy their pastor's dress mode; we won't need to copy, we shall be automatically translated into our Pastor/Shepherd's mode. Oh Jesus! I love You!!! Amen!!!

Learn righteousness and Love and keep your learning and abide in the same and you will receive the promise of Eternal Life in Christ Jesus!!!

The disciples were curious and confused about His leaving (going and being seen no more then in a little while being seen)! He still tried His best to assure them but still they didn't really fully understand till much later when the events came to pass!!!

Unlike our so called men/women of God who invite the cameras to witness their "shows", Jesus Christ shunned publicity wherever avoidable and in some cases gave stern instructions to those healed not to tell; so much so that this particular one did not know who healed him!!! Hmmmm... who are we really serving when we claim to be serving Him??? We shall all come under Judgement!!! Beware!!!

96th Day

GOD LOVES YOU, YES; BUT YOU MUST BELIEVE HIM TO ENJOY HIS LOVE BECAUSE HIS LOVE IS NOT CHEAP - GOD'S LOVE IS PRECIOUS!!!

This is the verse that many quote to justify their mindset that God Loves everybody unconditionally! Please kindly examine the Scripture both with your mind and by the Spirit of God (if you have the Holy Spirit). It does not say that God Loves the world unconditionally (man says that not God not the Bible)! It says God so loved the world alright, that He Gave His only begotten Son; but it goes on to say... "that whoever believers in Him shall not perish, but have eternal life". The Word and Blessing and Love is for those who believe!! That "whoever believes" is what the Word says; it's not for all and sundry! Those that do not believe stand condemned already if you care to read the very next couple of verses (John3:18 as above for example); so, be wise!!!

The above verse accentuates the previous one in exactly the same way! All the prophets witness to Him (the Old Testament testifies to the Lord Jesus Christ's story because He is from of Old and He is the Ancient of Days). Some still maintain that the Old Testament ceases to be relevant for today. Jesus Christ NEVER said so. He Said: He did not come to abolish the law (the Old Testament), but to fulfil it. Stop changing the Word of God - do not add to it or take away because a curse is upon whosoever does this!!!

Thomas wouldn't believe until he saw specific evidence! He was shown alright; then, he believed - but Jesus made clear that Blessed are you when you believe without evidence! That is faith; being sure of what you hope for and certain of what you have not seen. Rather different than today's seeing is believing self-proclaimed faith!!!

All of those people claiming to be working for God in so many ways... did God Send you to do all your doing or are you doing things for yourself in the Name of the Lord? Better wait on the Lord for Him to Send and Authorise you lest you work in vain!! The work of God is that you believe in Him whom He Sent!!! Amen. It's very clear but we tend to choose contraptions from our own minds conjured up for our own fleshly reasons!!! Beware!!! The wrath of God!!!

97th Day

BE ALERT and SOBER; ENEMY ABOUT!!!

How can you consume alcohol and get tipsy/drunk as a Christian and claim to be sober? Do you not agree with the common sense principle that anything that affects your brain functioning cannot be good for you quite apart from being Christian? The enemy prowls waiting for you to fall! Be and stay sober for your own sake and may God Help you and Help us all in Jesus' Name. Amen!!

Victory against satan is assured; so, endure patiently like a good soldier whatever trials/tribulations come your way and the Spirit of the Living God Will continue to Help you in Jesus' Name!!

You not only have to be sober, but be very vigilant and pray for a discerning spirit for satan disguises himself as an angel of light. Satan works through people not just in the spirit; and they will come as innocent and harmless. Remember that the Bible says a man's enemies will be the very members of his own household! Beware and take good care! Pray ceaselessly and believe!!

For a successful walk with the Lord, you have to submit yourself to the Authority of the Lord God Almighty in Jesus' Name and resist the devil/satan! Don't just sit back and take whatever satan throws your way; resist him - you have the power within you in Jesus' Name to resist, so resist the devil and he will flee because he hates your resistance!!!

You cannot live a holy life without being pure in heart! Since without holiness no one will see the Lord, it makes sense that the pure in heart are Blessed because they shall see God!! Be ye holy as I am Holy; be ye perfect as I am Perfect says the Word of the Lord! It pays to obey the Word of God!

The fathers of the faith were hopeful in faith for the Great Promise of God to come to pass and they died in their hope/faith! Though they longed for the promise, they lived as witnesses to the promise they did not see. However, their faith was not in vain because God was pleased with them and not ashamed to be called their God! What a testimony!! Lord Help me to please you so my testimony can be sure and rich in Jesus' Name I pray with thanksgiving. Amen!!!

98th Day

FAITH IN JESUS CHRIST ALONE OVERCOMES THE WORLD!!!

For everyone born of God overcomes the world. This is the victory that has overcome the world, even our faith. Who is it that overcomes the world? Only he who believes that Jesus is the Son of God. 1 John 5:4,5 NIV

A victory that overcomes the world (which is very tough to overcome) is being born of God as in being born again into Jesus Christ by faith in Him! The one that believes Jesus Christ is the Son of God overcomes the world! Also, to know that the Father and the Son are ONE even with the Holy Spirit!!! That is our faith!!!

If you want to please God, you must live a just life by faith in Him; this is a daily life of faith-living to please God. Without faith, no one can please God. If you don't even believe that God exists, how can you be in faith then? You cannot believe that He is a rewarder of them that diligently seek Him if you don't believe that He even exists in the first place!!!

It is by grace that one is saved through faith; not through works of the self, for it is the Gift of God such that no one can boast! God Gave us the Gift of Faith! But does everyone have this gift or will everyone get it? Not so. Because it is not for everyone; it is for those who choose to believe!!!

When I come into Jesus Christ, I give up my life in the flesh and take on a new life in the Spirit such that it is no longer I who lives but Jesus Christ who lives in and through me - i.e. the life that I live anew in Jesus Christ, I am living by faith in the Son of God, who loved me and Gave Himself for me!!! Not I, but Jesus Christ Lives in me and through me!!! Understand that somebody?

The Kingdom of Heaven is like a seed sown that receives the breath of God and yields a harvest thereby multiplying the original seed sown abundantly! This is likened unto yeast which you only need a little bit to work into a dough of flour and yet is so fast in multiplying itself till it works right through the whole dough so fast! The Strategy of God for the Growth of His Church therefore is not what man things through like as in worldly marketing strategies!!! Hmmmm... may God Help Save us from worldliness in the Name of Godliness!!! Amen!!!

99th Day

Only those who stand firm to the end will make it into Heaven! The joy of a race is not in starting alone but in finishing! The beauty of starting something is not ever the same as the beauty experienced in seeing it to conclusion! Many do not start well, but finish well and are satisfied! Many start well and finish badly and are dissatisfied! God, I plead with you to let me finish that which you began in me in Jesus' Name; for You Who Began the Good Work in me are more than able/faithful to complete it in Jesus' Name. Amen.

The righteous are supernaturally strengthened to the finish line in Jesus' Name. They flourish till old age; likened unto the palm tree and the cedar of Lebanon. Their path is like the light of dawn that shines brighter unto the full daylight is come! The fruits of righteousness are more than worth it for one to pursue righteousness. Help me o Lord to pursue righteousness and live a righteous life in Jesus' Name. Amen.

God Does not discriminate and although He often appears unjust is very very Just! He Will not only Save those He Assured Salvation unto; He Will also extend Salvation to some of those who hated Him who are willing to listen to the story of Salvation and choose to believe; so that everyone will have no excuse, but have every opportunity to make a decision. All will be judged according to what they claim to believe!! Amen!! Halleluyah!!

These are signs of the last days and when we look at these stated signs seriously, we would all agree that those times predicted are here upon us already! Many have a form of godliness and truly deny its power. The question is are we able to turn away from such people! Especially at a time when we just love to be liked, appreciated, acknowledged etc. We love the world so much and claim to be so eager to bring all to Jesus to save all as if we love mankind more than Jesus Christ Himself who has already told us that we should struggle to enter through the narrow gates!!!

Preach the Word by all means but know that you cannot of your own accord save anybody! May God Bless and Help us all!

100th Day

I have seen you in the sanctuary
and beheld your power and your glory.

Because your love is better than life,
my lips will glorify you.

I will praise you as long as I live,
and in your name I will lift up my hands.

This is my testimony! How can anyone say to me there is no God when I have beheld His Power and Glory? When I know that His Love which He Gave to me is better than life itself? I will praise Him from everlasting to everlasting! Somebody help me praise the Lord! HALLELUYAH!!

I sat down under his shadow with great delight,
and his fruit was sweet to my taste.

Psalm 91 comes readily to mind here... He that dwelleth in the Secret Place of the Most High... shall abide under the Shadows of the Almighty... where there is great delight and plenty of sweet fruits... leading unto the Banqueting house at the Lord's Table... in the presence of my enemies with His Banner over me... LOVE!!!

The righteous man will flourish like the palm tree,
He will grow like a cedar in Lebanon.

Planted in the house of the LORD,
They will flourish in the courts of our God.

This is the heritage of the righteous! A lot of people quote this verse as if it applies to them and claim it! YOU can claim it all you want! It applies only to the righteous!! I am not sorry, this is the Word of God. If I am unrighteous, I need not apply as they say when you fail to meet the relevant criteria when looking for a job! Truth!

Jesus' Judgement is Superior Judgement unlike that of a man! Jesus Said He Came into this world for judgement! People talk about love love love and more love forgetting completely that judgement may not appear to be loving or love at all! We need to get real in the Faith and stop chasing after shadows as we're doing at the moment. This is why even in the so called places of worship, righteousness is scarce as love is too!!!

How many times are you in a position to help a brother/sister and you withhold your hand or actually say you are not in such a position when you didn't even have to say anything? YOU forget that God Sees/Knows all things? Hmmm... The God of that time remains God anyway and very capable of similar judgements! God is Love; yes! But, He is also an All-Consuming FIRE!!! He Will LOVE sometimes and at other times He Will Consume!!!

101st Day

The Yoruba have a saying that my mouth will not kill me! It's a kind of prayer. What is the mouth if not the tongue? Self-control is critical to have in faith not just with the tongue though! We all meet evil; the issue is to turn from evil and do good. The path and option of peace is very readily available however not many take that option! But if you would love life and see good days, the instruction or counsel is very clear: keep tongue from evil and lips from deceit etc. candid and good advice. Who is listening though? This is a must if you want to prosper! No amount of prosperity preaching can give you God's Prosperity which is not only about money/wealth!!

The lip of truth shall be established for ever:
but a lying tongue is but for a moment.

Lying lips are abomination to the LORD:
but they that deal truly are his delight.
Proverbs 12:19,22 KJV

Lips, like tongues can be used interchangeably in Scriptural references almost for they do more or less the same job. Truth is a choice we have to follow; who wants to though? But know this: the Lord Delights in those who deal truly i.e. in TRUTH!

O LORD, who shall sojourn in thy tent?
Who shall dwell on Thy Holy Hill?
He who walks blamelessly, and does what is right,
and speaks truth from his heart;
who does not slander with his tongue,
and does no evil to his friend,
nor takes up a reproach against his neighbour.. Psalm 15:1-3 RSV

Who wants to ascend unto the Holy Hill of the Lord? Who wants to sojourn and or dwell in His Sanctuary? The Word is very clear. YOU must obey closely to achieve this lofty but not impossible feat. God is Great and with Him nothing shall be impossible; so, get on God's Side and get God on your side!!! Yes, you can!!!

Faith is driven to success by Love. Bible says the only thing that matters is faith that works through love! Love is not a feeling. Love is a choice and a decision and is very active not passive. So, you cannot really have faith without love for the object of your faith can you now? Therefore, if you have faith, your faith can only live if powered by love to "work"!!! Anything that is done had better be done if faith otherwise worth nothing in God's Sight!!!

102nd Day

HELP ME THANK THE LORD FOR MY LIFE!!!
STILL I LIVE!!! BECAUSE JESUS LIVES I CAN FACE EACH DAY!!!
THANK YOU JESUS FOR MY LIFE!!!

How could I ever forget to give You thanks o my Lord Jesus Christ?!! I will remember You every day of my life for the rest of my days! I will celebrate You on this Special Day as well as on my Birthday, 28th of February, for the rest of my days! For You Have Been so good to my family and I o Lord! Thank You Jesus!!! Exactly 6 years ago today! I went in for an emergency heart operation known as an aortic dissection!!! To the medical experts, please decipher and tell us what it means really!! For me, I was told that 80% of those diagnosed with aortic dissection are diagnosed "post mortem"!

You must understand what that means!! That means they are only diagnosed after they are dead!! for years on and though still in recovery because it's a very difficult operation to recover from fully with all manner of possibilities, for me it has been a miraculous recovery process as I have all my faculties back and am walking freely by God's Special Grace!! It was over 10 hrs on the surgeon's table!! It was supposed to be a 4/5 hr operation!! After the operation, I woke up into the tender hands of a Nigerian lady nurse who told me what I said as I came round so to speak! I spoke in Yoruba (remember I didn't know who was going to be with me and when you're coming round from anaesthetics imposed for the operation, you do not know anything).

I said: "Awa ti b'eegun ja, ati segun egungun; awa ti b'orisa ja, ati segun orisa; ati wa di orisa akunlebo fun awon ota wa"! Meaning: we have fought with the masquerades and have overcome them; we have fought with the gods and have overcome them; we have now become as gods to be worshipped on the knees unto our enemies!! So, I reiterate that it is the living that CAN praise the Lord Jesus Christ. The dead cannot!!

My wife did not become a sudden widow nor my children suddenly fatherless!! I do not rejoice over those that experienced such; am just giving due Glory to the God of all LIFE for sparing me to date! Praise be unto His Holy Name!!! I thank God for my wife and sons in particular and the very few friends who came to pray for me at the hospital and continue to uphold me in prayer to date and those who visited, called, sent texts etc. You are all highly valued and will be lifted up in Jesus' Name!!! My classmates from King's College and all highly valued. Thanks and God Bless y'all in Jesus' Name!!!

I praise You O Lord God of Heaven and Earth today that You Have Done me well and kept me alive to see this day which I celebrate as my kind of second birthday!!! The day the Lord Gave me a definitive second chance to live!!! I will praise Him and serve Him till I die; so, if you love and appreciate me and my ministry help me to thank God Almighty in Jesus Christ for preserving my life! Even if you do not love me and you can help me thank Him please feel free to do so!! Alaaye ni o ma yin Yin, oku ko le yin Yin!!! (The living will praise You, the dead cannot)! Halleluyah! Thank You Jesus for Loving me!!!

103rd Day

The pure are Blessed for they shall see God! The acts of righteousness undertaken by the pure, the righteous will never go unnoticed nor unrewarded! To the pure all things are pure. The pure at heart see with the eyes of purity; but the crooked see with the eyes of corruption and to them nothing is pure and that shows in all they think, say and do! Although he too may claim to know God, yet by his deeds which are unrighteous, he denies God in every way! So, it's not who proclaims God, purity and righteousness that has a pure heart; but rather, he who does/acts righteously is pure in his heart and will be Blessed!!!

We are fearfully and wonderfully made to and for God's Glory to be revealed in us for us to shine is a dark and evil world! God said let there be light and there was light. I decree a thing and it comes to pass according to God's Will. I decree Light upon and into your life right now in Jesus' Name. Receive LIGHT!!!

104th Day

He who is generous will be blessed

If you know in your spirit that a person is a servant of the Lord and because of that you lend a helping hand, you will not fail to be rewarded; if however, you hurt them, remember Touch not my Annointed. That means you will pay! No nice way of saying that; today, too much wickedness especially against the servant of the Lord!

Is this not the fast that I have chosen?

Is it not to deal thy bread to the hungry,
and that thou bring the poor that
are cast out to thy house?

When thou seeth the naked, that thou cover him;
and that thou hide not thyself from thine own flesh?

Then shall thy light break forth as the morning,
and thine health shall spring forth speedily:
and thy righteousness shall go before thee;
the glory of the LORD shall be thy reward.

Then shalt thou call, and the LORD shall answer;
thou shalt cry, and he shall say, Here I am.
If thou take away from the midst of thee the yoke,
the putting forth of the finger, and speaking vanity;

And if thou draw out thy soul to the hungry,
and satisfy the afflicted soul;
then shall thy light rise in obscurity,
and thy darkness be as the noon day:

And the LORD shall guide thee continually,
and satisfy thy soul in drought,
and make fat thy bones:

and thou shalt be like a watered garden,
and like a spring of water, whose waters fail not.
Isaiah 58:7-11 KJV

Fasting is very common and is a new type of religion especially amongst so called believers. They believe that fasting will do everything for them. Fasting is very good; don't get me wrong. But read the above and have a rethink! Whilst so called fasting you're doing whatever you want with your mouth and your body and your mind; you're wicked and unjust and unloving; and everybody must know that your fasting as you announce to the whole world. YOU ridicule yourself and put your faith to shame in the presence of unbelievers in particular and believers in general; even if nobody checks you, can't you check yourself?

Well, the Lord is Good (all the time) and His Mercies endure forever!!! Seek God and live!!!

105th Day

Blessed are the peacemakers; for they shall be called the children of God
Matthew 5:9 KJV

Remember as you work for peace with all men and reconciliation with both man and God that it is the Power of the Holy Spirit of the Living God that CAN achieve your stated objectives! So, do not be discouraged when you're appearing to be failing in your endeavour! Jesus Christ is on the Throne and at a time you're not expecting, there will be a turnaround in Jesus' Name. Don't give up!!!

If you want life, love and to see good days, you must consciously take charge of your tongue for good and against deceit and turn from all evil and do good, pursuing peace always relentlessly. This is profitable. But who will listen eh?

The counsellors of peace is joy! Proverbs 12:20 KJV

Wow! The counsellors of peace is Joy! Can we say the fruit of peace is joy? There can only be increased joy when there is peace starting from the family to the whole nation of peoples. Take heed of the Word of God!!!

Pray for the peace of Jerusalem!

"May they prosper who love you!
Peace be within your walls,
and security within your towers!"

For my brethren and companions' sake I will say,

"Peace be within you!"

For the sake of the house of the
LORD our God, I will seek your good. Psalm 122:6-9 RSV

Pray for the peace of your nation and in particular my nation Nigeria!!! The prayer applies to all lovers and well-wishers of Nigeria. So, stop badmouthing the nation. Bless always and stop cursing! Prophesy good upon Nigeria and it shall come to pass in Jesus' Name. Amen!!!

There will always be talk behind your back as a believer; no matter how much you seek to please the whole world which many are doing rather than seeking to please God! Just focus on the One that Sent you for He Will Give you all the Backing you need in His Service always. He Will never fail u; He Will not leave nor forsake you!!!

Hmmmm... Persecution ain't funny and ain't nice at all. Nobody wants it but it will happen with all who follow Jesus Christ so don't even bother to pray against it. It is Biblical that there is no one who will follow Jesus Christ and not face persecution!!! Just know this: you are Blessed, for great is your reward in Heaven and those before you, the Faithfuls went through exactly the same thing!!! Be fully encouraged in Jesus' Name. Amen!!!

106th Day

I am with thee to deliver thee; Work to See His Kingdom Come

"If you repent, I will restore you that you may serve me; if you utter worthy, not worthless, words, you will be my spokesman. Let this people turn to you, but you must not turn to them.

As a servant of God, you must dare to fearlessly, boldly trust and believe the Word of God completely! See from the Word above; as a sinner, all you need to do is to repent and be restored ready for service! It is the Lord that makes ready no man can make you ready except the Lord's Hand is with him to teach and train you in the Way of the Lord! No shortcuts!

You are not too small to serve God; once in His service, you're automatically exalted but you must receive this grace with full and maximum humility! No one will fight you and prevail from the moment your Sent. If you believe this Word, just run with it!!!

Even to speak sometimes is almost impossible as you can't find the words; do not panic! Relax for the Holy Spirit is with you!! Often we don't remember this, even as servants of the Lord, especially when in crises!

Do not let anybody shake or change the agenda God Gave you for your life. If you have not received an agenda yet, then wait on the Lord; He is Faithful to Deliver right on time! God's Time is the best we often hear; but, who is ready to wait?

The bottom line: The blood of bulls, goats, birds, fowls etc. cannot take your sin away or save you! Only the Blood of Jesus CAN do that and that is a FINISHED Work on the Cross at Calvary!!! Only JESUS can SAVE!!!

107th Day

Righteousness exalts a nation,
but sin is a reproach to any people.

In the same way the Blessings of a good and faithful servant applies to the good and faithful servant of State. A good citizen may not work for a government parastatal but is a servant of State. You have the choice to love your nation and pray for your nation and wish your nation well according to the Word of God and Pray for your leadership whether they do right or wrong. The whole essence of praying for leadership is so that God Will Touch their hearts to do right and godly by God and by the nation. Let us all be patriotic especially with regard to Nigeria. May my God, the God of Abraham, Isaac and Jacob Bless and Have Mercy on Nigeria, my fatherland in Jesus' Name I pray with thanksgiving for all He Has Done for us as a nation. Amen.

A wise servant shall have rule
over a son that causeth shame,
and shall have part of the inheritance
among the brethren.

A faithful servant is rewarded by God because promotion does not come from the East, West, North or South; but promotion comes from the Lord God Almighty. In due season your reward will come. Remain faithful when in service directly or indirectly.

This simply means that tests will always come in your life but not to destroy you for the Lord Has Said that He Will NEVER test you beyond that which you can cope with i.e. God Will not allow you to go through tests of life beyond your capacity to cope!!!

Righteousness exalts a nation,
but sin is a reproach to any people.

A servant who deals wisely has the king's favour,
but his wrath falls on one who acts shamefully.

Proverbs 14:34,35 RSV

May God Give our leaders the heart to deal wrathfully upon servants of State who act shamefully and same for parents and children and same for parents who act shamefully will be dealt with via the wrath of God Almighty since there is no Authority greater than God.

No eye service which is very plentiful in our communities; people who bless you when you're there and curse you behind your backs no matter how good or bad you've been to and with them. Are we really doing whatever we're doing as unto the Lord in expectation that the Lord Will Reward us according to our deeds good or bad???

The Word is meaningless without the Spirit; it is the Spirit that Gives Life to the Word spoken, written or thought no matter how used! The Spirit of the Word is the Spirit of Jesus Christ and is the Spirit of Prophecy. The whole world or earth was Created at the instance of the Spoken Word. God Said: "Let there be; and there was" and He's still Speaking today!!!

108th Day

We should follow His steps

For even hereunto were ye called: because Christ also suffered for us, leaving us an example, that ye should follow his steps:

Who did no sin, neither was guile found in his mouth:

Who, when he was reviled, reviled not again; when he suffered, he threatened not; but committed himself to him that judgeth righteously:

Who his own self bare our sins in his own body on the tree, that we, being dead to sins, should live unto righteousness: by whose stripes ye were healed.

Have you been through Jesus for the Cleansing Power? Are you Washed in the Blood of the Lamb? Are your garments sparkling are they white as snow are you washed in the Blood of the Lamb? ARE you washed in the Blood? In the soul-cleansing Blood of the Lamb? ARE your garments spotless are they white as snow are you washed in the Blood of the Lamb?

Because if you are, you will be more like Him in thoughts, words and deeds. Strive to be like Him and you won't regret it!!!

109th Day

Teach your children well "Let us be diligent then to Obey Him and teach our children to do the same..."

Let us remember that this was the Old Testament and compare with the New Testament where it says the servant of God must be the husband of but one wife and the wife and children must obey and respect him properly! To such a man God Entrusts much!!! Does it mean God cannot use others? No. But this is the Word of God!!! I would strive to obey if I were you as long as I have the opportunity to do so!!!

The instructions are very clear! What use is your faith if your children and their mother are not carried along? That is a recipe for family chaos as is evident in many homes. Through sincerity of purpose and prayers, such homes as are willing to obey the Lord are very possible!

The governments of the world say don't smack your children! What does the Word of God Say? Which will you obey? Your choice! There is a way that seems right to a man, in the end it leads to death. There is a way to discipline your children without government interference today! If you're willing and obedient, you will eat the best of the land. This is the Word of the Living God!

Preach the Word of God with your testimonies without fear or favour and the Lord Will Surely Back you up every time if you trust and believe Him!

You do your best! Not everybody will want what you want and that includes peace with you and you do not need to offend people before they war with you because satan is using them to try and destroy your faith and challenge your belief structures. Do not yield to satan. Resist the devil and he will flee is the Word of the Loving Living God!!!

110th Day

God's promise of salvation unto them that trust and hope in Him is secure and sure! If you trust and hope in Jesus' Christ our Lord God Almighty, you will never be put to shame and or disgrace that is the lot of the wicked and unbelieving!

The way of life of the wise must be evidenced by their faith and different than that of the foolish who do not believe. If you claim therefore to believe, your faith must be seen in how you live your life daily. Faith is not a matter of words but of power as faith is like the Kingdom of God itself. The Power of God must be evidenced in your daily living; there must be fruits to prove your faith walk!!!

But God shows his love for us in that while we were yet sinners Christ died for us. Since, therefore, we are now justified by his blood, much more shall we be saved by him from the wrath of God. Romans 5:8,9 RSV

God's Love is supreme as He Showed His Love whilst we were yet sinners. This should however not be mistaken for God loving everybody forever! God Showed His Love in this way; but those who believe set themselves up for receiving God's Love whilst those who refuse to believe in this Holy Sacrifice set themselves up for the wrath of God. God is Love and REAL and all in all but He is also the All Consuming Fire that will consume all His enemies and the wicked!!!

Teach me Your way, O LORD;
I will walk in Your truth;
Unite my heart to fear Your name.

I will give thanks to You,
O Lord my God, with all my heart,
And will glorify Your name forever.

For Your loving-kindness toward me is great,
And You have delivered my soul from
the depths of Sheol. Psalm 86:11-13 NASB

I need Thee every breath I take O Lord; lead me; teach me; break me; remold me; refill me with Your Holy Spirit... so I may be like You increasingly in life, in love and in Spirit day after day! You alone delivered me from death through your LOVE for me!!! Thank You Jesus!!!

Feed me till I want no more O Lord and fill me with the benefits of feeding on the Bread of Life. Enable me to eat Your Flesh and drink Your Blood so I may stand worthy and considered accordingly on that DAY!!!

I said it earlier that God is LOVE; yet He is a terrible God full with terror; make no mistake about it. God Will repay; vengeance is His!!! So, our preaching must include the full person of God and not present God to people in a one sided LOVE LOVE way without the other side, the terrible, terror side. Complete Knowledge of God is what is TRUTH and sets people free. Praise the Lord! Halleluyah!!!

111th Day

The world will put you down when God Has Called you; remember, one with God is majority in the Spirit! Be prepared in and out of season, especially to stand alone if needs be, for the sake of the Word of God. You can preach but you can't force anyone to come to the Lord and you can't save anyone; only Jesus Christ Can Do that and by the Power of the Holy Spirit. So, don't expect people to like or love you because they hated Jesus Christ first and they will antagonise you and speak all manners of ill against u; leave all judgments to the Lord Who Sent and Called you. He is Able; vengeance is His and He Will Repay!!!

(10) "For violence against your brother Jacob,
Shame shall cover you,
And you shall be cut off forever. Obadiah 1:10

Life and good; death and evil; the choice you make is entirely yours and for that you're going to be held responsible on that Day of Judgment! Choose well; choose life!!! Nobody else will be responsible for your choices in life unto death!!!

How much clearer can this be? We would rather die than obey the Word of God! We would rather die than follow God's Word. We love the world so much it shows in our daily living but every Sunday we cry unto God and shout Jesus Jesus Jesus yet all week long and even on the Sundays, we're filled to the brim and overflowing with worldly desires at home, work and at play. We love to deceive ourselves and others. Hmmm the Judge is standing at the door!!!

112th Day

The Disciples Sent Out

And he called unto him the twelve, and began to send them forth by two and two; and gave them power over unclean spirits;

And commanded them that they should take nothing for their journey, save a staff only; no scrip, no bread, no money in their purse:

But be shod with sandals; and not put on two coats.

And he said unto them, In what place soever ye enter into an house, there abide till ye depart from that place.

And whosoever shall not receive you, nor hear you, when ye depart thence, shake off the dust under your feet for a testimony against them. Verily I say unto you, It shall be more tolerable for Sodom and Gomorrah in the Day of Judgment, than for that city.

And they went out, and preached that men should repent.

And they cast out many devils, and anointed with oil many that were sick, and healed them. Mark 6:7-13 KJV

When the Lord Calls you, He'll Send you, when He Sends you out, He'll Empower you, when He Empowers you, He'll Help you and Watch over His Word to bring it to pass in your life and experience! When He Sends you out, He Speaks to you and expects you to believe His Voice and obey Him! If you meet and fulfil His Expectations of you, He'll Prove Himself Faithful to you too!!! He is the Lord God Almighty!!! Jesus Christ is His Holy Name; and at the mention of His Name, every knee shall bow and all tongues confess that Jesus Christ is Lord!!! Amen!!! Halleluyah!!!

113th Day

(6) Blessed are those who hunger and thirst for righteousness, For they shall be filled. Matthew 5:6

When you truly love the Lord, you will hunger and thirst for His Righteousness! Nothing else or less would do! Here's a promise from the Word of the Lord God Almighty: "You Will Be Filled"!

When you know your God and the potential for Blessings you will have when in contact and in tune with Him, then you will surely search Him out wherever He may be! He is near you right there in your mouth is His Word! Call on Him and know the difference! I am a living testimony and a witness that the Lord is Good and His Mercies endure forever!!!

This re-emphasizes what happens when you truly love the Lord! Because I love the Lord, my soul rejoices in Him and I delight greatly in Him. My knowledge of Him increases daily as I walk with Him! Will you join me? No matter where you're at, you can come along and share in this joy in this glory with me!!! Amen, thank You Lord Jesus!!! Halleluyah! Amen!!!

I form the light, and create darkness:
I make peace, and create evil:
I the LORD do all these things.

Drop down, ye heavens, from above, and
let the skies pour down righteousness:
let the earth open, and let them
bring forth salvation,
and let righteousness spring up together;
I the LORD have created it. Isaiah 45:7,8 KJV

Tell out my soul the greatness and the wonders of the Lord!!! Behold the Power and Beauty of the Lord God Almighty!!! He is too awesome to behold! Isn't He? Love Him, honour Him, worship and adore Him for He is Good and truly, His Mercies endure forever!!!

The LORD is exalted, for he dwells on high;
He will fill Zion with justice and righteousness;
and He will be the stability of your times,
abundance of salvation, wisdom, and knowledge;
the fear of the LORD is his treasure Isaiah 33:5,6 RSV

He is exalted, the King is exalted, my Lord is exalted on High... and I will praise Him... He is exalted forever exalted and I will praise His Name... He is the Lord... forever His Truth Shall Reign; Heaven and earth rejoice in His Holy Name... He is exalted the King is exalted my Lord is exalted on High!!!!

114th Day

He will rule in glory! The Authority of Jesus Christ is unquestionable! It is made very clear in the Scriptures about the Christ of God and the Authority in and of His Person! His Name is Established forever as being Higher than any other name and that at the mention of His Name, all knees must bow and tongues confess that He is the LORD! To Him and to His Name, all honour, glory, adoration, praise etc. is due and His Name shall endure forever and ever. Amen!

He will rule from sea to sea and
from the River to the ends of the earth.
All kings will bow down to Him
and all nations will serve Him.

May his name endure forever;
may it continue as long as the sun.
All nations will be Blessed through Him,
and they will call him blessed.

Praise be to His Glorious Name forever;
may the whole earth be filled with His Glory.
Amen and Amen. Psalm 72:8,11,17,19 NIV

It shall come to pass in the latter days that the Mountain of the House of the LORD shall be Established as the highest of the mountains, and shall be raised above the hills; and all the nations shall flow to it, and many peoples shall come, and say:

"Come, let us go up to the Mountain of the LORD,
to the house of the God of Jacob;
that He may teach us his ways
and that we may walk in His paths."

For out of Zion shall go forth the law,
and the Word of the LORD from Jerusalem.
He Shall Judge between the nations,

and Shall Decide for many peoples;
and they shall beat their swords into plowshares,
and their spears into pruning hooks;
nation shall not lift up sword against nation,
neither shall they learn war any more. Isaiah 2:2-4 RSV

Also, the Mountain of the Lord is to where all will go ultimately to learn of His Ways that we may walk in His Ways. His Way is the way of LOVE! From Zion therefore, judgment will flow forth to all nations until the Peace of God is established with and in God's Love!

Believe in Jesus

When we love others, we know that we belong to the truth, and we feel at ease in the presence of God. But even if we don't feel at ease, God is greater than our feelings, and He Knows everything. Dear friends, if we feel at ease in the presence of God, we will have the courage to come near Him. He will give us whatever we ask, because we obey him and do what pleases Him.

There is incontrovertible evidence that Jesus Christ is the Lord God Almighty! When we belong to Him, we love instinctively; and that's how we know that we belong to the Truth and we increase in confidence in Him regardless of our feelings! The only thing that matters is faith that works through love; in obedience to God's Commandments to keep us one with Him and He with us. His Holy Spirit Given to us evidences our oneness with Him who loves us so!!!

There is more to this passage than meets the eye! It's about "intent"! Even in law, intent is considered before final judgment is delivered! This is applicable in all of living in and for Christ Jesus and not just relevant to adultery. Guilt is established even before the offence is effected. To think is to do! To think by looking with purposeful intent is deemed to have commitment embedded; therefore in the heart, guilt is established. Now, this is very serious!!! What do you think???

115th Day

Saved by Faith - Fulfilling Our Duty to God:
By Faith In Christ Jesus

What a Mighty God we serve! What love? What opportunity? The purity of God's Love is incomparable with anything else life has to offer! At what cost? Just to believe! Is that too much to ask? Is God unjust? He Wants all to be saved and wants none dead! God's Love is not cheap! Make no mistakes about it; and God Knows exactly what to do with and how to protect and defend His Love!!!

Verily, verily, I say unto you, He that believeth on me hath everlasting life. I am that bread of life. John 6:47,48

What benefit is it to you to gain the whole world and lose your soul; especially when you have the choice to have Eternal Life and to feed on and drink the Body and Blood of Jesus Christ?

By grace are ye saved through faith. Ephesians 2:8 KJV

You cannot pay for or buy salvation! You cannot earn it; neither can you work for it! It is entirely by Grace... So that none may boast!

Thy faith has saved thee; go in peace. Luke 7:50 KJV

When you have faith in Jesus Christ, He Gives you the Peace of God that passeth all understanding! Come to Him today!!!

Hmmmm! Satan used the fear of the unknown to trap the woman using deceit and seduction; deceit in that the tree was good for food when God Said Don't touch it! Seduction in terms of the senses - pleasantness to the eyes and also in gaining wisdom, which is about power! Satanic strategy does not change; Why change what works every time eh? To overcome a known enemy, you must study the enemy and not take him for granted! That's the enemy's way! Now let Godly Wisdom be activated in you right now in Jesus' Name to understand this message!!!

116th Day

(20) For where two or three are gathered together in My name, I am there in the midst of them." Matthew 18:20

What began the Church of Jesus Christ in the early times - small prayer cells and especially in homes/families - is highly despised today; especially encouraged by today's popular anti-family lifestyles! To your tents o Israel! When you engage in this way, you are considered as despising the gathering together of believers! Does it mean that the early Church erred according to the Word of God? I say no! Small prayer/fellowship/cell meetings are as effective and relevant in the earlier times as today! May the Lord Continue to Lead His Church aright in Jesus' Name!!!

He's got the whole world in His Hands!!! Peace, be still; be still and know that I Am God!!! Jesus is a Mighty God!!! Heaven and earth bow before Him!!! Every knee shall bow, every tongue confess... That Jesus Christ is LORD!!!

117th Day

The righteous perisheth,
and no man layeth it to heart:
and merciful men are taken away,
none considering that the righteous
is taken away from the evil to come.
He shall enter into peace:
they shall rest in their beds,
each one walking in his uprightness. Isaiah 57:1,2 KJV

We are confident I say, and willing rather to be absent from the body, and to be present with the Lord. to Corinthians 5:8 KJV

God's Ways are very different! This world is not for us really; we who believe are sojourners here on earth. The is a better place for us yonder! Painful as it is when one of us leaves this earth, we ought to rejoice that they are going to a better place! We fear death yet it is inevitable! Just live each day one day at a time and as if it's the last! Difficult but not impossible!!!

118th Day

He Pardons all our sins

Corrie ten Boom used to say that God puts our sins in the deepest part of the ocean... and then puts up a "No Fishing!" sign. Glory!

Men Ought Always To Pray - We need revival, saints. As the household of God first, we are called to repentance; judgement begins with us.

Oh! What a wonderful God we serve! Please take note of 2nd Chronicles 7: 14; humility, prayer/meditation (not as in yoga), seeking God's Face, turning from sin/wickedness is absolutely critical and essential BEFORE pardon! God's Love and or Pardon is NOT cheap!!! I'd rather do it God's Way!!!

119th Day

He Leads and Guides Us

He restoreth my soul; He leadeth me in the paths of righteousness for His Name's sake. Psalm 23:3

They shall not hunger nor thirst;
neither shall the heat nor sun smite them:
for he that hath mercy on them shall lead them,
even by the springs of water shall he guide them.
Isaiah 49:10 KJV

I will direct their work in truth. Isaiah 61:8 KJV

Thou shalt guide me with Thy counsel. Psalm 73:24 KJV

He found him in a desert land, and in the waste howling wilderness; he led him about, he instructed him, he kept him as the apple of his eye. As an eagle stirreth up her nest, fluttereth over her young, spreadeth abroad her wings, taketh them, beareth them on her wings: So the LORD alone did lead him, and there was no strange god with him. Deuteronomy 32:10-12 KJV

Whether you turn to the right or to the left, your ears will hear a voice behind you, saying, "This is the way; walk in it." Isaiah 30:21 NIV

And the Lord shall guide thee continually.
Isaiah 58:11 KJV

Current Blessings Are Ours
The Lord Will Lead Us and Guide Us... there's a natural mystic blowing in the air... If you listen carefully now you will hear... God is a Spirit; all who worship Him must do so in Spirit and in Truth!!! For you to be Led and Guided by the Lord God Almighty, you must humble yourself and pray and submit to Him with fear and trembling... With plenty of patience and waiting!!! Will you? Is this a priority for u???

120th Day

Bottom line is this: if you want to see the Kingdom of God, you must be born again... so repent, humble yourself and submit yourself to God. YOU may not understand everything immediately; but in humbling yourself and submitting to God, God Will Take you from there, Bless you and Teach you through the Power of the Holy Spirit!!! Again, the choice is very much yours to make!!!

(3) Jesus answered and said to him, "Most assuredly, I say to you, unless one is born again, he cannot see the kingdom of God." John 3:3

Jesus is very authoritative and clear about the condition for seeing the Kingdom of God (again proof that almost everything God Does is Conditional). I use the word "almost" because I know that God Alone Reserves the right to Do as He Wills in any situation. God Can Choose to Bless a sinner if He Wants to. He is God. After all, Jesus Said He did not come to call the righteous, but sinners to repentance (again to repentance not to continue in sin and be Blessed anyway)!!!

121st Day

The statutes of the LORD are right,
rejoicing the heart:
the commandment of the LORD is pure,
enlightening the eyes.

The fear of the LORD is clean,
enduring for ever:
the judgments of the LORD are true
and righteous altogether.

More to be desired are they than gold,
yea, than much fine gold:
sweeter also than honey and the honeycomb. Psalm 19:8-10 KJV

(32) Those who do wickedly against the covenant he shall corrupt with flattery; but the people who know their God shall be strong, and carry out great exploits. Daniel 11:32

Flattery corrupts so beware of flatterers and do not flatter others to their detriment and yours! Flatterers do not mean well! However, know your God and reap the results!!!

122nd Day

Instructions to specific groups for Holy Living! Act with the fear of God. The Fear of God is so lacking today! Get the Fear of God back in your heart. Ask the Lord for His Holy Spirit and for the Fear of God to flood your heart, mind and spirit in Jesus' Name. Then you will be transformed. Whatever you do, have in your mind that you're doing it for the Lord; that will prevent you focusing on whether people appreciate or not. Know this; there will be no partiality and there will be reward for every deed, good and or bad!! Yet, God is Love!!! But He is Just!!!

123rd Day

For who makes you different from anyone else? What do you have that you did not receive? And if you did receive it, why do you boast as though you did not? 1 Corinthians 4:7 NIV

But by the grace of God I am what I am, and his grace to me was not without effect. No, I worked harder than all of them--yet not I, but the grace of God that was with me. 1 Corinthians 15:10 NIV

Humble yourself in the Sight of the Lord and He Will Lift you up! The Grace of God is sufficient for you; remember this always and that wherever you are is not by your power or might but by the Grace of God through His Holy Spirit! Remember this when you're dealing with other people when your looking down on others less well off than you or when envious of those you feel are above you! !! Will you be a sheep or would you rather be a goat! Goats do not hear His Voice! Only sheep, His sheep do!! Repent!! For the time is short... and be baptised in Jesus' Name so you can receive the Gift of the Holy Spirit which is a promise for you and your household and for all the Lord our God Will Call!!!

124th Day

For thou art an holy people unto the LORD thy God: the LORD thy God hath chosen thee to be a special people unto himself, above all people that are upon the face of the earth.

The LORD did not set his love upon you, nor choose you, because ye were more in number than any people; for ye were the fewest of all people:

But because the LORD loved you, and because he would keep the oath which he had sworn unto your fathers, hath the LORD brought you out with a mighty hand, and redeemed you out of the house of bondmen, from the hand of Pharaoh King of Egypt.

And repayeth them that hate him to their face, to destroy them: he will not be slack to him that hateth him, he will repay him to his face.

Thou shalt therefore keep the commandments, and the statutes, and the judgments, which I command thee this day, to do them. Deuteronomy 7:6-11 (KJV)

Out of all peoples, God Chose a peculiar people, considered them Holy, Favoured them amongst all others, He Loved and Loves them especially. So, God Does not love everybody and definitely not equally. God chooses whomsoever He Gives His Love to. He Keeps His Covenant and Mercy with them that love Him and Keep His Commandments (definitely not with anybody). But He repays those that hate Him to their face to destroy them!!! Why would He destroy those who hate Him if He loves them regardless!! It's your choice what you believe but I would rather believe the truth of God's Word!!!

Know therefore that the LORD thy God, he is God, the faithful God, which keepeth covenant and mercy with them that love him and keep his commandments to a thousand generations!!!

125th Day

Lord, loose me from all my infirmities in the Holy Name of Jesus! Loose me regardless of my circumstances and the expectation of others around and about me! Set me free that I may serve You without fear or favour in Jesus' Name I pray with thanksgiving!!! Amen!!!

126th Day

The Lord is Faithful to us; it's us that are not faithful to Him! The Lord can therefore bring charges against us for which we must as a matter of course confess and seek forgiveness and Blessings. Who shall bring a charge against the Lord God Almighty eh?

Forgive me o Lord when I have erred against you and even when I do for I am not perfect. However, help me Lord for I want to be perfect as Your Word says be ye perfect even as I am perfect; be ye holy even as I am holy!

Teach me Your Ways o Lord and help me to follow; for without You, I can do nothing good! Help me in Jesus' Name I pray Amen!!!

127th Day

For the kingdom is the LORD's:
and he is the governor among the nations. Psalm 22:27,28 KJV

A voice is calling, "Clear the way for the LORD in the wilderness; Make smooth in the desert a highway for our God. Let every valley be lifted up, And every mountain and hill be made low; And let the rough ground become a plain, And the rugged terrain a broad valley; Then the glory of the LORD will be revealed, And all flesh will see it together; For the mouth of the LORD has spoken." Isaiah 40:3-4 NASB!!!

128th Day

Don't worry or be anxious and think positive and good thoughts. Focus on these things and God Will be with you. So, if you're worrying, know that it does not pay you at all. It pays however to obey God's Word and heed His Counsel!!!

129th Day

And this gospel of the kingdom shall be preached in all the world for a witness unto all nations; and then shall the end come.
Matthew 24:14 KJV

Sing and rejoice, O daughter of Zion;
for lo, I come and I will dwell
in the midst of you, says the LORD.

And many nations shall join themselves
to the LORD in that day,
and shall be my people;
and I will dwell in the midst of you,
and you shall know that the LORD of hosts
has sent me to you. Zechariah 2:10,11 RSV

May His Kingdom Come! At the end of the day, every knee shall bow (in Heaven and on earth) and every tongue shall confess that Jesus Christ is the Lord! Nations will come, men and women, with gifts! For, unto the Lord be the Glory, great things He Has Done and greater things He Will Do. Just believe!!!

130th Day

God - He Who Justifies! No-one but God can bring any charge against God's elect. The same God Who Justifies is the only one who can condemn!!! Does He not have the Power to do so? Is He not qualified to do so? He Can Do and Undo; can't He? How can a so called Christian then say to me that God Does not condemn? If God Does not condemn, how can He Judge? Do these so called Christians have any revelation of the Judgement of God? They talk as if the Love of God is so cheap as to be unconditional!!

And what is the exceeding greatness of His power toward us who believe, according to the working of His mighty power which He worked in Christ when He raised Him from the dead and seated Him at His right hand in the heavenly places, far above all principality and power and might and dominion, and every name that is named, not only in this age but also in that which is to come.

If the Love of God is unconditional and we have nothing to do at all and that it's simply automatic whether or not we live in sin, what and who do we take God to be? May God Have mercy on us all in Jesus' Name. Be wise folks!! Whether you want to accept it or not, Truth is Truth as Revealed only by God to His elect!!!

Man makes up lots of stories and they take it to be Gospel truth whereas it's all lies!!! Nowhere in God's Word does God give us any inclination that His Love is unconditional or that He Loves everybody!!! He Said Jacob I have loved but Esau I have hated. He Said He chooses whom He Blesses and those He Will curse He Will curse!!! That is my God!!! Greatly to be feared and revered!!

What a Faithful, Gracious God We Serve!!!

131st Day

I acknowledged my sin to You,
And my iniquity I did not hide;

I said, I will confess my transgressions to the LORD;
And You forgave the guilt of my sin.

You are my hiding place;
You preserve me from trouble;

You surround me with songs of deliverance. Psalm 32:5,7 NASB
He who covers his sins will not prosper,

But whoever confesses and forsakes them will have mercy.
Proverbs 28:13 NKJV

If we say that we have no sin, we are deceiving ourselves and the truth is
not in us.
If we confess our sins, He is faithful and righteous to forgive us our sins
and to cleanse us from all unrighteousness.
1 John 1:8,9 NASB

Somebody says to you that God's unconditional Love is yours even if you
refuse to repent (which the same person says causes you to lose your salvation
and your then hell bound); what kind of unconditional love is that then?
Sin is sin and God hates sin. This is why God Speaks all through the Bible
that if you do this, I Will Do this and this for you. If you obey my Word/
Commandments, then I Will Bless you. That is my understanding of God's
Love and so His Love cannot possibly be unconditional. Every Promise of
God in the Bible is conditional! Can we separate His Promises from His Love;
especially when those promises are tied to His Love for us and our Love for
Him made manifest in our obedience to His Word? I say NO!!!

What a Faithful, Gracious God We Serve!!!

132nd Day

God's Love is NOT unconditional and God Does not Love everybody!!!

God Said: "Jacob I have loved but Esau I have hated!" How can He suddenly love everybody? Hmmmm do not believe a lie!!!

The sins of some men are obvious, reaching the place of judgment ahead of them; the sins of others trail behind them.

In the same way, good deeds are obvious, and even those that are not cannot be hidden. 1 Timothy 5:24,25 NIV

Therefore, putting aside all filthiness and all that remains of wickedness, in humility receive the word implanted, which is able to save your souls.

But prove yourselves doers of the word, and not merely hearers who delude themselves. James 1:22,23 NASB

And, behold, one came and said unto him, Good Master, what good thing shall I do, that I may have eternal life?

And he said unto him, Why callest thou me good? There is none good but one, that is, God: but if thou wilt enter into life, keep the commandments.

He saith unto him, Which?

Jesus said,
Thou shalt do no murder,
Thou shalt not commit adultery,
Thou shalt not steal,
Thou shalt not bear false witness,
Honour thy father and thy mother:
and, Thou shalt love thy neighbour as thyself.
Matthew 19:16-19 KJV

I don't understand why we would keep saying that God's Love is unconditional? Just read what Jesus says below and meditate on it for yourself and come to a spiritual judgement on the matter! We suggest to people that they do not need to do anything to earn God's Love even though Jesus Christ says to keep and obey His Commandments and He Spells out some of His Commandments!

So, many behave as they like and do whatever pleases their lustful souls believing that they're loved unconditionally anyway!! Well, not what the Bible says. Nowhere in the Bible does it actually say that God's Love is unconditional! I stand to be corrected on this.

Also, nowhere in the Bible does it say that God Loves everybody let alone unconditionally. All that God singled out for Blessing, there has always been something attached to it. Abraham believed God and it was accounted unto him as righteousness!!! He believed God!!!

133rd Day

Faith is not about visibility; does not make sense. Faith believes the impossible, the improbable. The only connection faith has with knowledge is in knowing that by believing, the impossible, the improbable, becomes possible in Jesus' Name!!!

134th Day

ARE YOU PUTTING IN YOUR ALL??? Jesus clearly had a preference for putting in your all, even in your poverty; not to talk of when you do actually have plenty!!! In short, put in your best!!!

135th Day

Follow the leader - but not just any other leader doing whatever they like; do not follow just anyone simply "seen" as a leader; but you may emulate someone that is tried and tested to be doing right in the Eyes of God and man... be wise!!!

136th Day

If you have any encouragement from being united with Christ, if any comfort from his love, if any fellowship with the Spirit, if any tenderness and compassion, then make my joy complete by being like-minded, having the same love, being one in spirit and purpose.

Be Like Christ - in short if you have anything to do with Jesus Christ, then love like Him; being one in spirit and purpose! Do not let prideful vanity or selfishness drive you; rather humbly consider others better than yourself and don't look only to things that concern you, but also to things concerning other people!! That's what you do when driven by the Love of Jesus Christ!!!

137th Day

NO BETTER THAN OTHERS

When touching lives, remember where you were coming from before and that you are no better than the sinner you're Sent to help. No need for arrogance and prideful attitudes because you're under God's Grace; but for this Grace, where would you be???

138th Day

BE DILIGENT IN WORK AND THE REWARDS WILL COME IN SUCCESS! DO NOT FOLLOW FALSEHOOD; BE PREPARED!!!

If you are lazy, change your approach to life; only diligence in hard work brings wealth. A wise son gets his timing right even in harvesting or planting; timing is critical and crucial to success. However, when you are lazy, timing is insignificant; of course with dire consequences in poverty! Lord, Give me strength of purpose to be diligent in my approach to life and not lazy and crown my efforts with success in Jesus' Name. Amen!!!

If you are a thief, of course you will know that you are; change your ways though. Get a decent work ethic. Practice to work for your keep so that God Will Bless you and you will be able to bless other people. Father, do not allow satan to take over my heart to steal; rather to have a good work ethic and to earn my keep in Jesus' Name. Amen!!!

If you have land and till it following the right times for planting watching and harvest, you will most likely have plenty of food and succeed. If however, you follow after emptiness, you will have poverty due to laziness and chasing after the wind! Faithfulness will be Blessed; but faithlessness leads to a get rich quick approach which will reap punishment as a reward. Lord Help me to be faithful so to be Blessed in Jesus' Name. Amen!!!

The lazy person does little or next to nothing; hence, looks for short cuts to everything which leads to many failures and eventually, poverty and criminal activities. However, the diligent's soul shall be made rich and fat in prosperity because of good wise planning, counsel and advice! Lord Help me to be faithful, diligent and prosper in Jesus' Name. Amen!!!

Many deceivers abound; be wise and do yourself justice in learning and mastering the Word of God diligently! Then, you will not fall victim to lying spirits and prophets etc.! Even satan will produce great signs and wonders; yet not of the Lord. Be wise and very diligent to follow after the TRUTH alone! Even regarding the coming of the Lord; there will be impostors. Know that it will not be a hidden phenomenon at all. All eyes will behold Him when He Comes but not all will go with Him. Lord, Help me to decipher Truth from the inner man and follow only the TRUTH in Jesus' Name. Also, that I may not miss out at Your second coming in Jesus' Name. Amen!!!

Be prepared in and out of season; be very ready for any eventualities. This is the best form of change management known to man! Prepare yourself and arm yourself for any eventualities. Likewise in handling the Word of God, prepare for success and dangers; there will be both along the way. You will definitely face persecutions and threats. Help me Lord Jesus to be prepared in and out of season always in Jesus' Name. Amen!!!

139th Day

ETERNAL LIFE IS JESUS CHRIST AND THERE IS ONLY ONE WAY TO ETERNITY. JOURNEY WITH THE LORD IN SPIRIT AND TRUTH!!!

In this Scripture, I believe God Gives us a brief "taste" of Eternity! When we all get to Heaven, what a day of rejoicing that would be! When we all see Jesus, we'll sing and shout the victory! No more hunger, thirst, pain, tears, heat nor evil; the all-sufficient Lamb of God will make every Provision to meet all needs. We shall have access to the Springs of Living Water; God shall wipe away every tear and make all things well and beautiful! O Lord, I don't just want a taste of Eternity, Grant me and my family to have Eternal Life for all Eternity in Jesus' Name. Amen!!!

A day is coming as prophesied in the Word of God; when the Lord Jesus Christ shall return to the earth with pomp, pageantry and a great noise/ shout and music! The dead in Christ shall arise first from their graves as they did when Jesus rose from the dead. Those alive shall be caught up together with the Lord and the Hosts of Heaven in the clouds and be with the Lord Jesus Christ forever! O Lord, please Help me and my family not to miss this glorious reunion for Eternity in Jesus' Name. Amen!!!

Have you got the Son? If not, you risk not making it to Eternity. Eternal life is ONLY in Jesus' Christ, the Son of God; our Lord God and King. This is the mystery of faith; just to be believed and received in faith for the mystery to be REVEALED! Only in the Son can you truly have the Life. Without the Son, you do not have life! Do you want Eternal Life? ONLY in Jesus Christ! Amen! Father God, please Grant me and my family Eternal Life and Peace in Christ Jesus. Amen!!!

Lord, please Give us the wisdom and discernment to decipher the truth in Your Word and have revelation from You to know exactly what You are saying to us at any given time in Your Word. I pray with thanksgiving in Jesus' Holy Name. Amen! On that Day of the Lord o Father, let me and my family find Favour Divine with You o Lord in Jesus' Name to be Saved. Amen!!!

If you are in the Lord, you had better be true to the utmost! Otherwise, you will be cast out at the end. If blessed, do not be arrogant and trust in your wealth; the Lord Sees all things and will Judge all! When the Lord rebukes you, take heed; because He disciplines those He Loves and does not want them to be lost! If you do not take heed, you will end up being lost! Be zealous for the Lord and repent of your sins and live holy. When you hear His Voice or His Knocking, take heed and open the door for Him to let Him in! Then He Will dine with you and vice versa! If you love Me you will obey my Commandments and the Father and I shall come and make our home with you says the Lord Jesus Christ! O Lord, I long for you; Help me to obey Your Commandments. Please I need You. Come and make Your Home with me in Jesus' Name. Amen!!!

140th Day

WHEN YOU WALK WITH AND HOPE/WAIT/TRUST IN THE LORD, HE WILL GIVE YOU VICTORY, POWER, STRENGTH AND COURAGE!!!

Be of good courage, and He shall strengthen your heart, all ye that hope in the LORD. Psalm 31:24 KJV

When you put your trust/hope in the Lord and wait on Him; combined with obedience to His Word and Counsel, your hopes and expectations of Him will never be cut short nor dashed! He Will Strengthen your heart, deliver and empower you; and give you victory and save you too in Jesus' Name. Amen! Lord, Keep me abiding and trusting in You all my days in Jesus' Name. Amen!!!

He gives power to the weak, And to those who have no might He increases strength. Even the youths shall faint and be weary, and the young men shall utterly fall, but those who wait on the LORD Shall renew their strength; They shall mount up with wings like eagles, They shall run and not be weary, They shall walk and not faint. Isaiah 40:29-31 NKJV

If you are weak and heavy laden, put your trust in God. Hope in Him, look up to and wait on Him; your hope will never be disappointed nor your expectations cut short. He Will not deny you any good things in life; you will not tire nor faint. You will be taken up high as in flight like an eagle. There is great benefit in following the Lord faithfully and obediently in spirit and in truth through Christ Jesus. Amen and Amen. Father, Help me and mine to follow You to the very end in Jesus' Name. Amen!!!

I had fainted, unless I had believed to see the goodness of the LORD in the land of the living. Wait on the LORD: be of good courage, and he shall strengthen thine heart: wait, I say, on the LORD. Psalm 27:13,14 KJV

Because I believed that I will be Blessed by God the Lord in life, I wait on Him with courage, without fear; and He Makes my heart strong and bold. I am not stressed nor depressed because my faith in Him is unshaken!

Lord, I look to You; and I trust that You Will NEVER leave nor forsake me. My needs will be met in Jesus' Name. Amen!!!

Do not be downcast o my soul; continue to hope in God. God is Faithful to deliver and save you from death and or destruction. God Will Save my eyes from tears, feet from stumbling and Enable me to walk in His Presence in the land of the living. I Bless His Holy Name. O Father, Continue Your Goodness to my family and I in Jesus' Name. We shall continue to exalt Your Name, honour You, offer our praises and adoration with fear and reverence in Jesus' Name. Amen!!!

'Then you will be handed over to be persecuted and put to death, and you will be hated by all nations because of me. At that time many will turn away from the faith and will betray and hate each other, and many false prophets will appear and deceive many people. Because of the increase of wickedness, the love of most will grow cold, but the one who stands firm to the end will be saved. And this gospel of the kingdom will be preached in the whole world as a testimony to all nations, and then the end will come. Matthew 24:9-14

There shall be persecution for all who believe in diverse forms including imprisonment and death. Do not let your faith weaken nor faint; rather be fully encouraged and emboldened in Jesus' Name. Amen! Even though the faith of many and their love will weaken, faint and fail with many false prophets deceiving many, you will be kept safe in Jesus' Name. Do not stop preaching and doing the works of God; the end will surely come and then you will be vindicated. Have faith to the very end in Jesus' Name. Amen. Father, Keep me to the very end in Your Presence; and my heart with You o Lord in Jesus' Name. Amen!!!

God Promised in His Word that He Will not be angry with mankind forever; so when He disciplines and punishes us, it's never forever. He Shows Mercy! I'd rather be judged by God than man because God is Kind at heart and Merciful and the heart of man is deceitful and desperately wicked! At the same time, no man lives forever on earth; God set a time for man of around a hundred and twenty years! Of course this may vary according to God's Will! Lord, Grant me long life and prosperity in good health I pray in Jesus' Name. Amen!!!

141st Day

EVERYBODY NEEDS CONFIDENCE! FROM WHAT SOURCE THOUGH? THE LORD IS MY CONFIDENCE

When you fear the Lord, your confidence will be fully in Him and He Will be the source of your confidence! If that is the case, it cannot be hidden and all who fear Him will be drawn to you for mutual edification and confidence building. When you believe in the Lord, your heart would be increasingly blameless towards God's Word as you obey and shame will be far from you. Lord, my soul therefore faints with longing for Your Salvation; because my hope if fully in Your Word. Help me o Lord; that my confidence is fully drawn from and in You though Jesus Christ my Lord God and King. Amen!!!

For this reason I also suffer these things, but I am not ashamed; for I know whom I have believed and I am convinced that He is able to guard what I have entrusted to Him until that day. to Timothy 1:12 NASB

Even though there is much suffering and persecution in believing and serving the Lord my God, yet, I will not be ashamed nor put to shame for His Name's sake. I know Him Who I have believed and I am fully persuaded that He is ABLE to keep me safe with everything I have entrusted to Him in Christ Jesus. Blessed be His Holy Name!!!

When God Said to follow Him in Jesus Christ and you will be Blessed; He meant everything. He is very Faithful to His Promises which are Yes and Amen in Christ Jesus! Those He Favours will be blameless when Jesus returns! We are reconciled to God through Jesus Christ and by His Grace. He is the Lord God Almighty!!!

Many deceivers abound claiming already to be Jesus Christ. They have many followers too! Hmmm! May God Help us who believe not to be deceived by hollow fancy intellectual rubbish presented by impostors.

There are definitive signs of the coming of the Lord and the end times. May God Enable us to decipher these and to watch and pray! The Lord Jesus Christ is coming back again; soon and very soon! Please let me be right standing when You come o Lord in Jesus' Name. Amen!!!

Be subject to governing authorities is what the Bible says! Every authority in place is sanctioned by God. When you rebel against authority, you are rebelling against God. I didn't write the Holy Bible! Do good and you will not suffer dire consequences from the one in authority. Those in authority are supposed to be ministers of good to the governed from God; hmmmm, if they are not, they must be told with due respect to their offices for their position is very delicate in the Eyes of God! That is why many lives have been needlessly lost in the name of "fighting" for the masses! Be very careful how you tackle or correct those in authority. Be wise. Lord, Give us wisdom to deal with those in authority over us who are not doing what is right or who we perceive not to be doing so in Jesus' Name. Amen!!!

142nd Day

MANY SEEK TO BE WEALTHY! HOW MANY GO THROUGH THE GOD WHO GIVES THE ABILITY TO CREATE WEALTH?!!

But remember the LORD your God, for it is he who gives you the ability to produce wealth, and so confirms his covenant, which he swore to your forefathers, as it is today. If you ever forget the LORD your God and follow other gods and worship and bow down to them, I testify against you today that you will surely be destroyed. Like the nations the LORD destroyed before you, so you will be destroyed for not obeying the LORD your God. Deuteronomy 8:18-20 NIV

God Said in His Word that if you obey His Word, He Will Bless you; and He fulfills His Word. Will you remember Him and bow only to Him in praise, adoration and exaltation? If you do and refuse to bow to or follow other gods, God Will Surely Bless you. Then you will not be destroyed; but rather have life and more abundantly in Jesus' Name. Amen. Help my family and I o Lord to obey Your Word; so to be Blessed abundantly and never to bow to other gods in Jesus' Name. Amen!!!

He that tilleth his land shall have plenty of bread: but he that followeth after vain persons shall have poverty enough. A faithful man shall abound with blessings: but he that maketh haste to be rich shall not be innocent. Proverbs 28:19,20 KJV

Hard work pays off in the end. If you work hard, the likelihood is that you will succeed and have plenty for yourself and to help others less fortunate! Keep faith with God and man in all that you do; then you will be truly Blessed. If however your desire is for quick riches, you will fall victim to satan's evil ploys and your heart will be corrupted! Lord, Help us Your children not to fall into satanic traps to get rich quickly; but rather to work hard with faith and wait for God's Blessings in Jesus' Name. Amen!!!

As for the rich in this world, charge them not to be haughty, nor to set their hopes on uncertain riches but on God who richly furnishes us with everything to enjoy. They are to do good, to be rich in good deeds, liberal and generous, thus laying up for themselves a good foundation for the future, so that they may take hold of the life which is life indeed.

1 Timothy 6:17-19 RSV

If you are Blessed to be wealthy in this world, then do not become cocky by letting your wealth get into your head! God gives and takes away at will. No condition is permanent! You can lose all in an instant as has happened before to others! Be good and do good with your wealth; thereby creating for yourself a future of life everlasting in spirit and truth! Do not put your hope in your wealth but rather in God Who Gives the ability to create wealth for your security. Vanity, all is vanity. Lord, Help me to be wise in my relationship with wealth in this evil world in Jesus' Name. Amen!!!

God wants us to give a tenth (the first fruits) of our harvests or earnings to His and His Causes and or through His servants. But be wise in giving otherwise you will fall into traps set by very clever and intelligent fake servants who claim to be of God! Obey God in giving this way and watch Him Bless you so much you won't have room enough for His Blessings! Lord, Help my family and I to be wise in giving and to be generous in Jesus' Name. Amen!!!

For all who hold on to the worldly vain things like great achievements and vainglory like big houses and constructions like big cities etc., God Wants you to know that Heaven and earth will pass away; only the Word of God shall remain for all eternity! Everything else is vanity upon vanity! The signs of the times are rife everywhere; but who's on the lookout? Who's preparing for Eternity? Hmmm! Lord, Help me to be wise and appreciate that this world and all that is in it is vanity upon vanity; to make me work and strive towards Heavenly goals in Jesus' Name. Amen!!!

Lord, please do not let my family or myself be like seeds that fell amongst thorns; choked up with the cares of life and bear no fruit. Help us to be as seeds that fell on fertile ground; bearing the Word of God with a noble heart, bearing fruits with patience for and in the Name of Jesus Christ! So Help us o Lord in Jesus' Name. Amen!!!

143rd Day

THE POTENTIAL OF GOD'S LOVE FOR HUMANITY IS IMMEASURABLE; HOWEVER DON'T TAKE IT FOR GRANTED!!!

"Then it shall come to pass, because you listen to these judgments, and keep and do them, that the LORD your God will keep with you the covenant and the mercy which He swore to your fathers. And He will love you and bless you and multiply you; He will also bless the fruit of your womb and the fruit of your land, your grain and your new wine and your oil, the increase of your cattle and the offspring of your flock, in the land of which He swore to your fathers to give you." Deuteronomy 7:12,13 NKJV

God's love is not unconditional. Read above meditatively again; and know the truth to be free! "Because" is an "if"; both are "conditional"!

If you obey the Lord's Word/Commandments, He Will Keep His Covenant with you by His Mercy and LOVE, Bless and Multiply you etc. in the land that He Promised to give to you, which He Will Give you! O Lord, Help us to understand that Your Love demands our sacrificial obedience to receive and enjoy in Jesus' Name. Amen!!!

The LORD, your God, is in your midst, a warrior who gives victory; he will rejoice over you with gladness, he will renew you in his love; he will exult over you with loud singing! Zephaniah 3:17 RSV

God is Present in the midst of His people; so let us bow before Him, for He Heals the broken-hearted! He Has turned our darkness into Light; our night into Day! O what a victory He Gives! Rejoice over me please my Lord and Renew me in Your Love! Exult over me o my Lord with loud singing because I know that You are present in the midst of Your children in praise and worship of You! Help me to give over all my battles unto You; for Yours Lord is the battle and I have the victory because You Give me the Victory in Christ Jesus! Thank You my Father Lord and God in Jesus' Name. Amen!!!

The love of God for us like I postulated earlier has huge potentials! Still sinners, He Showed us unparalleled love in Giving Jesus Christ (Himself) for us whilst we were yet dead in our transgressions! However, for us to enter into His Kingdom, we must believe that He did this and believe in the Holy Sacrifice of Jesus Christ. We must also show our love for Him in obeying His Commandments and committing to Holy Living. Only then can we get to enjoy His Love freely in our daily lives and be Blessed in Jesus' Name. Amen. Lord, Help us to understand Your Love and the need to not take it for granted in Jesus' Name. Amen!!!

God affirms His Covenant Love with and for the children of Israel in this Scripture, thereby proving His Faithfulness and His Commitment to His Promises which are Yes and Amen in Christ Jesus! By His Spoken Word, we know that He is Faithful; especially when He Promises and Brings it to pass! Father, Speak Your Word into my life and Bring it to pass in Jesus' Name. Amen!!!

Perhaps and perchance if we spend some time trying to understand the potential good embedded in trials and tribulations, we would look at such as opportunities rather than be stressed! The above Scripture proves the point. However, we must read, meditate and learn such wisdom for it to be effective in our lives! Help me Lord Jesus to appreciate adversity as an opportunity for Blessing to flow into my life. Help me to give all to You, for You Take Care of things far better than I can ever do for myself in Jesus' Name. Amen!!!

144th Day

JESUS CHRIST IS THE PEACE OF GOD! THERE IS NO PEACE FOR THE WICKED! SO YOU WANT PEACE?!!

When your heart is set to do good and you are so determined so to do, you will have peace like a river; because you heart so set is drawing upon the peace of God! With a peaceful heart, you will be able to think clearly to do the right things of God with gratitude. The Word of God will dwell richly in you. Whatever you do will be done in the Name of Jesus Christ. To God be all the Glory in Jesus' Name. Amen!!!

If you are not wicked, you cannot be in between being wicked and good. You cannot be a little wicked and a little good. You are either one or the other! You are either good or wicked! If good, you will have peace like a river; but if wicked, there will be no peace for you. Peace is not for the wicked; rather, it's for the good! May God Enable us to be good always in Jesus' Name. Amen!!!

Have no anxiety about anything, but in everything by prayer and supplication with thanksgiving let your requests be made known to God. And the peace of God, which passes all understanding, will keep your hearts and your minds in Christ Jesus. Philippians 4:6,7 RSV

When you lose sleep over issues, you erode the peace in your life and it's not worth it. Anxiety does not help peace grow in the heart but increases and nurtures worry! But is we cultivate a habit of praying and committing all our cares unto the Lord Jesus Christ; taking everything to the Lord in prayer, the peace of God that passes all understanding will keep our hearts and minds on and in Christ Jesus. So let it be for us o Lord in Jesus' Name. Amen!!!

"The steadfast of mind You will keep in perfect peace, Because he trusts in You. Trust in the LORD forever, For in GOD the LORD, we have an everlasting Rock." Isaiah 26:3,4 NASB

Those who are faithful in the Lord and stand steadfastly upon His Word in everything and every way have God's backing! Because they trust in Him, the everlasting Rock, He Gives them and Keeps them in Everlasting and Perfect Peace! I want Your Peace o Lord; Grant me in Jesus' Name. Show me the paths of Peace and Help me to follow the paths of Peace in Jesus' Name. Amen!!!

God is determined to Save humanity; but humans are so proud and stubborn and rejecting the Lord God Almighty! You have to make up your mind to perish or to live forever; I have decided and chosen life everlasting for my household and self! I do not want to be like Jerusalem nor suffer the consequences accordingly! I want to see my Lord and be with Him in His Glory in Jesus' Name. O Lord, Grant unto me Your Salvation. Reveal yourself to me in Jesus' Name. Amen!!!

The Word of God is written for us not for fun; but rather for us to be Saved and to give us peace, patience and hope in Jesus Christ! O Lord, Feed us increasingly with Your Word; that we may enter into Your Sabbath Rest and Righteousness in Jesus' Name. Amen!!!

145th Day

WHAT DRIVES YOU AND WHERE TO? THE DEAD WILL LIVE! THE VOICE I HEAR I FOLLOW! VENGEANCE BELONGS TO GOD! THE GOOD NEWS IS FOR REAL! JESUS ALIVE FOREVERMORE!!!

Let go of the past and move on with life. Be sure to have a focus; and be careful regarding what drives you! I choose the Higher Calling for my goal and the Holy Spirit to drive me in Jesus Christ! What your choice is in these matters determines your ultimate destination! Lead me by Your Holy Spirit o my Father in Jesus' Name. Amen!!!

We are running a race! Run yours in such a way that you will win. Apply strict self control which is what differentiates the Believer from all others and identifies the true Believer! You cannot do just what you want and express your anger willy nilly. That's what all others do. You must not be like the world. Be wise. Discipline yourself strictly in Jesus' Name and your life will become inspirational for others to follow your example as a model of character and spirit in Jesus' Name. Amen! Help me o Lord; for with You, nothing shall be impossible. Amen in Jesus' Name. Amen!!!

Eternal Life is not Given to just anybody unconditionally. This is the Highest form of Love available ever! It is not unconditional at all. It was never meant to be! You must hear and believe the Word of the Living God to gain Eternal Life! Then you will not come into judgment! You have passed from death into life only then. Otherwise, you remain in death! Lord, I want to hear Your Voice and live; Help me in Jesus' Name. Amen!!!

I'd rather be a sheep in the pen of my Lord Jesus Christ than be a goat roaming freely in the freedom provided by the wily serpent, satan. I need Your Yoke around my neck o Lord; let me be enslaved to You as my Master, Lord and King; such that no one can snatch me from Your Hand! Train and Teach me to know and be able to discern Your Voice o my Lord in Jesus' Name. Amen!!!

The legacy of satan is monumental but leads and ends ultimately in hell. Satan's followers love to destroy whatever God stands for and or is building as a routine. However, God Will always have the Victory because light must and will always overcome darkness! The blood guilt is upon the disobedient and the brood of vipers who follow not the Lord our God nor His Ways eternally! Strive to be a part of the new generation, a holy nation, Called by and living in Christ Jesus our Lord God and Saviour. Amen. Sanctify me o Lord and all Your saints to do Your Will in this life and that to come in Jesus' Name. Amen!!!

Establish in me and my family and all who come to You o Lord; Your Gospel - so that the Good News super saturates me and flows from within me out onto those You Have Predestined to receive it in Jesus' Name. Help me and be with me; Lead me to do Your Work day after day till the very end in Jesus' Name. Amen! Help me to be a change agent for the good and for the Good News, the Gospel of my Lord Jesus Christ! I am and will forever be satisfied doing Your Will o Lord; so Help me Lord in Jesus' Name. Amen!!!

146th Day

DO NOT BE ASHAMED OF THE GOSPEL OF JESUS CHRIST OR PERSECUTION FOR SAME! EMULATE THE RIGHTEOUSNESS OF GOD AND NOT THE HYPOCRISY OF THE PHARISEES ETC.!!!

There is a lot of suffering and persecution experienced as part of exercising Faith in Jesus Christ! Do not be ashamed; rather glorify God in gratitude that you share of the Lord's Sufferings! Do not suffer for nothing. Any suffering that comes not as a result of Faith in Jesus Christ is in vain. Suffering for and in the Name of Jesus shall be sweetly and faithfully rewarded by God on that Day! Lord, Help us to bear up suffering for Your Name's sake in Jesus' Name. Amen!!!

Glory in the fact that you're suffering persecution etc. in Jesus' Name yields patience, experience and hope, which never puts one to shame. Basically, no cause for shame because the Love of God is showered upon the believer suffering for the Holy Name, from above into our hearts through the Holy Spirit Given to us in Christ Jesus. Amen. Lord, Help us to look at suffering for Jesus aright and bear up with it, considering the glory to be revealed in and through us in Jesus' Name; and the rewards released to us in Jesus' Name. Amen!!!

In the Faith, you must study yourself and present yourself to God as approved; a workman, not ashamed of the Word, but who rather handles the Word of God/Truth correctly! You must be prepared in and out of season because nobody knows when the Lord shall come! Lord, Prepare me; to be a sanctuary... pure and holy... tried and true... with thanksgiving, I'll be a living, sanctuary, for You in Jesus' Name. Amen!!!

Because I am not ashamed of the Gospel; I am so eager to preach at any given opportunity regardless of man's judgements! This Gospel is the Power of God for the believer's salvation for all; first for the Jew, then for the Gentiles too! Salvation is available to all who choose to believe in the Holy Testament (Gospel) of Jesus Christ! Lord, I know that You Will NEVER put me to shame with regard to the Gospel because You were never ashamed nor put to shame. Whatever was supposed to be shameful, You Converted to Glory in Jesus' Name. Halleluyah! Amen!!!

In this evil world of sin, hatred, evil and wickedness, anyone who is ashamed of the Lord Jesus Christ and His Gospel, Jesus also will be ashamed of such people when He returns in His Glory of the Father with the Holy Angels of God! Is shame preventing you from doing what you know to be the Will of the Lord? Are you more concerned about what is spoken of you than doing the Lord's work? Hmmm! You must choose whom you shall serve; mammon or Jesus Christ! I have decided to follow and serve Jesus Christ; for me, there is no turning by and no turning back. So Help me o Lord in Jesus' Name. Amen!!!

When you present yourself on the outside as holy and righteous and you are more concerned about being seen as such than actually living and or being holy and righteous, you are a hypocrite! You deceive none other than yourself; because not only does God See through you, but human beings too can tell that you are fake! Strive to be holy and perfect; even as your Father in Heaven is Holy and Perfect! O Help me Father by the Power of Your Holy Spirit to be perfect and holy in Jesus' Name. Amen. For I believe that with You, nothing shall be impossible! Amen!!!

God's Judgements are always trustworthy and right! No matter how ridiculous His Judgements may appear to man, especially because the heart of man is deceitful and desperately wicked! Father, Help us who believe to trust and hope in You fully; so that we can benefit from Your Love and Blessings even unto Eternity in Christ Jesus! Amen!!!

147th Day

REMEMBER WHEN YOU ARE TEMPTED TO SIN THAT YOUR SIN IS PRIMARILY AGAINST GOD! ARE YOU JOYFUL IN SIN? HMMMM!!!

The Bible says that the only thing that matters is faith that works through love. That is often the solution to our problems but we hardly ever look to it as a solution. There will always be temptation! If however we consider faithful love seriously, we would be guided in the rightful direction in Jesus' Name. Lord, when tempted, Lead me by the Power of Your Holy Spirit to be guided aright by faith in love in Jesus' Name. Amen!!!

David knew that he had sinned and probably hoped it would not be exposed. However the man of God knew by revelation from God that David had sinned and he confronted him. David did not deny; but rather confessed and affirmed that he had sinned against the Lord. The Lord was however Merciful to David and forgave him his sin and so David was not destroyed. O Lord, if it pleases You, let me be one of those whose sins You shall not count against them in Jesus' Name. Amen!!!

God Grants unto some that their sin is covered, forgiven and not counted against them. I believe David was one such man at least! True that all have sinned and fallen short of the Glory of the Lord. If that be the case, how will God Judge mankind and not find all guilty? I believe that God's Judgement will be by Grace and He said in His Word that He Will Show Mercy to whomsoever He Will; and to whosoever He Chooses He Will not show Mercy. Father Lord, please let me be one of those that will receive this Divine Mandate for Mercy, Forgiveness, Covering and not counting my sins against me in Jesus' Name. Amen!!!

When we walk in the Light of God, He Abides with us and Sheds His Glory on us so much that we desire to have fellowship with like minded people wherever He Leads us! The Blood of Jesus Christ thus cleanses us from all sin. In His Justice and Faithfulness, when we confess our sins and seek His Forgiveness earnestly, He Forgives us and cleanses us from all iniquity and unrighteousness! Thank You Jesus for the kind of God that You Are Who is Willing and Able to forgive our sins and cleanse us from all unrighteousness in Jesus' Name. Amen!!!

The hypocrisy of cleaning the outside of the cup and dish not minding the insides is highlighted here. It's best to deal with the inside and the outside will follow suit; because uncleanness comes from within and the manifestation is seen outside. Likewise the sorting out should be done from within and the manifestation of cleanliness will be seen on the outside. Help me Lord not to be hypocritical in my approach to matters of faith, love and life in Jesus' Name. Amen!!!

When you live a life that is not righteous and yet judge others living likewise, you have no moral standing to do so at all. You yourself will be judged by the same standard you use to judge others and you will not escape judgement. Therefore, judge yourself; lest you be judged! However, mercy prevails over judgement. The final judgement belongs to and is in the Hands of God and will be executed by the Lord Jesus Christ. Father, prepare me to be a sanctuary for You in my life and Keep me so that I will not fail in the judgement to come in Jesus' Name. Amen!!!

148th Day

TO ENJOY THE FAITHFULNESS, MERCY, TRUTH AND LOVE OF GOD IN JESUS CHRIST, YOU MUST BE BORN AGAIN! LEARN TO SOW BOUNTIFULLY! IT'S BETTER TO GIVE THAN TO RECEIVE!!!

If you do not want God to abandon you, you must obey His Commandments to show and prove your love for Him. God does actually desire that you love Him. Yes God so loved the world and all of that; but this love is not unconditional. God Expects you to love Him in return. That is the very first commandment and is a very serious matter. Get it wrong at your own peril. I will not argue the point with anybody. I do not preach for fame or riches; so keep your accolades, your money and attention to yourself. This is between my God and I only! Thank you very much indeed. Father, please keep me in You and Your Word to the very end in Jesus' Name. Help me to earnestly desire to please You rather than man's applause in Jesus' Name. Amen!!!

God is not like men and does not tell lies. God is the Father of all Truth and all Right and the truthful and righteous! He does not have to repent for anything because He Knows best and is absolutely perfect! When He Speaks or Promises, it's sure that His Word and Promise shall come to pass. Alewi lese; Alese lewi! The One Who Speaks and Does; Who Does and Speaks! He is alone God. His Name is JESUS! He is Yahweh! The Great I AM!!!

In Christ Jesus, we must die, live and endure with Him; so we can live and reign with him. Don't even think you can deny Him and get away with it because He Will deny you too. However, your lack of faith does not move Him to be faithless like you. He Will remain Faithful. Lord, Help me to die to my flesh, endure adversity, persecution and to know You and the Power of Your Resurrection in Jesus' Name. Amen!!!

There is a law of giving and receiving that many have learnt to tap into for real and it works for them. It's high time that believers tap into this power of giving and receiving in order to receive God's Blessings! God Loves a cheerful giver; not a grudging giver! When you give, let it not be out of necessity! This is affecting many givers today as they do not see increase in the Name of the Lord because their giving is not cheerful; but rather grudging and out of necessity! You should not need to be begged to give! God multiplies when the giving is right. Lord Help us to give appropriately to please you and not to prove a point; as in giving grudgingly or out of compulsion and or necessity in Jesus' Name. Amen!!!

You must be born again. You need to study the Word of God so you know exactly what that means and so you understand for yourself the Word of God. Ask for God's Help in this! Yield yourself to the Lord Jesus Christ and His Holy Spirit in Jesus' Name. Amen! Repent of your sins and prove your repentance with deeds commensurate with repentance. Being born again is all of these things and more; like I said you need to study the Word of God yourself to discover the truth and live by it to be free in Jesus' Name. Amen!!!

149th Day

WHO IS LIKE OUR GOD? IS HE NOT THE WORD? GOD EXALTED HIS WORD OVER HIS NAME! THE WORD OF GOD IS ETERNAL!!!

Wouldn't you like to know and experience the Word of the Living God? Do you know that God Created everything by His Word? If only we humans would value the Word of God and do right by the Word of the Living God! The key to relating with the Word is by Faith that works through Love! If you can combine faith with love sincerely, you would be on the right track and you will know the Truth and the Truth will set you free! The Word lives forever and if you have the Word in you by faith that works through love, you stand yourself in good stead to live forever! O Lord, please Give us a Revelation of Your Word to transform our lives for You in Jesus' Name. Amen!!!

Your Creation o Lord is designed to remain forever. You've got the whole world in Your Hands. Yours Lord is the Honour, Glory and Majesty forever and ever. Amen! The Heavens are Yours as the earth is Yours. Who besides You could have laid the foundations of both? You Are very Great beyond measure o Lord. Blessed be Your Holy Name! Halleluyah. Amen!!!

On the Day of the Lord, the Lord's own shall all be rescued. Spectacular developments shall occur; like the rising from the dead from graves of those who have died (slept) in the Lord. Some shall rise unto everlasting life and others to everlasting contempt and disgrace! The wise ones shall shine brightly as the Sun; just as those who obeyed the Lord's command to lead others to righteousness! The Mouth of the Lord has Spoken, who can reverse it? The Lord's Will shall be established in Jesus' Name. Amen!!!

When adversity comes, be very careful not to act out your distress lest you displease the Lord your God! Saul did this and paid dearly for it! Different roles Given by God to different people! Learn your role; beseech the Lord to know His Will for your life and don't look at circumstances nor look at others' acting out their destiny and you want to be like them or copy them. You are an individual; don't let envy, jealousy and discontentment lead you astray. Trust in the Lord without shaking and God Will Make straight your paths in Jesus' Name. Amen!!!

150th Day

GOD HATES PRIDE AND ARROGANCE; FEAR GOD AND OBEY HIS COMMANDMENTS! SEEK PARDON AND BE TRANSFORMED!!!

Pride and arrogance always end in stumbling and destruction. Why engage in what does not profit? Is it not better to embrace profitable humility which begets much grace? Help me to be humble o Lord; I pray in Jesus' Name. Amen!!!

Apart from the wicked and violent, God also hates perverse speech, pride and arrogance! If you are perverse in speech, proud and arrogant; you deceive yourself claiming God Loves you! You had better submit yourself to God wholeheartedly and be transformed into the image and likeness of Jesus Christ for whom nothing shall be impossible, only believe. Lord transform me into the model which is Jesus Christ; I want to dwell in Your courts forever in Jesus' Name. Amen!!!

Many do not or cannot understand that failing to submit to and put their trust in the Lord is prideful and arrogant; basically, a lack of humility! Hence, they wittingly or unwittingly stir up strife wherever they go and wonder what's going on. Efin ni iwa (behaviour and attitude are like smoke) and cannot be hidden. Yours follows you like an odour! If it's poorly or good, that's what follows you around! When you trust you heart like some advice you to do, you are foolish! But when you trust/hope in the Lord you are wise and shall be made fat and be delivered! You choose. I have made my choice forever to humble myself and walk with my God, following Him to the very end in Jesus' Name. Amen!!!

When you are proud and arrogant; you will not walk in the way of the Lord; but rather in the way of the world. It takes humility to keep away from sin/evil and walk away from strife and wickedness! You will be rewarded with reproach and contempt to accompany your behaviour and attitude! Keep the Lord's testimonies and Word though; and be free from reproach and contempt in Jesus' Name. Amen. Again, the choice is yours!!!

When arrogance and pride grips you, you begin to have lofty thoughts and ideals beyond normal, rational human limits. Basically, you begin to think and act like you are God; even in your dealings with fellow human beings. Hardly anything or anyone means anything to you at all. You think, sound and act in your prideful, arrogant and boastful manner. You fool! Do you own your own life? Do you not think for a moment that your life could end immediately? Cannot the One who Created you; whether you acknowledge Him or not, can He not bring you crashing down? Lord, Teach us to be wise and humble; that we might strive to please You and not live our lives anti-God. I pray in Jesus' Name. Amen!!!

You cannot say because you give to God, His servants or work, you will be justified; when you refuse to factor in the more important issues around justice, mercy, faithfulness and love! You will regret bitterly and it will be too late! If however, you combine these with your giving; factoring all of the above, you will be very Blessed and stand yourself in good stead, made ready for the Kingdom of God! Help us to do the right and shun the wrong o Lord; that we might please You and not our own selves in Jesus' Name. Amen!!!

All said and done, what matters most before God is for humans to fear God and obey His Commandments! God is the Judge of every work and secret thing, good or bad; and He Will Judge all. So, whether you embrace love, goodness and righteousness or evil and wickedness, know that the Judge is waiting at the door! All shall be rewarded according to all they have done. Father Lord, please count us worthy to live for You; that we might not end up as castaways from Your Presence and Kingdom in Jesus' Name. Amen!!!

151st Day

PARENTAL RESPONSIBILITY IS GODLY; DO NOT TOY WITH IT OR FACE THE WRATH OF GOD! BE DILIGENT AND BE BLESSED!!!

The Word of God is Life and gives LIFE. The Spirit begets spirit as flesh begets flesh. Do your utmost to get the Word of the Living God in your life and you owe it to God and to your children to pass on the Word of God to your children so the Word of God can pass on from generation to generation! This is so that generations will remember and not ever forget the Lord; but rather have the Lord God Almighty and His Word inherent in their psyche and daily lives. This way, they can walk in the Love and Blessings of God always in Jesus' Name. This is the Word of God! Obey and be Blessed; disobey and remain under a curse! I choose to obey in Jesus' Name. May God Help me and my family in Jesus' Name. Amen!!!

Likewise, parents owe it to God and also to their children, to train the children in the Way of the Lord, so they will never depart from it in Jesus' Name. Parents must also be very diligent to ensure that their children are not discouraged through parental unwarranted anger. This calls for discernment and sensitivity in dealing with our children; because not only the children, but God will not be pleased with us if we anger the children and they will react to that anger and that may lead them astray and we would bear that responsibility to God Almighty! Father, Teach us how to be parents and fairly so to our children in a godly, just and righteous way in Jesus' Name. Amen!!!

When you have learnt from childhood the Way of God and His Righteousness, if you are convinced of this, then you have a responsibility to continue in that Way! Especially knowing those from whom you have learnt the Way are trustworthy! This Way will make you wise for salvation by faith in Jesus Christ and help you help others into salvation likewise as you put to practice your learning. Help us o Jesus; that we might touch others' lives with our faith for Your Name's sake in Jesus' Name. Amen!!!

Be very wary and careful of and with the accursed breed; who are not interested in entering the Kingdom of God and are doing things that would only serve to keep those who are interested from entering in! Effectively, they shut the doors to the Kingdom of Heaven in people's faces rather than lead people in! Help us to follow good role models of Faith in Jesus Christ and not be led astray by detractors, deceivers, etc. who are leading many astray in Jesus' Name. Amen!!!

What spirit has possessed you? You know by your own fruits! You surely can see the evidence of your faith in your daily living! As for the true believers in the Christian Faith in Jesus Christ, they received not the spirit from this world to live for the sake of worldliness. But rather, for the sake of the Holy Spirit, the Spirit from the Lord God Almighty - for the sake of the Kingdom of God! Father, fill us with Your Holy Spirit; that we might know You and the Power of the Resurrection of Jesus Christ. Amen!!!

152nd Day

THE WORD OF GOD IS PRESENTED IN PARABLES; IT TAKES GODLY WISDOM AND THE HOLY SPIRIT REVELATION TO DECIPHER!!!

God's Thoughts and Ways are different than man's! Is it human to give more to who has and take from who has not? The one who has gets an abundance; whereas the one who does not have loses the little he has. Those who see don't see and those who hear don't hear. Does this make sense? So, don't ever toy or play games with God; He is not a man to lie or change His Mind. He is Holy and True! Pray to God for His Holy Spirit and for discernment. When your heart is calloused, your senses may work, but your spirit is deadened. However, if you submit yourself to God's Holy Spirit, He Will Wake you up. He Will Arouse your heart and unclog it so your senses come alive with the Holy Spirit; then the difference is clear! Please open the eyes of my heart Lord, that I may see You in all I experience in life in Jesus' Name. Amen!!!

The Kingdom of God works as a farmer who sows seeds and waits patiently for the harvest. Before the harvest, the seed that was sown transforms from stage to stage until the harvest! The Kingdom of God is hence very developmental! A time for everything! God Help us do right by You and be patient to know and understand the signs of the relevant times to act or not in Jesus' Name. Amen!!!

Father, in Jesus' Name, please Help us to have the discernment to know when and where to sow seeds; in order to maximise our harvest potentials in Jesus' Name. Amen! You cannot just sow seeds willy nilly whilst expecting a bountiful harvest! You need wisdom, knowledge and understanding of the relevant timings for the whole process of sowing right up till reaping! Teach and Lead us Heavenly Father in this evil world; that we might succeed in Jesus' Name. Amen!!!

As a believer, it is expedient to count all things as a loss compared with the supremacy and excellency of knowing Christ Jesus and the Power of His Resurrection! Help us o Lord to have fellowship in spirit and in truth with the Lord our God and in His sufferings right unto death; that we might attain unto the resurrection from the dead in Jesus' Name. Amen!!!

The role of a servant of God includes to preach the Kingdom of God; teach about the Lord Jesus Christ confidently! With God's Backing, all who come against to hinder you shall be put to shame in Jesus' Name. You will march on and succeed in your ministry in Jesus' Name. Amen! Lord, so let it be in Jesus' Name. Amen!!!

153rd Day

WHATEVER YOUR NEEDS, ASK (ASK SEEK KNOCK) GOD! DIE TO WORLDLY PASSIONS - WANTS NOT NEEDS! DO GOD'S WILL!!!

By faith, whatever your needs, feel free and be confident to ask the Lord. Is it not safer and better to have your conscience clean in the Name of the Lord? When your conscience is clogged up, you lose the confidence and moral standing/grounding to ask God for your needs because of guilt! However, were the Lord to draw a line for sin, who could stand or cross? For all have sinned and fallen short of the Glory of the Lord, so ask, seek and knock anyway in faith and trust/believe God will answer and He Will Deliver in Jesus' Name. Amen! A case of nothing ventured, nothing gained; no pain no gain! No sowing no harvest! If you do not sow, how do you expect a harvest? Even when you sow, there is a timing and a time for everything! May God Help us to sow aright and at the right time in Jesus' Name. Amen!!!

When we sin and repent, choosing to willingly return to the Lord and to His Word; as in "to your tents o Israel", then God Will Favour us as it is written! May God Give us the wisdom to act in a way as to get His attention for Divine Blessings and Favour in Jesus' Name. Amen!!!

Before all things, we are requested and expected to Love the Lord our God with all our hearts, minds, souls and all! When we do this, we position ourselves perfectly for Divine Visitation, Blessings and Love! Even we have confidence to ask anything in His Name by faith and our expectations shall not be cut short in Jesus' Name. Amen!!!

This promise is not for every and anybody willy nilly! It is for those who fear the Lord and love Him; proving their love by obeying His Commandments! Such people, God Will Favour and Honour in Jesus' Name. O my Father, Lord, God and King, Touch me afresh and turn my everything towards you in every way; that I might enjoy the very best of You in Jesus' Name. Amen!!!

Ohun kohun to le de mi lona iye, Metalokan, bami mu kuro! Whatsoever will bar me from the Kingdom of Heaven, Three in One, Lord God, Help me remove such! You must be willing to let go of all evil and its appearances from your life (heart, mind, soul, psyche, etc. in thoughts, words and deeds) completely! There are many things and in many ways; we love to pretend and deceive ourselves. We do know many things that we do that will not please God; we convince ourselves that these things do not matter to God and that God does not care about such, so we continue freely. On that Day, there will not be another chance to repent and give these up! Quit deceiving yourselves and honour God with your bodies and lives in Jesus' Name. Amen! Father, Lord, Help us not to deceive ourselves; but to give up worldly ways willingly to be saved in Jesus' Name. Amen!!!

154th Day

ARE YOU YOUR OLD OR NEW SELF? NEW SELF DID AWAY WITH LIES! LIARS NEVER ESCAPE JUDGMENT! DO AS THEY SAY NOT AS THEY DO (JESUS' ADVICE; SO NOT NEW AT ALL)!!!

Although you may be clothed with your new self, you are still predisposed to tell lies! You have to take control of your life and stop telling lies; because satan is always on your back - trying to trip you up all the time! You have to become increasingly Christ-like! Jesus Christ is our Creator!!!

If you keep telling lies and it appears you are getting away with it, trust me, you will not get away; there is One Who Sees, Hears and Knows everything! He is the Judge standing at the door; His Name is Jesus!!!

Be truthful in all things! Truth has become such a scarce commodity, even though readily available! Hmmm! Even when we judge, do we apply the standards of truth? This applies not just to those entrusted with justice in the law courts; but also to people in all walks of life! God hates lies, injustice and perjury! Do you honour God? Will you? Obey the Word of God and enjoy His Love and Blessings; disobey at your own peril!!!

Not just anybody can dwell on God's Holy Hill or in His Presence or Tent! The Word of God makes very clear that you must be blameless, righteous and truthful to gain access to the Presence of the Lord! Can you strive towards this? Hmmm! May God Help us all to achieve what is clearly a lofty ideal for humanity born in iniquity; in Jesus' Name. Amen!!!

Many religious leaders are daily accused of not practicing what they preach; this is not new! Jesus Christ Himself advised the people to do as "they" say (who have the responsibility of the Word of God in their possession) and not as "they" do! They know what to say according to the Word of God but themselves to not obey. Therefore you have the responsibility to monitor and discern to be sure they're leading you aright. Otherwise, you ought to just listen to them and if they're telling you the truth of God's Word, don't look at how they act, speak or think, just obey the Word of God!!!

Seek first the Kingdom of God; seek it as if your life depends on it! Meditate on the above example! Whatever you do, get the Kingdom of God! You can only enter as a little child! Otherwise, no chance for you or anybody who will not come as a little child! Hmmmm! May God Help us in this quest for the Kingdom of God in Jesus' Name. Amen!!!

155th Day

FOR YOUR MERCY I PLEAD O LORD; FOR I AM A SINNER! HELP ME TO LIVE FOR YOU! JESUS CHRIST IS THE LORD!!!

Father Lord God, please establish Your laws in my family; on our hearts and minds. As for me and my household, o Lord, we shall worship and serve only You o Lord! Forgive our sins and remember them no more; so that ours will be a case of blessed is the man whose sins the Lord Does not count against him in Jesus' Name. Amen!!!

As long as you have life, there is hope; a live dog is better than a dead lion! As long as there's life in you, you still have an opportunity to call upon the Lord, who is worthy to be praised! You have a chance to change your life and sin no more. You have a chance to cry out for God's Mercy over your life and ways and for a Touch from the Master over your life. Why don't you do it now? You don't have all the time in the world; once dead, you can't repent anymore. Think on that! Help me o Lord to change my ways in Jesus' Name. Amen!!!

I don't know why He loves me but I know He does. I know that Jesus doesn't deal with me as my sinfulness deserves. I do not even deserve to be alive; although no one lives for ever! I must continue to fear Him sincerely because of His Love. My mother taught me that "eni to ba fe'ni la and beru"; meaning: we fear the one who loves us! We don't want to offend the one who loves us; it puts us to shame to offend such a one that loves us! Take Your rightful place in my life o Lord in Jesus' Name. Amen!!!

God does not ever vent His full anger or fury on those who fear and love Him. He doesn't even count the sins of some of them at all. But, only God alone Knows those He puts in such a category. I would play safe if I were you; rather than assume that you are in such a category and be belatedly disappointed. Strive to please God always in holiness, righteousness, love and faithfulness in Jesus' Name. So, Help me o Lord to please You in Jesus' Name. Amen!!!

Who is Jesus to you? Who is the Messiah to you? To many of you, He's no more than a son of David! Especially my brother who challenged me recently (I won't mention names)! Again, the above Scripture leads you in the right direction! How can Jesus Christ be the son of David and yet David refers to Him as Lord? Hmmm! Food for thought. Clearly the Bible says who is the Lord except our God and who is God except the Lord! Father, let Your Truth be Revealed through me in Jesus' Name; that many may believe and come to You in Jesus' Name. Amen!!!

When you are poor you are rich; when you are weak you are strong! God Knows wherever you are at in any given situation and at any given time! Even though you may appear to be in want, the Lord considers your richness according to His Grace and Mercy upon your life and things money cannot buy! So, folks, are you rich, strong or poor, weak? I know what and who I am in Jesus Christ. Lord, I am satisfied with You in every way in Jesus' Name. Amen!!!

156th Day

WHEN YOU WALK WITH THE LORD; NO NEED TO FEAR ANYMORE! SONS OF GOD ARE LED BY THE HOLY SPIRIT!!!

The judgement of whatever we do is secure even here on earth apparently! According to the Word of the Living God! If you live a wayward, complacent lifestyle, the same will kill and destroy you. If however, you live for and in the Name of the Lord and by His Word, you need fear no evil; for you will live in safety and at ease. Lord, Help us to do what is right by You in Jesus' Name. Amen!!!

When you walk with the Lord in the Light of His Word, what a glory He Sheds on your way; whilst you do His Good Will, He Abides with you still, as will all who will trust and obey! There is on other way! The Lord Himself will teach your children and great will be their peace; whilst you shall be established in righteousness, far from fear, terror and oppression! Lord, please keep us abiding in You in Jesus' Name. Amen!!!

When you look upon the Lord absolutely for all things, He Will be your Keeper and will preserve you from all evil; even as you go and come daily and forevermore in Jesus' Name. Will you choose to hope and trust in the Lord? I have decided to do so myself and my household with me. We shall serve the Lord! Help us o Lord to serve You sincerely and diligently to the very end in Jesus' Name. Amen!!!

When you submit yourself to be led by the Spirit of God, then you become a son of God. The Spirit you submit to is not one of slavery leading to fear; but one of adoption as a son. Then you can cry out freely unto the Father; as in crying Abba Father! The Holy Spirit will witness to your sonship unto your spirit so that you know! I want to be and remain as Your son to the very end o Lord; Help me in Jesus' Name. Amen!!!

Here I am Send me; if my Lord needs somebody, here I am Send me! This Glory, this Great Spirit is poured into this pot of clay (the fleshly body). You no longer desire sacrifices nor offerings of birds, lambs etc.; but rather that mankind would simply do Your Will o Lord God Almighty! You have done away with the first system to establish the new; through the Holy Sacrifice of the Body of Jesus Christ! Help us to understand and live by Your New order o Lord in Jesus' Name. Amen. Help us to do Your will and submit ours in Jesus' Name. Amen!!!

The more Jesus Christ overcame the tests from the Sadducees and Pharisees, the more they tested Him and devised new tests! This time they touched on the very core of the Lord's Commandments and Jesus Christ summarised everything for them concisely! The greatest commandment is to Love the Lord with all your heart, soul and mind! The second is to love your neighbour as yourself! All the Law and Prophets hang on these two! Thanks to God for such an Executive Summary of the Commandments of God. Lord, Help us to get right with You and obey Your Commandments in Jesus' Name. Amen!!!

157th Day

THOSE WHO TRUST/HOPE IN THE LORD SHALL NEVER BE PUT TO SHAME! HE'LL GUIDE, DIRECT, PROTECT AND BLESS THEM!!!

The Lord Will not just Direct anyone's paths willy nilly because He is God and Love! You must trust/hope in Him wholeheartedly and not lean upon your own understanding as many are wont to doing! It is expedient that you acknowledge Him in all your ways. Then you can expect by faith to get His attention; and for His Love, Blessings and other benefits to flow forth unto you from the Throne of Mercy and Grace. Lord, Help incline our hearts towards You increasingly; to trust/hope in You all the days of our lives in Jesus' Name. Amen!!!

The steps of a righteous (good) man are ordered by the Lord; not just anybody's steps. Please take note! God's Love is not cheap and definitely not unconditional! Were it unconditional, there would be no need for any expectations of us from God before we receive His Blessings! As it is, all over the Holy Scriptures, there are these requirements from God for us to enjoy His Love and Blessings! Take heed; the Word of the Living God in Jesus' Name. Amen!!!

When you show the Lord that you need Him and Him alone and you take hold of His Hand and behave yourself according to His Word and requirements, He Will never let you down! Then, He Will Guide and Direct your paths unto eternity in Jesus" Name. Help me o Lord to draw near to You so that You will draw near to me and never leave me alone in Jesus' Name. Amen!!!

No man shall be able to stand before you all the days of your life. Just as I was with Moses, so I will be with you. I will not leave you or forsake you. Be strong and courageous, for you shall cause this people to inherit the land that I swore to their fathers to give them. Only be strong and very courageous, being careful to do according to all the law that Moses my servant commanded you. Do not turn from it to the right hand or to the left, that you may have good success wherever you go. Joshua 1:5-7 ESV

When the Lord puts you in leadership and you not only put your hope/ trust in Him, but encourage those you are leading to do likewise, then you will have good success! The Promises and Blessings of God shall be yours and you shall overcome all enemy actions over your affairs! Is it not good for a leader to hope/trust in the Lord always? You must however combine boldness and courage with your faith in God in order that fear will not take root in your heart and psyche! The Word of God clearly says that the fearful will not get to Heaven! Lord Help me to combine boldness and courage with my faith in Jesus' Name. Amen!!!

Man loves to test and ridicule the Word of the Living and Loving God! So much so far removed are some from the Word of the Living God that they believe that if they kill believers, they will have so many virgins waiting for them in Heaven to enjoy; as if there will be sexual activities in Heaven as on earth? Some believe these and on these fake beliefs, go round killing themselves and many others at the same time. O no! It is a disaster to play with the certainty of hell fire and eternal damnation! Lord, Help us to believe in the Way, Truth and Life in Jesus' Name. Amen!!!

Suffice unto you to test and examine yourselves just as per being and remaining in the Faith; as against measuring yourselves with those people who commend themselves amongst each other - measuring and comparing themselves likewise - alas, a fruitless endeavour! Is Jesus Christ in you? You need to be very sure; in case you are running your race in vain! Father, please come into my life and stay forevermore in Jesus' Name. Amen! I need you every breath that I take o Lord in Jesus' Name. Amen!!!

158th Day

IN HUMILITY, AFTER JESUS CHRIST, COMES THE LITTLE CHILDREN; EMULATE THEM AND BE BLESSED! YOU WILL NOT LOVE THE WORLD IF YOU HAVE THE FATHER'S LOVE !!!

God places a great value and premium on humility! So much so we are told that God opposes the proud and gives grace to the humble! Jesus Christ is our prime example! Next to Jesus Christ are the little children! So much so that we are told in the Holy Scriptures that there is no place for anyone who will not come to Jesus Christ as a little child in the Kingdom of Heaven! God Favours the humble always in every way possible! How can you resist the devil for him to flee except with humility? Humility helps you even to avoid sin! Humility is what keeps you godly in your mindset. Would you not rather have God on your side? I would. So, I choose to yield to God! Please o my Father, Teach me humility so I can enjoy the very best of You in Jesus' Name. Amen!!!

You love the world! Do not deceive yourself! If the Love of the Father is truly in you, then you will begin to hate the world and all it stands for! However, if you arrogantly refuse to yield to God, then the world will just simply eat into you all the more and you will regret ultimately! Lord, please Help me not to love the world; remove the love of the world from my heart. I want to be Your friend and not Your enemy; so Help me o Lord in Jesus' Name. Amen!!!

159th Day

WHEN YOU PRIORITISE LOVING THE LORD, HE BLESSES YOU; AND WITH THE FRUITS OF THE SPIRIT TOO! GIVE TO CEASAR AND TO GOD WHAT BELONGS TO THEM!!!

In the Word of God, Loving the Lord is the number one priority; even over and above loving your neighbour as yourself! Meditate on the above Scriptures very seriously! God has great treasures for those who love Him; such that eyes have not seen, nor ears heard, or minds conceived - and He treasures them! With this, I cannot see how God's Love can be unconditional; because clearly, God has an expectation for all believers - indeed all humans to Love Him as a matter of priority! Not only are we to love Him, but also to keep His Commands; so to receive His Love and Blessings! We are to love Him with all our strength, heart, passion, our everything! We are to learn and master His Words and Commandments and teach them to our children so His Love and Blessings for us and our children can endure from generation to generation! Help us o Lord to Love You like You want us to in Jesus' Name. Please Touch our hearts in Jesus' Name. Amen!!!

The Spirit of the Lord Jesus Christ is the Spirit of Prophesy! Who does not know that that same Spirit is the Spirit of the Living God? Yet, some still doubt the Lordship and Godhead of Jesus Christ! Hmmm! May God Help us indeed to be wise to know Him and the Power of His resurrection! Jesus Christ Knew their hearts and what they were up to and He always had a Word for them and they never overcame Him; nor were they ever able to trap Him like they planned to! Father, Give us wisdom to be more like Jesus in every way; in thoughts, words and deeds in Jesus' Name. Amen!!!

The fruits of the Spirit are the same as the fruits of Love; because essentially Love is synonymous with the Spirit! God is Love and God is Spirit! If you claim to be in Jesus Christ, then you must be sure to crucify your flesh with its passions and desires! Have you? What I see today is the free reign of the fleshly passions and desires amongst those who vehemently proclaim to be in the Christian faith! May God Help us not to deceive ourselves in Jesus' Name I pray with thanksgiving. Amen!!!

160th Day

TRUTH IS PLEASING TO GOD FOR THE FAITH WALK; ESCHEW ALL MALICIOUS BEHAVIOUR AND FUTILE SACRIFICES!!!

Check your heart! Stop telling lies; God is not pleased with lies nor liars! Stop toying with hell fire; it will not be fun! Never swear falsely in the Name of the Lord! Hmmmm! May God Help us in Jesus' Name. Amen!!!

Stop the hypocrisy; going after whores and homosexuals as if all other sins are tolerated by God? Meditate carefully and sincerely on the above Scripture and make relevant confessions and eschew all evil and its appearances. Strive to please God by faith not through works. The Judge is standing at the door! Help us o Lord to live for You in Jesus' Name. Amen!!!

Do not emulate the wicked; and submit your life and heart to God for a renewal of your mindset which is born astray from the Ways of God! Strive for holiness and righteousness to be saved in Jesus' Name. Amen! Help o Lord; please Save us in Jesus' Name. Amen!!!

Do you forget that humankind are connected one to another? That's why the Word of God says to love your neighbour as yourself! Be truthful to each other and cut out the unproductive, sinful and dangerous lies that will let you end up in hell! O Lord, we need Your Help; please do not forsake us in Jesus' Name. Amen!!!

Stop the pretences and hypocrisy; you can fool people, but even so, not all the time. But can you fool God? Can you hide your true self from God? My son wrote this morning: "be careful who you pretend to be; you might forget who you are!" How true! Cut out all malicious behaviour with all appearances of evil! Father, Help us to forsake all evil and its appearances in Jesus' Name. Amen!!!

When you love the Lord and witness to others about Him, many will persecute you and try to trap you in your words as they did to Jesus Christ relentlessly! If only you will learn from the Master! Jesus dealt with issues and people in a particular way. His wisdom is learnable and teachable! Strive to emulate and imbibe the Wisdom of God. Father, Teach us Your Wisdom in Jesus' Name. Amen!!!

Your way of life is abominable to God; and He Sees through all your pretences because He is the All-Knowing God unto whom all hearts and minds are open and all desires known! You cannot fool God! So, because He's not pleased with you, when you call Him, He won't answer! If however you stay in obedience to His Word and on HIs right side and call on Him, He Will Answer you. Father, Help us in this wicked and evil world to stay on Your right side in Jesus' Name. Amen!!!

161st Day

GOD DESIRES TO GLORIFY HIS SON; ARE YOU READY TO YIELD TO AND BE LED BY HIS HOLY SPIRIT? ONLY BY SUBMISSION AND OBEDIENCE TO HIM!!!

Jesus Christ IS God in human form; He came to show us the Way. He obeyed the Word of God and did His bidding until He returned to His Position in the Godhead as Lord of everything! To Him belongs the Royal Majesty with all the Power forever and ever. Amen! Every knee shall bow and all tongues confess to His Lordship to God's Glory in Jesus' Name. Amen! Lord Give me understanding with Your wisdom to know this TRUTH!!!

Having been fully obedient to the Word of God, Jesus Christ, Himself the Word of God, asked God to Glorify His Son; and God DID in every possible way! Jesus Christ is the Revealed God, Eternal Life! Help me o Lord; that I might know Him, Christ Jesus and the Power of His Resurrection!!!

When the nobility hear Your Words, they will bow in praise, adoration, exultation and glorifying Your Name and Your Ways o Lord! You who are highly exalted yet You do not despise the lowly! Truly You Are God! The haughty and arrogant you oppose! Blessed be Your glorious Name! Help us who believe to be increasingly like You in Jesus' Name. Amen!!!

There is a time, a place and a season for everything in the earth under the sun! There is appropriateness in everything for every time, place and season accordingly. Lord Help us to learn what is timely, due placement and seasonal, appropriate for all at all times in Jesus' Name. Amen! That way, we will not get caught out and have cause to regret, even forever in Jesus' Name. Amen!!!

This is the TRUTH of all stories of creation! Believe by faith the Word of God and be rooted in the knowledge of the Truth and be set free unto salvation of your soul in Jesus' Name. Amen!!!

162nd Day

JESUS CHRIST WILL TAKE GOOD CARE OF ALL WHO COME TO HIM FOREVER; SEPARATE YOURSELF FROM THE WORLD! IF YOU DON'T FOLLOW JESUS, OTHERS WILL; YOUR LOSS!!!

You cannot be yoked with unbelievers (the world) and expect to please God! Stop deceiving yourself; in wanting to satisfy the world so they can like you, as against pleasing God as a priority! If you will separate yourself out for God's sake, God will receive you and be Father to you. Nothing short will do for God! Lord, Help me to separate myself from this evil world and live for You alone o Lord in Jesus' Name. Amen!!!

Jesus made this promise and He is true to His Word! Dare to believe. How did Jesus reveal Himself even though He is no longer with us physically? Is it not by the Holy Spirit? Yet, many still doubt that Jesus is God's Holy Spirit! If Jesus Christ is God's Holy Spirit, then how can He not be God? Can anybody be the Holy Spirit if not God? When we all know that God is a Spirit (not a ghost)? Please God, Reveal Yourself in and through me to others, that they might believe that You are the Lord Jesus Christ. Amen!!!

When God Promises almost exactly like Jesus in the penultimate Scripture that He Will be with His own, He means business! This promise here was made in Genesis, long before Jesus Christ Came into the world in the flesh! Why do many still doubt that Jesus Christ is God who Came to us in the human flesh form? The promises of God are Yes and Amen in Christ Jesus! Thank You Lord for revealing Yourself to me; I appreciate You my Father, God and King in Jesus' Name. Amen!!!

As long as you come to the Lord and lay all your troubles, hopes, aspirations and your everything on Him, He Will Keep you safe in every way. He Will Provide for you all your needs forever. He Will Deliver you from all evil and protect your goings and comings in Jesus' Name. Amen! Lord, I give my all to You; do with me as You wish and I will be fully satisfied in Jesus' Name. Amen!!!

When you honour people and they trample on your gesture; don't keep begging or pleading with them. That would amount to casting your pearls unto pigs. Transfer such honours to those you would normally consider as undeserving randomly and in an unplanned way and watch how they will appreciate you and God Will Bless you and they will bless you too! Learn from the Master and be wise in Jesus' Name. Amen!!!

When you have love, you are not insensitive, unbelieving, hopeless; nor will you lack endurance! Love copes with all things and situations to the best of one's ability! Likewise, love causes one to believe and not feel that because others have been unfaithful, become wary of everyone. Love gives chances to others. Love never loses hope and always endures. People may call you a fool; but to Love (God) there is wisdom from God in you. So, choose who you want to emulate today; God or man! Likewise, who do you want to trust? God or man! Father, Help me to trust You all the days of my life in Jesus' Name. Amen!!!

163rd Day

GOD IS THE CREATOR OF ALL THINGS GOOD AND PERFECT! IF IN NEED, ASK HIM WITH FAITH! GOD IS LIGHT! JESUS IS GOD!!!

Jesus Christ is the Light of the world and He is the Father of all lights! He is our Heavenly Father! Yes, He shed His Blood for humanity that we might be reconciled back to Him simply by believing and pledging a good conscience unto Him. We must also in so doing, obey His Word and live for the sake of righteousness! He does not shift like shadows as humans do! God is GREAT and greatly to be praised, worshiped and adored!!!

God is Good all the time; and He Gives all their fair share of chances in life in everything and in every way. He avails Himself to us to ask anything we desire of Him! He says to Ask, Seek and Knock (fascinating acronym, ASK); but when we ask, we must believe - i.e. to ask with faith! He Has reserved the best for His children. Eyes have not seen, nor ears heard, neither has the mind understood yet; what the Lord Has in store for those who love Him! Lord increase my faith and confidence to come to You for all my needs to be met in Jesus Christ I pray thankfully, Amen!!!

God is Light! No darkness in Him at all! You cannot claim to fellowship with God whilst walking in darkness! If however you walk in the light, then you will fellowship with other believers! God inhabits the praises of His people; therefore, as you fellowship together, the Blood of Jesus Christ, Son of God cleanses you all from all sin! O what a privilege to know the One and ONLY true God; Rock of all ages! Thank You Lord Jesus for Loving me (us)! Help me to follow You faithfully o Lord; in spirit and in truth in Jesus' Name. Amen!!!

The heart of man is deceitful and desperately wicked who can know it? Hmmmm! An invitation to dinner, totally shunned and disdained, with violence meted out to the messengers, some of who were actually killed! However, wickedness will kill the wicked; whilst goodness will be the lot of the good! Those who perpetrate and perpetuate wickedness to others, their spouses and children will share in the rewards of wickedness in due season! Be wise, emboldened to flexibly change your decisions when people fail to appreciate goodness planned or meted out to them! God Give me the wisdom to act appropriately in different circumstances in my life in Jesus' Name. Amen!!!

(1) In the beginning God created the heavens and the earth.

Genesis 1:1

In the beginning was the Word and the Word was with God and the Word was God, He was with God in the beginning! Nothing was created without Him! Jesus Christ created all things. He is the Word of the Living God! The Creator of all! King Jesus. Thank You o Lord Jesus! I have reasons to praise Your Name. Father, please continue to give me reason to praise Your Name in all the earth in Jesus' Name. Amen!!!

164th Day

HAVE FAITH IN GOD AND DO GOOD; SHOW LOVE AND LIVE LIFE IN LOVE IS WHY WE ARE ALIVE! BLESS THE LORD!!!

To enjoy God and God's best, it's not a matter of unconditional love at all. You have work to do! You need to love God and trust Him; delight yourself in Him; commit your ways to Him and He Will Bless you with His manifold Blessings. Please do not let anybody deceive you as if you can continue in wilful sinfulness and yet be enjoying God's Love and Blessings. Not so! Lord, Teach us how to live for You in our daily lives in Jesus' Name. Amen!!!

To show or prove that you love the Lord and have given your life to Him, your heart must be prepared! Then you stretch forth your hands unto Him and everything in your life would begin to turn around for the good, better and best in Jesus' Name. Your star would shine and you would dwell in safety in Jesus' Name. Amen. May God Bless us to love Him and have the relevant evidence in obeying His Commandments in Jesus' Name. Amen!!!

Jesus Calls out to all who are thirsty, hungry, destitute, impoverished, oppressed, depressed, etc.! In short, all who labour and are heavily laden; the Lord is reaching out to you. Will you open up to Jesus? Will you come to Him? If you do, you will enjoy an everlasting covenant of Love with Him with Mercy, Grace and Blessings in Jesus' Name. Are you ready for Jesus? Come now, for tomorrow may just be too late! Be prepared in and out of season for the Lord may Come anytime now! Lord, Help us to be prepared for Your Coming so that we shall not live in eternal damnation and unending suffering with great pains in Jesus' Name. Amen!!!

165th Day

IF ONLY THE NATIONS WILL TREAD HIS PATHS AND WALK IN HIS WAYS, HOW GREAT WILL THEIR PEACE BE!!!

The justice and righteousness required by the Lord in following Him is not only applicable to leaders in any nation but also to followers too! Leaders are chosen from amongst the people; of the people are not versed in doing rightly and justly with each other, how easy would it be for them to learn when in leadership? Hmmm! Study the Scripture above carefully and learn; hopefully, obey the Word of God and live the best you can on the earth and make the most of the life that you have been Given by God. Lord, Help us to learn to live and apply justice and righteousness in our daily living with each other in Jesus' Name. Amen!!!

At the end of the Day, God Will Have His Way! He Will Rebuild the ruins of Jerusalem and put His Spirit in His Chosen; and they will live according to His Statutes, Commandments and Laws. Justice will flow with Righteousness. There will be no more need for war anymore and peace shall abound like a river; with the Lord rebuking even the strong nations from oppressing the weaker ones! Wow! What a Mighty God we have and serve! Father, may it be unto us according to Your Promises; Help us o Lord, Teach us to live justly and do righteously in the lands and according to Your Holy Word in Jesus' Name. Amen!!!

The owner of the vineyard represents leadership; and possesses the power to act against all evil doers as far as his business and other interests are concerned! All wrongdoing shall be punished; for he does not hold the rod/staff of authority for nothing! Leadership have a privilege and authority to act to punish and make right! Lord, Help us to apply Your Word to our lives daily and be prepared for leadership opportunities even as we live our daily lives with our brethren in Jesus' Name. Amen!!!

Whenever God Blesses you with spoils belonging to His enemies, He Knows that their ways are very attractive and will be so to His children. However, God Counsels us not to follow their evil ways and practices; but rather to obey the Commandments of the Lord our God and act according to His Counsel to us. This way we shall continue to live and enjoy His Love and Blessings! Otherwise, we shall come under His wrath. Hence, Blessings for obedience and curses for disobedience! To enjoy God's Love and Blessings, we have a part to play. That is fully conditional and will never change! May God Give us the wisdom to learn and know the truth; that we might be truly free. For, only the Truth can set us free, in Jesus' Name. Amen!!!

166th Day

WISDOM OF LEADERSHIP; ASSOCIATED SUFFERINGS AND EVIL! A VITAL PART OF CREATION'S STORY!!!

When in leadership such as a king, you ought to for the sake of God Almighty, reign with the fear of God at heart. You ought to be driven by the fear of God and reign in righteousness and with justice. Then the people you reign over will be encouraged to live in faith in your leadership and there will likely be peace and love amongst them. Then, each man will look out for his brother and be his brother's keeper; as a shelter and refuge from the wind and storm; and a comfort from every trouble and distress! O Lord, Give us a heart to understand and do Your bidding and follow Your Counsel and Word in Jesus' Name. Amen!!!

Father, I pray that Your children everywhere will be encouraged to lead according to Your judgments and with your righteousness whether in leadership or not. For each is in leadership in one way or another in life. The important thing is to live by Your Word and according to Your Counsel. Then Your children will judge each other (Your people) with righteousness and justice (including the afflicted, oppressed, and underprivileged, etc.). Then the children of the needy will be saved and the oppressor crushed. I pray in Jesus' Name. Amen!!!

The Bible says that the heart of man is deceitful and desperately wicked; who can know it? In the above story, when the landowner was renting the vineyard to the farmers, they were alright with him then. However, when the time came for harvest, they had a problem with him; so much so that they dealt mercilessly with his servants. The landowner then sent his son, thinking that they would at least offer the same or similar respect to his son as they have for him; alas, they killed the son too! Does this not show their mindset towards the landowner? Suddenly, they would want to take over his land completely! That is the mindset of mankind for you! May God Save us from all evil and Help us to flee from all appearances of evil in Jesus' Name. Amen!!!

God is the original Man. He made man in His image and according to His likeness. One of the critical purposes of man's creation is to have dominion over the earth and all that is in it! This tells us that we must look after the earth (environment)! Man, know your place! Lord, Help us to know our place and purpose in this earth and in our lives that You have Given to us and to do rightly and act justly towards fellow humans and our earth (environment) in Jesus' Name. Amen!!!

167th Day

BLESSINGS FOR OBEDIENCE; THE OPPOSITE APPLIES FOR DISOBEDIENCE! ROYAL PRIESTHOOD! INTEGRITY!!!

And it shall come to pass, if thou shalt hearken diligently unto the voice of the LORD thy God, to observe and to do all his commandments which I command thee this day, that the LORD thy God will set thee on high above all nations of the earth: And all these blessings shall come on thee, and overtake thee, if thou shalt hearken unto the voice of the LORD thy God. Blessed shalt thou be in the city, and blessed shalt thou be in the field. Blessed shall be the fruit of thy body, and the fruit of thy ground, and the fruit of thy cattle, the increase of thy kine, and the flocks of thy sheep. Blessed shall be thy basket and thy store. Blessed shalt thou be when thou comest in, and blessed shalt thou be when thou goest out. The LORD shall cause thine enemies that rise up against thee to be smitten before thy face: they shall come out against thee one way, and flee before thee seven ways.

The Word of God is not a joke! Whether you are born again or not, the Word of God, the Commandments of God are to be obeyed! To disobey is perilous. Meditate on the above very seriously; so you know the advantages of obeying God's Word! We are lulled into believing that God's Love makes no demands or requirements of us; this is untrue. We must obey the Lord's Word! To disobey is at your own peril. There are conditions for God's Love and Blessings; obedience is key! Lord Help me to be wise to know the truth and be free in Jesus' Name. Amen!!!

When you give your life to Jesus Christ you become all of the above! You are special to God; created to bring Him Glory in your daily living and throughout your life! You must refrain from sin, fear God and live a holy life; such that your adversaries, foes and enemies see your good works and glorify God on account of you. Lord, Help me to remain in You; that I may continue to benefit from Your Love and Faithfulness in Jesus' Name. Amen!!!

When you put your hope in Jesus Christ and become born again, you have made the confession that Jesus Christ is the Son of the Living God! Those who insist that God has no son do not belong in this category; so God does not dwell in them! The difference is very clear! Lord, Help me live with my conviction according to my confession in Jesus' Name. Amen!!!

As a believer, it is imperative that you do not lack integrity. You must be demonstratively honest and let your yes be yes and no be no. You should have no need to swear and or take the Name of the Lord our God in vain, lest you fall into judgement! Lord, Help me to have integrity and to be consistently so; so that I do not fall into judgement in Jesus' Name. Amen!!!

168th Day

THE GRACE, PEACE, STEADFAST LOVE AND MERCY OF OUR LORD NEVER ENDS; RATHER RENEWED EVERY MORNING!!!

As a believer, I have a tremendous potential advantage in my life to receive an endless run of the Grace, Peace, Steadfast Love and Mercy of the Lord Jesus Christ, with His Faithfulness! The Lord is my portion in the land of the living. He is always so good to me; I will forever hope and trust in Him! I will wait in quietness and trust for His Salvation! He is my Redeemer, Lord and Saviour. He Will Deliver me! Thank You Lord Jesus for the Love you freely give to me in Jesus' Name. Amen!!!

The Grace of our Lord Jesus Christ, the Love of God and the sweet fellowship of the Holy Spirit is with me both now and forevermore in Jesus' Name. Amen. My Lord Satisfies me with every good thing, with every blessing day by day; His Love is unshaken and is renewed every blessed morning of my life! Heaven backs me up by His Grace and Mercy always; and the Windows Of Heaven open up to me in pleasant places all the time! The Lord has Chosen me before the foundations of the world were laid. He Granted me to be adopted as a son of His in Jesus Christ according to His Will, I am accepted in the Beloved; unshaken, unrelenting, no matter what satan's plans are, the Will of God Shall prevail over my life in Jesus' Name. Amen!!!

169th Day

THE WORD OF GOD TASTES SWEETER THAN HONEY BUT SOURS UP THE STOMACH; CURSES TURN TO BLESSINGS; AND GREAT IS THE LORD AND WORTHY TO BE PRAISED!!!

The psalmist said the Word of God is sweeter than the honeycomb; and we read in the Word of God that the Scroll above (which I believe to be the Word of God) turns the stomach sour. This is largely because the Word of God, when taken in, if taken in, brings about change. Change is hardly ever a pleasant experience. That unpleasantness is the souring up of the stomach experienced in letting the Word of God "Touch" us to create the change we need. Lord, Help us to yield to your Word; that change may come to us in Jesus' Name. Amen!!!

Whom the Lord has Blessed, no one can curse! I am of the stock of Abraham; I am his seed. The Blessings of Abraham are active in my life and experience! All who bless me shall be blessed and those who curse me shall be cursed. This is the Word of the Lord to me. The Rhema of God! I receive and accept Your Word of Blessing over my Lord o Lord and reject anything contrary from any quarters in Jesus' Name. Amen!!!

It is good to tell out the Goodness and the Greatness of the Lord as rendered above! Then the awe of God can fall on us and we can fully and truly appreciate the handiwork of the Lord upon our lives and experience. The Lord Gives and Takes away; Blessed be His Glorious Name. May the Lord not hide His Face from us and that He Sends us His Spirit increasingly day by day in Jesus' Name. Amen!!!

Instead of humbling ourselves to simply believe the Word of God, we arrogantly intellectualise everything! However, the Word of God is best received by faith not by questioning and rationalising everything intellectually! Knowledge puffs up but love builds up! The people we despise and do not expect to receive the Word of God for whatever reason, are those that actually end up believing faithfully because they humble themselves and appreciate the Word of God more! May God Grant us the wisdom to humble ourselves to receive the Word of God and to obey in Jesus' Name. Amen!!!

In today, come in to stay; come into my life/heart, Lord Jesus. Amen!!!

170th Day

NOBODY IS PERFECT; EXCEPT GOD ALONE IN JESUS CHRIST! HOWEVER, HE SAID BE YE PERFECT AND HOLY AS HE IS!!!

The fear of God is what enables a righteous and wise man to submit to instruction, teaching, rebukes and admonition; for which reason, they get even wiser and increase in learning. If you want to be wise and righteous or claim to be, you must be likewise in attitude! Lord, Help me to submit to Your Authority and sound instruction and teaching that will improve my lot in Jesus' Name. Amen!!!

A son who is wise accepts and submits to his father's discipline, not to talk of God's! However, a scoffer does not listen to rebuke! Which are you? How do you respond to discipline (your father's or even God's)! Do you not know that it is written: "A father disciplines a son that he loves!" Help me o Lord to accept discipline for my life in Jesus' Name. Amen!!!

Jesus Christ led an exemplary life in every way including in the area of His response to discipline, suffering, the whole lot! Why? He, in fleshly man, entrusted Himself to the Just Judge, who judges righteously; who is the Lord God Almighty! What a great exemplary humility. The Great Judge submits himself; the One to whom all must and will submit, submits Himself! Hmmmm! O what a story! Thank You o Lord for Teaching us submission and humility; Help us to follow Your example in all things in Jesus' Name. Amen!!!

The humble introduce peace into a volatile situation by speaking soft words and answers in response to the harsher words spoken in wrath by other parties! However, grievous words only fuel the fire of anger in such situations! The humble wise ones apply their knowledge rightly in every situation they're involved in; however, the foolish pour out folly! Lord Teach and Help us to be wise and humble in life's situations; only by Your Strength o Lord. In Jesus' Name. Amen!!!

When the Power of God manifests through anybody; or when in authority of any type, your (or that) power authority will be questioned, tested and challenged! If the authority and power of the Holy One of Israel was tested, how do you not expect that yours will likewise?! Lord, Help me to be wise in authority and in the use of power in Jesus' Name. Amen!!!

When for example as a Christian, you relate with non-Christians; but when in the presence of other Christians, you "pretend" that you do not, that is hypocrisy! This was what the Apostle Paul challenged, rebuked and admonished his brother Apostle Peter for! Was he justified or not; especially in public? Half a word is enough for the wise! O Lord, forgive our hypocrisy and lead us aright in Jesus' Name. Amen!!!

171st Day

ON MARRIAGE: TOW THE ANCIENT PATHS; BE TRANSFORMED VIA RENEWAL OF YOUR MIND! DON'T CONFORM! LET GOD!!!

God's Standard is supreme for a successful marriage! As Jesus Christ loved the Church, husbands, love your wives! Meditate on the Word of God about marriage seriously and put to practice the Word of God! Your wife is a part of you; your very own body! Love your neighbour as yourself! Your wife is not your neighbour; you have a primary responsibility to love her! She is effectively a part of you. Love her as you. Fulfill your responsibilities to her! God Grant us who trust and hope in You, to love like You Do and as You recommend and Counsel that we do, even with our wives in Jesus' Name. Amen!!!

Your wife is your fountain! The Bible says that he who finds a wife finds a good thing and obtains Favour from the Lord! Your wife is a channel of Blessing to you from the Lord! Be satisfied with her love and loving her. Do not let in any other "loves" that will let you lose your focus, even with God Almighty! Honour the Lord's Word and be Blessed. Father, Teach us Your ways; for no man can obey Your Word, unless You Touch their hearts. Teach us o Lord and Lead us in Jesus' Name. Amen!!!

Wives, be subject to your husbands, as is fitting in the Lord. Husbands, love your wives, and do not be harsh with them. Colossians 3:18,19 RSV

Wives, be submissive to your husbands; this pleases God and is honourable in God's Sight! Husbands, show love to your wives and don't be harsh with them; and thus displease the Lord! If both husbands and wives will do things God's Way and simply apply the principles of God's Love as laid out in 1 Corinthians 13 and everywhere else God Gave us His Word on Love and Marriage, humanity would be fulfilled in love. Father, Help us to obey Your Word and Counsel in Jesus' Name. Amen!!!

This is God's Way! No matter what satan and "wise" men and women say about love and marriage! God's Word is supreme! God Created male and female and intended marriage definitely to be between man and woman. Anything else is a counterfeit; it's ungodly, sinful and will incur severe consequences from God! The two (man and woman) in marriage shall become ONE! Note that if you unite yourself with anyone, you are one with them; if with the wrong person (not your husband or wife), you are outside of God's original Will for man! Father, forgive us for we have sinned; create in us a new heart that will bow to Your dictates in Jesus' Name. Amen!!!

This world has its own teachings on life and including marriage and love etc.! Do not be conformed to worldliness. Submit yourself to the transformation that comes only from renewing your mind through the Grace of God and the Holy Spirit. In so doing, you prove what is good, acceptable and perfect; you prove the Will of God! Thank You Lord Jesus for such an opportunity to change our lives for the better in Jesus' Name. Amen!!!

172nd Day

IN GOD THROUGH JESUS CHRIST IS ALL TRUE COMFORT, REST, STRENGTH, PEACE, JOY AND LOVE! PRAISE, GLORIFY HIM! HEAVEN IS FOR CHILDREN! I MUST PREACH THE GOSPEL!!!

A call to all who are burdened and tired into the Lord's Rest rings out continuously in life! Anyone listening? There is a yoke that is bearable; a lesson to be learnt from the Lord, who is gentle and humble at heart! The reward if you learn this lesson is peace and rest for your soul; with an easy bearable yoke and a light burden! What a gracious alternative we have! Still many opt to remain bound in their worldliness to the heavy yoke and huge burdens that destroy the soul, then the person. The choice is yours! Father, Grant that I choose what is right in Your Eyes and good for my soul in Jesus' Name. Amen!!!

We have a God who is our refuge and strength in times of trouble; hence, we shall not give in to fear, no matter what comes our way; whatever! O my Lord; I pray that I may trust and hope in You to the very end in Jesus' Name. Amen!!!

Let the redeemed and Blessed of the Lord praise Him. His praise from such folks is sweet in His Ears! He does not ever despise your affliction; don't stop crying out unto the Lord! He hears and will deliver you in Jesus' Name. Amen. Hear my cry o Lord in Jesus' Name. Amen!!!

God is with the righteous and all who fear the Lord! God Restores their captivity always in Jesus' Name. He Will Save them who live holy in the Fear of the Lord! O Help me Lord to fear Your Name and live for You in Jesus' Name. Amen!!!

Out of the mouth of babes, the Lord Has Ordained praise! Little children are Blessed and Favoured tremendously by the Lord God Almighty! So much so that He said: "Let the little children come unto Me; for theirs is the Kingdom of Heaven!" If you cannot come to God as a little child, there's no place for you in Heaven! Grant me this child-likeness o Lord; that I may make it into Your Kingdom in Jesus' Name. Amen!!!

I need not boast that I preach the Gospel; for woe unto me if I do not! I preach as a necessity and love outreach in Jesus' Name. Amen. Please Help me o Lord to do so effectively in Jesus' Name. Amen!!!

My reward for preaching the Gospel freely without abusing the Authority placed upon me in so doing is Heavenly! My reward is in Christ Jesus, even Eternal Life! Do not let me lose focus nor miss the Crown of Life o Lord in Jesus' Name. Amen!!!

173rd Day

WHEN YOU GIVE YOUR LIFE TO JESUS, SUPERNATURAL JOY IS RELEASED INTO YOUR LIFE! STRIVE FOR GODS' APPROVAL!!!

Every living soul praise the Lord; the Most High Reigneth in the believer's life daily! The believer is accompanied with joy in peace in their going and coming and the whole of nature created is in harmony, celebrating! Just trust God and believe; His Words never fail! Amen! Halleluyah!!!

Righteousness begets much joy with rejoicing and salvation, as manifested in the tabernacle of the righteous; combining melody with harmony to create a godly atmosphere always in Jesus' Name. Amen! Father, grant me this with my family as our portion in Jesus' Name. Amen! Grant likewise unto all believers in Jesus' Name. Amen!!!

The Joy of the Lord is communicated to the believer through the Word of God Spoken into our spirit via diverse means. May the Lord Bless us increasingly with His Joy through His Word in Jesus' Name. Amen!!!

When the Lord Blesses His people, they are filled with God in the great Power of God made manifest! He Gives them things they do not deserve to have and enjoy all the time! He Plants His chosen ones wherever He likes in any nation (including nations not their home nation) and Blesses them richly! When God Blesses you this way, you are so Blessed that you might observe and keep His Laws and Statutes so others can see and give honour to His Name as you do! Take note believer! Father, Help me; that my life may show forth Your Praise in Jesus' Name. Amen!!!

The Redeemed of the Lord will return to the Lord's City (Zion) with great joy forever; where sorrow and mourning will be no more! Pure bliss! Would you like your life to tow this line? Then you must come to the Lord Jesus Christ; to know Him and the Power of His Resurrection! I want to go to Heaven when I die to hear Jordan roll! I want to experience this great Joy o Lord; please grant me Divine Favour in Jesus' Name. Amen!!!

Wherever Jesus Christ went, the atmosphere changed from the ordinary to the spectacular every time; even in death! He made provision for every situation including the impossible. The people saw Him as the prophet from Nazareth in Galilee! Jesus Christ, however, is the Lord God Almighty!!!

Only God's approval makes any lasting sense and is for real! Man's approval is meaningless. Is presenting yourself to God for approval, it's not automatic you see! You have a part to play. You need to know the Word of God and be capable of understanding and communicating the Word of God to others accurately, boldly and without shame nor fear! You must shun all evil: in thoughts, words and deeds; and shun all idleness. Evil teaching will spread like gangrene (cancer); you must keep firmly in line with the straight and narrow path in Jesus' Name. Amen! Father, Help my family, myself and all believers to tow the line of holiness and righteousness in Jesus' Name. Amen!!!

174th Day

TRUE CHRISTIANITY IS PRIMARILY A CALL TO SUFFER HUMBLY WITH AND FOR JESUS CHRIST! SOW UNTO THE HOLY SPIRIT!!!

Anybody who follows Jesus Christ will as a matter of course face many trials and persecution; this is not a bad thing at all. Rather, His followers must rejoice in partaking of His sufferings; so when His Glory is revealed, they would be glad with great joy. Lord Help us to emulate Your Example in readiness and willingness to suffer for Your Name's sake in Jesus' Name. Amen!!!

Persecution for the sake of righteousness is inevitable for the followers of Jesus Christ. Often unjust and very negative experience, the believer is to bear up under such a yoke of injustice with a positive countenance. It is important to know that believers who went before, those present and those to come have been through and will experience the same. However, for this experiences, the believer shall be fully recompensed in Jesus' Name. Lord our Father, please remember us according to Your Promise in due season in Jesus' Name. Amen!!!

The believer's Call is for the purpose of suffering! I did not write the Holy Scriptures; they were Inspired by God Almighty and I believe them to be the Word of the Living God! Jesus Christ suffered for us tremendously and we are to follow in His Footsteps and example! Father God, please give us a heart to follow in Jesus' Footsteps in Jesus' Name. Amen!!!

Jesus Christ's every need was met Supernaturally! He was always surrounded with people who met His every need! When Called, do not worry about your needs being met; for the One who Called you shall make sure all your needs are well covered in Jesus' Name. Amen! Help me o Lord not to think or bemoan adversity, challenges, persecution or unmet needs in my Call; but rather to look up to You, the Author and Finisher of my faith for all my needs to be met in Jesus' Name. Amen!!!

Many go through life as if all the evil they engage in will be swept under the carpet! No, not so! Every action is a seed sown; no man can mock God. Mocking God is thinking that God cannot see nor punish wrongdoing and evil! If you follow after your flesh in sin and evil, you cannot mock God; God Sees and will Judge every wrongdoing including words spoken. If you sow unto the flesh you will reap corruption; and if you sow unto the Spirit, you will by the Spirit reap Eternal Life in Christ Jesus! Amen. Lord, Help us to sow unto the Spirit; that we may reap Eternal Life in Jesus' Name. Amen!!!

175th Day

GOD EXPECTS TRUTH, HONESTY AND INTEGRITY IN HIS FOLLOWERS! ARISE AND SHINE; FILLED WITH HOLY SPIRIT!!!

Believers must avoid all appearances of evil; including every form of falsehood, dishonesty, greed, etc.! They must strive always to act with integrity, truth, honesty and love; in order to live long! The expectation of God from children to their parents (honour) has exactly the same value/reward attached to obeying this instruction. Lord, Help us to obey Your Word and be Blessed in Jesus' Name. Amen!!!

God made man in His Image; and the expectation is that man takes God as his role model. Therefore, since God is not a liar, nor the father of lies (which satan is fully), man must put on the new man and cast off the old man with his deeds. Man ought to embrace holiness, righteousness, truth, purity and everything positive; thereby manifesting the goodness in the new man, renewed in knowledge after the image of the creator. Help us o Lord; that we may be more like You every day in Jesus' Name. Amen!!!

We are fearfully made, we are wonderfully made, we belong to God, we resemble Him. That's why the devil trembles whenever he hears us singing, we are God's own, we are the apples of His Eyes! We must display and manifest the attributes of the new man, once we are born again; putting off all falsehood - embracing only the holy, righteous nature of God in spirit and in truth in Jesus' Name. Amen. Help us o Lord to do this more and more in Jesus' Name. Amen!!!

For those who claim that we are under a New Covenant devoid of the Old Testament; are we not supposed to obey the Commandments of God as summarised in The Ten Commandments and further summarised by Jesus Christ Himself in the New Testament as in "Love the Lord your God with all your might, power, strength etc. and love your neighbour as yourself"? There is no truth at all in such claims; discard them fast! Help us o Lord to discard and never entertain untrue teachings in Jesus' Name. Amen!!!

To Arise and shine, we must receive the Light! Only Jesus Christ can give the Light, because He's the Light of the world/earth! As we know that God is Light and only Jesus Christ can give light; that can only be because only Jesus Christ possesses and has the Power to give Light. He is the Light. The Bible makes clear that God is Light! How can it be that this Jesus is not God? Be wise and not foolish; earnestly desire to understand the Will of God. Be drunk; but not with alcohol or other intoxicants, but rather with the Holy Spirit! Encourage each other with psalms, hymns, songs of praise, spiritual songs, etc.; making melody in your hearts unto the Lord with thanksgiving unto God always for all things in the Name of our Lord Jesus Christ. Amen! Father, Help us who believe to do this more and more in Jesus' Name. Amen!!!

We know that we are God's children who believe in Him; and that the wicked one sways the whole world (which is potentially under satan's control)! We know that the Son of God (Jesus Christ) came to give us understanding to know the Way, Truth and Life (again Jesus Christ). We know that when we believe, we are then in Him who is true, in God's Son, Jesus Christ who is referred to again above as the true God and Eternal Life! Jesus Christ is Eternal Life and is the true God! Jesus Christ is the Lord! Halleluyah! Amen! May this Gospel never leave my heart and may I share it till the very end without fear or favour in Jesus' Name. Amen!!!

176th Day

GREATEST LOVE IS IN SACRIFICING ONE'S LIFE FOR OTHERS! PERSEVERE! ALL POWER BELONGS TO JESUS! ABIDE IN HIM!!!

Do not give up on love and loving nor in doing good; for you labour in such a direction will never go in vain, but always rewarded positively in Jesus' Name. Amen! Especially towards believers, extend love and goodness always! Help us to obey Your Word o Lord; that we may be Blessed in due season!!!

If you want your prayers to be answered, then you need to abide in Jesus Christ and let His Words abide in you! His Love cannot be unconditional! There are conditions attached to every promise of God to humanity; especially to His beloved children! Likewise, if you want your life to bear fruits for the Lord God Almighty, to His Glory, abide in Him and let His Words abide in you! O Father, unless You Favour us to let Your Words abide in us, we can't make it; so Help us o Lord in Jesus' Name I pray thankfully. Amen!!!

Strive always to sow good seeds! It is often very challenging and with much sorrow at times to do this; however, there is a great reward at the end of such an investment! Tearful, sorrowful sowing leads to joyful harvests with rejoicing, gladness and shouting with thanksgiving and praise! O Lord, let this be our portion in Jesus' Name. Amen. I know not many will say Amen to this prayer; because none of us want to suffer the sorrowful, tearful sowing - which is inevitable for best results in terms of harvests! My people in the Yoruba culture say: "ohun ti a ko ba jiya fun, se kii le t'ojo; ohun ti a ba fi gbogbo ara sise fun, nii pe l'owo eni!" Meaning: what you do not suffer to accrue hardly ever lasts for long; but what you work very hard to accrue lasts long in your possession! We need Your Help o Lord; please Help us in Jesus' Name. Amen!!!

Jesus Christ (the man God in the flesh) declared that He Possessed all Power and Authority in Heaven and on earth! Who has such except God Alone? Hmmmm! If you remain unconvinced that Jesus Christ is the Lord God Almighty, may God Open your eyes eventually in Jesus' Name. Amen! He Gave us a commission to go out and disciple all nations (God is not racist) and baptise them in the Name of the Father, Son and Holy Spirit! Why? Because Jesus Christ Knows that they are ONE and the same! Also, that we should teach them all what He Taught to us for all to obey; He Will never leave nor forsake us in so doing! Thank You Lord for we have assurance that You Will be with us to the very end!!!

If you persevere and not give up, your case will come to the attention of the Lord and you will have your opportunity to present your case before Him. He Will have compassion on you and Touch you and your need shall be met in Jesus' Name. So, don't give up; pray ceaselessly, give thanks in all situations, stand firm and praise God always! May the Lord Grant us Divine Favour in Jesus' Name. Amen!!!

No pain no gain; nothing ventured nothing gained! Love is not free! There is a price to pay for Love; there are conditions attached to love! Love is not cheap! Love is invaluable! Love sacrifices; the greatest love is to sacrifice one's life for friends! That is the ultimate in love! Jesus Christ calls and relates to those who obey His Will and Commands as friends! You are not His friends if you do not obey Him. Your obedience is your affirmation of love for Jesus Christ; your words are meaningless without obedience! He Reveals the heart of the Father to those who love Him and obey Him. Lord God Almighty, please Help us to be obedient to Your Commands and Will in Jesus' Name. Amen!!!

177th Day

THE LORD OF REVIVAL; A STRONG TOWER; HUMBLES; A FUTURE FOR MAN OF PEACE; PERSEVERE REGARDLESS!!!

In life's experience, you will notice that the Blessing of God is truly upon the righteous! There surely is a future for the man of peace. The Bible says for I know the plans I have for you; the plans of peace, to give you a future and a hope... etc.! The future of the wicked will be cut off with their hopes and expectations. They will be destroyed as sinners! Choose today! Righteousness, peace or wickedness, war? You will reap and have to bear the consequences. Lord, please make me a channel of Your Peace; I want to be a man of peace and reap accordingly in Jesus' Name. Amen!!!

You can fool some of the people sometimes; but you cannot fool all of the people all of the time! You end up fooling only yourself! God is good... all the time; all the time... God is good! The Name of the Lord is a Strong Tower; the righteous run to it and they are Saved! The Lord is a sure and effective stronghold in times of trouble and He Knows those who take refuge in Him! Where are you taking refuge? Does the Lord Know you? Father God, keep me close to You all the time; whether in times of peace or war and trouble in Jesus' Name. Amen!!!

O Lord of true revival. Revive my family, myself and all who trust and hope in You in Jesus' Name. Amen! Only You commending me makes sense to me o Lord. Commend and recommend me according to Your Word and Truth o Lord. I'd rather You Honour me than be honoured by man! I will praise You from everlasting to everlasting; even with musical instruments and my voice, for Your Faithfulness in Jesus' Name. Amen! Help me o Father in Jesus' Name to do so increasingly till the end of my days here on earth!!!

Fear is not our portion because we have a great and mighty God; our refuge and strength, ever present Help in times of trouble. No matter what we face and or whatever happens around us ever, we shall trust in the Name of the Lord our God and refuse to give in to fear. Lord, Help us never to give in to fear; but rather to trust and hope in Your unfailing Power to deliver us in Jesus' Name. Amen!!!

Like these two blind men above, I will call upon the Lord; who is worthy to be praised! So shall I be saved from my enemies! The Lord Reigneth; and Blessed be the Lord; and may the Rock of my Salvation be Exalted! The Lord Reigneth; and Blessed be the Lord; and may the Rock of my Salvation be Exalted! No human rebuke, discouragement or bullying will I give in to; until I receive my full deliverance from the Lord my God in Jesus' Name. Amen!!!

God allows "thorns in our flesh" to keep us humble! In going through your thorny issues; don't be discouraged even if you are unable to overcome the thorny challenges! The Grace of God is sufficient for you! The Lord's Strength is made perfect in weakness! So therefore infirmities are not necessarily an evil thing; and there is good that can come from thorny situations in life! Behind every cloud indeed; there is a silver lining! Out of darkness comes the Light! Shine Light into my darkness in Your mercies o Lord I pray in Jesus' Name. Amen!!!

178th Day

THE LAW IS INSPIRED AND NOT EXTINCT FOLKS; OBEY THE LAW OF GOD AND LIVE; LIFE IS NOT ALL ABOUT FOOD AND SENSES!

Many are out there teaching people that the Old Testament laws are extinct and only the New Testament is relevant to the Christian Faith! The Word of God does not say that please! Jesus Christ said clearly that He did not come to abolish the law but to fulfill it! Be careful what and or who you believe! Believe, trust and hope ONLY in the WORD of the Living God! Father, Help us to believe Your Word and do only Your Will; living our lives only to please You in Jesus' Name. Amen!!!

Do you want to remain in the Love of God in Christ Jesus? Then, refute the teaching that His Love is unconditional! The Bible doesn't say so; man did! You need to keep His Commandments. Whilst on earth, Jesus Christ Himself kept the Commandments! He didn't just read or hear the Commandments of God, He obeyed them and lived by them. Father, please Help us to refute falsehoods in Jesus' Name; and to obey Your Word as hearers and doers, in Jesus' Name!!!

Stop deceiving yourself; because God is neither mocked nor deceived - a man will reap whatsoever he has sown! Don't be like the one who looks at his face in a mirror and instantly forgets what he looks like. But rather, be like the one who looks into the perfect law of God, the law of liberty, which is the WORD of God with perseverance; and you will be very Blessed! Bless us o Lord; even as You Enable us to do the right and shun the wrong in Jesus' Name. Amen!!!

We love to be first and most important wherever we go! The heart of man is deceitful and desperately wicked; who can know it? God's Way is different though! Whereas man wants to be the head so he can be served, Jesus Christ recommends for whomsoever wants to be the head to be the chief servant and or slave of all! Are you a leader? What kind of leader are you? A worldly leader or a godly one? Is your leadership about serving or being served? Father Lord, please Help us to lead by following Your example in Jesus' Name. Amen!!!

Life is not all about feeding our senses and meeting our needs! Food for the stomach; stomach for food - God Will destroy both! Live not by bread alone to stay alive; but by the Living Word of God if you want to live forever! Only by the Word! Jesus Christ is the Word of the Living God; He is the Living Word! Jesus Christ is the Living God personified; who came to mankind as man! Teach us o Lord to know the Truth; that we may be set truly free in Jesus' Name. Amen!!!

Ori rere l'ori mi o... ori rere (2ce)! Mo ti kekere m'oju Oluwa... ori rere... mo si tun d'agba sinu imole... ori rere... a to'ba jaiye l'Omo Maria... ori rere... ori rere l'ori mi o... ori rere! Meaning: My head is a good head (2ce)! I've known the Face of the Lord since my childhood... a good head... and I grew up in the Light... a good head... the Son of Mary is worthy to enjoy life with... a good head... my head is a good head... a good head!

I have used this Yoruba (Nigerian) song to attempt to convey the message above in terms of knowing the Lord from childhood and the benefits laid out therein. The Word of God is all Inspired by the Holy Spirit (God) and beneficial to all humanity for living a good and godly life in Jesus' Name on earth and training in righteousness. The Word of God is needful to complete the man of God; that he be equipped for every good work. O Lord, please remember me for Your Goodness in my lifetime; that I may serve you and fulfill my destiny in You - I pray in Jesus' Name. Amen!!!

179th Day

THINK AND EMULATE THE GODLY, POSITIVE, ALWAYS; HEAR AND DO; CAN YOU DRINK THE CUP? GOD'S JUDGEMENT IS SURE!!!

Norman Vincent Peale wrote the Power of Positive Thinking! This is exemplified in Biblical Wisdom which is superior to all human wisdom! Why would the Word of God come to us as stated above? Except it be for our own good; but who cares to obey? If you will obey the Word of God, again, you will be so very Blessed in Jesus' Name. Amen! Lord, Help me cleanse my mind and that of my family members and all who truly love You; that we may receive Your Blessing to think Godly and positively always in Jesus' Name. Amen!!!

If your mind is clean, positively inclined, driven and godly intended, you would be free from fleshly lusts that war against your soul. Also, your behaviour and attitude would be so excellent that your adversaries and foes who slander you as evil doers because you do not live like them would glorify God for the reason of your excellent behaviour and attitude in the day of visitation. The world does not read the Bible; rather, they read the believer's behaviour and attitude. Hmmmm. Lessons for the believers here indeed. Lord, Help us to be more like Jesus Christ in every possible way in Jesus' Name. Amen!!!

When you obey the Word of God, then you are like the wise man who built his house on the rock! When the storms come, your house shall stand! When you disobey the Word of God, you are like the foolish man who built his house in the sands and when the winds blew, the house fell apart! Be a hearer and doer of the Word for maximum benefits and Blessings in Jesus' Name. Amen. Father, Touch my heart to willingly obey Your Word in Jesus' Name. Amen!!!

Everyone wants to go to Heaven; but who wants to die? Very interesting indeed! Many people desire the Blessings of God in their lives; but how many people want to live according to the righteousness and holiness of God Almighty? Hmmmm! We love to deceive ourselves and our brethren!

We must be able to drink the cup that leads us into the Blessings of God! There is a sacrifice to be paid as a price! No love is unconditional! Unconditional suggests nothing is needful for the love. Love sacrifices and you sacrifice to receive love's best! Grant us Divine Wisdom for living life o Lord in Jesus' Name. Amen!!!

Judgement awaits all for every foul word spoken or deed done. As in nothing ventured and nothing gained! Action begets a reaction! The laws of sowing and reaping kicks in with every individual in life! If you follow after lies like your fathers did before you and perished, you will perish likewise; however, if you follow after and live the Truth according to the Word of the Lord to His followers, you will likewise reap bountiful blessings that are godly in Jesus' Name. Help us o Lord to value Your Word and Name in Jesus' Name. Amen!!!

180th Day

GOD: THE ORIGINAL MAN! DO NOT BE A SLUGGARD! JESUS CHRIST KNEW HIS FATE! MAN TAKE CHARGE OF THE GARDEN!!!

The sluggard is quarrelsome, boastful and always very tired because of abuse to his body! He clearly does not value his life nor his body; always ready and open to and for a fight or brawl! Even to eat is problematic for him; and he thinks he can outwit anyone with his wisdom. He is unaware of his folly nor myopia! You will be wise not to be a sluggard. May God Help us not to walk in the way of the sluggard; and to value life in Jesus' Name. Amen!!!

When I look into Your Holiness, gaze into Your Loveliness; when all things that surround become shadows in the Light of You o Lord! I worship You; for the reason I live is to worship You! You o Lord, like Your Word unto me are like a mirror. When I look into Your Eyes or Word, I see my true self and my filth; then I desire to be more like You. I therefore rise early to worship You and do likewise through the day and watches of the night! I seek out those who fear You to share with of all You have done for me. I see Your Hand all around me in my life. Father, Teach me Your Ways and Help me to walk in Your Ways in Jesus' Name I pray with thanksgiving. Amen!!!

Jesus Christ spoke prophetically of His fate to His disciples; although they didn't really understand and were not happy to hear His particular words in this regard! However, His Words came to pass and they saw, realised and believed that He IS who He claimed to be and who it IS written that He IS! He became the Atoning Sacrifice for our sins and iniquities; He is Alive forevermore! Amen! Lord do not let anything in life cause us to give up our faith in You in Jesus' Name. Amen!!!

God is the Original Man! He Made man in His Image and gave him dominion over His creation! Man is made to be in charge! But where is man today? O Lord Have mercy on us and restore man to his original position so that life may be more bearable for us in Jesus' Name. Let all men everywhere lift up holy hands unto the Lord God Almighty; and pray, seeking the Lord's Face. Perhaps the Lord Will Show us mercy and grace to overcome all our challenges and live a peaceful and godly life as God Purposed for mankind in Jesus' Name. Amen!!!

God's Instruction to man is to take charge! If only man stuck to God's Instruction obediently, we wouldn't be in the mess we're currently in right now! Right from the time of Adam and Eve when man fell from grace; the same way of that fall then still applies to mankind today! O Lord God Almighty, please Help us to simply obey Your Word and Instruction! All Your laws and statutes are for our good and beneficial to us for life. Help us in Jesus' Name. Amen!!!

In the very beginning, God entrusted the care and charge over His creation to man. He gave man instructions as to what to and not to do; with the freedom to roam freely and peacefully. Man disobeyed God and we live with the consequences until the end of time. We have the sure word of God; even today, our hearts still stray. Rather than obey God, we desire the world so strongly. O Lord my Father, please give me a heart that would desire to honour and obey Your Word in Jesus' Name. Amen!!!

181st Day

DO YOU BELIEVE IN GOD? DO YOU REALLY HAVE FAITH? IF YES, THEN DO NOT FEAR; BECAUSE GOD HAS GOT YOUR BACK!!!

Jesus Christ performed awesome miracles! Miracles that induced fear in the beholders. However, the fear of God will do for them with faith, who believe! There will always be fear wanting to attack or actually attacking a believer or anybody else; just do not give in to fear, but rather hold on to your faith in God or submit to God fully! Lord, Help my infirmity! Strengthen my heart and resolve. Give me a faith that will not yield to fear in Jesus' Name. Amen!!!

If the Lord God is Holding your hand or you believe that He Will; and He Will Help you, you need fear nothing at all, no evil nor weapon fashioned against you shall prosper! He, the Lord, is the Redeemer of Israel! Just be sure you are the Israel of God in Christ Jesus! Be and stay on the right side of God Almighty in Jesus Christ! Father, please let Your Word be true and manifest in my experience in Jesus' Name. Amen!!!

When the enemy comes against you like a flood, remember the battle belongs to the Lord! Have faith in and trust the Lord God Almighty for victory assured! Sudden fear must not shake you o believer; remember that it's not your battle to fight, just stand in the Name of the Lord God Almighty in Jesus Christ and watch the victory He Will deliver! O Lord my God, I stand in awe of You! Give me victory over all my enemies and situations in my life that threaten my family or my life in any way in Jesus' Name. Amen!!!

Evil surrounds us all the time in this wicked crazy evil world! Dogs of men with angry lions prowl around like the devil looking and waiting for whom to devour! They boast and are so much more powerful than the believer and myself included! You are the ONE that can Redeem my life; only You Ransomed me in Jesus Christ, even unto Eternal Life! You o Lord my God Will Deliver me in Jesus' Name! Father, I give all authority over my life into Your Holy Hands and I run to Your Holy Name, the Strong Tower, where I will be Saved and Safe! Even though I die, yet shall I arise to see Your Face and Behold Your Holy Awesome Presence in Jesus' Name. Amen! Yes Lord! I say yes to You; both now and forever! Amen!!!

Who can justify? Can man justify? Man may try; but only the justification of the Lord God Almighty shall stand the test of time! Who shall God justify? The hearers of the law and testimony or the doers? Alas, it is the hearers and doers of the law of God that will be justified! Do not just be a hearer, but also a doer of the law! Your obedience is your evidence and proof of love for God! Give me a heart that will submit to and obey You o Lord I pray in Jesus' Name with thanksgiving. Amen!!!

182nd Day

HE WHO THE SON SETS FREE IS FREE INDEED! IN CHRIST JESUS, WE HAVE TRUE AND SURE REDEMPTION! BLESSED!!!

Our redemption in Jesus Christ is made complete with the forgiveness of our sins and cleansing with His Blood! We have been Blessed through the Grace of God lavished on us; full with wisdom and understanding. O how great is our God! I will praise Him from everlasting to everlasting! Father Lord God, please do not let the death of Jesus Christ be meaningless in my life; but rather, maximise its potential to transform me into His likeness increasingly, in Jesus' Name. Amen!!!

The blood of birds, rams, goats etc. did not set us free; no, no, no! We are set free and redeemed fully by the she Blood of the Lamb of God that takes away all our sins! Through the Blood of Jesus Christ our Lord and Saviour. He Will purge our conscience from dead works to serve the Living God in Jesus' Name. Amen!!!

Who is clean? If the Lord measured sins by His Standard, who can stand? But, we thank God for the Gift of God in Jesus Christ, our Redeemer, who mercifully bore our iniquities on the Cross at Calvary and reconciled us back to God even when we were still in sin! Such love! How excellent a sacrifice so complete! He is Just and only He can truly justify those who choose to have faith in Him. O Lord, count me (and my household) worthy to receive Your Grace and Mercy in Jesus' Name. Amen!!!

In following Jesus Christ, no loss... only profit! Whatever appears as your loss will turn out for your gain in Jesus Christ many times over! A big bonus is also promised by He who never fails; Eternal Life! He does things His Way not our way! The first shall be last and vice-versa. To God be the Glory in Jesus Christ our Lord and Saviour. Halleluyah! Amen!! Thank You Lord Jesus! Lord, help me to follow You faithfully in spirit and in truth; and my household with me in Jesus' Name. Amen!!!

This is what it took out of my Lord for me to be set free and truly REDEEMED! I am redeemed and make bold to proclaim it! The signs and wonders didn't stop even at His death; rather, more spectacular! To crown it all, He Arose! He Lives forevermore! Jesus Christ is alive forevermore. Amen! Thank You Lord Jesus for Your Blessed Assurance to me and all who choose to have faith in You!!!

183rd Day

BE SOBER AND VIGILANT; THE ENEMY DISGUISES! SUBMIT TO GOD; RESIST THE DEVIL, HE WILL FLEE! WITH GOD NOTHING IS IMPOSSIBLE; HE'S NOT A MAN!!!

Be sober, be vigilant; because your adversary the devil, as a roaring lion, walketh about, seeking whom he may devour 1 Peter 5:8 KJV

In Christ Jesus, you need to be sober, vigilant and alert; otherwise, evil will creep up upon you without your knowledge and wreak havoc upon you, your household, business, community, nation or what have you! The devil is very active and dynamic; looking to devour whomsoever or whatsoever he may find or gain access to. If you are not sober, vigilant or alert, then you are giving him free and easy access to your own detriment. Beware. O Lord, Protect and Deliver us from evil in Jesus' Name. Amen!!!

God's Judgement upon the devil is already secure! I've heard people ask questions of conscience of Christians to discredit our faith. Questions like: why did God create evil? Why is the devil doomed and not forgiven? Why was Judas not forgiven etc. No answer you give these people will ever satisfy them because very often their questions are not sincere! All I know is that come what may, The Judgement of God upon evil is secure and done! God's Will Shall Manifest in Jesus' Name. Amen! Father, please keep my family, myself and true believers safely on Your Side and far away from the reach and or influence of satan and his cohorts in Jesus' Name. Amen!!!

Because of satan's negative and evil intentions, he wouldn't want to be recognisable when on the prowl or attack! He therefore disguises himself to keep himself very subtly present and if possible unnoticed whilst he gains access and wreaks havoc as intended! Likewise, his agents are equally wily in their strategies and approach. Their judgement is secure! Stay submissive to God; resist the devil and he will flee. This is not impossible as long as you receive discernment from the Lord God in Jesus Christ and use it as required! May God Bless us with the Holy Spirit to help us discern between good and evil; and stay away from satan and his wiles in Jesus' Name. Amen!!!

Riches almost as a matter of course causes the wealthy to become very arrogant and prideful; very opposite to faith. Faith by nature is needs-led and driven! If you have no need for anything, there's hardly any incentive to have faith and or pray or hope for anything! Hmmmm! This is a chief deception for those who are very Blessed in this world. This is why the wealthy are counseled in the Word of God to win/make friends for themselves in the Heavenly Kingdom; i.e. use their wealth for Godly purposes. Hence, the above Scripture! But with God, nothing is impossible; He Makes a way even where there seems to be none anyway. Trust and hope in Him alone! May Your Will be made manifest in our lives o Lord; to You be all the glory in Jesus' Name. Amen!!!

When the Lord Speaks a word, He always brings it to pass and never fails. His words never fall to the ground because His intentions are just, upright and righteous; even in punishing people and or nations! God chooses whom He Blesses; who can reprimand Him or change His Mind? He will have mercy on whom He wills also; who can judge Him? So, it's not of man's making, running or will that things happen; but according to God's design and Sovereign Will and Mercy! Lord Grant us Divine Favour to enjoy Your Mercy all of our lives in Jesus' Name. Amen!!!

184th Day

THE WORD IS TRUTH; IS SANCTIFIED AND SANCTIFIES BELIEVERS! ALL SINNED; AND SAVED IN JESUS CHRIST! GOD'S KINGDOM IS FOR LITTLE CHILDREN; LOVE LIKE THEM OR LOSE!!

Sanctify them by the truth; your word is truth. For them I sanctify myself, that they too may be truly sanctified. John 17:17,19 NIV

The Word sanctifies! The Word is Truth; therefore Truth sanctifies just like the Word because they are one and the same! God is the Word, Way, Truth and Life! If you want to live, then get the Word, Way, Truth and Life at all costs; give everything else up to get this and you will be rewarded with life forevermore! Jesus Christ, the Word, sanctified Himself by the Word that we who believe may live and be truly sanctified! May God be pleased with us to sanctify us in spirit and in truth in Jesus' Name. Amen!!!

All of us have sinned and fallen short of the Glory of the Lord! But Jesus Christ redeemed us by His Sacrifice (being crucified on the Cross, like a sheep to the slaughter and He went like a lamb without protesting or complaining)! Yet, He was Exalted to the Highest place ever, The Throne of The Almighty God! It pleased God (for what was to be achieved) to bruise Him so that His end may justify the means! The Will of God shall prosper in His Hand! He took what the vilest in the land deserve just to set us free and reconcile us back to God and cleanse us from all iniquity! For this, He is Crowned the King of all; revealed as the Lord God Almighty who came to humanity in the flesh to show us the way to Him! Halleluyah! Amen!! Thank You Lord Jesus for everything You have done!!!

Blessed are the little children; so do not hinder them, but rather, give them free access to come to the Lord Jesus Christ. Teach them young; lead them to Jesus Christ as a matter of right and urgency. Teach them so that when they are older they will not depart from the Word, Way, Truth and the Life! Lord, please Teach me and all mine how to live in this world as little children; I know this takes Your Wisdom and only You Can Give it. Help me in Jesus' Name. Amen!!!

The only thing that matters is faith that works through love! There's nothing better than child-like love! You may have all things (including good gifts and things) that life has to offer; without love, you have absolutely nothing! You can do good better than all who do good; yet without love, you have absolutely zero, nothing! The value of love is laid out here! Love is the most valuable thing in life; and should be treated as such and never abused! Love is the greatest and best emotion in life ever! Love is stronger than death and hatred put together. Love is a healer like nothing else! Please o Lord God Almighty Father, Bless us with love in Jesus' Name. Amen!!!

185th Day

TO WHOM MUCH IS GIVEN MUCH IS EXPECTED! WE NEED TO OBEY GOD TO RECEIVE HIS BLESSINGS (LOVE INCLUDED)!!!

God's Word is to be obeyed, not for fun! All through the Holy Scriptures in the Holy Bible, God Counsels us to obey His Word so we shall be Blessed. When we do His bidding, He Rewards us! Punishment is due to any human being who does not obey the Word of God! Obedience is better than sacrifice. We are implored to fear God and keep (obey) all His Commandments; that it might go well with us and our children for ever! The man who trusts God and whose walk is blameless and who fears the Lord will enjoy all good things; for God withholds no such things from such a man! Therefore, clearly, God's Love is fully conditional; if you do this, I will do this He Says throughout His Word. May God Grant us the wisdom to listen, hear, obey and be Blessed in the Word of God! Amen!!!

Father Lord God, please, Sanctify my household and I by Your Truth, which is Your Word. As You Sanctified Yourself o Lord for my sake that I might be truly sanctified, so let it be unto me in Jesus' Name I pray with thanksgiving in Jesus' Name. Amen!!!

The Word of God is potentially for all who will accept, believe and obey; not for everybody willy nilly! The Word of God, like His Love, is not cheap! So, really, the Word of God is targeted at those who love the Lord and will prove their love by obeying the Word of God Sent to them! As for eunuchs, some were born that way, some were made that way by mankind and some choose to live that way for the sake of the Kingdom of God (Heaven)! Accepting the Word of God is a choice never enforced on anyone; but rather for those who are can and are willing to accept it! Help my household and I o Lord; that we might be willing in our hearts to accept Your Word in Jesus' Name. Amen!!!

You cannot expect to gain the rewards of the obedient when you sin without the law; you will perish accordingly! Likewise, if you sin in the law. However, it's not the hearers of the law that will be justified in the

Sight of God; but rather the hearers and doers of the law (the obedient)! So, obedience is key all round with regard to the Word of God! May God Guide our hearts not just to be hearers of the Word and Law; but to be doers as well in Jesus' Name. Amen!!!

186th Day

THE PATH TO THE ANCIENT OF DAYS IS THE ANCIENT PATH; NO OTHER! JESUS CHRIST IS THIS PATH (WAY, TRUTH AND LIFE)!!!

This is the Word of the Lord if you want rest for your soul! Follow the Ancient Paths for their ways are good. Walk in those ways and you will find rest for your soul. I thank God who has Shown me these Paths and has Given me rest for my soul! Dig into the Word of God and discover the Ancient Paths that will lead to the Ancient of days for there is no other reason for even bothering to try except that you might find Him! Jesus Christ is the Ancient of Days! O my Father, how excellent is Your Name in all the earth! Please Help me to find and stay on the Ancient Path to You in Jesus' Name. Amen!!!

Position yourself to find the Ancient Paths with your roadmarks and guideposts! Whatever you can do to find them shall not be in vain! In this quest, you will do well to study and observe the Mosaic Laws so as to keep them. Some say they are archaic; I say not! May God Lead and Guide us into the Truth of His Word in Jesus' Name. Amen!!!

How can we know the way? Jesus answered, "I am the way and the truth and the life. No one comes to the Father except through me. If you really knew me, you would know my Father as well. From now on, you do know him and have seen him." John 14:5b-7 NIV

You want to find God? There is only one Way! It's not a new way, it's an Ancient Way! His Name is Jesus, the Way, Truth and Life! No one finds the Father except through Jesus Christ. Know Jesus and you know the Father too. See Jesus and you have seen the Father. Jesus Christ and the Father with the Holy Spirit are ONE! O Lord, thank You for this glorious revelation. Help me to show others the Way in Jesus' Name and Help me not to lose or even change tracks in Jesus' Name. Amen!!!

God hates divorce but due to the hardness of man's heart, Moses permitted it. However this was never part of God's plan for marriage! So, divorce being permitted has now become a tool for man to use in manipulating the marriage process for changing husbands and wives! Marriage is an institution honoured by God so much so that His relationship with man is likened unto marriage; and the marriage bed must be kept pure and holy. You cannot do whatever you like even on your matrimonial bed! God our Father, please Help us to have the right attitude to and honour marriage as an institution in Jesus' Name. Amen!!!

Do not allow any frustrated "believers" to get into your head and psyche to change or distort your vision from Jesus Christ's holy way and righteousness! These people will say all manners of discouraging things to your hearing just to draw you away from the narrow ancient paths to Jesus Christ and to Heaven! You will be tempted with gold and other precious metals to store up and to wear on your bodies. Yet these things are abominable to the Lord! They become our new calves today and our hearts are in these things over and above the Lord God Almighty to our own detriment! Be alert and aware of the wiles of satan and do not give in. Do not celebrate ungodliness! Celebrate God! Celebrate Jesus Christ!! May the Lord Grant us the Holy Spirit; so we can discern the Way and follow no matter how narrow or rough in Jesus' Name. I pray with thanksgiving. Amen!!!

187th Day

WE ARE BLESSED BECAUSE JESUS DIED AND AROSE; SECURE IN THE LOVE OF CHRIST. DO NOT FALL FOR FALSE PROPHECY.

The Jesus Christ experience that I have has changed my life; for I was "Touched" in a most profound way. I have thus been crucified with Him; and the life that I live now is not me at all, but Jesus Christ living His Life through me! This is all enabled by faith in Jesus Christ, the Son of God; He loved me and gave Himself up for me and in my place. O, how I love You Lord; because You first loved me! Please o Father, do not let Your Sacrifice be in vain over my life family and ministry, in Jesus' Name. Amen!!!

Nothing this evil wicked and cruel world throws at me to dislodge me in their father's name (satan) shall separate me from the love of Jesus Christ. No matter what guise they come in, I shall not be moved. I refuse to look and or focus on circumstances; I shall keep my focus firmly upon the Christ, who died for me and set me free from bondage to sin and this world/flesh. I will praise Him from everlasting to everlasting. I will live for Jesus day after day; come what may! I will obey His Holy Spirit. Please o Lord, Help me in Jesus' Name. Amen!!!

When the Lord is unhappy with mankind, He punishes us in His own special way. No man can escape the Judgement of God! As man cannot escape, so nations do not escape His Judgements! However, God Provides a way of escape mostly. He said in His Word that if My people who are called by my Name will humble themselves and pray, forsaking their evil ways; I would hear from Heaven, answer their prayers and heal their land! God may use famine, the sword, or things we call "natural disasters" to punish mankind; and allow things that we see as most vile to happen. Many often get so angry and speak rashly about God rather than humbly seek His Face and petition Him for mercy!

In the midst of all of this, there are some who ought to know better; they claim the Lord has Sent them and prophesy good upon the land and keep assuring the people that all is and will be well. Rather than instructively admonish counsel and warn the people to desist from iniquity, they prophesy good. God says He will punish them and those who listen to them. This means everyone has the responsibility to draw near to God and seek out His Will for themselves otherwise face the wrath of God. Father, Help us to stay on the right side of Your Word and when we fail, Help Guide us back home to You in Jesus' Name. Amen!!!

188th Day

DO NOT BEFRIEND THE WORLD, FOR THAT IS ENMITY TOWARDS GOD! HUMBLE YOURSELF, FORGIVE; YOU WILL BE BLESSED IF YOU DO!

Most of us are ashamed and afraid of the world around us. We fear to lose our jobs or other privileges; hence, we do not want to be associated with God's Word in Spirit and Truth! Hmmmm! At the end of the day, who is the Provider? Your choice! Not that I do not understand; please don't get me wrong! However, Love compels me to write these words! We prefer to befriend the world so the world can accept, like or even "love" us; whilst we forsake the true Love of all, the Word of the Living God! Whereas we harbour pride etc. in our hearts like multiple jeopardy! God jealously desires His Spirit Given to us; He's opposed to the proud, but gives Grace to the humble! Therefore, resist the devil and his wiles and he will flee from you. Submit to God in Jesus' Name. Father Lord God, Help us to be bold and courageous in our walk with you and not fear man in Jesus' Name. Amen!!!

I'm stressing humility always because God opposes the proud and gives Grace to the humble! If you are humble, God Will exalt you and bless you! Put all your trust in Him; even when you are facing trials and tribulations, cast all your anxieties on Him because He cares for you like no one else can! You need to be sober minded at all times so your mind is on full alert in order to be watchful for the devil's plans to devour whomsoever he can get a hold of. Resist the devil and remember that other believers are going through diverse issues that are satanic in nature. May God in His infinite mercies keep you safe from the evil one in Jesus' Name. Amen!!!

A man who received mercy and goes on to refuse mercy to another man does not know God! He neither appreciates God's goodness to him. He deserves whatever he gets! Comfort is given to you so that in due season you may give comfort to the needy; likewise mercy! Gratitude to God is also about being kind and loving to others according to the love received by you from God. God never fails to reward love and loving; God is Love! Please Father Lord, Help us to love our fellow human beings whenever others are in need of love in Jesus' Name. Amen!!!

Abraham's Blessing is transferable unto the faithfuls in Jesus Christ! Joseph received the Blessing as above. So can you. But do you believe? Nobody can submit to nor love a God they don't know. Get to know God; and the more you get to know Him, the more you will love Him! The more you love Him, the more you will obey Him. He desires your obedience as evidence of your loving Him. If God's love was unconditional, then He doesn't need your love; if He didn't need your love, He would not say in His Word that you should prove your love for Him by obeying His Word and when you do, He would Bless you. Please be wise. Seek the Holy Spirit for yourself to Help you decipher and understand the Word of Life! Help us o Lord so to do in Jesus' Name. Amen!!!

189th Day

IN LIFE, THE EVIDENCE, WISDOM AND KNOWLEDGE OF GOD IS MADE MANIFEST DAILY; THE KINGDOM, LIKE GOD, IS DYNAMIC! BELIEVE IN JESUS CHRIST AND LOVE ONE ANOTHER!!!

There is a time for everything in life; including a time to stop and start something. Get it wrong; and untold misery beckons. Get it right; and blossom magnificently! God's Counsel, Wisdom, Knowledge and Understanding is therefore manifested daily in life. There are principles attributable to God; if adhered to, they make life more bearable in this cruel and evil world. Otherwise, life is so frustrating and miserable! Lord, Grant us the wisdom and all we need to live life maximally and successfully in Jesus' Name. Amen!!!

For to us a child is born, to us a son is given; and the government shall be upon his shoulder, and his name shall be called Wonderful Counselor, Mighty God, Everlasting Father, Prince of Peace. Isaiah 9:6 ESV

This is instructive prophecy! Just take a look and meditate on what this says about our Lord Jesus Christ (then yet to be born)! God's Government shall be upon His Shoulder! Look at the names we call Him today and compare with these names as prophesied! Wow! Does anybody still doubt that Jesus Christ is the Mighty God, Everlasting Father, Prince of Peace, Wonderful, Counselor and much more? O Lord, please Give Faith to Your children; that they may come running to You in Jesus' Holy Name. Amen. Praise the Lord! Halleluyah!! Amen!!!

Who possesses the wisdom to search out everything about God and succeed? Who can fully know His Mind or Counsel Him? Yet, God is in all and all in all! How great is our God and His Name! Would You accept that the Name of the Lord is JESUS? The Strong Tower that the righteous run into and are saved? If we can only tap into the depth of wisdom and knowledge that God Possesses! Lord my Father, Help me to tap into the depths of Your wisdom and knowledge in Jesus' Name. Amen!!!

Many people are so proud and arrogant that when in crisis, they pity themselves beyond normal reasoning and can't believe that "they" are in such a situation! Their thinking is then notched up into "what would people think of me now" mode! This is the destructive mode of pride and arrogance! It is dangerous to put yourself up on a very high pedestal and assume you can never go wrong or be in trouble; and that if you are, then you are no good and unworthy etc. etc.! This servant humbled himself and was willing to beg/plead with the master. Lo and behold, the master had mercy on him! What if he never begged? Hmmmm! Wisdom is known by her children and she knows her own children too! Be wise always. Many have committed suicide needlessly for such reasons. As long as you have life, hope is not ever lost. So, don't give up! Lord, Help us to trust in You and never give up hope in Jesus' Name. Amen!!!

God's Commandments can be learnt and meditated upon for a richer and deeper understanding! Then we would find out that what God requires of us as human beings in not really much at all. However, the human heart is deceitful and desperately wicked as the Bible says. Hence, we always tend to want to do everything contrary to the Word of God. Doing God's Will takes extra effort and discipline; and we mostly don't want to sacrifice what it takes. This is why we are perpetually in trouble and hardly ever at peace! Lord, please Give us a heart that is willing to do Your Will and Give us peace in Jesus' Name. Amen!!!

190th Day

THE WILL (PLAN) OF GOD FOR MANKIND IS GOOD; TRUST, OBEY HIM! FORGIVE AND HAVE FAITH IN THE WORD OF GOD!!!

The Lord Promises to take good care of you; and He never fails in His Promises! He's got the whole world in His Hands including your life and mine! Can we just leave things in His Hands and stop trying to "help" and or play God both in our lives and those of others? Let Him have His Way in your life and then you can see and confirm that He does everything far better than you can ever imagine! If you can have faith and trust in Him alone, then His Promises shall prove true to you and your circumstances and life. Lord, Help us who believe and hope in You to trust fully in You without shaking and have total and absolute faith in You in Jesus' Name. Amen!!!

The Lord's plans for those who trust in Him and do not look unto other gods nor to the proud are many and beautiful. He stops at nothing to do wonders for them and do the impossible! If we were to recount the Lord's mercies and goodness to us who believe, they would be too numerous to declare. However, we shall not stop counting the blessings and giving thanks unto the Lord our God in Jesus' Name. Give us o Lord more and more reasons for thanksgiving unto You in Jesus' Name. Amen!!!

You show Your love to me o Lord not just when I'm in my comfort zone; but also, in the presence of my enemies! How wonderful, beautiful and excellent are Your gestures towards my family and I o Lord! I am fully convinced that goodness and mercy flowing from You shall never depart from my family, myself and all true believers and followers of Your Holiness and Righteousness in Jesus' Name. Amen! We shall dwell in Your Temple forever and ever in Jesus' Name. Amen. Lord, Help us to dwell in Your Presence forever in Jesus' Name. For, in Your Presence, there is fullness of Joy!!!

In terms of forgiveness, how often should we forgive our brethren who offend us? Indeed is forgiveness only for our brethren? I believe forgiveness is for all and sundry who might offend us. It is not in our best interests to hold on to unforgiveness which leads to bitterness and many sorrows which are unnecessary. Basically, the Lord's Teaching on forgiveness basically says we must always be willing to forgive just as stipulated in our Lord's prayer! Lord Jesus, Help us to forgive one another no matter how painful in Jesus' Name. Amen!!!

Faith is a gift from Heaven and from God! However, the Bible makes clear that faith comes and grows through the hearing of the Word of God. So you can feed your faith by reading, studying and meditating on the Word of God. Just keep doing it; even if it seems you are not seeing results. Just believe that you are receiving faith and being built up. Faith will manifest in due season and grow as you increase in your investment in faith as stated! Lord, Help us to have and nurture faith in our lives in Jesus' Name. Amen!!!

Do you know that many are ashamed of the Gospel? They don't want others to know that they have faith. They won't proclaim the Gospel. They keep looking for reasons not to engage in anything Gospel especially so as not to displease other people. Yet, these other people are never ashamed to foist their beliefs no matter how evil and perverse on us all. I will not be ashamed. I refuse to be ashamed of the Gospel of Jesus Christ; for it is a revelation of the righteousness of God by faith unto faith. Indeed, the righteous, the believer must live by faith. Father Lord, Help me (us) to live by faith in Jesus' Name. Amen!!!

191st Day

BROUGHT OUT OF DARKNESS INTO MARVELOUS LIGHT;
I SHALL NEITHER RUN NOR LABOUR IN VAIN IN CHRIST
JESUS. AMEN!!!

We shall not stop praying for those that God Sent us to (the same prayers we say for ourselves in Jesus' Name)! They all (including you reading this sincerely wanting change in your life to know Jesus Christ and the Power of His Resurrection) will come to know His Power. That they may increase in His Knowledge and be delivered from darkness into light and lead others likewise. Jesus Christ is our Alpha and Omega; the Beginning and End of our faith! He created all things; both good and evil - whether thrones, dominions, principalities or powers! Just trust in Him! He Will Deliver us and see us through this evil world till we attain unto Eternal Life in Him in Christ Jesus. Amen!!!

In Christ Jesus, we learn to obey our Instructors in Christ not just when they are around us but even when they are away. This is faith! We strive to work out our salvation with fear and trembling; knowing that our God is an all-consuming fire! He loves and will punish if He deems it necessary! Whatever you do, do as for the Lord Jesus Christ without murmurings, disputing, etc. Do this so as to be blameless, harmless sons of God in the darkness all around you; whilst you shine as lights! This way, the labours of our forefathers in the faith shall not be in vain and if passed on accurately, nor will ours in Jesus' Name. Amen!

Help us o Lord to watch and pray for nobody knows when our Lord shall come. Help us to keep our garments on; lest our nakedness be seen and we be shamed! Help us to live and walk aright so as to please the Lord, our Commanding Officer; so that at the end of time, we shall receive the Crown of Life that will never fade away in Jesus' Name. Amen!!!

192nd Day

BE A GIVER; GIVE APLENTY, CHEERFULLY! LOVE NOT THE WORLD AND ALL IN IT! YOU WILL BE BLESSED IF YOU OBEY!!!

Giving is a sowing! When you give, do so willingly and not grudgingly. Give freely and give abundantly as God Gives unto you. The Bible says it is better to give than to receive. It is not wrong to receive; just better to give! Givers never lack; and when in need, givers always find help! Giving is not supposed to be under compulsion; because God loves a cheerful giver. Nobody can be cheerful as a giver under compulsion! Lord, Help my family, myself and all who truly love You to be cheerful givers; and to give aplenty in Your Holy Name, Jesus. Amen!!!

When you give, give freely, willingly, positively and do not begrudge in your heart, grumble or complain or be under compulsion; know that for your giving in the right mindset and attitude, God Will Bless you in every way in Jesus' Name. Amen! Lord, Help us; especially those of us who truly believe in You to give aright in Jesus' Name. Amen!!!

Father Lord God Almighty, You Know all things and You See into our hearts and Know our every thought and plan. Grant unto us a cheerful giving heart; that we might give with Your leading and with joy always in Jesus' Name. Amen! Help us to please You in every way in Jesus' Name. Amen!!!

Jehovah! Please Help keep away the love of and for the world from our hearts in Jesus' Name. The way of the world is very tempting and sweet to the human heart which is deceptive and desperately wicked! With lust as its chief tool, the world/flesh struggles to gain control of my life o Lord. Do not let me give in to the evil of the world/flesh; Help me to overcome and resist all temptations from the world/flesh in Jesus' Name. Amen! Help me Lord to do Your Will and abide forever in Jesus' Name. Amen!!!

193rd Day

WHAT A WONDERFUL OPPORTUNITY WE HAVE IN CHRIST JESUS; A GOD WE CAN GO TO FOR ANYTHING! HE IS LORD!!!

ASK! Ask Seek Knock! Hmmm what an acronym! Wow! A God that gives us the freedom to ask Him anything as long as we ask in faith and according to His Will! A God that actually answers prayers! The asking itself is a prayer unto our God! Who dares to believe! If you dare to believe, then ask and it will be given to you; seek and you will find; knock and it will be opened unto you! Everyone who ASKs receives! If you seek, you will find; and it will be opened unto you if you knock! So, what are you waiting for? Let your faith go to work for you in Jesus' Name. Amen!!!

The Lord promised never to leave nor forsake His own! So, all you need to do is ensure that you do not stray away from the Lord your God! Whatever the enemy has afflicted you with; what you've done to yourself, or even God Himself punishing you? Take it all to the Lord in prayer and He Will answer and deliver you in Jesus' Name. Amen! If you have been displaced from your roots or homeland, God is Able to restore you back to your homeland! Trust Him! He promised to give you a heart that will return to Him wholeheartedly! God, let this be my family's portion in Jesus' Name. Amen!!!

Tomorrow may be too late for you to seek and find the Lord! Seek Him right now! You who are wicked and unrighteous should forsake your ways and thoughts, so the Lord may show you mercy and abundant pardon! God's Ways and Thoughts are supreme and far higher and richer than man's! Lord enter into us that we might seek You in spirit our Lord God and Saviour! Amen!!!

If you believe the Word of the Living God, whatever you bind or loose on earth will be bound and or loosed in Heaven! If two people or more agree on anything they're asking God for, they will receive it in Jesus' Name! Where two or three gather in His Name, He is there with them. This is the foundation of the Church from the beginning. Help us to believe o Lord in Your Word and also in You in Jesus' Name I pray with thanksgiving! Amen!!!

Faith is so crucial to anything God does for mankind! Without faith no one can please God! The blind men had faith (believed) that Jesus Christ could heal them if He wanted to and Jesus Christ Knew that and worked with their faith to heal them. O Lord, increase my faith in Jesus' Name and that of my family and all who are seeking Your Face in Jesus' Name. Amen!!!

194th Day

FOR CHRIST JESUS, I CONSIDER ALL THINGS LOSS; JUST TO KNOW HIM AND THE POWER OF HIS RESURECTION

Nothing compares with having the Lord Jesus Christ in my life. I would willingly give up all else just to have Jesus Christ in my life! Just to see Jesus, I'll do anything; just to see Jesus, I'll do anything! I will climb the highest mount; go beneath the lowest valley - just to see, just to see... the Face of my Lord! I want to be found in Him alone! I want to know Him and the Power of His Resurrection! Who wants the fellowship of His sufferings enh? We mostly love the goodies and blessings that come in the Name of Jesus! How many of us will stand for the fellowship with His sufferings as well? Hmmm! Christ Knows those who are truly His! O count my family and I worthy o Lord in Jesus' Name. Amen!!!

Jesus Christ is Eternal Life and the whole idea of Eternal Life is that we who believe might know Him the only true God and that He Sent His Christ in His Person to Reveal God unto mankind in Jesus' Name. Amen! Give us the wisdom and understanding to know You o Lord and the Power of Your Resurrection! Amen!!!

Man's wisdom, might and riches will not last nor save man! It is useless to boast in these futile things! If you want to boast, then boast that you understand and know the Lord God Almighty! He who practices steadfast love, justice and righteousness on earth! If you will delight yourself in these things that are clearly of the Lord; and put them to practice, then the Lord will be pleased with you and Bless you in Jesus' Name. Amen! Lord, Help us to do what is right by You in Jesus' Name. Amen!!!

This is a Biblical example of how to deal with issues as believers! Is anyone listening? Does anyone care today? Hmmm! God is Watching all! Remember that every matter must be established by the testament of two or three witnesses; especially accusations against elders! If you follow this prescribed procedure and nothing comes of it, then we are encouraged to treat people guilty of such behaviour as you would treat unbelievers (as not part of your fellowship)! God Help us with the wisdom and knowledge to do what is right every time in our lives. Amen!!!

If you have the Spirit of God, you would have something to show for it! Some of the manifestations are mentioned in the Scripture above! I notice that most people would rather have everything but longsuffering! Very few see longsuffering as virtuous! Even, many pray against suffering of any type! There is joy in longsuffering which many do not see for they have no faith! Thank You Jesus for Your Power invested in the believer to endure all situations and circumstances. Amen!!!

195th Day

THE GOD OF ABRAHAM, ISAAC AND JACOB! HE REIGNS IN
POWER AND MAJESTY!! VALUE EVERY LITTLE BLESSING!!!

Are you God's own? Do you know His Name? Do you even know the
meaning of knowing His Name? Hmmmm! Teach my family, myself and
all who truly seek after You o Lord; that we may know Your Name in Jesus'
Christ, Amen! To know the Name of the Lord is to believe, trust, hope
in and serve Him without fear! To know His Name is to love Him and
prove your love by obeying His Word! To know His Name is to take your
lovely feet upon the mountains to proclaim your knowledge of His Name
and His Gospel; so as to effect passionate change and transformation in
lives! To know the Name of the Lord is to receive His Joy and share this
joy with people and affect people positively with this joy all the time and
release joy into their lives! To know His Name is to receive His Comfort
and share with others. These all prove that you have been redeemed to
help reconcile others to become redeemed in Christ Jesus too! Praise the
Lord! Halleluyah!!!

The Lord reigneth let the earth tremble! Wherever the Spirit of the Lord is
there is liberty; and Strength is released tremendously! He established the
whole world, the earth and all in it such that they cannot be shaken unless
by Himself! He IS from everlasting to everlasting; unmovable, unshakable
rock of all ages - established from of old! He is the never changing yet ever
changing God! He reigns and rules supremely amongst men! I submit
myself to You o Lord with all humility and invite You to come reign in my
life, family, ministry and all in Jesus' Name. Amen! Glory! Halleluyah!!
Amen!!!

You have to learn to value yourself and all that God Gives to you no matter
how little it seems that you have! That is faithfulness! How can you say you
are faithful to God if you do not value even your life and those of others
or even what gifts God Has Given you? That's why if you have ninety nine
treasures out of a hundred; which means one is missing - you go after and
find the missing one, leaving the ninety nine behind in safety to look for

the missing one! That missing one is valued is why you would leave the others to go looking for it! That is a demonstration of faithfulness to God's gift to you! Lord, teach us to be faithful to You in every way and to value all that You have Blessed us with in Jesus' Name. Amen!!!

Look out always for God's Hand all around you! It is good, right and meet to observe and take note of the Goodness of the Lord all around you, including in your own life! Including all the trials and tribulations because they all lead to victories and for the Name of the Lord to be glorified! The only exception is when God punishes! However, unless you are completely wiped out, killed; God always leaves room for thanksgiving even in disciplining His children. It is written that a father disciplines the son that He Loves! O Lord, Help us not to miss Your Hand in our affairs and all around us in our daily life; that we may give You Your dues in Jesus' Name. Amen!!!

196th Day

YOU CAN ENTER INTO THE SONSHIP OF THE LIVING GOD; SUBMIT YOURSELF; ALLOW THE HOLY SPIRIT TO LEAD YOU!!!

The Bible says that as many as are led by the Holy Spirit, such are the sons of the Living God! To belong in this group of "sons", you must submit yourself to God and prove your love to Him by obeying Him. Then you will receive the gift of the Holy Spirit! Then the Holy Spirit will confirm that you are a "son" of God and co-heir with Jesus Christ. But, you must suffer with Him, so to be glorified with Him; remembering that the suffering you go through in His Name is with Him and is incomparable with the glory to be revealed in you ultimately in Jesus' Name. Amen!!!

Abraham's blessings are mine. I am blessed in the morning, afternoon, evening and night! Yes! Abraham's blessings are mine! God changed his name from Abram to Abraham; and promised Him that he would father many many nations. God assured him that his children shall be as the sand of the sea, which cannot be measured or numbered! God always told them that He would punish them for the whole world to see if they disobeyed His Commandments; but that if they returned to Him, He would likewise Bless them for the whole world to see. Hence, the Word that came forth from the Throne of Mercy that where He condemned them and said they are not His people, likewise, it shall be said of them that they are sons of the Living God! Sela!! Halleluyah!!! Amen!!!

If only you will receive and believe in Jesus Christ, you will receive the right to become a child of God! Then you will be born not of blood nor of the will of the flesh nor man, but of God! That is being born again by the water and the Spirit; in being baptized and receiving the gift of the Holy Spirit after you have obeyed His Word and Commandments in proving your love for Him truly! God Help us to live for and obey You in all that we think, speak and or do in Jesus' Name. Amen!!!

"These little ones" I believe are those who receive and believe in the Name of the Lord Jesus Christ and in His Testimony! They are not to be despised because they are so special to God. There angels in Heaven are always in the Presence of God and see His Face! God Will do anything to protect, defend, honour and let His Glory Shine in and through them! It pays to become as one of "these little ones" who must not be led astray! Jesus my Lord, please count my family and I worthy to belong to this special group in Jesus' Name. Amen!!!

This is the prophetic word spoken when John the Baptist was born! Jesus was queried at a point that it was said in the Word of God that Elijah would come first before the Lord; and Jesus told them that if they were willing to believe, Elijah had come first! He was referring of course to the words of this prophecy; according to the ministry of John the Baptist which suited the purpose of going before the Lord in the Spirit and Power of Elijah to turn the hearts of the fathers to the children; and the disobedient to the wisdom of the just, to make ready a people prepared for the Lord! Selah! The Word of God never fails; it shall always come to pass! O Send me o Lord! Here I am Send me! When You need to Send somebody, Send me o Lord in Jesus' Name. Amen!!!

197th Day

PREACHING IS FOOLISHNESS TO THOSE PERISHING BUT THE POWER AND WISDOM OF GOD TO THOSE BEING SAVED! WORK HEARTILY AS UNTO THE LORD ALWAYS!!!

When you work or serve, your attitude should be such as you are doing the work for Jesus Christ always, rather than for any man! What a difference this would make to your service or work life's effectiveness and diligence to do your work! Especially as the Lord is a Rewarder of all who diligently seek Him! In serving as though serving Him, you are seeking His Hand always in your affairs and this is very good for your faith in Jesus Christ. Lord, Help us to serve and work as if we are working directly for You in Jesus' Name. Amen!!!

I wish and pray for me to have people who will commit me to God and the Word of His Grace to build me up and give me this inheritance amongst the sanctified! This is a great message of goodwill and a prayer in Jesus' Name. Amen!!!

What is this inheritance that I pray to be built up to receive? That is incorruptible and undefiled, that will never fade away? This heritage of those who like me and my desire, are kept by God's Power through faith unto salvation to be revealed in the last days! It has to be the "Crown of Life"! This is my heart's desire and my goal! Please God, let me achieve and attain it in Jesus' Name. Amen!!!

When you preach like Noah, the righteousness of God, don't expect to be popular! Do you imagine that Noah got along excellently with his neighbours and was part of their revelling etc.? Think again! His preaching and message was foolishness unto them and they persecuted him as Jesus Christ was persecuted and very unloved! Especially those who would perish! However, to those who were to be saved, his preaching and message was the power and wisdom of God! Sadly, they were just members of his immediate household! O Lord, please count me worthy, amongst those being saved in Jesus' Name. Amen!!!

God is so intent on our living holy and righteous lives; such that we are counseled to get rid of any of our body parts that cause us to stumble. This calls for discipline as opposed to cutting off your actual parts as they do in sharia! God's Wisdom is not the same as man's wittiness! The Word of God needs the Holy Spirit for interpretation for the sake of Godliness! Teach us o Lord to discern Your Word and have Revelation in You through Jesus Christ our Lord God and Saviour. Amen!!!

198th Day

OUR LORD GOD IN JESUS CHRIST IS MERCIFUL, FORGIVING AND VERY LOVING! DO NOT TAKE HIM FOR GRANTED!!!

If you know you are unclean and want to be cleansed in the Name of the Lord, then come forth right now in Jesus' Name and repent of your ways and receive forgiveness! All you need is a willingness to change and follow up with an actual change of heart and ways and you will be done and dusted! You may even think you are beyond forgiving; come and try Jesus Christ! The Lord of all sinners who forgives the worst offenders who are willing to receive Him and repent of their ways! God's Ways are very different and far Higher than the ways of mankind! No comparing ways; it's a futile exercise!!!

The Lord our God does not get angry easily because He is the epitome of Love; indeed He is LOVE par excellence! He neither punishes nor chides forever! His Love like His Ways are so great towards those who fear Him (definitely not to everybody as some would like to believe and preach)! Only He Can remove our transgressions far away from us! O Lord, please take away all sins and unrighteousness from my family and my life in Jesus' Name. Amen!!!

You who deliberately put stumbling blocks in the way of your brethren or others; know this, God is personally on your case and it will not bode well for you! All stumbling blocks and those who constitute them or bring them forth shall fall by the Right Hand of the Lord God Almighty in Jesus' Name. Amen! Strive to Love and not be a stumbling block or put such blocks in the paths of your brethren. Strive to please God always in Jesus' Name. Amen!!!

Hmmmm! Even the fearful will partake of the lake of fire! Why then do you give in to fear when it is a sin unto the Lord? Fear is not for man! Only the fear of God which is the beginning of wisdom is sanctioned by God! All other fears are not from God nor sanctioned by God; therefore they are unprofitable for man! Do not fear! May the Lord remove every fear from us in Jesus' Name. Amen!!!

199th Day

BELIEVERS ARE AMBASSADORS OF A COVENANT KEEPING GOD! REVERE GOD; PRAY IN THE SPIRIT; AND BE CHILDLIKE!!!

I urge you to be reconciled to God; if you don't know how, then please get in touch with me urgently and I'll show you the way! Once reconciled, you become an ambassador for Jesus Christ. The reason for His sacrifice is that we might become the righteousness of God in Jesus Christ! Help us o Lord to be like You in every way in Jesus' Name I pray with thanksgiving. Amen!!!

God is a covenant keeping God! He made a covenant with Levi, a faithful priest in God's House! If you obey God, He Will keep His covenant with you! Do you revere God? Is true instruction in your mouth with nothing false on your lips? Do you walk with the Lord in peace and uprightness and turn many from sin? Do your lips preserve knowledge and is Godly instruction in your mouth when people seek you out as a messenger of the Lord God Almighty? Well, if you can answer yes to all of these, then you stand in good stead with the Lord and have nothing to worry about! But if not, you are in trouble and need urgently to seek the Face of the Lord, repent and seek forgiveness! You need to amend your ways with the Lord's Help in Jesus' Name! O Lord Help me for I am a worthless sinner that does not deserve the mercy, love and grace that I enjoy in Your Name. Help me o Lord to appreciate You in Jesus' Name. Amen!!!

Pray in the Holy Spirit at all times and persevere with your prayers and supplications for all believers and for me especially as I need your prayers! Pray for me that I may be bold in proclaiming the gospel mystery with words Given me by God as an ambassador in chains! Father, Help me to discharge my duties for which You Called me into my role in the world and Body of Christ in Jesus' Name I pray. Amen!!!

No matter how old or wise you are, you need the innocence of a child to discharge your duties in the Name of the Lord and to enter into the Kingdom of Heaven! There is space only for the likes of such little children in Heaven's Kingdom and no alternatives are acceptable! Be gentle, innocent, pure and humble like the little child and welcome such because as you do so, you welcome the Lord Jesus Christ! Amen!!!

In Christ Jesus, you are not to murder or be angry with your brethren; not even to call them fools! The use of foul language and insults etc. is alien to the ways of Jesus Christ! Who are we really following in our faith? Hmmmm! Please Jesus! I stand personally very guilty and sinful; help me to find true love as You exemplify in every sense of the word. Help me to enjoy the fruits of truly following and serving You o Lord in Jesus' Name. Amen!!!

200th Day

NEW CREATION? IS THAT YOU BELIEVER? HAVE YOU BEEN TRULY RENEWED IN YOUR MIND AND WAYS? BORN AGAIN!!!

When you are born again, you are supposed to be a new creation; no more in condemnation, because you stand afresh in the Grace of God! All negativity within you must be let go and replaced with all positivity, freshness, goodness with the grace of and faith in Christ Jesus our Lord God and King! You must become increasingly loving, kind, tender hearted and forgiving even as God forgives you. You are renewed truly and born again if you are living this new life; otherwise, you deceive only yourself!!!

Being born again, you must get rid of anger, rage, malice, slander and filthy language as a way of life. Refrain from and strive not to engage in such negativities again in your daily living! Whereas telling lies used to be a way of life; in your new life, strive always to tell the truth and no more lies. No more lying to yourself or to others. The old self must be discarded and the new self embraced fully; which is renewable daily in knowledge, wisdom and the image of your Creator! Jesus Christ is the Supreme One! Love and fear Him!!!

You must in the new life in Jesus Christ, discard all your old rustic and outlandish behaviour including all the malice, hatred, deceit, envy, slander and hypocrisy! You must crave pure spiritual milk like an infant; by which you will grow up unto salvation. Especially, now that you have tasted that the Lord is good and His mercies endure forevermore! Live by faith not by sight in Jesus' Name. Amen!!!

Growing in grace and power is not restricted to the leadership of the faith in Christ Jesus at all. If you have faith like a mustard seed, you can say to this mountain: "move from here to another place" and it will obey you; nothing shall be impossible for you in Jesus' Name! The disciples wanted to know why they couldn't perform a healing on a particular boy in a particular situation. Jesus told them the pure truth! They had little faith; they didn't believe that they could! Having faith is not about "you"! It's about having faith in the Name of Jesus that He, the Lord Jesus Christ is Able to do that which He Promised to do! Just believe; and for you, nothing shall be impossible! Lord, Help me to have faith in You. Amen!!!

201st Day

TO INHERIT GOD'S KINGDOM, WALK IN THE SPIRIT AND FORSAKE THE FLESH! CHRIST SUFFERED; GIVE THANKS!!!

If your mindset is worldly, fleshly, then you will be very hostile to God and His Word or servant; hell-bound, not subject to the laws of God! However, with a godly, Spirit mindset, you are life-bound with peace in subjection to the laws of God and pleasing God! Help my family and I o Lord; that our mindsets are conformed to the likeness of that of the Lord Jesus Christ in Spirit and in Truth in Jesus' Name. Amen!!!

If the above includes your lifestyle and what you revel in, then you do need help in Jesus Christ to change urgently! Jesus Christ is coming and tomorrow may be too late for you! Come now! Come running whilst it is day and the Lord will receive you. Leaving it all till later may not yield fruits for you because you do not know how long you have on this earth! Be wise. Act NOW in Jesus' Name. Amen!!!

We shall testify in our generation and to the next generation of Your Goodness and all o Lord Jesus! We shall show Your praise to all generations. This is our duty, calling and faith. Help us o Lord to do so increasingly in Jesus' Name. Amen!!!

Without faith no man can please the Lord. Even if God Speaks to you, without faith, you will continue to miss it. It is faith that works with Love that leads the faithful to obey the Word of the Living God! Even when God Sends a helper, you may not recognise him without faith; faith can move mountains where love rules! Give my family and I love o Lord so full and complete so that our lives here on earth may be meaningful and complete in Jesus' Name. Amen!!!

Who is standing in the Name of the Lord? Hmmm! If you are sure that you are standing, then you had better stand firm so you do not fall! When you have done all to stand, yet, stand! The reality of satan is such that he will take down anyone that is complacent! Be on your guard! Guard your spirit; resist the devil and he will flee. Help us o Lord to stand firm for You in Jesus' Name. Amen!!!

202nd Day

OUR POTTER! WE ARE YOUR CLAY YOU ARE OUR SHEPHERD! BE MERCIFUL TO US LORD DO NOT VEX FOREVER WITH US!!!

We are but flesh o Lord and very far from perfect; so we vex You always. However, we need Your mercy o Lord. Do not vex with us forever; we are Your clay and You our Potter. Only You Can Make us right! Forgive our iniquities and sinfulness o Lord; revive and restore us in Jesus' Name o Lord I pray in Jesus' Name. Amen!!!

You do things and think they are hidden from the Lord our God? How foolish! Better to always remember that our God Sees and Knows all; including the thoughts not yet formed nor expressed by mankind! Stop turning things upside down! Do what is right! Can you keep questioning Your Maker as to why and how He made you one way and not another? Hmmm! Wisen up folks. God is GOD!!!

Take cognisance of the fact that God is our Creator and our God and Father! We are His people and sheep in His pastures. Relate with Him with this at the back of your minds; hold Him in awe and fear Him! Obey Him and Honour Him! Give Him thanks and praise all the time and bless His Holy Name; for He Has Done Great things for us!!!

The awesomeness of the transfiguration and the Voice that spoke had the disciples present in awesome fear and they fell face down to the ground until Jesus Christ "Touched" them to revive them. He told them not to broadcast what they had witnessed until He had been raised from the dead! Unlike our ministers of today who take a camera to wherever they are going for exactly the opposite reasons!!!

When we play too clever for our own good, we always lose out! Whenever we act wiser than our means and resources likewise, we always tend to lose out! Look at the end result of this episode by reading it up please. Take the trouble to do so! May God Enable us to humble ourselves and be wise in the way of the Lord and not of the world in Jesus' Name. Amen!!!

203rd Day

LORD, I DELIGHT TO DO YOUR WILL; HELP ME OVERCOME MY FLESH IN JESUS' NAME. AMEN!!!

Your Law is inscribed on the tablet of my heart o Lord and You Know that I delight to do Your Will as revealed to me! My flesh is always warring against Your Spirit within me o Lord. Help me overcome my flesh so I can do Your Will perfectly in Jesus' Name o Lord. Amen!!!

Who is on the Lord's side? If you are on the Lord's side, then prove it with your deeds! Are you doing your own thing or are you striving to do the Will of God? The harvest is so ripe and the workers are few; pray to the Lord of the Harvest to send workers into His Fields. Have you? Are you enrolled into the Lord's Army to serve Him? Are you a worker or willing to be sent into the fields to gather in the harvest into the Lord's barns? Hmmmm! If you love the Lord, the proof is in obeying His Word! Are you ready? Are you willing? O Lord, Help me and my family with me, the Grace to do Your Will in Jesus' Name. Amen!!!

When righteousness is your focus and heart's desire and you delight in it, then your mouth will utter wisdom and your tongue shall speak justly. For the Law of the Lord is in your heart; hence, your feet shall not slip. The Lord Shall uphold you with His Mighty Right Hand! Give me oil in my lamp o Lord and keep me burning till the break of day! Give me strength o Lord to remain on Your side to the very end in Jesus' Name. Amen!!!

You are evidence of the workings of the Lord through us unto you! We have ministered in the Name of the Lord to you and you have imbibed our teachings in the Name of the Lord. This is clear for the whole world to see. Therefore you are our epistle and of Christ Jesus, not ministered or written with ink; but rather by the Spirit of the Living God which is Holy Spirit on the tablets of your fleshly hearts and not on stone! Amen!! Halleluyah!!!

In the course of the transfiguration of our Lord Jesus Christ in the presence of Peter, James and John, Peter was moved and He voiced out that if it pleased the Lord, he would put up three shelters. One each for Jesus Christ,

Moses and Elijah! But the Lord was not finished. A bright cloud covered them and a voice thundered from the cloud saying: "This is my Son, whom I love; with Him, I am well pleased. Listen to Him!" If the disciples had any doubts of the Authority and Sovereignty of Jesus Christ, those would have been immediately laid to rest! God Proves His Anointing upon His Anointed always! Lord, Prove Your Hand upon my life for the whole world to see that You Sent me o Lord in Jesus' Name. Amen!!!

Let us remember that this same Solomon was the son borne to David by Bathsheba, with whom David committed adultery and had her husband killed in the thick of battle to which he requested that he be sent! It is Solomon that became king after David! God was so pleased with David that his son Solomon was a delight unto God. So God wanted to bless him; and asked him what he wanted! Solomon was already blessed with a wise heart; whether he knew it or not. He asked for wisdom and understanding to rule the people justly. This pleased God so much that He not only Granted his request but gave him much more blessing than he imagined! Hmmm! O Lord, yes You Can change my story! I look up to You and wait upon You o Lord in Jesus' Name. Amen!!!

204th Day

SERVING WELL AND WITH INTEGRITY PAYS OFF IN THE LORD; SERVE IN A WAY THAT GOD WOULD COMMEND YOU!!!

When called to serve, do so diligently as if you are doing such for the Lord Jesus Christ! Everybody has a Calling. Discover your calling and run with it! Your calling is your vision! If you serve well and with integrity, you will be very blessed in Jesus' Name. Take note!!!

If you hear the Voice of the Lord and open the door, He Will come in! Once in, your life will be transformed and never be the same again! You become more than a conqueror and a crown of life that will never fade away awaits you in Heaven above in Jesus' Name. Be therefore diligent to obey your calling and serve diligently in the Name of Jesus!!!

Part of your calling and thus service is to love daily! You love in service. If you love, you fulfil the Royal Law and thus you do well. As you serve people, you are serving God. Be careful how you entertain strangers for you might be entertaining the Lord Jesus Christ without knowing it! Whatsoever you do unto one of My Brothers, that you do unto Me! Jesus Christ said so Himself! Watchout!!!

Jesus Christ Revealed Himself and His Glory to Peter, James and John specifically; not to all the disciples. Hmmm! That's for you proponents of God loves us all equally. No. God does not love us equally. He is God. He chooses whom He Blesses. He does not bless everybody either! Hmmm! Believe if you like; it's your choice. The Lord Has Spoken!!!

What have you wasted in your life! What has the enemy stolen from you due to your own negligence? Do you know that you can go back to the enemy's camp and take back what he stole from you? Satan is under your feet! Do not be like Esau; selling your birthright is not an option. Guard your heart and spirit diligently. Do not take the Grace of God for granted. Do not cast your pearls unto pigs either! May God Bless you and yours in Jesus' Name. Amen!!!

205th Day

BE PREPARED TO DO WHATEVER IT TAKES IN THE NAME OF JESUS CHRIST AND FOR HIS GOSPEL!!!

This is speaking of a level of humility with godly flexibility! You cannot say you became a witch or wizard in order to win them for Jesus; that would be very wrong and absurd! For the sake of the Gospel, we can become flexible to accommodate a diversity of people and situations in order to bear fruit for the Lord Jesus Christ! This takes a lot of wisdom; so as not to malign the Name of the Lord! May God Help to Teach us the way to go about serving Him fruitfully in Jesus' Name. Amen!!!

This "new" commandment has been from of old. LOVE! Bind us together O Lord with cords that cannot be broken; bind us together with LOVE in Jesus' Name. By this, people will know that we are yours truly in Jesus' Name. Amen!!!

If you obey the commandment to LOVE, then you have done well in the Name of the Lord; so, will you or can you love in Jesus' Name? Help us o Lord to love in Your Name Jesus. Amen!!!

We shall all be judged. The Judge is standing right at the door! Jesus Christ is His Name! Who can Judge this world except God! Is this not another way for us to know that Jesus Christ is the Living God? The words that follow about not tasting death before the coming of the Lord is understood only by revelation by Jesus Christ's Holy Spirit Himself! Don't even try to intellectualise it at all; it won't work! God is Great; His Word is presented in parables and only by the Holy Spirit can we decode it! May God Grant us wisdom and discernment to understand, appreciate and know His Word in Jesus' Name. Amen!!!

A day of Judgment is coming! Be prepared in and out of season; there will be no exemptions! God is Just! Jesus Christ is His Name! Trust in Him and live for Him; thank You Lord Jesus for Your Supremacy and the gift of Your Holy Spirit that Enables us to live a holy life in Your Name. Amen!!!

206th Day

THE LORD CAN DO AND UNDO; PRAY! FREEDOM IN CHRIST, YES; USE YOUR FREEDOM RIGHT! JESUS WILL FINISH UP!!!

Mercy o Lord! You fashioned me the way You want me; please do not destroy nor consume me! Save me o Lord; unworthy though I am, please Lord, be merciful to save me in Jesus' Name. Amen!!!

Make me righteous o Lord; so that my Calling and Anointing may be worthy in Your Sight! Let Your Light so Shine in and through me, that others may be lit up through me in Jesus' Name. Amen!!!

In Christ Jesus, we have freedom; but not to sin or exalt the flesh! Stop battering, biting and devouring one another; lest you consume each other and all come to nought! Follow after and walk in the Spirit; so you do not fulfil the desires of the flesh! May God Help us on the right path in Jesus' Name. Amen!!!

When Jesus starts a work in my life, that work is good and He Will finish it in Jesus' Name. Amen! I wait upon Your goodness o Lord; that I may taste and experience for myself that You are so good and that Your mercies endure forevermore! Amen!!!

To be a disciple, you must deny yourself in walking the faith, carrying your cross and following Jesus! No point in trying to save your life; but if you lose it for Christ's sake, you will find it! Your soul is not worth losing for the world! Guard your spirit! God has given you what is precious, it's up to you to do the right thing for your life with God's Help! Amen!!!

No matter how much God loves you, if you engage in evil, God will warn you; if you change, you will be spared! If you do not change however, God will punish you and may destroy you; He Has the Power so to do. Who can question Him? Try God at your own peril! As for me and my household, we shall serve the Lord!!!

207th Day

IN CHRIST JESUS WE ARE HIS WORKMANSHIP; HE WILL NEVER ABANDON HIS WORK! HE STARTED AND WILL FINISH!!!

The Lord deserves our praise, adoration, worship and all; because of His Love and Faithfulness! His purpose for His children shall be fulfilled; He shall not abandon the works of His Hands in Jesus' Name. Amen! With Jesus Christ, I remain work in progress! God exalted His Name and His Word above all things! His Love endures forever; and He Loves me fully although I am unworthy!!!

Show me mercy o Lord for I trust and hope in You absolutely! I hide myself in You o Lord; You Will Protect me from all afflictions and evil in Jesus' Name. I will continue to cry out unto You because of the great and mighty things You do for me. Help me o Lord in Jesus' Name. Amen!!!

I have every confidence in the Lord that You who began the good work in my life, will bring Your work in my life to completion in Jesus' Name. You will not leave me half way; nor will You leave me undone! Amen and Amen!!!

Whilst the human instinct avoids stress, troubles, persecution etc., Jesus Christ explained all He would suffer to His disciples. The human spirit sometimes leads one to act "good" in our eyes; but our such actions in the Eyes of the Lord are "evil"! This is what we see of Peter in this passage! Jesus sternly rebuked him: "Get thee behind me satan!" Hmmm! Who amongst us can take this type of rebuke?

No one! No one has seen God nor ascended to Heaven except He who came down from Heaven. Who is He? Jesus Christ of course! Many of us still can't understand that Jesus Christ is the Living God! Yes, He is! Just believe and be saved. There is no other. He is God the Father, Son and Holy Spirit!!!

208th Day

CHOSEN? WALK IN LOVE! DON'T BE HYPOCRITICAL! THE KEYS TO THE KINGDOM OF HEAVEN IS YOURS! WIN SOULS!!!

As those chosen by God, let the Beauty of Jesus be seen in you; all His wondrous compassion and purity! Let the Spirit Divine, all your nature refine, till the Beauty of Jesus be seen in you! Demonstrate the goodness of God in your daily living so as to impact positively on lives you come in contact with. Bless the Lord with your life and be a blessing so God can Bless you always in Jesus' Name. Amen!!!

As a believer, you really ought to be a prisoner for the Lord! Hmmm! Who wants to serve the Lord this way today? Who loves the Lord so much as to be a prisoner for the Lord? Combine love with humility; as only in humility can love truly work by faith in Jesus Christ! Always work for peace and unity amongst fellow believers in Jesus' Name. Amen!!!

In ministry we are neither afraid nor ashamed to go through adversity patiently and with long suffering and love with the Help of the Holy Spirit always! We believe and know that this is pleasing to God Almighty who has Called us unto a Holy Calling in Christ Jesus! Emulate us in this if you are truly of the Faith in Jesus' Name. Amen!!!

Not everyone knows that Jesus Christ is the Messiah; now will everyone believe this. However, faith in Jesus Christ is rooted in and built on this rock. Likewise, we have been empowered to bind and loose on earth and it will be done in Heaven for us too in Jesus' Name. Amen!!!

It is hypocrisy to spend lots of money travelling to win souls and turn them into children of hell likewise due to wrong and dangerous teachings. Repent now! Tomorrow may be too late! Jesus is coming back again very soon!!!

209th Day

SEEK THE LORD AND YOU WILL FIND HIM; HE FORGIVES AND SO MUST YOU! VENGEANCE IS HIS; HE WILL REPAY ALWAYS!!!

When man forsakes God, God forsakes man! That is how God operates even with His Love and Blessings! If you love Him, you will be loved and blessed by Him! God is God! You cannot ever force your unconditional love agenda on Him; preach it all you want, it's not His way nor is it His style! God reserves the right to act however He wants; even if He wants to love the undeserving. He is God! However, that does not mean that God's Love is cheap or unconditional!!!

When you obey the Lord your God, your life will change according to the Word of God. God Will release His Love and Blessings upon you in Jesus' Name. Amen! Meditate on the above!!!

God's leadership is by example! In Psalm 23, we learn forgive us our trespasses as we forgive those who trespass against us! If we want to be forgiven, we must forgive! Very straightforward! No adding to nor taking away from the Word of Life! When you repent of your ways, God forgives you! Many of you claim to forgive even though the other person has never repented! Hmmm! What God did for us in sending His Son is a set standard! To receive the blessings, we must accept the sacrifice, believe and receive His forgiveness for His Love and blessings to be activated by faith upon our lives! There is a part we have to play in God's Love!!!

We need to expose evil in order for the Word of God to take root and the blessings of God will flow accordingly in Jesus' Name! When people act badly and or ungodly, there is a tendency that others will emulate their behaviour especially if they're perceived to suffer no consequence! However, let us imitate good and not evil. He who does good is of God but the one doing evil has neither met nor seen God! Touch us today o Lord that we may know You and the Power of Your Resurrection in Jesus' Name. Amen!!!

210th Day

WHEN YOU CONSIDER THE GOODNESS OF THE LORD, YOU WILL BLESS AND MAGNIFY THE NAME OF THE LORD!!!

There is a Yoruba (from the Wester parts of Nigeria) saying that if a servant or slave can think deeply, he or she would be thankful or grateful! It is good to meditate on the Word of God and reflect on the goodness and blessings of God in one's life! Only a soul and mind that does that can and will appreciate God enough to be able to bless and magnify the Name of the Lord! From the above Scripture, it is very clear that magnifying and blessing the Name of the LORD is prompted by a deep reflection on what He Has Done for human kind or the person. O Father Lord God Almighty in Jesus' Name, I bless and magnify Your Holy Name and worship and adore You in Jesus' Name. Thank You O Holy Spirit!!!

Again we see in this Scripture above that Mary burst forth into praise; magnifying and blessing the Lord and His Name on a deep reflection on the Lord's Hand upon her life and experience. In her words expressed, we can clearly follow what appears to be a part of her life's journey in the Name of the Lord God Almighty who did "great" things for her. Indeed o Lord, Your Name is Holy!!!

The teeth that a dog uses in playing with its puppies are used likewise to bite them for discipline! This does not liken the Great God unto a dog; no. Just an analogy to allow my reader to grasp the depths of the Lord God Almighty's Power! I have said it repeatedly that if we obey God, we are in for a blessing and for a time of abundance and satisfaction! However, if we disobey Him and His Word and engage in evil and not good, we shall surely suffer His wrath and judgment! Make no mistake about this! God is good and we all say all the time; but God Will, in His Goodness, punish sin, evil and wickedness, in order to purge mankind of evil and restore man's soul. Those who turn from their evil ways shall be saved; but all who continue in their evil ways shall be destroyed in Jesus' Name. Amen!!!

211th Day

GOD HAS GIVEN YOU A LOVE (DOING GOOD) MANUAL (THE WORD OF GOD); USE IT! NO EXCUSES ON JUDGMENT DAY!!!

We cannot say that God has been unkind or harsh to and or with us at all; for God has Given us His Word to obey and told us what to do in living to please Him! If we fail, it's out of our choice to disobey His Instructions!!!

The Word of God is not far-fetched from us at all; nor is the Word of God too difficult for us to obey either! It is made very clear. We are to love the Lord our God wholesomely, walk in His ways, keep and obey His Commands and love one another. Then, He Will Bless us! This does not sound like unconditional love to me at all! This God's Love is fully conditional! Obey and be blessed; disobey and remain under a curse and face the consequences! God's Love works that way folks!!!

The Pharisees and Sadducees were always testing Jesus Christ and looking for ways to catch Him out! Then they asked for a sign! Jesus is presented as so loving and kind etc.; but He never danced to the whims and caprices of mankind! Jesus Christ was very firmly focused on His Ministry and Destiny! He castigated them and never gave them a sign. Is that because He couldn't? Clearly not!!!

I urge you children (if you have parents, that makes you a child regardless of age) to take heed of this injunction from the Lord; you will be very blessed if you do! It is almost customary for children to despise parental advice and positions on life matters generally and disobey at will! However, it will go well with the children who obey the above commandment from the Lord God Almighty even though it hurts!!!

212th Day

GOD IS THE POTTER AND WE ARE THE CLAY; WHO IS IN FULL CONTROL? MANKIND? GOD? SUBMIT TO GOD AND HIS WAYS!!!

Only a foolish human does not know that God has overriding Powers over humankind and their lives, living and all! Can not God do whatever He likes with His creation? Be very careful and act wisely so as not to incur the wrath of the Almighty God!!!

Don't I have the right to do what I want with my own money? Or are you envious because I am generous?' Matthew 20:15 NIV

When a man has riches and or power, you have to be careful when dealing with such a person because their power can easily be used against you. Likewise, learn contentment and patience; because such a person has jurisdiction to do as they please with their belongings! Be wise and very careful!!!

But indeed, O man, who are you to reply against God? Will the thing formed say to him who formed it, "Why have you made me like this?" Does not the potter have power over the clay, from the same lump to make one vessel for honour and another for dishonour? Romans 9:20, 21 NKJV

If man or a government has power and the Bible urges us to accept that all power/authority instituted on earth is sanctioned by God and we must give due honour/respect to such; how much more do we owe to God, the Creator of all! Grumble/complain less and be more humble and compliant with the Word of God and be blessed! All Power belongs to Jesus Christ! God has all power; so know this: that Jesus Christ is God!!!

We acknowledge o Lord that You are our Maker and we submit to Your authority fully! We ask for Your Mercy, Grace and Love in dealing with us o Lord; lest we fall away from You and into the hands of our enemies and perish! Have Mercy on us o Lord according to Your great compassion and loving-kindness in Jesus' Name I pray. Amen!!!

When Jesus' Hands are in a matter, the matter is sorted/resolved fully and absolutely! Wow! He Provided for the followers who wanted help to eat miraculously and there was so much left over; enough to feed another multitude! All Power belongs to Jesus! All Power belongs to God! O Glory Halleluyah! All Power belongs to God!!!

You cannot afford to be complacent with the issues of God! That to God is the same as being neither hot nor cold; being lukewarm, which makes God very upset and He will spew such people out of His Mouth! You must take sides; either with God and be blessed or against God and be accursed! Whose side are you on? I am settled firmly on the Lord's side in Jesus' Name. Amen!!!

213th Day

WALK IN THE LIGHT; REFRAIN FROM WORLDLINESS AND SIN!!!

What a mighty God we have! Just having hope in Him purifies the believer! Wow! We have great potential in Jesus Christ! He's coming back again and we shall be as He is and see Him likewise! Jesus Christ is our Light! Blessed be His Holy Name! Halleluyah! Glory! Amen!!!

When He appeared with His LOVE, Grace and Mercy. He Sacrificed his life for us. Believing His Sacrifice and His coming and His story and His testimony, gives us new birth! We then follow up with denying all worldliness and ungodliness as we look up for the hope of His appearing; the Great God and Saviour, Jesus Christ! Jesus Christ is the Lord God Almighty! Just believe!!!

The description of Jesus Christ here again confirms His Godhead! For those who have ears to listen and hearts to believe! Can anyone be in any doubts as to who the Bible is referring to here? How can someone have these qualities as God and not be God? It is very clear to me that God came as Man (Jesus Christ) and He is the Holy Spirit!!!

All have sinned and fallen short of the Glory of the Lord! No one is without sin. Truth be told! Better to confess sins and seek forgiveness from the Lord and cleansing from all unrighteousness than to deny sins! God is Able and Kind to forgive us and cleanse us in Jesus Christ our Lord God and Saviour!!!

Were it not for the Lord's mercies, I would have been consumed long ago! He is Faithful and Just to forgive, protect and defend me. He is my Saviour indeed! I recommend my Lord Jesus Christ to you who are looking for salvation from any situation in your lives! It's better to bear the yoke when young; do not fret nor worry! God is Able! Just put your trust in Him!!!

Submit yourselves to Jesus Christ and give up all your fleshly lusts and sinfulness. Is not God worth it? I say He's worth far more than what we can give. Let us go for godliness and strive for righteousness in Jesus' Name. Amen!!!

214th Day

A PROPHETIC OUTCRY FOR REVIVAL IN THE NAME OF THE LORD JESUS CHRIST! REVIVE US O LORD, OUR HOPE/LIFE!!!

We are overwhelmed o Lord, we need You to Lead us to the Rock that is Higher than us! How we have fallen from Your Grace o Lord! I make confession on behalf of myself and all who will be truthful and are seeking for restoration and revival! Save us o Lord! Cause Your Face to Shine upon us o Lord; and we shall be saved in Jesus' Name. Amen!!!

Even though You have allowed me to face discipline in diverse forms, I know I have deserved Your discipline! However, in You, I have hope for revival and restoration because I know that You do not vex with me forever! Your anger o Lord lasts a very short while compared with the duration of Your Love to me over my faulted life! Restore and revive me o Lord my God in Jesus' Name I pray. Amen!!!

Whenever you are facing adversity, always remember that God allowed it to be; and that you can go back to God to seek for solace, revival and restoration in Jesus' Name. I call out to all who are facing tribulations, adversity, hard times reading this prophetic word right now to come, let us return to the Lord our God. He has caused grief but will likewise restore and revive. Let us not be weary in crying out to Him. Only Jesus Can Save!!!

My enemies are many (mostly unseen). Many more are the enemies I do not even know or see than those that show their faces o Lord. I do not take Your Love, Mercy and Grace for granted o Lord! I need Your Mighty Right Hand to Save, Revive and Restore me o Lord! Do not forsake me or my ministry in You o Lord. I have been so imperfect that I do not deserve Your Mercy; but I cry out to You because of the Blood of Jesus Christ shed for me! Overlook my misdemeanour o Lord! Overlook my offense, my sin, o Lord. I have no other besides You o Lord. I stand guilty before You of all my iniquities. Save me o Lord in Jesus' Name. Amen!!!

I desire mercy o Lord not to sacrifice. Let my sacrifice to You be of praise singing and thanksgiving in Jesus' Name for Your wrath has come down hard on the land and the people do not know what they are doing anymore. Your Word is scarce in Spirit and Truth. Reveal Yourself o Lord please! Remember the Blood of Jesus and be merciful I urge and appeal to You o Lord. I know that You are a merciful God. You will not leave nor forsake me now! I plead o Lord Jesus. Amen!!!

215th Day

ONCE YOU PUT YOUR HOPE/TRUST/ALL IN JESUS CHRIST, NO MORE REASON TO FEAR! BE BOLD AND COURAGEOUS!!!

When the Spirit of the Lord is upon my soul, with the knowledge that the Lord is on my side; and because I know that He LIVES, all fear is gone from my life forever! When Jesus came into my life, He gave me power, love and a sound mind with discipline! I am not the same as I used to be! I must neither be ashamed of the Testimony of my Lord Jesus Christ, nor to testify/witness for Him. I have a holy calling upon my life which I must fulfill with the help of my God in Jesus' Name. Amen!!!

I am a son of God as long as I yield to the leading of the Holy Spirit of God! I received the Spirit of adoption that Enables me to cry Abba Father; His Holy Spirit bearing with my spirit that I am God's son/child! O blessed be the Name of the Lord Most High in Jesus' Name. Amen!!!

Imagine the Blessings I have bestowed upon my life as enumerated above just because the Lord is my Shepherd! Hmmm! Assurances of never lacking, peace and prosperity in serenity! Protection against all odds and or eventualities/negativities. A boldness as against fear even as I walk in righteousness with His Help always! Comfort with Provision in abundance all in His Name with the anointing of God that breaks every yoke. God's goodness and mercy follow me all life long and in appreciation, I will dwell in His House forever serving in His Courts in Jesus' Name. Amen!!!

Wherever Jesus Christ went, He was doing good whilst He walked this earth in His physical body. He continues to do good today through His Holy Spirit as He is present wherever there is a need for Him. Jesus Christ Ministers to needs and Meets needs wherever He is made welcome! Will you welcome my Lord today into your life? Then you will experience a great change!!!

(34) He beholds every high thing; He is king over all the children of pride.'
Job 41:34

Leviathan referred to in this verse is likeable unto satan, the true king of all pride and the prideful! I'd rather have Jesus and the humility that comes with knowing Him than satan and all the pride that comes with him. Lord protect and defend me from satanic influences; for they are so powerful and enticing to the human mindset. Give me a Godly mindset with accompanying wisdom and understanding in Jesus' Name. Amen!!!

216th Day

BELIEVERS! TRUST JESUS CHRIST: HE ORDERS YOUR STEPS, UPHOLDS AND PROTECTS YOU! HE'LL KEEP YOU SAFE!!!

I believe that the Scripture above is referring to the Lord ordering the steps of a righteous man. Being good does not necessarily get you into Heaven. It's safer for you to be in Jesus Christ! Even though the righteous fall, the Lord shall uphold them in Jesus' Name. Amen! I look up to You o Lord; do not let me get lost into the world. I need You more than anything o Lord, help me in Jesus' Name. Amen!!!

Do not worry about anything! Be care free, stress free, and worry free! Take all your concerns, petitions, requests, etc. to the Lord in prayer! Then the peace of God that humans cannot understand shall rest upon you and keep your heart and mind focused on and in Jesus' Christ. Halleluyah! Amen!!!

To be born again is a big deal only in so far as recognition and emphasis is given to the fact that it's ONLY brought on by and through God's Mercy. This living hope is obtained only through the resurrection of our Lord Jesus Christ from the dead! By this we who are born again are promised and assured of an imperishable heritage that will never fade away; held in trust in Heaven for us. This is protected by God's Power through faith for salvation to be ultimately revealed in the end time in Jesus' Holy Name. Amen!!!

Look at Jesus' dealings with an "undeserving" woman at the well and her response to His words! Wow! How many women today will take such from a man, let alone a servant of God! Such exemplary humility and grace in the face of what today would be termed extremely harsh judgment! Her response qualified her for what she didn't deserve! I pray that God Touches my heart to respond to negative situations in my life in such a way that would qualify me for that which I am not qualified to receive in terms of goodness and mercy in Jesus' Name. Amen!!!

Jesus Christ today would be accused of rudeness, insolence and insubordination, considering His response to Pilate, the ruler here!

This proves that God's Ways are indeed different than man's and really incomparable! However, did He speak the truth? I say yes! Remember, no one has power over you unless given from above; and even that power is not permanent! God, please give us wisdom to tackle our myriads of daily problems encountered in Jesus' Name. Amen!!!

217th Day

DO YOU KNOW THAT FAITH IS GIVEN TO YOU BY GOD'S GRACE BUT NEEDS TO BE BUILT UP? BUILD WHILST YOU CAN NOW!!!

As a believer, you need the Holy Spirit. Your faith will grow only if you build it up; so you do have work to do. The more you trust God and believe Him, the more testimonies you would have. We are made strong and overcome by the Blood of the Lamb and by the words of our testimonies (and or the Testimony). What is your testimony? This is what you have to witness to Jesus Christ and His Power made manifest in your life. These will build you up and your faith with you; and you pray without ceasing! The more God Answers your prayers, the more your testimonies; and the more you will be built up in Christ Jesus. Amen!!!

The Gospel of Jesus Christ is actually the Power of God leading unto the salvation for all that choose to believe Jesus Christ's testimony! In this, there's no discrimination; as it is for the Jew, so it is for the Greek and gentile! It's a revelation of God's righteousness by faith unto faith; for the just (righteous) shall live by faith! Faith is what pleases God; partly why the believer must continue to build up their faith in holiness and righteousness in Jesus Christ. Amen!!!

Not everybody you share the Gospel or your testimonies with will believe or accept! You as a believer must come to understand that. You do not need to force or push anyone to believe! You do your bit and leave God, who is the Master Fisherman to fill your nets! Faith of course comes through hearing; and hearing what? Hearing the Word of God of course! Thank You Jesus; for You designed all for Your good pleasure such that You are in full control and all in all. Amen!!!

Out of the abundance of the heart the mouth speaketh! Simply put, whatever comes into the mouth goes into the stomach and then passes on out of the body. However, the things that contaminate and defile the person come from the heart. Sins are hatched from deep within the hearts of mankind and followed through to execution with the full knowledge and consent of the heart. This is what defiles a man and not the washing of hands before eating or not! O the depths of the knowledge and wisdom of God Almighty! Fill me o Lord with Your Wisdom and Knowledge and Power in Jesus' Name. Amen!!!

On the day of judgement, for you who buy security on earth with your great wealth etc.; your wealth will be fully useless on that Day! Get right with God so He will get right with you. Strive to do your best to be on the right side of God in Jesus' Name. Amen! Same for one and for all in Jesus' Name! Amen!!!

218th Day

PRIORITISE GOD'S KINGDOM AND HIS RIGHTEOUSNESS! QUIT DECEIVING YOURSELF; AND BE VERY BLESSED BY GOD!!!

When you align yourself with the world (pagans), you become like them and miss out on the blessings and heritage of God! They run after primary needs (food, drink, clothing, etc.); but do not prioritise to know God and or His Ways. You must not emulate them; rather you must seek first the Kingdom of God and His Righteousness and all your needs shall be met thereafter. Stop worrying for the morrow; sufficient are the troubles for each day! Live one day at a time believer! Who will receive this word? We live in a world where everyone thinks they are wiser than everyone else and nobody can teach us anything; and we can't learn anything from anyone else! Lord God Almighty! Please Help us to humble ourselves in Jesus' Name and be willing to add to our learning in Jesus' Name. Amen!!!

God has given us reasons to praise Him; because He causes us to remember His Mighty works amongst us! God is Gracious and full of compassion and Love especially unto them that fear Him. He's a covenant-keeping God. He shows the Power in His works so as to give his followers the heritage of the heathen (pagans)! O what a God! What a mighty God we have!!!

Those who are the Lord's will never be left alone, forsaken nor put to shame! Amen! This is to let all know that He is the Lord and there is no one else like Him! I have absolute confidence in my Lord and God and King; in Jesus Christ! Will you join me now?!!

It takes God's Wisdom to understand the Word of God! How else can you have understanding of this Word above? It's not what goes into a man's mouth that defiles him; but rather, what comes out of his mouth! Hmmm! Fill me with Your Holy Spirit Lord Jesus; to help me decipher, discern and have knowledge and understanding of Your Holy Word in Jesus' Name I pray thankfully. Amen!!!

This is a warning from God against complacency in faith and religion! Sometimes we get arrogant in thinking and assuming that all is well with us and we tend to want to rest on our oars! We even give ourselves and or fellowships or ministries names that suggest that we are alive! God Knows that we are dead and adjudges that we are dead. He Ministers this to us and we turn a deaf ear because He did so through a human vessel! Beware! The Word of God! Watch and pray! Look out for the weaknesses and weak ones around you and within you fellowships so they do not die off too! You have not attained perfection yet; take heed of the Word of Life! Receive and repent NOW! Otherwise the Lord Himself will come upon you like a thief and deal with you! Father, forgive us; be patient with us! We are mere mortals! Lead us, Guide us, Help us to a place where You want us to be in Jesus' Name. Amen!!!

219th Day

LORD JESUS, HELP ME TO INCREASE IN OBEDIENCE, HOLINESS AND LOVE IN MY DAILY LIFE; SO TO IMPACT OTHERS TOO!!!

Pray for me saints of God, that I might increase in love in my daily living; so to be able to discern what is good, perfect and acceptable to the Lord and be pure and blameless till Jesus returns! With our Lord Jesus Christ, nothing is impossible; and He is a prayer answering God. So, I beseech you humbly, please pray for me in Jesus' Name. Amen. Meanwhile, I pray the same for you all who receive this in Jesus' Name right now. Amen!!!

Faith without works is dead; therefore, faith, like love is an act of will (an action). Therefore, as you must do with your faith, act out your love in every way possible daily. For if you do, you are obeying the Lord Jesus Christ's Command to LOVE and your reward is that you will never be barren nor unfruitful in the knowledge and understanding of our Lord Jesus Christ! Again, we see that the Love of God is not unconditional; everywhere throughout the Holy Scriptures, God's Instructions and Ordinances have always followed a pattern of: "Do this and I will do this for you"; "obey my Commandments and I will Bless you"; "disobey and you are under a curse"!

Even in John 3: 16-18 (16 For God so loved the world that he gave his one and only Son, that whoever believes in him shall not perish but have eternal life. 17 For God did not send his Son into the world to condemn the world, but to save the world through him. 18 Whoever believes in him is not condemned, but whoever does not believe stands condemned already because they have not believed in the name of God's one and only Son.), it makes clear that the blessing is for those who believe; those who do not believe stand condemned already. Children of God; do not be deceived, be wise!!!

But the path of the righteous is like the light of dawn, that shines brighter and brighter until the full day. Proverbs 4:18 NASB

No matter how much darkness the righteous face, their paths are always lit up with the likeness of the light of dawn, shining brighter and brighter until the full day arrives! Righteousness pays off in the short and long run; try it! Lord, please Grant unto me Your Righteous Spirit to live my life in righteousness and holiness until Your Return in Jesus' Name. Amen!!!

It is great hypocrisy to take the Name of the Lord upon your lips constantly without giving your heart to Him nor doing His Will! Man may see your acts of hypocrisy and your make-believe style of living as if you are a faithful believer; however, God Knows the truth about you. You cannot deceive God. Your professed faith is in vain!!!

If you are truly in the Lord and in the faith sincerely, you ought to grow and be able to impact others through your living and your words in teaching others the way of the Lord. However, most people are found wanting! They remain like babies who still need milk perpetually! Solid food (feeding and leading to maturity in the Lord) is for those who have been used to exercising their faith in obedience to the Word of God and growing into maturity thereupon in Jesus' Name. Lord, Grant me the Grace in Jesus' Name so to grow in Your Word. Amen!!!

220th Day

WHETHER THE TIMES ARE GOOD OR BAD; PRAY WITHOUT CEASING! PRAY WITH FAITH AND BELIEVE YOU ARE HEARD!!!

Pray all the time; and remember to pray not just for yourself, but for the saints of God (other believers)! When you pray, believe that God has heard your prayers and will do for you what you desire of Him in Jesus' Name. When you pray, pray in the Holy Spirit of God. Amen!!!

There are many times you want to pray but don't find the words. At such times, the Holy Spirit within you is activated and helps you with sounds (moanings and groanings). These come from the Holy Spirit interceding for you at those times. I would place speaking in tongues in this category; as I think it is appropriate! However, groanings and moanings may come out in other ways too. Thank You Jesus for letting Your Holy Spirit so intercede for us!!!

Those who fear the Lord and live by His Word and bind themselves to Him in spirit and in truth will enjoy God bringing them to His Holy Mountain and giving them Joy. Remember that the Joy of the Lord is the believer's strength! God Will accept their offerings. The House of the Lord will be called a House of Prayer for all nations! No discrimination with God in true worship! Though of many nations, we must not forget; that we all are brothers with a common debt in Christ Jesus. Amen!!!

221st Day

THE WORD OF GOD (BOTH OLD AND NEW TESTAMENTS TOGETHER) IS FULL AND VERY RELEVANT TODAY! BE WISE!!!

I garner from this above Scripture that the Law opened us up to Jesus Christ; it is a revelation of Christ Jesus. How then can the student set aside the teacher as irrelevant as some are doing in the Name of Jesus Christ? Impossible! Jesus Christ said He did not come to abolish the law; but rather to fulfill it! He also said a man that is well versed in both the law and the Kingdom of God is like a farmer that brings out treasures from his barn (both old and new). The Word of God is full and relevant for all time in Jesus' Name. Amen!!!

The pharisees and sadducees were always looking for ways to "get" (i.e. fault) anything Jesus Christ did! Jesus here answered the foolish according to their folly! He laid on them squarely their evident hypocrisy, which nullifies the Word of God for the sake of their traditions! Hmmmm! The Wisdom of God is Supreme. Lord God Almighty, please teach us Your Wisdom; that we might be wise for this age and make it into Eternal Life in Jesus' Name. Amen!!!

222nd Day

LOVE; NOT JUST BY MOUTH, BUT IN ACTION, SPIRIT AND TRUTH! LORD BE MY HELP AGAINST HATERS; REWARD AND BLESS ME!!!

If you claim to have God's love and love someone and see them in need yet do not help them, how is that consistent with the love of God in you? Love is not about what is said really; but rather love is about what you do! Love is not theoretical; love is very practical; love is action. Love is about what you do not what you say! Lord Help us to love like Jesus did in action not just in words. Amen!!!

When you follow after the goodness of God and love in spirit and truth, you become a threat to those to whom you become like a mirror. They begin to see their shortcomings in you. Hence, they are vexed in their spirit and start to hate you and like love, hate is acted out not just in words. Father Lord God Almighty, You are my hope and defence against such haters. Protect and vindicate me in Jesus' Name. Amen!!!

If only people would understand and appreciate God's Word! To you who are striving to live a righteous life; understand that haters do not need a justifiable reason to hate you. However, like-minded righteousness loving folks strive to take care of you, even if they may be few and far between! Also, don't be like a fool in venting out all your feelings like a rudderless ship. It is simply unfruitful. A lot of noise making and anger that leads only into deeper troubles; because anger does not bear good fruit! Learn to control yourself and your emotions. You do not have to vent all your feelings, frustrations etc.; you look and sound so unwise when you do and you will not know it at the time. However, the results will prove your folly to you for sure. Exercise restraint always!!!

Aa kin ri omo'ba ka'ma ri dansaki l'orun re; meaning: we do not see a King's child without a royal insignia on him/her. There will always be a sign that this is a King's child on him or her! Likewise, everywhere He went, Jesus was always doing good; Almighty Healer, He Healed the sick at will. When the weak, sick and possessed saw Him, they were Healed immediately. Jesus Christ was always doing good. This is why as soon as they climbed into the boat, the wind died down; and the occupants marvelled and acknowledged Him. He is the Lord!!!

The age we live in is surely coming to an end some day very soon. Then, the evil and wicked people will be gathered and separated from the good and upright! The former will be cast into everlasting torment of hell fire whilst the latter will be led into eternal salvation of bliss and peace with joy and harmony. Amen. Come, Lord Jesus!!!

223rd Day

AS A BELIEVER WHERE IS YOUR MIND FOCUSED? ARE YOU PREPARED TO SUFFER FOR JESUS? JESUS SAVES HEALS DELIVERS BUT WILL JUDGE ALL ALSO IN DUE SEASON!!!

Keep your focus as a believer on Heavenly things not worldly or earthly things. When you came to Jesus Christ, you died to your flesh and previous self and put on the new man thereby hiding your new life in Jesus' Christ who is God. At the Revelation of Jesus Christ in His Glory, the believer will also be revealed with Him in Jesus' Name. Amen. Are you ready? Have you decided or chosen your focus? Do not be like a rudderless ship without a focus? My people perish because of a lack of vision. That is the bottom line here. Vision. Focus. Lord, Help my family, self and all believers to keep our eyes on Jesus Christ, the Author and Finisher of our faith; our Alpha and Omega! In Jesus' Name. Amen!!!

Whatsoever you do unto one of my brothers, that you do unto me! This comes into play significantly here; as the Apostle Paul commends a brother who demonstrates true love for Jesus Christ by caring for the welfare of believers. He is very much unlike most others who basically look out for "number one"; which is the message of the world to it's own. No, not so for the believer! Have a change of heart now! Have a heart; not just for yourself but for others too in Jesus' Name. Lord, Help us. Touch our hearts afresh; so that we can put our brethren's interests in perspective to care for other than ours in Jesus' Name. Amen!!!

Our Lord Jesus Christ; the One we ought to model our lives after, suffered for us in the flesh a lot! Why do we shy away from suffering in His Name? So much so that we see anyone who suffers as basically being ungodly and under some kind of "punishment" from God! Hmmm! What and where is the faith? When Jesus Christ returns, will He indeed meet faith on earth? In the Will of God, we must suffer in the flesh so that we do not live our lives in the flesh for worldly lusts, but rather for the Will of God! Help us o Lord to live for You in Jesus' Name. Amen!!!

The Holy Spirit filled Peter the Apostle and he was moved to speak to the rulers and elders of Israel! He spoke the Gospel Message as a witness to the people! He explained to them that the miracle they had witnessed was attributable to the Lord Jesus Christ; and that only in the Name of Jesus Christ can anyone be saved. The people knew that Peter and his fellow believers had been with Jesus Christ; this was obvious to them! With the evidence of the man that had been healed, they had nothing to say against them or the miracle; as they saw that Peter and his company were unschooled ordinary men! What a Mighty God we serve. He chooses like no man does. He chooses the humblest amongst men and not the powerful and mighty! Lord Have Mercy on us in Jesus' Name. Amen!!!

Out of disobedience, the people loved blood and shed it freely in the land so God pronounced judgment on them in these words above. Lord, please deal mercifully with my family, self and all who hope in You; for not one of us is able to keep Your Word without straying. We need Your Help o Lord in Jesus' Name. Amen!!!

224th Day

HAVE CONFIDENCE IN JESUS CHRIST; HE IS FAITHFUL! IF GOD BE FOR US, WHO CAN BE AGAINST US? EAT GOD'S WORD!!!

Let us hold fast the confession of our hope without wavering, for He who promised is faithful; and let us consider how to stimulate one another to love and good deeds, Hebrews 10:23,24 NASB

Let us not faint with doubt for any reason at all nor be discouraged. God is faithful; when He Promises, He Delivers every time! Be bold and courageous even in encouraging each other to do good always even whilst waiting upon the Lord. Please Jesus, we wait for Your Mercy and Goodness daily; Strengthen our resolve to wait patiently in Jesus' Name. Amen!!!

We are assured and encouraged about the faithfulness of God who called us into this glorious fellowship with and in His Son, Jesus Christ our Lord God and Saviour! O thank You Lord Jesus for Your Faithfulness. Amen!!!

In addition to God working for the good of those who love Him and are called according to His purposes; He has Predestined us in conformity to the likeness of Jesus Christ our Lord! We therefore have a Blessed heritage and need not fret nor be fearful of anything for any reason at all. We must know and believe that because God is for us, nothing, no one can came against us successfully in Jesus' Name! Amen!!!

The Word of God is so Powerful and Effective! The Word of God is sweeter than the honeycomb! However, because of the Power to bring about desired change, it serves as bitter in the stomach! Be careful what you are feeding on; to be sure you are feeding on the Word of God. For you to experience the transformation required in Christ Jesus, the Word of God will churn your stomach! So, if it's not having the required effect, question it! Is what you are feeding on the Word of God?!!

225th Day

JESUS LOVES ME YES I KNOW; THE BIBLE TELLS ME SO; LITTLE ONES TO HIM BELONG; THEY ARE WEAK, BUT HE IS STRONG!!!

My God is a special lover of the oppressed, poor, impoverished, hungry, thirsty, underprivileged, underdogs, widows, orphans, etc.; He takes care of the needs of the needy (whatever their needs are)! He's a lover of the righteous and all who fear, obey Him and tremble at His every word! He is a Friend to and watches over the alien. Are you an alien (living in a strange land)? God Knows what you are facing; trust Him, call on Him, put all your cares in His Hands and you will be alright in Jesus' Name. Amen! O! God is GREAT and Good; He is just and upright! Bless His Holy Name. Amen!!!

This is a prophetic word which I receive for my fatherland, Nigeria today! If you are so inclined, you can also receive it for your country. I receive the same word for my homeland, Ekiti in Ekiti State of Nigeria in Jesus' Name. Please do likewise if you are so inclined. It's a very free world. May God Bless my fatherland, Nigeria; and my homeland, Ekiti in Ekiti State of Nigeria. Nigeria shall be saved and free in Jesus' Name as will Ekiti State. Amen!!!

Covenant-keeping God! There is no one like You; Alpha Omega! There is no one like You! O Lord apply this word in my life and family; in my state and country in Jesus' Name I pray with thanksgiving in Jesus' Name. Amen!!!

Jesus' way of meeting the needs of the people included feeding them supernaturally. He caused an increase in the food available such that the people were all fed and loads of leftover food! A total of five thousand men; not counting the women and the children. Wow! What a Saviour we have in Christ Jesus. His Hand is not too short at all! He Knows all things and can do all things! He is the Lord!!!

Everybody wants to go to Heaven; but nobody wants to die! Yet, the only formula for life and living is to seek the Lord God Almighty! Otherwise, He Will Break out and devour you! He owns you anyway; whether you believe in Him or not is irrelevant to the Truth! If you seek Him, He Will be with you. Do not seek evil; lest you die! I am talking about everlasting life and or death! God! Help us who trust absolutely in You to live eternally in Jesus' Name. Amen!!!

How Great is our God? How Great is His Name? He's the Greatest God! Forever the same! He Rolled back the waters, of the mighty red sea; He says I'll never leave you, put your trust in Me! The Power of the Lord is made manifest daily in life; believe and trust in Him and you will live eternally! Don't just say you trust and believe Him and not obey Him; because the proof of your love for God is in obeying Him. Please Help us o Lord to live for You; in obedience to Your every word and in the fear of You in Jesus' Name. Amen!!!

226th Day

THE LORD CAN/WILL CAST OFF IF HE DEEMS FIT; BUT NOT FOREVER! HE WILL YET SHOW HIS GOODNESS; BE FAITHFUL!!!

I have confidence in faith that no matter what I go through in life, no matter how challenging, no matter how negative, no matter how adverse, I will yet see the goodness of the Lord in the land of the living! Therefore, I will wait upon the Lord. He Will Strengthen my heart; that I might wait for Him to Act on my behalf and restore my fullness and my joy!!!

Every adversity is known unto God. No leaf falls even from a tree without the Lord Knowing about it. Therefore, anything that happens to man, God has allowed it. However, when the Lord casts one off or causes grief, it's for a time; after, He Shows mercy and compassion. The Lord does not willingly nor willfully cause grief or affliction upon mankind. Thank You Lord that You are not a man and that You show mercy in Jesus' Name. Amen!!!

Who have I in Heaven but You... there is nothing on earth I desire besides You... my heart and my strength, many times they fail... but there is one truth, that always will prevail... God is the strength of my heart and my portion forever. Amen and Amen! The righteous are saved only of the Lord; He Gives them strength in times of trouble and adversity. God Helps and delivers the righteous from the wicked; because He is their refuge. They rely absolutely on Him as their fortress and refuge in Jesus' Name. Amen!!!

Jesus Christ was not happy with the beheading of John the Baptist although He must have known it was going to happen because of who He (Jesus Christ) is! He therefore withdrew Himself to a quiet and solitary place to mourn him quietly. When the crowds heard of this, they followed Him en mass. He saw them and yet had compassion on them and ministered to their needs; healing those who were sick amongst them! Merciful God!!!

Your lack of appreciation and respect for my work in the Lord within and amongst you has compelled me to act like a fool in boasting about what the Lord Has accomplished through me in your lives! Whereas you ought to commend and appreciate me, you prefer others who have not fared better than I have with you. The only thing that I have not done with you is to make myself a burden unto you. For this, I apologise, I pray you forgive me. Otherwise, the Lord Almighty is Witness between us that I have served you faithfully and in uprightness in Jesus' Name. May He Reward me accordingly in Jesus' Name. Amen!!!

227th Day

PASS ON YOUR KNOWLEDGE AND WISDOM OF GOD TO YOUR CHILDREN WITH INSTRUCTION TO DO LIKEWISE! THEN THEY WILL NOT BE SUBJECT TO FALSE PROPHETS ETC.!!!

Make it a way of life for your family with a view to teaching your children the Word of God. Affix God's Word into your hearts and minds in order to facilitate this lifestyle of holiness, godliness in righteousness in Jesus' Name. Amen! May God Help us to do so increasingly in Jesus' Name. Amen!!!

Can God entrust His Love and Word to you or I? Are we prepared for God really? God does not do anything without first revealing it to his prophets! Hmmm! Abraham was his chief prophet as the father of the Faith then (I can safely conclude?)! Lord please prepare me to be a sanctuary, pure and holy, tried and true; with thanksgiving, I'll be a living, sanctuary for You! In Jesus' Name. Amen!!!

Discipline your children so they will make you proud when they grow up. Spare the rod and spoil the child. It is not evil to discipline children. May God Help us in this evil world of today where children are left to their own devices! Give us a vision from You o Lord so we do not perish. Help us in the pursuit of the vision from You o Lord with Your Guidance in Jesus' Name. Amen! Help us to keep Your Law in Jesus' Name. Amen!!!

I'd rather be a gateman in the Household of my God; than be a king in this evil world! Please Help me o Lord; that Your Word be entrenched in my spirit/heart and that I may follow through with Your Word in my daily living in Jesus' Name. Amen! I want to be where You Are; dwelling in and surrounded by Your Presence in Jesus' Name. Amen!!!

(24) For false christs and false prophets will rise and show great signs and wonders to deceive, if possible, even the elect. Matthew 24:24

Many people are following after signs and wonders (miracles) today and are getting these! But, are these from the Lord God Almighty? Hmmm! Beware believer! Not all that glitters is gold! Follow Jesus Christ faithfully as opposed to following so called men and women of God?!!

Satan, the king of darkness will use deception and evil powers to create miracles, signs and wonders so he can increase in following. Believers please beware to follow the Word of God to the letter and very closely so you are not deceived. Please Help us o Lord; Protect us from satanic deception in Jesus' Name. Amen!!!

Judgment Day is coming and there will be plenty of surprises! Many who assume that Heaven is theirs will be shocked! Jesus Has Truth on them and will rebuke them and reject them on the last day! Lord, please Help my family, self and all who look up to You not to fail on that Day in Jesus' Name. Amen!!!

228th Day

HUSBANDS AND WIVES ARE URGED: BY FAITH, LOVE AND ENJOY ONE ANOTHER; AND THE WIFE TO RESPECT HER HUSBAND!!!

Marriage is essentially about two people becoming as ONE; united by faith in God's Love! This is a profound mystery when we consider. However, likewise with Jesus Christ and the Church! The husband MUST love his wife as himself and the wife MUST respect (honour) her husband! Are you obeying the Word of God?!! Hmm!!!

Who cares about these Godly values and instructions to women for today? How many women care about sobriety, loving the husband and children, being discreet, chaste, home keepers, good, obedient to their husbands etc. today? How many husbands remain in the Word of God to lead the home with God's Love? It's no wonder that things fall apart in marriages today; the Word of God is dishonoured and disobeyed generally! In disobeying the Word of God, we malign the Word of God and cause others to do likewise. May God Help us to return to our first Love!!!

Instead of abandoning your wife in a state of neglect, you should strive to enjoy life with her; as this is an opportunity Given to you by God Almighty in the short time you have together as husband and wife on earth! Please Help us o Lord to receive Your Wisdom to live life according to Your Word in Jesus' Name. Amen!!!

Faith is very crucial if we hope to please God; and is it not in our best interests to please God? To please God, you must come to Him alright; how can you come to God unless you believe that He exists and actually rewards all who diligently seek Him? Thank God, praise Him and pray ceaselessly in Jesus' Name. Amen!!!

229th Day

YOU WANT TO ENJOY PROTECTION, SAFETY AND LIVE LONG? THEN FEAR GOD AND OBEY HIS WORD/COMMANDMENTS!!!

Length of days is relative to your obedience to the Word of God! Honour your father and mother is also linked to life span! I urge all not to try God nor take Him for granted because He's a Loving God but also an all-consuming fire! Obey the Word of God and live long; honour your parents and live long. This is the unshakeable Word of God! To obey is better than sacrifice!!!

Do you believe God? If you do not know, then please find out. But if you know that this word applies to you, then know for sure that God is Faithful to His Word always. When He Promises, He NEVER fails! His Promise is very clear; He Made you and has been with you ever since and will be with you till you are old and grey! He Will protect, sustain, deliver, carry and rescue you etc. He is true to His Word! Halleluyah! Amen!! Thank You Lord Jesus!!! I have a great heritage in Christ Jesus!!!

So you want wisdom and understanding? Well, if you will fear the Lord, you will begin to get wisdom; and if you learn to know Him, you will accrue understanding! However, mankind finds this so difficult to do because of sin. It is a big battle for us to fear God and learn to know Him, even though, He readily makes Himself available to all who would humble themselves and come to Him as little children! Hmmm! Lord, Help me to humble myself in Jesus' Name; so I can learn to fear You and learn to know You in Jesus' Name. Amen!!!

Look at the manner of persecution suffered by John the Baptist! Good Lord! Have mercy! Herod didn't like the man because he rebuked him for sleeping with his brother's wife. Herod obviously passed on his hatred of John the Baptist to his wife, who at the earliest opportunity prompted her daughter to ask for John's head! The king's word had gone out and could not be changed to give the young lady whatever she asked for! Alas! She asked for the head of John the Baptist! Hmmm! Did John do anything to deserve this? Why did God allow it? Didn't Jesus Christ know what was happening? Why didn't He Help John? The thoughts and ways of God differ from those of man indeed! God is all-knowing, all-wise and all in all! If God allows a thing, it is for His Good, Acceptable and Perfect Will's sake. Therefore, fret not folks!!!

This God is so Great! He does whatever pleases Him! Who can challenge Him or tell Him how to run His creation? Hmmm! He is to be worshiped, feared and adored! He puts checks and balances in place; He Knows exactly how to punish even those He Loves who go out of line in order that they might be saved ultimately! The above are a type of people created for a purpose ordained by God to discipline nations. So, everything you see and are experiencing is known to God and actually part of God's Sovereign Plan! God is Great!!!

230th Day

"WORK AND EAT"; EARN YOUR PAY/WAY; ENJOY YOUR LABOUR! RIGHTEOUSNESS ATTRACTS PERSECUTION! SATAN COMES ALSO WITH LYING POWER, SIGNS AND WONDERS. BEWARE!!!

There is a football game we used to play as children growing up in Ibadan, Nigeria called "work and jeba" or "work and eat" (another name for "o", "j", "o", "ojo")! You allow the ball to bounce three times and the game starts. It's a local fair play way of starting the game without favouring any of the two teams playing. In a way it's about struggling for the ball from the start and if your team scores, that's your gain! Reflect on this in terms of the Scripture above and it begins to make new sense though the contents are very obvious. The message is very clear; do not be idle. For the devil finds work for idle hands according to the wisdom of our elders. Otherwise you become busy bodies and gossip mongers when idle. The Word is laid down that if a man will not work, there shall be no food for him. You must work for your takings and or food or things you need! May God Help us to understand and appreciate this principle emphasizing value for hard work which is today lacking in most societies! In Jesus' Name. Amen!!!

Life is never easy for the lazy man at all; his life is not enviable. Do not be like him; it will not profit you at all. However, laziness is not part of righteousness; for the life of a righteous man is made plain, less complicated. This is the Word of God. Take heed and be blessed in Jesus' Name. Amen!!!

If God Grants you means to acquire wealth and riches, He Enables you to profit from, benefit and enjoy from your largess! This is God's way of Rewarding your bother or your hustle Rejoice, be grateful to God and remember the poor; because all of this comes from the Lord and it will pleas God that you remember the poor!!!

Righteousness always attracts persecution. Jesus Christ was so targeted ultimately as was John the Baptist, whom Herod had reason to hate and want dead because he preached against him having his brother's wife. He later killed him. When he heard about Jesus Christ he thought John had arisen from the dead to haunt him perhaps. This is the Word of God; nobody who follows Jesus Christ faithfully will not be persecuted. May God Grant us strength with courage and resolve to follow Him faithfully in Jesus' Name. Amen!!!

The Day of the Lord will not come until the lawless man of perdition has been revealed, the man of sin! The revelation of that man will include and involve the manifestation of satanic power with the working of miracles, signs and lying wonders. This will occur with the unrighteous deception amongst those perishing because they did not receive the love of truth unto salvation. For this reason, God Will Send them a strong delusion to believe lies so they can be condemned who rather than believe the truth revealed in unrighteousness! Beware and be warned! If you want to be saved, work according to and walk in the way of righteousness in Jesus' Name. Amen!!!

231st Day

NOTHING WILL COME BETWEEN THE LORD JESUS CHRIST AND I; WHETHER I HAVE OR WANT, I HAVE MY SUFFICIENCY IN JESUS!!!

I love my Jesus; my Jesus loves me; no circumstances can change my decision! Heaven and earth shall pass away but the Word of God Stands forever in Jesus' Name. Good or evil; nothing shall come between the Lord and I. Nothing will pluck me from His Holy and Mighty Hand. I am His and He is mine forever. Amen!!!

I am confident that the Lord Will Save me from all evil and negativity that may come against me in my life. So, no matter what I face, I will never give in to fear; because fear is not of God and will only lead one to hell. I want to go to Heaven when I leave this earth; so, I will trust in the Name of the Lord Jesus Christ. I'll live for Jesus. day after day; I'll live for Jesus, then come what may; His Holy Spirit, I will obey; I'll live for Jesus, day after day!!!

I have learnt to live with and without; I have learnt to survive in plenty and in dire need (including hunger). I have strength to do all things through Jesus Christ who gives me strength! Therefore, I am Blessed in my coming in and going out; in the fields and at home; in whatever I do or not, I am so very Blessed. For this reason, I give thanks endlessly even as I pray unto the Lord Jesus Christ, my Lord, God and Saviour. It is well with me and mine in Jesus' Name. Amen!!!

For no just cause, people will take offence against the true servant of God no matter what you do. Remember, they did the same and worse to our Lord Jesus Christ and hold your peace! You will not always have success spiritually wherever you preach or witness to the Word of God; not because God is not listening or has left you, but because the people themselves lack faith! A prophet is without honour in his own home, town and abode! Take heed the Word of God!!!

Every prophetic word is confirmed; because if the Lord Said it, He'll bring it to pass! The Word is God is Light that shines in darkness! One day, the Day shall dawn and the Morning Star shall arise in our hearts (those of us who believe). Behold, no prophecy in Scripture is of private interpretation. Prophecy is not inspired by the will of mankind; but rather by the Inspiration of the Holy Spirit (note not ghost)! The Word of God came not by man's will as many believe and teach; but rather by the Holy Spirit of God Almighty in Jesus' Name. Amen!!!

232nd Day

BE COMPLETELY HUMBLE ALWAYS AND REMEMBER THAT IN LEADERSHIP, YOUR AUTHORITY WILL BE QUESTIONED!!!

The Lord God Almighty loves the humble; and because they humble themselves, God Raises them up in every way. It pays to be completely humble in every way. How many will heed this word and actually strive for complete humility in all ways? Help my family and I o Lord and all who look faithfully unto You to be completely humble in all ways and always in Jesus' Name. Amen!!!

The Lord our God is upright and although He is God, He does not despise mankind. This is why He considers sinners who humble themselves and pray to Him for forgiveness and the grace to live clean. He Teaches sinners as He does the humble His Way. O Lord, consider me favourably and Teach me Your Ways o Lord and Help me to live within The Way in Jesus' Name. Amen!!!

The poor are almost always humble because of the very nature of their circumstances; therefore, like the humble, they increase in the joy of the Lord (which is their strength), the Holy One of Israel!!!

When you are Called of the Lord, be prepared; for your authority will be questioned even to the point of ridicule almost wherever you turn. This happened first to our Master/Teacher, Jesus Christ; so don't be surprised! Even your circumstances and the people's knowledge of you will be used against you; to ridicule you and even malign your name - all in their effort to challenge/question your authority when the Lord is Working through/ in you!!!

Young people in particular should take note of the above as well as older people who have lived according to the Word of God. The former, so they can heed the Word of God and the latter so they know not to stray from the Word of God. Respect elders and be humble in disposition always; for God opposes the proud and gives grace to the humble. Who is on the Lord's Side?!!

233rd Day

LIVE IN THE LIGHT OF LOVE; LOVE FULFILLS THE LAWS OF THE KINGDOM OF GOD (PEARLS, A TREASURE)! ARE YOU A DISCIPLE OF LOVE'S TERRAIN?!!

Do you hate your brother/sister or indeed anyone? No, you can't do that and yet have love in you! You live in darkness! You will live in Light only if you love; then nothing will make you stumble! God Will Hold you up if you will just love! The choice is yours; and that's the truth. LOVE!!!

For some of you folks, you do not need to be taught about brotherly love because God Has already taught you about love and in practice, love is evident in you. I congratulate you. This is for you who do not hate your brethren or anyone. Will those who truly have love please stand up and identify yourselves!!!

As those Chosen by God (believers) you must wear a heart of love; you must forgive each other and bear with each other always. Love must be at work in your lives and in your midst always in Jesus' Name. This is the only way the world will see you and know that you are of the Lord! Take note and comply for your own good!!!

Jesus Taught them and asked them if they had understood. What a Great Teacher our Lord Jesus IS! Every one versed in teaching the Law and the Prophets who has also become versed in the Word of God, in the Kingdom of Heaven is like one who owns a house and brings out treasures, both new and old! Therefore it is beneficial to the Faith that we are well versed in the totality of God's Word. No part of the Word of God is archaic at all!!!

You must not conform to the way of this world! Present your body to God, holy and acceptable, as a living sacrifice by God's Mercies! This is your responsibility unto the Lord as a service. Your mind must be renewed, transformed into the likeness of that of God and the way of God, holiness and righteousness. This way, you may prove in your living the good, acceptable and perfect Will of God daily in Jesus' Name. Amen!!!

234th Day

PATIENCE IS A VIRTUE; IT CAN BE LEARNT! LEARN PATIENCE; IT'S THE VERY FIRST ASPECT OF GOD'S LOVE!!!

Be patient until the Lord returns; as the farmer waits patiently for his plantings to come to fruition, then harvest time comes! The Lord's coming is near; don't look at circumstances. Continue to live in hope of the expectation of Glory which shall be revealed with the Lord's coming because He is Coming!!!

Doing good can at times seem so boring and exhaustive; don't give up - because at the right time the harvest will come if you don't give up! As the opportunity arises, do good unto all people, especially those who are believers. This is the Word of the Lord to all believers and all who will obey this word. God Will Bless and never forsake your doing good in Jesus' Name. Amen!!!

Suffering is not such a terrible thing as many make it out to be; for through suffering we develop strength spiritually! Perseverance, character, hope etc. all develop in the individual afflicted with suffering. When these virtues are acquired, it's of tremendous benefit to the believer! But if you suffer, let it be for the sake of Jesus Christ; not for the sake of wrongdoing or sin!!!

In Christ Jesus, you become a new being; the old having passed and the new made manifest. Through Jesus Christ, God reconciles mankind unto Himself; forgiving their sins and giving them a new slate so to speak! So, now in Jesus Christ, you become an ambassador for Jesus Christ with the ministry of reconciliation; i.e. doing what Jesus did for you for others through your witnessing Jesus Christ unto them. Remember that Jesus Christ was made sin in our stead that we may be the righteousness of God in Christ Jesus. Jesus Christ is the Lord God Almighty!!!

The Lord God is Almighty! Heaven is His Throne and the earth is His Footstool! What house can you really build for Him that will ever contain Him? None! However, He abides with the poor and contrite in heart and spirit, who trembles at His Word! God is particularly close to the broken hearted!!!

235th Day

IS YOUR FAITH AND LOVE GROWING? FAITH THAT WORKS THROUGH LOVE IS ALL THAT MATTERS IN CHRIST JESUS!!!

We ought always to thank God for you, brothers, and rightly so, because your faith is growing more and more, and the love every one of you has for each other is increasing. Thessalonians 1:3 NIV

Is your life and mine worthy of thanksgiving unto the Lord when reviewed by others? Is your life indeed edifying at all? Can people benefit or learn from your life? Test (check) yourself, are you still in the Faith? The above Scripture is a testament to the lives of those the words are directed at. It is basically saying that thanksgiving is due and in order because their faith and love are growing and increasing respectively. Blessed be the Name of the Lord God Almighty in Jesus' Name. May our lives incur such a blessed testament and be an encouragement to the lives of others in Jesus' Name. Amen!!!

I press toward the mark for the prize of the high calling of God in Christ Jesus. Let us therefore as many as be perfect be thus minded; and if in anything ye be otherwise minded, God shall reveal even this unto you. Nevertheless, whereto we have already attained, let us walk by the same rule, let us mind the same thing. Philippians 3:14-16 KJV

As believers we must emulate the Apostle who wrote these words for us in the Name of the Lord Jesus Christ! We must keep pressing forward towards the purpose of God for our lives which is the Call in Jesus Christ and maintain such a mindset. If there are areas where this mindset is absent in us, may the Lord Reveal such to us and Correct us in Jesus' Name. But we ought to live according to our faith (wherever it's at). The just shall live by faith according to the Word of the Living God!!!

Regardless of whatever happens, the righteous with clean hands will increase and grow stronger and higher in Jesus' Name. Yorubas say oke loke l'owo afunni ngbe (the hand of the giver will always be right on top). Righteousness pays off; let us all strive for holiness and righteousness always in Jesus' Name. Amen!!!

Although our God is High and Mighty, He never forsakes the weak, lowly and downtrodden! However, not so for the arrogant, prideful and haughty; whom the Lord Knows from afar! The Right Hand of the Lord Delivers the righteous who fear the Lord always from the power of their enemies. The steadfast love of my Lord never ceases; His Mercies never come to an end. They are renewed every morning; great is His Faithfulness! The Lord's purpose for my life shall be fulfilled in Jesus' Name. Amen!!!

Do you want to delight yourself in the Lord so He Will Delight in you? Then obey His Commandments! Not just about the Sabbath; but in all of His Ways and His Word! Then the Lord Will Bless you and take you on High. He Spoke this Word and if you obey Him, He Will Deliver in Jesus' Name. Lord, please Help us who follow You sincerely to obey your Word and Bless us in Jesus' Name. Amen!!!

236th Day

THE LOVE OF GOD IN JESUS CHRIST IS MULTIFACETED; WORTHY OF REFLECTION UPON! COUNT YOUR BLESSINGS!!!

We love Him because He first loved us. 1 John 4:19 KJV

Oh how I love Jesus... oh how I love Jesus... oh how I love Jesus... because He first loved me! Even if you love Jesus Christ truly, never forget that He first loved you; and it was your choice, by His Grace, to accept His Love and believe in His Name and Sacrifice and then follow Him. Never forget this!!!

Loving Jesus may be spoken by anybody; however, the one who loves Jesus truly is the one who first of all has His Commandments and obeys them. Whoever does this will be loved by the Father and the Son and He Will show Himself to such a person! Indeed the Word of God says that He and the Father will come and make their home with such a person! So, will you love the Lord? Would you want the Father and the Son to make their home with you? The choice is yours now folks; the Lord Has Spoken!!!

A prayer for the saints; that the Lord Jesus Christ, the Father, the One who has Loved us and given us hope and eternal comfort by His Grace. May He comfort and strengthen our hearts through His Word and every good work. Nobody does any good all by themselves. God Enables all goodness. May God Bless us in Jesus' Name. Amen!!!

Another analogy for the Kingdom of Heaven is like the fisherman's net which was let down and catches fishes of all sorts (good and bad). It is easy to assume that all fishes are good. Hmmm. Not so, according to the Word of God. Then comes the sorting; when the good fishes are collected and separated from the bad ones which are thrown away. Again, this is indicative of the end time when the angels of God will separate the wicked from the righteous and the wicked will be thrown into the eternal furnace with gnashing of teeth and weeping. The righteous will proceed into Eternal Life in Jesus Christ. Amen!!!

There will be times of intense need, a scarcity indicative of the wrath of God. But during such times, there will be plenty available unto the elect of God. So, even though there will be a famine of common foodstuffs; the oil and the wine will be plentiful. This represents the fellowship and all that it will take to keep fellowship alive in the Name of the Lord. Also, the oil and the wine (fruits of the vine and produce from it) shall not be scarce in Jesus' Name. So, pray and strive for righteousness so that in the famine, you will not lack in Jesus' Name. But rather, you will have an abundance in Jesus' Name. Amen!!!

237th Day

JESUS CHRIST: SAVIOUR, FORGIVER OF SINS, COMING BACK AGAIN! GOD'S KINGDOM: A GREAT TREASURE; GET IN NOW!!!

She will give birth to a son, and you are to give him the name Jesus, because he will save his people from their sins." Matthew 1:21 NIV

This prophecy is specifically about the advent of the Lord Jesus Christ as Saviour; and it came to pass. The rest is history. Very apt and significant for all who care to believe!!!

The disciples went around witnessing to the advent of Jesus Christ, whom they had experienced personally. Though now, Risen and Ascended unto Heaven, yet still very present in the Holy Spirit, which the world cannot see. With Jesus Christ, justification is by faith in the forgiveness of sins and primarily faith in Him and in His Name. Amen!!!

It is appointed unto mankind, once to die and after that judgment; likewise, Jesus Christ was offered once for the sins of all mankind. He's however coming back a second time. Jesus is coming back again; soon and very soon. He's coming back for those who eagerly await His Coming!!!

The Kingdom of God is so seriously significant and valuable that it is likened unto a great treasure and or pearls hidden in fields. When found, the finder sells everything he/she has to buy the field where it is found. God is Great; and so is His Kingdom. Strive to enter in at all costs!!!

The Body of Christ is of immense value and believers must eat of it and drink also of His Blood in remembrance of the sacrifice of Jesus Christ. However, before partaking of the eating and drinking, each person is to examine him/herself to be sure that they partake in a worthy manner, discerning and deserving of being a partaker. Otherwise, they drink and eat judgment upon themselves. God is Love and God is so good; but we must fear God and deal sensitively, truthfully and in holiness and righteously with Him always!!!

238th Day

HE'S COMING BACK AGAIN; MY LORD IS COMING BACK AGAIN! JESUS CHRIST IS COMING BACK AGAIN! HE'S THE JUDGE!!!

The Lord Will Perform outstanding feats that will leave no one in doubts about who He Is. As a result, the nations and kings of the earth will fear the Lord and revere His Glory! He Will rebuild Zion and appear in His Glory. He's Coming back again; Jesus Christ is coming back again!!!

The Lord Will Cause the whole world to remember Him by His mighty deeds and they will turn to Him and worship before Him; for His is the Kingdom and He's the Ruler/Governor over all! Jesus Rules. God Rules!!!

A Voice (the messengers of the Lord) telling all to basically prepare and make way for the coming of the Lord. Every valley shall be raised and every mountain be made low; rough grounds shall be made plain and rugged terrain shall be made into broad valleys in readiness for His Coming. They shall the Glory of the Lord be Revealed for all flesh to see and behold. The mouth of the Lord Spoke this and it shall come to pass in Jesus' Name. Amen!!!

The Lord Shall Send His angels to purge out His Kingdom; they shall weed out all causes of sin and evil and all that is evil and sinful. They shall be thrown into the fiery furnace where there shall be everlasting weeping and gnashing of teeth. But the righteous ones shall shine like the sun in the Lord's Kingdom. He who has ears, let him hear what the Spirit is saying to the Church. Forsake evil now and embrace good; faith that works through love. The time is very near now! Be prepared in and out of season!!!

Even though most if not all that were close to Him disappeared from Him in the end, God did not allow Him to have no help at all even in death. God stirred the heart of a man, Joseph of Arimathea to go to Pilate and request for the Lord's Body to take good care of His Body and place Him is a brand new resting place (tomb) fit for kings. He is the Lord!!!

239th Day

THERE IS TREMENDOUS BENEFIT IN PLEASING THE LORD BUT DO YOU REALLY CARE TO PLEASE GOD IN YOUR LIVING?!!

When our hearts do not condemn us, then our consciences are clear and we have confidence to approach the Throne of Grace to ask whatever we desire. This is because we are obedient to His Commandments and please Him in our daily living! What is His Command? Just simply to believe in the Name of Jesus Christ, His Son; and to love one another as He Commanded! Who cares? Well, I do! Please o Lord, Help me to serve You diligently and conscientiously in Jesus' Name. Amen!!!

Believers ought to have an ambition; to please God, whether at home or absent. There will be judgment for all. For we shall all appear at the Judgment Seat of Jesus Christ to receive our rewards for our thoughts, words and deeds whilst in the body (good or bad)!!!

Approval by God for anyone is about how much the person can endure pain with the mind of God when suffering unjustly. Who can endure this way? That is a test of true faith; not avoiding or praying against suffering! Alas! Wrong teaching endures! When you do right and suffer for it and you take it with patience because you know that God Will Make it alright, then you have God's Approval! This is following Jesus Christ's example! Are you following Jesus' example? Who is your role model?!!

In the parable of the sower, the sower of good seeds is the Son of Man (Jesus Christ)! The world is the field. The good seed are the children of the Kingdom of God whilst the weeds are the children of the evil one (believe that both exist in this world), the seeds of which are sown by the devil! The harvest is the end of the age/time and the angels of God are the harvesters! O Lord, Help my family and I and all who truly are Yours to be amongst the Kingdom seeds to be harvested unto the Lord Jesus Christ at the end in Jesus' Name. Amen!!!

How quickly people's faith can be destroyed without constant encouragement and feeding. If you are being fed, please appreciate it; if not, learn to feed for yourself. As believers we ought to appreciate and encourage each other as iron sharpens iron for mutual sustenance in the faith in Jesus' Name. For maturity is about learning to feed yourself spiritually based on lessons learnt from those who fed you before. I do not want to bow to any idols in my life o Lord; feed me till I want no more o Lord in Jesus' Name. Amen!!!

240th Day

BLESSINGS FOR OBEDIENCE; CURSES FOR DISOBEDIENCE - AN ORDINANCE ETERNALLY RELEVANT! BEST TO OBEY!!!

The Word of God is so very clear on this! But mankind choses to malign God's Word and do what pleases them rather than God! Obedience truly attracts God's attention for Blessings; disobedience on the other hand automatically incurs a curse whether you are aware of it or not. This is the Word of God. Thank God for Jesus Christ. O yes! But has the principle changed? I say no. So, be careful to strive towards obeying the Word of God who Justifies the doers of His Word not the hearers. Hmmm!!!

This is the beginning of the delivery of the Ten Commandments to the children of Israel with the admonition to listen and take care to obey (do) the Commandments of God. Has this changed today because of the advent of Jesus Christ? Again, I say no. Jesus Christ made clear that He did not come to abolish the law but to fulfill the law! I cannot accept that this renders the law irrelevant and archaic! Rather a confirmation of the need to obey the laws of God!!!

Who is your family? Jesus made clear that His family are those who obey the Will of the Father! Should we not emulate Him? Do we? If not what is stopping us? Disobedience and sin! Let us set aside the attractions and sweetness of sin for the discomfort and pains of sticking to truth and obeying the Word of God; meaning to discipline ourselves - because it takes discipline to obey the Word of God as we have to die to our fleshly nature!!!

The power and benefit of humility and perseverance is evident in this short story to the Glory of God! The woman could have said Jesus was arrogant and unkind to her and thus gotten upset and left without her desire being met. But no, she humbled herself and took what was said to her and responded sincerely with wisdom and faith which got the attention of Jesus Christ and her desire for her severely demon possessed daughter to be healed was met immediately, at that particular hour! O what a God we serve and follow. Thank You Lord Jesus for Your Mercy and loving kindness!!!

241st Day

SOON AND VERY SOON, WE ARE GOING TO SEE THE LORD; HE'S COMING BACK; JESUS CHRIST IS COMING BACK SOON! BETTER BE PREPARED IN AND OUT OF SEASON!!!

Meditate on these words from the Throne of Grace and Mercy! The Word of God stands firm forever; but there will be lustful scoffers who will challenge the Word of God freely, with "logical" arguments that would make "sense" to people of a feeble mind and nature who do not have faith nor the Holy Spirit! The silence of a lion is not that of cowardice (Yoruba saying: didake ekun bi ti ojo ko)! The Lord is not slow concerning His promises at all; but rather offering a very long rope for those willing to be saved. Soon and very soon, there will be finality and the Lord Will come for sure!!!

The Lord encourages us who believe to be gentle and humble in disposition unto all mankind; ready and willing to teach, patient in every way as we do the work of an evangelist! God is Able to Touch the hearts of mankind unto repentance; so they can free themselves from the snare of the devil by believing in the Name of the Lord Jesus Christ!!!

I am facing diverse calamities o Lord; yet I will hope and trust in you steadfastly in faith that You o Lord will deliver me. You o Lord will defend and uphold my cause even with my enemy who surround me night and day ready to destroy me. You will not let them see their desire come to pass over my life and family in Jesus' Name. Save me o Lord; I trust in and lean on Your unfailing Grace, Mercy and Protection. You will never leave nor forsake me o Lord in Jesus' Name. Amen!!!

This is a sneak preview of what it will be like on the Day of the Lord! Be prepared folks in and out of season; because the Lord Will come at a time when no one is suspecting. He is coming and it will not be so long. Remember that a day in the eyes of the Lord is like a thousand years and vice-versa! May God Help us to stand on that Day in Jesus' Name. Amen!!!

242nd Day

IT WILL NOT GO WELL WITH THE DISHONEST AND ARROGANT ULTIMATELY; IN HELPING ANYONE, HUMBLE YOURSELF! A SURE REWARD AWAITS THE OBEDIENT AND RIGHTEOUS!!!

What is it to do what is listed above? Deception and dishonesty of sorts. Who is wise and clever in their own eyes? A fool. Please God Help us to be wise in Your Eyes not in our own eyes in Jesus' Name. Teach us Your Wisdom and Give us the heart and spirit to obey Your Word and keep to Your Teaching and Wisdom in Jesus' Name. Amen!!!

Nobody is perfect and without fault; for all have sinned and fallen short of the Glory of the Lord! However, some would be available to help those who fall to stand again. These would be the spiritual ones amongst the people. Such must help the others with humility and due care and diligence so you are not tempted into sin too! Help carry each other's burdens in the love of Jesus Christ! Pride and arrogance even in thinking one is something when one is not is deception! Stop deceiving yourself!!!

Humans love themselves to the point of arrogance which is not the type of love God recommends for us. Self-approval is meaningless in the scheme of things according to God; it is not when you commend and approve yourself that you are so. Rather, whom God approves and commends is the one that stands so! Submit to and humble yourself before God and He Will Bless and Lift you up in Jesus' Name. Amen!!!

Whenever you lend a hand to others in any way thereby showing love, you do this for the Lord Jesus Christ and your reward awaits! Do works of charity as the Lord Leads you. Even if unsure it's the leading of the Lord, do it anyway. Remember, whatsoever you do unto one of My brothers, that you do unto Me says the Lord Jesus Christ. Selah!!!

243rd Day

THERE IS POWER FOR TRANSFORMATION, HEALING AND PROTECTION FULLY IN THE BLOOD OF JESUS; ON HIS SIDE!!!

The Lord God Almighty never promised that when you are on His Side you will never have enemies that will come against you time and time again! No! However, He gives us full assurance that our enemies will be defeated in our presence (before us)! Even though they might come against us from one direction (could be more), they will be dealt such a blow that they will flee in multiples of seven directions per line of attacking us! This is a great message from the Lord for they that believe! Do you believe? So, why do you fear so much? Fear not; at least not if your hope and trust you put firmly in the Lord God Almighty in Jesus Christ! Amen!!!

Why has the Lord made these promises? Of course there is a reason behind everything God does. He's not a flippant nor an idle God! It's all so we may serve Him fearlessly; but in holiness and righteousness before Him all the days of our lives! Who is on the Lord's Side? Who is prepared to serve Him as He Designed it to be? Who is ready to follow His pattern and standard! We make all sorts of excuses just not to do His Will; including saying that His Standard is archaic and must be "modernised"!!!

The Lord Empowers those who believe in Him to condemn every accusing tongue in judgment; and will never allow any weapon formed against us to prosper. He will frustrate all the plans of our enemies and foil their attacks! This is the heritage of God's servants and their vindication from the Lord!!!

Still on the Kingdom of Heaven; Jesus told the people that it's potential is such that it will spread like a little yeast that is mixed into a sizable amount of flour that works through all of the flour. Jesus always spoke in parables in fulfillment of Biblical prophecy; that He would speak in parables about things hidden since the world began! O! The depths of the richness of the Wisdom of God!!!

Now the Lord is Reaching and Calling out to all and sundry to come and listen; learn fearfully (of God) of the ways of God and the fear of God which is the beginning of all wisdom. Wisdom is crying out in the street corners and every nook and cranny! Anyone listening? Hmmm! Yes Lord! I want the Wisdom of God for my life; please give me Your Wisdom in Jesus' Name. Amen!!!

244th Day

THE KINGDOM OF HEAVEN POWERED BY FAITH COMES ALIVE AND IS BRIGHTLY LIT UP!!!

The mustard seed is the smallest of all seeds; it is however completely transformed when it is planted! It then grows into a great big tree with lots of branches where birds come and perch; with a great big shade where mankind come to rest awhile from the scorching heat of the sun! What great potential in a tiny mustard seed. Jesus used this analogy in the parable to explain to the people what the Kingdom of Heaven is like. Hmmm. How very interesting. I want that Kingdom. I want to be a part of that Kingdom. I want to be in that Kingdom. I want to spend Eternity in that Kingdom. Anyone joining me? Jesus please make it possible for me to be with You in that Kingdom. The great big Kingdom Powered by faith. So much so that if you have faith as small as a mustard seed, you will say to this mountain, be removed and located in the sea and it will obey you! Hmmm. That is the power of faith. Amen!!!

What is faith that makes it so powerful as a force; so powerful that it lights up a whole life or even race? Faith is not seeing is believing. Faith is being sure of what you hope for and certain of what you have not seen. Faith is the substance of things hoped for and evidence of things unseen! Even though you have not seen it, you believe you have received it. Faith does not make sense; it's not supposed to! Faith is not about sense (common or not)! Abraham was called to go out to a place he knew not and without a clue as to what would happen to him or how things would pan out! He just got up and went! That place was his inheritance (he was given that place). Had he not obeyed, he would have lost his heritage! This is the lot of the disobedient! Will you obey henceforth? Hmmm! Please Help us o God!!!

245th Day

JESUS CHRIST DELIVERS NOT JUST FROM EVIL AND WICKEDNESS, BUT ALSO FROM DEATH! HE WILL DELIVER YOU!!!

When needy and or faced with evildoers (the wicked), cry out to the Lord, for He Will Deliver you! When afflicted and there's no one to help you, lean upon the Lord, cry out to Him, He Will Save you! When you are weak, needy, afflicted, oppressed, etc., even unto the point of death, there is a Saviour who will take pity on you if you will just cry out to Him; and He Will Deliver you. He is the King of kings, Lord of lords, Prince of peace, He is Jesus Christ our Lord God and Saviour! Put your hope and trust in Him!!!

The Lord has chosen Zion for His Temple forever! However, for us who trust and hope in Him, do you understand what or where our Zion is? Let me tell you what the Lord Told me. Zion for us represents our bodies. Does not the Bible tell us clearly that our body is the Temple of the Living God and must be kept holy? The Lord is coming back again and what will He Take with Him? His Temple! We shall all be changed in the twinkle of an eye; from mortality to immortality! Your body is the Temple of the Holy Spirit of God which is God the Father, Son and Holy Spirit! Stop abusing your body or doing what displeases God with it! God Will Deliver you from all evil if you ask Him! Have you asked Him before giving up?!!

The owner of the vineyard has servants tending the land for him and they came to ask him how come weeds are growing as well as the good seeds in his field. He told them not to pull them up for they might also pull up the good wheat seeds with the weeds. Rather, to let them grow together until the good seeds are ready for harvesting. Then he would instruct that the weeds be gathered first for burning up then the wheat gathered and taken to the barn! What wisdom. O Lord! Please Help us to be wise in all of our undertakings in Jesus' Name. Amen!!!

When things are not going our way, we say rash things about God; a reflection of our thinking, which serve as guide for our actions! During such times, it looks as if our faith is in vain and there is no profit for our believing God. Hmmmm! At such times, we think that all our humbling ourselves has gone in vain etc. But why? It's because we see the evil doers and those who do not fear God prosper. So, we join up with the world and begin to call the proud and arrogant blessed. Those who disrespect and show disdain for God and His Word, we see to be exalted in the lands and are impressed. Hmmm! Don't buy the lie! Appearances deceive! Even though what you observe may be true; it is only an appearance and soon enough the wicked will be cut down and their wealth is held in store for the righteous! Trust God and strive for holiness in living always! Honour God always for this is profitable in the long run!!!

246th Day

BE A BLESSING; BE HOSPITABLE TO ONE ANOTHER! LOVE SEES AND MEETS NEEDS NOT JUST OF SELF BUT OTHERS TOO!!!

Do we even think of others' feelings enough to think about meeting their needs? Even in our immediate families let alone outsiders? Many of us claim to be faithful to God yet we deceive ourselves daily in failing each other and those that God Sends our way daily! If only we would obey God; the Name of the Lord would spread to the unbelievers increasingly through us! May God Help us to be faithful to Jesus Christ and obey His Word to LOVE one another; through which the world would see and know that we are His disciples!!!

When you see your brethren are in need and you are in a position to help and you don't; what do you think you are doing? You are shutting up your bowels of love from your brethren! Does that show that you have the love of God? Is it not easy to love with our mouth? I love you I love you I love you! Sweet to hear but very painful when not followed up with action! Lord, Help us to love one another truly as You Taught us in Jesus' Name. Amen!!!

When you see and meet others' needs, you are meeting the needs of our Lord Jesus Christ whether you are aware of it or not! Your reward is sure when you do this! Otherwise, your reward is also sure; but in the opposite sense! For God cannot be mocked; we shall all reap whatever we have sown. To obey is better than sacrifice!!!

Hmmm! So, don't be surprised that there's a good measure of insincerity, hatred and general chaos wherever the Spirit of God is at work today! Satan is on the prowl looking for whom to devour! God has His Plan and Purpose though; for the believer, God's Plan and Purpose is good, acceptable and perfect in Jesus' Christ!!!

The body of Christ must be built up through Godly Standard made available through the Gifts of the Holy Spirit to the body of Christ. This is to help steady the ship so that believers will be rock solid as should be in

Jesus Christ! Only then will they no longer be tossed up and down with diverse winds of doctrines, trickery, cunning, craftiness and deceitful plotting that humankind is capable of! Better to obey God and be on the safe side in Jesus Christ than fall for man's falsehood at the behest of false prophets etc. who have gone out amongst believers. May God Help us to stay on track and on the Lord's side in Jesus' Name. Amen!!!

247th Day

WHO HAS TRUE RICHES? THE RICH/WEALTHY PERSON OR THE ONE WITH FAITH WHO INHERITS THE KINGDOM OF GOD?!!

It's easy for all to despise those who are not rich in the eyes of the world; however, their Maker Has the Power to Choose them for far greater honour that money cannot buy or make happen! The Creator has chosen them to be rich in faith that entitles them to inherit the Kingdom of God which God Promised to those who love Him! This, money cannot buy or make happen! So, who is the greater than an overcomer here? Given the choice, which would you choose? I know which one I have chosen right now; how about you? Hmmm! May God Help us to choose aright in Jesus' Name. Amen!!!

You may not be aware; but when you mock or make fun of the poor, this is considered a reproach to God. Also, when calamities make you happy, God will punish you. So, you had better be very careful how you see life and especially how you see others! God is real and watching everything in life and will give to each one of us according to our attitudes/behaviours!!!

Riches are very deceptive and very nice and can give humankind a false sense of security. If your trust is in your riches, the Bible is saying that you will fall! However, the righteous do not think that way; and they will flourish like the green leaf!!!

Whoever has ears, let them hear. (Matthew 13:9 NIVUK)

The Word of God is written and sometimes spoken! Ignore at your own peril! The wise (who have ears to listen) would be well blessed to listen, hear and heed the Word of God! For those who choose not to heed the Word of God, there will be sure consequences!!!

I believe that God has hardened the hearts of Boko Haram for now and in due season, they will get the "pharaoh and his army" treatment in Jesus' Name! This is my same prayer for those pursuing you and I without a just cause! Evil will not prevail in our land in Jesus' Name. I implore the righteous not to relent in their outcry unto the Lord God Almighty! Our Father in Heaven is a just God!!!

248th Day

WHEN YOU ARE IN THE LORD JESUS CHRIST, YOU NEED NOT FEAR; NO FEAR IN LOVE! TRUST JESUS TOTALLY; FEAR NOT!!!

In life, we're surrounded with fear, but they that trust in the Name of the Lord shall renew their strength and fear not. To overcome fear, you must believe that you are covered from and against all evil and wickedness! This is faith. Without faith, you cannot please the Lord anyway! Faith can and does move mountains. Do you believe this? If not, you will fear. If you do however, you are on your way to "no fear"! Lord Help me to believe in You and to overcome fear; come what may, in Jesus' Name. Amen!!!

God reminds and Counsels us of His being there for us and to trust in HIM and not fear any man or things in life; but is anyone listening, let alone believing Him? Faith comes by hearing; hearing by the Word of the Lord! To believe, first you have to hear! Humankind listen but do they hear? Hearing is deep! Anyone can listen; but it takes the grace of God for anyone to hear, let alone believe. Therefore, faith is truly a gift from God. Lord, Help me to receive the gift of faith from You; that I might hear Your Word and increase my faith in Jesus' Name. Amen!!!

But in all these things we overwhelmingly conquer through Him who loved us. For I am convinced that neither death, nor life, nor angels, nor principalities, nor things present, nor things to come, nor powers, nor height, nor depth, nor any other created thing, will be able to separate us from the love of God, which is in Christ Jesus our Lord.

Romans 8:37-39 NASB

In Christ Jesus, we are not given the spirit of fear; but one of Power, Love and a Sound mind! Satan works with and uses fear to trap and destroy souls. Satan causes us to fear mankind, things and situations. Resist the devil and he will flee; easier said than done one might say. However, with God all things are possible; it is very doable! Lord, I am more than a conqueror because I trust and hope ONLY in Your Name (JESUS)! Nothing shall separate me from Your Love in Jesus' Name. Amen!!!

If we're truly willing to learn from the Word of the Lord and be obedient, this passage above is such a blessing! Being subject to authority is a hugely beneficial thing; who cares though? At every excuse (and we usually have many; because no authority is perfect), we disrespect, slander, curse, hate and malign authority in our lives and nations! We forget the Word of God and that we ourselves are not perfect and live by God's Grace! We lack mercy and love and hence fail to pray for those in authority over us and our nations. May God Help us to understand and obey His Word in Jesus' Name. Amen!!!

The Word of God impacts people at differing levels. Some can only handle the milk; which is really the starting point, from which the believer is expected to grow! Gradually, the believer grows into solid food of the Word of God; which is for those who have entered into maturity. They due to constant use (i.e. hearing and obedience by faith), have become able to discern good from evil! The Word of God is a life changer! Prepare for the Word of God; accept the Word of God and use it for daily living for greatest impact by faith (believing the Word Works for you) in Jesus' Name. Amen!!!

249th Day

GIVE THANKS IN ALL SITUATIONS AND REJOICE ALWAYS! WHO CAN DO THIS? WITH GOD ALL THINGS ARE POSSIBLE!!!

No matter what comes my way; positive or negative, I will rejoice in the Lord with a grateful heart! How can anyone rejoice unless there's cause for rejoicing? Rejoicing comes largely if not solely from gratitude! Therefore, you have to cultivate an attitude of gratitude to be able to rejoice all the time and in every situation! Lord, please Help me to see the positive in every situation; that my heart may overflow with rejoicing unto Your Holy Name in Jesus' Name. Amen!!!

Even though I do not see my Lord in the physical, I love Him and believe in Him. I have faith in Him. This faith somehow fills me with inexplicable and inexpressible glorious joy because I am saved. I am free. I know the truth now and the truth has set me free. O thank You Lord Jesus. Halleluyah!! Amen!!!

Those that the Lord my God has redeemed like myself will return to the Lord with joyful noises; filled with everlasting joy, devoid of sorrow, sighing and gnashing of teeth. The joy of the Lord is my strength!!!

If you have faith in the Lord Jesus Christ, you will overflow with love, especially for all the saints (fellow believers)! Faith without love doesn't work. The only thing that matters according to the Word of God is faith that works through LOVE! Love is all in all!!!

250th Day

THE HOLY SPIRIT: OUR DEPOSIT, A GUARANTEE, COUNSELOR TO LEAD US INTO ALL TRUTH AND ALL RIGHTEOUSNESS!!!

Jesus Christ Knew that He was leaving the earth physically and assured His followers that He will not leave them unattended. He Told them that He would come to them; the world would not see Him but His followers would. He Promised them His Holy Spirit "personified"! The world cannot accept "Him" because they cannot see Him and do not know Him! However, the disciples know Him; He lives with them and will be in them! When you have the Holy Spirit, you know! Do you believe? I have the Holy Spirit and believe! Thank You Lord Jesus for a promise fulfilled! You NEVER fail!!!

I will pour out my spirit unto you, I will make known my words unto you. Proverbs 1:23b KJV

In the Word of God, we are promised an outpouring of the Holy Spirit (not ghost); who will reveal the Word of God to us and lead us into all truth and righteousness! The One who Promised is Faithful!!!

This sprinkling of clean water is symbolic of the Holy Spirit; for only the Holy Spirit can cleanse us from all filthiness and all idolatry. Who else can remove our hardened hearts and give us a heart of flesh? Who else would put His Spirit in us and cause us to walk in His Ways and according to His Word? Only the Holy Spirit can do that. Thank You o Lord; for the gift of Your Holy Spirit in Jesus' Name. Amen!!!

We who receive the Holy Spirit must understand that we have not received a worldly spirit; and there is a worldly spirit! However, we have received the Spirit of God and from God, so that we would understand the free gift of God!!!

Now, the gift of God to us which is His Holy Spirit, we carry in our body, which is the temple of the Living God! We must understand and appreciate that the Holy Spirit, the Spirit of God dwells in us; hence, we cannot do as we wish with our bodies! We must not defile our body; otherwise God will destroy us! The temple of God is holy and must be kept holy in Jesus' Name. Amen!!!

251st Day

IS THE LORD YOUR REFUGE? DON'T DECEIVE YOURSELF BECAUSE HE KNOWS THEM WHO RUN TO HIM FOR REFUGE!!!

Many claim to take refuge in the Lord but are only deceiving themselves because they don't. Does God not know those who take refuge in Him? Can anyone mock God? Will not all reap whatever they sow? God is good; that is for sure. He is very reliable in times of trouble as an ever-present help!!!

The LORD also will be a refuge for the oppressed, a refuge in times of trouble. And they that know thy name will put their trust in thee: for thou, LORD, hast not forsaken them that seek thee. Psalm 9:9, 10 KJV

The Lord is not there for any and everybody willy nilly; I keep saying this, but many refuse to take heed! God favours the oppressed and people in specific conditions like orphans, widows, the helpless etc.! God favours those who know His Name and put their trust in Him. He specifically and deliberately takes good care of them!!!

If the LORD delights in a man's way, he makes his steps firm; though he may stumble, he will not fall, for the LORD upholds him with his hand.

Psalm 37:23,24 NIV

When God delights in a man's way, He upholds him. Even when he's about to fall, He holds him up and prevents him from falling. His Hand is firmly upon such a man. Likewise, He causes the enemies of such a man to come back and bow at his feet! Is it not better to be on the Lord's side? As for me and my household, we will serve the Lord in Jesus' Name. Amen!!!

Do not give in to people judging you in your faith based on the old order of things like eating or drinking certain foods or not; and or following after certain festivals etc.! Those are only a shadow of the things to come in the Name of Jesus Christ! Focus on the substance which is Jesus Christ our Lord God and Saviour and you shall not go wrong. Selah!!!

252nd Day

IF YOU BELIEVE AND HOPE IN THE LORD JESUS CHRIST, YOU MUST BE OBEDIENT, CONFIDENT AND COURAGEOUS IN HIM!!!

Be of good courage, and he shall strengthen your heart, all ye that hope in the LORD. Psalm 31:24 KJV

Those of you who fear the Lord and hope in His Name must not be given to fear; be bold and courageous. The Lord shall strengthen your heart; and give you victory. You shall not suffer loss. All things shall work for your good; for you love Him and are called according to His purposes in Jesus' Name. Amen!!!

He gives power to the weak, And to those who have no might He increases strength. Even the youths shall faint and be weary, And the young men shall utterly fall, But those who wait on the LORD Shall renew their strength; They shall mount up with wings like eagles, They shall run and not be weary, They shall walk and not faint. Isaiah 40:29-31 NKJV

When you believe in the Lord, you must believe in the Power of His Might to give you strength whenever you are in need. Even though the strength of the youths shall fail them and the young lions shall go hungry and thirsty; those who wait upon the Lord shall renew their strength. All their needs shall be met as the needs arise in Jesus' Name. This is for certain. Amen!!!

I had fainted, unless I had believed to see the goodness of the LORD in the land of the living. Wait on the LORD: be of good courage, and he shall strengthen thine heart: wait, I say, on the LORD. Psalm 27:13,14 KJV

The testimony of the witness here is that the only reason he did not faint strength-wise is because he believed that he would see the goodness of the Lord in the land of the living. We are encouraged to wait upon Him faithfully believing that He Will come through for us. We must be courageous and be of good cheer and He Will Strengthen our hearts in Jesus' Name. Amen. Do I have a witness? I believe!!!

God is so merciful. When He's going to deal with a nation or a people, He gives them advanced warnings and opportunities for repentance and obedience to His Instructions. Failing this, He then acts decisively. Can we then say He is unjust? The prophecy in the above Scripture came to pass according to the written Word because the people mainly failed to heed the warnings and instructions of the Lord. Hmmm! To obey is better than sacrifice! May God Help us to stay on the Lord's side and obey His Commandments and Instructions in Jesus' Name. Amen!!!

253rd Day

THE MESSENGER OF GOD IS LIKE A FARMER WITH THE WORD OF GOD, SOWING SEEDS; WHO IS RECEPTIVE THOUGH?!!

"Listen then to what the parable of the sower means: When anyone hears the message about the kingdom and does not understand it, the evil one comes and snatches away what was sown in their heart..." Matthew 13:18, 19.

A lack of understanding of the spoken word of God heard by someone is as though the seeds sown in that person's heart fell on the path. The evil one snatches it away even as birds of the air eat the seeds all up! You need to be prepared (with roots) for the Word of God to be rooted in you; otherwise, you're like rocky hard in your heart and the word heard gives you temporary joy, but trouble and persecution cause you to be quickly discouraged and give it all up! The Word of God (seeds) that fall on the thorny heart is unfruitful due to the worries of life and deceitfulness of wealth! The one who hears the Word of God and it is fruitful for him is the one that hears and understands, applies it correctly and for him it yields a bountiful harvest! The Word of God that you hear; what do you do with the Word of God? Is the Word of God working in your life? May God Help us all to let the Word of God bear a bountiful harvest in our lives in Jesus' Name. Amen!!!

Never mind do not murder; just being angry with your brethren could earn you God's judgment, especially without a cause! Even when there is a cause, in your anger do not sin! Simply calling your brother a fool endangers you towards hell fire! So, we all must be very careful with our behaviour and attitude to each other! May God in His Infinite Mercies Help us in Jesus' Name. Amen!!!

254th Day

I AM BLESSED TO HAVE YOU LORD; MAY THOSE WHO FEAR YOU LOOK TO ME! YOU GIVE ME GLORY NOT SHAME!!!

I am completely sold to You o Lord; to Your Word, Salvation and life in Your Ways! Make me approachable to those who fear You. Also make my heart blameless with regard to Your decrees that I may not suffer shame. I am weak with longing for Your salvation o Lord. My hope is in Your Word. Help me for life o Lord in Jesus' Name. Amen!!!

For the scripture saith, "Whosoever believeth on him shall not be ashamed." Romans 10:11 KJV

I will not be put to shame because I believe in You o Lord; this is Your Word to me and I believe!!!

For this reason I also suffer these things, but I am not ashamed; for I know whom I have believed and I am convinced that He is able to guard what I have entrusted to Him until that day. Timothy 1:12 NASB

If and when I suffer for Your Name's sake, I need not feel ashamed; for I know and trust the One that I believe in. I am also certain that He is Able to keep all I have entrusted to Him until the last Day of Judgment!!!

But blessed are your eyes because they see, and your ears because they hear. For truly I tell you, many prophets and righteous people longed to see what you see but did not see it, and to hear what you hear but did not hear it. Matthew 13:16-17 (NIVUK)

I am very Blessed to know the Name of my Lord God and King and experience His Holy Spirit in my life. I didn't experience Him physically or see Him walk the earth; but I experience His Presence as if He is with me physically! Hmmm! Many prayed for and longed to have my experience but didn't; for this, I am eternally grateful!!!

How could the bride be ready except the Lord Made her ready for Himself! It is the Lord's doing and it is marvelous in my eyes! I am privileged to be part of the Lord's bride, the Church of the Living God! I am blessed. The Name of the Lord is a Strong Tower; the righteous run to Him and they are saved. The Lord is my Light and my Salvation; I am fully satisfied in following Him and will do so till the very end in Jesus' Name. Amen!!!

255th Day

MIND YOUR OWN BUSINESS; WORK HARD; BE KINDLY TO THE POOR; AND SRIVE TO ENTER THE KINGDOM OF GOD!!!

Make it your ambition to lead a quiet life, to mind your own business and to work with your hands, just as we told you, so that your daily life may win the respect of outsiders and so that you will not be dependent on anybody. 1 Thessalonians 4:11,12 NIV

Make yourself useful by working gainfully; live quietly working with your own hands; and mind your own business. By this, you will be respecting yourself and others will respect you also; because you would have gained their respect by not depending on anybody! This is wise living according to the Word of God! Be wise!!!

Diligence rules; laziness will earn forced labour. The lifestyle of the lazy folks is never encouraging at all and only multiplies poverty. Hard work however does the opposite; you will have enough even to give to those in need when you work hard. God does not want His children to live idle lazy lives; but rather to be gainfully employed, hardworking and so blessed!!!

When you are kind to the poor, you lend to their Maker; when you despise the poor, you insult their Creator! When you consider the poor kindly, you will have Divine Favour from their Creator! He Will Bless you and Protect you and yours in every way. He Will Defend you. Even when you're sick, God Will be with you and Help you recover! All have sinned and fallen short of God's Glory; therefore, I pray Thee o Lord to be merciful to me. Heal my soul o Lord, that I might live in Jesus' Name. Amen!!!

When Jesus was queried, He made very clear in His answers that He IS a KING (but of a different type than humans think)! It is also clear that it was the Jews that wanted Him dead (they had the Word of God)! Jesus' destiny is made very clear in this Scripture passage! Jesus Christ is the way, truth and life; He came to bear witness to the Truth. Those of the truth hear His Voice! Hmmm. Do you hear His Voice today? Are you of the truth? Test yourself and submit yourself for the testing of the Holy Spirit! Who is on the Lord's side?!!

256th Day

JESUS CHRIST IS THE LIVING GOD, SAVIOUR OF ALL MANKIND; STILL UNSURE? HMMM! JUST BELIEVE AND BE BLESSED!!!

Do you trust in the Word of God? You cannot trust or believe in a God that you neither know nor have a clue about! How can you trust in a God you neither fear nor love? Trust is a very big word. Who can you trust; especially by faith, in a world that teaches you seeing is believing? So, when I confess to you that I put my hope in a Living God; the Saviour of all mankind, especially of those who believe, well, I do know what I am talking about! Just believe and submit your life to Him!!!

You must be born again to see the Kingdom of Heaven! This is not about returning into your mother's womb because that is impossible! You must be born of the water (be baptised) and of the spirit (receive the Holy Spirit). You become baptised after acceptance of the Gospel message of Jesus Christ; in accepting Jesus Christ as Lord, God and Saviour! Then you await the indwelling of the Holy Spirit to help you walk the faith! The flesh gives birth to the flesh; the spirit to the spirit!!!

God showed His love for mankind in sacrificing Himself once for all; but the blessings/benefits accrue only to those who choose to believe the facts of this singular action. All who do not believe stand condemned and cannot enjoy the fruits of this great love! This love shown to mankind is not due to the righteousness of man, but rather by God's Grace and Mercy. This also through the washing of regeneration and renewal by the Holy Spirit freely poured out on us in Jesus' Name; Him being our Saviour! We thus become justified by His Grace and heirs according to the hope and promise of Eternal Life in Jesus Christ. Amen!!!

257th Day

WHO HAS THE HIGHEST PLACE AND IS FOREVER GLORIFIED? MANY YET DESPISE HIM, THE EXACT IMAGE OF GOD!!!

God Exalted His Word above His Name. The Highest place is Given to and reserved for Him; so much so that at the Name of Jesus, every knee shall bow in Heaven and on earth and every tongue confess that Jesus Christ is the Lord! His Name is the Highest and He Sits Enthroned on High forever and ever. Halleluyah! Amen!!!

When the hour came, Jesus Christ looked up and called upon the Father to Glorify His Son, that the Father would likewise be Glorified in the Son (equality stressed here heavily)! This is neither for the Father nor the Son; but for us and those who will be Granted to believe in the Gospel of Jesus Christ and those to whom they will witness and who will in turn believe in the Lordship of Jesus Christ!!!

It is written that the kings of the earth will give thanks to the Lord on hearing His Word; and they will sing of His Ways! This is God's Way and Design, that this be so! The Lord is Great in Glory and in the Fear due to His Name! Even though He is so exalted, He does not ever despise the lowly (humble); but the prideful, arrogant and haughty, He knows from afar and discountenances!!!

I pray in Jesus' Name that the prophecy of Isaiah the prophet is not fulfilled in my life and family! I reject the spirit of hearing and never understanding; seeing and never perceiving. I reject a callous heart combined with the ability to hear and see with my ears and eyes. I pray that the Word of God ministers to me and causes my heart to turn to the Lord and fill up with His Holy Spirit in Jesus' Name, that I might be Healed! Amen!!!

Clearly in the Word of God, there is Power and in the Name of Jesus, every knee shall bow and every tongue confess His Lordship! For Jesus Christ is the brightness of the Glory of God and the exact representation of His

Being! He is the One written and spoken of in the Holy Scriptures; that He sacrificed His Life for our sins, crucified, died and was raised again and lives forever. It is He who is seated at the Right Hand of the Majesty in Heaven! Jesus Christ is the Lord God Almighty! The Great Judge!!!

258th Day

TRUTH IS VERY CRITICAL AND CRUCIAL TO THE KINGDOM OF GOD; WITH CONSEQUENCES FOR EMBRACING DECEPTION, FALSEHOOD AND LIES!!!

How often do we lie, deceive each other and swear by God's Name when we know we're not telling the truth; thus profaning the Name of the Lord?! Do we even care that there are grave consequences for doing these things? Ought we not to remember God in all we think, speak and do? Hmmm! There is a God; and He Will Judge justly!!!

Did you know that fear is a sin as much as lying, unbelief etc.? The Word of God is not to be taken for a joke nor ride! The wrath of God is sure to be visited upon those who err according to His Word! May God Have Mercy on us who follow Him sincerely; for we are not perfect and without sin, in Jesus' Name. Amen!!!

In your hearts you devise wrongs; your hands deal out violence on earth. The wicked go astray from the womb, they err from their birth, speaking lies. Psalm 58:2,3 RSV

When we sin willfully; whether we think of the Word of God and the wrath of God or not, we are nevertheless culpable! Truly we devise all sorts of unholy schemes in our hearts, which we execute to the letter! We often speak of the wicked without thinking we are wicked for our own actions! O Father, please Help us in Jesus' Name; forgive our trespasses in Jesus' Name. Amen!!!

To the children of God, God speaks clearly; unlike to the people in general, when He speaks in parables! The knowledge of the secrets of the Kingdom of Heaven is Given to us; however, to those who have, more is given, but from those who do not have, even what they have is taken and given to those who have! This is the Wisdom of God and cannot make sense to the carnal mind! Be holy and perfect therefore; even as God IS in Jesus' Name. Amen!!!

When God Speaks a word, He brings it to pass; even as He Spoke the curse over mankind! Shouldn't we fear God, the One who speaks and it comes to pass? Why has mankind become so fearless of God? Is it not because of taking God's Grace and Mercy for granted? Hmmm! Whatever we encounter, is it not of our own making? Hmmm! May God show us mercy on that Day; o please God in Jesus' Name. Amen!!!

259th Day

WALKING WITH JESUS CHRIST IS A LONESOME JOURNEY; BE WELL PREPARED! YOU MUST BE READY TO GO IT ALONE!!!

God's Word is very clear on how to follow Him; we are the ones making up our own rules as we go along! There is only one standard and this has and will never change! Only when you follow Him by this one standard are you his sons and daughters; otherwise, you deceive yourselves. God is not mocked; we shall reap what we have sown! We are called to be separated from the world. This is a very lonesome journey; because many do not want to be separate at all! Be prepared to walk alone in your journeying in Jesus Christ!!!

Jesus Christ will never leave nor forsake His followers! Is that you? You will never fail to have His Comfort! The world will not see Him; but you will (hmmm how wonderful)! Because He lives, we shall also live! In due season, on the appointed Day, we shall know that Jesus Christ is in the Father and vice-versa! All we need to do is take a decision to follow Him and stick to that decision for good!!!

We have the blessed assurance that God will remain with us as long as we remain with and in Him! Everywhere we go, He will be with us. He Promised to bring us back to our land of origin; I am trusting Him to His Word in Jesus' Name. It shall come to pass in Jesus' Name. Amen!!!

The Kingdom of God is like a farmer sowing seeds and not knowing which would thrive or not! Some seeds sown fall along the path, rocky places, thorns and good soil; all with attendant results. The bottom line is that only the seeds that fall on good soil shall thrive and yield a bountiful harvest! God will make a way even where there seems to be no way in Jesus' Name for all who truly follow Him!!!

The testimony of John states that he is a brother and companion in tribulation, kingdom and patience of Jesus Christ. That is self-explanatory. All for the Word of God, in witnessing to the reality of Jesus Christ! As for me and my household, we will serve the Lord! I have decided to follow Jesus, no turning by, no turning back! Though friends, family, others forsake me; no matter how difficult the journey, still I will follow. May God Help me along in my faith walk in Jesus' Name. Amen!!!

260th Day

SEEK FIRST THE KINGDOM OF GOD ABOVE ALL ELSE; THIS WILL OPEN UP THE WINDOWS OF HEAVEN UNTO YOU FOR ALL YOUR NEEDS TO BE MET IN JESUS' NAME; AMEN!!!

When you strive please God in all ways in all you think, speak and do, He Never forgets; He Will remember and Bless your whole life! This is expedient to do; and effective for answered prayers!!!

When you strive for and live a life of righteousness, you will not live in vain; you are living to please God and will surely be rewarded and blessed! You will eat the fruits of your labour; and will never labour in vain! It shall be well with the righteous! In Jesus' Name. Amen!!!

Who are those who would take refuge in the Lord? Are they not His righteous ones who strive daily to live a holy life unto Him? They shall be rewarded with the joy of the Lord for their strength; and sing for joy, rejoicing in Him. They will be surrounded with Godly Favour as a shield and protection! Selah!!!

Wherever Jesus Christ went, He was Doing Good; this attracted large crowds of people to Him always! So much so that He had to get into a boat whilst the people remained standing on the shore so He could address them without a commotion being caused; and from there He met their needs! Jesus' Presence was all that was needed; and even for those who believed, He didn't have to be present physically for their needs to be met! What a Mighty God we have!!!

Jesus used parables to describe the Kingdom of God in teaching the peoples. He likened the Kingdom of God unto a field where a man sowed good seeds and the enemy came and sowed tares in it! Both the good seeds and tares grew together. Wonder not about what to do; let them grow together until harvest time! In fact, you will gather the tares first; but for bundling and burning together! Then, the good seeds would be harvested and gathered into the barns! God's Judgment is going to be swift and just; be prepared in and out of season!!!

261st Day

IT TAKES GOD'S GRACE TO LIVE A GODLY LIFE; I PRAY THAT GRACE INCREASES IN OUR LIVES IN JESUS' NAME. AMEN!!!

Finally, brothers, we instructed you how to live in order to please God, as in fact you are living. Now we ask you and urge you in the Lord Jesus to do this more and more. For you know what instructions we gave you by the authority of the Lord Jesus. It is God's will that you should be sanctified: that you should avoid sexual immorality; that each of you should learn to control his own body in a way that is holy and honourable, not in passionate lust like the heathen, who do not know God; 1 Thessalonians 4:1-5 NIV

If you believe that you are standing in the Lord, then stand firm; so you do not fall! You who are obedient to the instructions in the Name of our Lord to live a life pleasing to God, be encouraged to continue to do so increasingly. Flee from sexual immorality; there is a morality that is very common but very ungodly. It allows for so much sexual perversion in passionate lust and it is said that as long as you are married, it is acceptable! No, it is not! Watching and doing pornographic scenes and acts is very ungodly (with all the associated positions etc.)! Everything is indeed permissible, but not everything is beneficial for me as a follower of Jesus Christ!!!

You can only bear fruit, let alone much fruit, if you remain in the Vine (which is Christ Jesus)! This proves and evidences your discipleship! No faking it nor deceiving yourself! By your fruits you shall be known; and by your deeds you shall be judged! Make no mistakes about this!!!

Let us not take the freedom assured by the Holy Spirit of our Lord Jesus Christ, who is ONE with God and the Holy Spirit, for granted! Godly freedom in Jesus Christ must not be taken for license to sin! We are being transformed into Jesus Christ's image by the Holy Spirit! So, we ought always to flee from sin outright and not say because we have freedom in Jesus' Name, then begin to do whatever we like. We must please our Commanding Officer!!!

Who is my family in Christ Jesus? My family (from the example of Jesus Christ above) are those who obey the Will of our Father in Heaven and His Word! They are my mother, brothers, sisters etc. It is them that I recognise; not in saying but rather in doing God's Will! I will not be distracted from my walk in the Faith by anyone including family members, no matter how well-meaning they appear!!!

Draw me to Yourself that I might be a worshipper and true; let Your Presence come and flood my heart, till all I see is You! For no one can come to Jesus unless the Father (He) Draws the person; and whomsoever He Draws, He will raise up on the last Day!!!

262nd Day

HUMILITY BEGETS MUCH GRACE; SERVANT LEADERSHIP IS THE SIGN OF FAITHFUL LEADERSHIP! IT IS SELF EVIDENT AND ATTRACTS GOD'S ATTENTION AND FAVOUR!!!

Contrary to man's futile thinking, greatness is God-Given, not man-made. Man can ubiquitously promote mankind even to positions of power and authority; and God would sometimes allow this to happen because of the heart of man. However, greatness cannot be manipulated into mankind; no, that is God-Given! Those who exalt themselves in pride and arrogance will be humbled; God exalts those who humble themselves! Stop wasting your time, energy and life on what is absolutely fruitless!!!

God does not despise the cry of the genuinely afflicted, oppressed, impoverished, widowers, orphans, destitute, sick etc. (the humble and or humbled readily get God's attention)! He Judges in their favour; that mankind may oppress no more! But does anyone care? Is anyone listening? Take heed; for God Will Act in due season!!!

The recommendation for young men is to humble themselves under the Mighty Hand of God; and subject themselves to their elders (of which parents are chief of course)! Disrespect, disobedience, disdain, etc. for parents is largely borne out of rebellion, fueled by pride and arrogance. Remember God; He opposes the proud and gives grace to the humble! God rewards pride/humility and (un)faithfulness in all that we think, speak or do; He rewards for sure!!!

If you are a follower of Jesus Christ, then you must consider yourself as the "elect" of God. There is a standard for you to follow as per living your life anew; forsaking the old way of life and submitting your mind and all for transformation by the Holy Spirit. This is so as to live a new life in Jesus Christ! In so doing, the only thing that matters is faith that works through love; allowing the Word of God to dwell richly inside of you and the Holy Spirit to drive you in all ways! Encourage each other with the Word of God as in psalms, hymns, spiritual songs etc.; doing everything in the Name of Jesus Christ our Lord, with thanksgiving!!!

May God give us who believe the wisdom to understand godly times and seasons; so as to act wisely and godly at every given time and opportunity. This would help us maximise our potentials as believers in Christ Jesus. Whatever you do, seek for wisdom; because there is a time for everything!!!

263rd Day

GOD IS OUR SAVIOUR, LORD, KING AND JUDGE! THOUGH OUTWARDLY WE MAY WITHER, INWARDLY, WE ARE RENEWED!!!

The LORD lives! Praise be to my Rock! Exalted be God my Saviour!

Psalm 18:46 NIV

My Lord is ALIVE forevermore; and He is Exalted accordingly! You are better off giving Him all Glory, Praise, Honour and Adoration. Help us o Lord to give to You Your dues in Jesus' Name. Amen!!!

When we judge ourselves, we are wise; as we will then not come under judgment. However, when the Lord Judges us, it's discipline for us; so that we shall not be condemned eternally with the world! God, Help us to accept Your Judgment and indeed to judge ourselves in Jesus' Name. Amen!!!

When you face adversity, do not be discouraged or give up hope; because there are inherent benefits accruable like: patience, experience, hope etc. that will work in your favour to keep shame far from you. This is due to the love of God poured upon you from abroad by God into your heart by the Power of the Holy Spirit Given unto you by the Almighty God. Help us to key into this Word from God o Lord; that we might benefit in Jesus' Name. Amen!!!

All things work for the good of those who love the Lord and are Called according to His Purposes! You ought to give endless thanks and praise unto the Lord for His Mercies that endure forevermore! No matter what is happening to your body/flesh, your inner man is fully intact and being renewed constantly and consistently. Do not look at circumstances; because the visible, tangible "realities" are dubious and very temporary! The true REALITIES are invisible and intangible; yet eternal! The intangible Life Force controls the true realities of the visible, tangible life that is seen! May God Help us to be wise in His Word and for His Name's sake in Jesus' Name. Amen!!!

Jesus predicted (prophesied) His brutalisation! True to His Word, the religious powers that be were hatching a thick plot just at that time to arrest and kill Him in secret. But God's Plan and purpose was about to be fulfilled; but they didn't know this! Whatever happens in life, God's Will Prevails irrespective of man's plans and schemes! God, Help us to yield to Your Word and Ways in Jesus' Name. Amen!!!

Babylon the great shall come under the wrath of God; the kings and queens and the powerful of the earth who covenanted with her through fornication etc. shall weep and lament for her and what would become of her. Vanity, all is vanity! Work not for vanity's sake; but rather, that your name may be written in the Lamb's Book of Life! Lord, Help us to live our lives with Godly Wisdom and yield to Your Person and Being in Jesus' Name. Amen!!!

264th Day

THE POWER OF THE LORD IS MADE PERFECT IN THE BELIEVERS' WEAKNESS; HIS GRACE IS SUFFICIENT FOR THEM!!!

God Loves it when you praise Him; declare His Power, Goodness, Mercy, Salvation and Love! "Bigging up" each other might encourage one another, true! However "Bigging Up" the Lord our God is the "real deal"! Lift Him up! Give Him Praise. He gets so excited that He Comes to Inhabit the praises of His people! Praise invokes God's Spirit like nothing else! How much more so when your praise is coming from a heart that fears and obeys Him?! O Lord, Grant unto us that loving and grateful heart that elicits glory, praise, adoration and love for You from us in Jesus' Name. Amen!!!

Look unto the Lord in times of trouble and adversity and believe that He Will Give you victory! Don't look at nor dwell upon circumstances because they do not move God; your faith is what moves God to act on your behalf! He Will Give you Strength and Power supernaturally to overcome; such that the least amongst you will be as David, whose house shall be as God, even as the Angel of the Lord before you. Lord, may Your Word come true in our experience in Jesus' Name. Amen!!!

God Favours His beloved (that is us who truly follow and believe Him); such that His Grace meted out unto us will bring more glory and thanksgiving unto God for all He Has Done and continues to Do for us. Jesus, may we continue to enjoy Your Goodness, Mercy and Love; that for our sakes and on our behalf, more glory, thanks and praise may come to You in Jesus' Name. Amen!!!

You know the Truth of the Gospel of the Lord and the Word of God in this particular regard; that God Stengthens the weak, opposes the proud and gives grace to the humble. Therefore, strive to encourage one another! Strengthen each other and tell the weak and anxious not to fear. Encourage all in the Name of the Lord and assure all that God is on their side and will fight for, avenge, defend, deliver and save them in Jesus' Name. Amen. Lord, encourage and comfort us; that we in turn may encourage and comfort one another in Jesus' Name. Amen!!!

This woman did something honourable and of immense quality and expense to the Lord Jesus Christ. She was seen differently than how Jesus saw her because of this very act. She was probably at her weakest in life and beliving and hoping in the Name of the Lord, she came with her very best, to Bless Him! Of course, He is Lord; and He recognised her sacrifice instantly and accepted her offering! So much so that her story will forever be told whenever the Gospel is preached forever! What a testament! How about you? Hmmmm! Lord, Guide and Direct our hearts to love and serve You meritoriously in Jesus' Name. Amen!!!

Arguments on circumcision and the likes are nothing; just a diversion from the real issues of the Word of God. Fear God! Keep and obey His Commandments; and you will please God. This is all that matters really. Is it not? Hmmm. May God Grant us the wisdom and discernment that we need to follow, serve, worship and lift Him up in our lives and amongst all the people in Jesus' Name. Amen!!!

265th Day

THE FIRST COMING AND REJECTION OF THE MESSIAH
LORD JESUS CHRIST WAS PROPHESIED IN SCRIPTURES!!!

Prophecy re: Coming:

Read and meditate on the Holy Scriptures above. The little town of Bethlehem shall bring forth the Ruler in Israel whose Roots are from of old, from everlasting. Jesus Christ is the Ancient of Days: who was, is and is forevermore. Very accurately delivered prophetically! Help us o Lord to learn, know and live Your Word out for and in our lives in Jesus' Name. Amen!!!

Fulfillment:

"Now when Jesus was born in Bethlehem of Judea in the days of Herod the king, behold, there came wise men from the east to Jerusalem, Saying, Where is he that is born King of the Jews? For we have seen his star in the east, and are come to worship him." Matthew 2:1-2

Jesus Christ according to the prophecy of Scriptures, was born in Bethlehem. His birth was not hidden at all; as three wise men from the East say His Star and followed it right to Jerusalem. They recognised the significance that was lost on the leaders of the faith at the time; the Lord Jesus Christ! They came to "worship" Him! O Lord, Grant that we would be able to discern the signs of the times with wisdom acquired from You in Jesus' Name. Amen!!!

Prophecy re: rejection:

"He is despised and rejected of men; a man of sorrows, and acquainted with grief: and we hid as it were our faces from him; he was despised, and we esteemed him not." Isaiah 53:3

The One who came to Save mankind; although seen, was fully rejected by mankind. He was despised and rejected; a Man of sorrows, acquainted with grief. He was not esteemed at all; and we kind of hid our faces away from Him! O what a shame upon mankind. Alas! But, it was all in the Master

Plan of the Almighty; who had prepared Him as a Living Sacrifice for mankind! He was predestined to take upon Himself all of the sinfulness of mankind; that we may be reconciled unto God, but by simple faith in Him and in His Holy Sacrifice. O Lord, Help us away from unbelief, into faith in Jesus Christ, our Lord, God, Saviour and King in Jesus' Name. Amen!!!

Fulfillment:

"Which of the two do you want me to release to you?" asked the governor. "Barabbas," they answered. "What shall I do, then, with Jesus who is called Christ?" Pilate asked. They all answered, "Crucify him!" "Why? What crime has he committed?" asked Pilate. But they shouted all the louder, "Crucify him!" Matthew 27:21-23 NIV

When push came to shove, who did the people choose to set free? Not Jesus the Christ, the Messiah! Barabbas, a known marauder and a thief in prison for his crimes was preferred over and above Jesus Christ; and he was set free in the place of Jesus Christ! Wow, what a wickedness in mankind. Certain evidence of the rejection of Jesus Christ via Scriptures. However, it was all in God's Plan! Lord, Help us not to crucify the Lord again and again by rejecting Him or not obeying His Commandments and living a life of unrighteousness in Jesus' Name I pray with thanksgiving. Amen!!!

Not only was Jesus Christ rejected, a man, Judas Iscariot was willing to sell Jesus Christ to the "enemy" (chief priests)! He sold Jesus Christ for thirty pieces of silver! Wow! Our Lord's worth in the eyes of the world! To us who believe, Jesus Christ is our everything! Priceless! However, we all have the same evil potential! Only Jesus Christ Can Wash us clean and Give to us His Holy Spirit to Enable us to live a life of holiness and righteousness in Jesus' Christ! Father, please Help us not to be ashamed of our Lord and Saviour; and also not to reject nor sell Him out or crucify Him again today, in Jesus' Name. Amen!!!

Living for and in Jesus Christ is like going into a battle with and against the world! We need to be fully equipped for this battle. Although, the battle is the Lord's and the victory is ours, we have a definite part to play in it. This is why I tell people what the Lord Taught me that His Love is not designed to be unconditional! We have a price to pay. Yes Jesus Christ Paid "The Price" for our Salvation! There is always a price for Love! Love is never unconditional! For the Love and Salvation that He Purchased, our price to pay is to believe and obey His Words to benefit maximally! We need to put on the whole armour of God; and know out enemy! To ignore the enemy and or have no information nor knowledge of the enemy is foolishness when you go to battle! Lord, Help us to live our lives as wise in the knowledge and wisdom of God about our entire lives in Jesus' Name. Amen!!!

266th Day

EVEN WITH GOD, HONESTY IS THE BEST POLICY! GOD VALUES HONESTY! STOP CHEATING YOUR BRETHREN OR NATION!!!

The LORD abhors dishonest scales, but accurate weights are his delight.
Proverbs 11:1 NIV

The Lord Almighty delights in honesty and abhors dishonesty. That means God hates dishonest people as much as He hates the wicked. In fact, dishonesty is seen in the Eyes of God as a type of wickedness. If you truly want to please God, obey His Commandments. Love does not cheat his neighbour! Lord, Help us to have purity of heart which will make us honest followers of Jesus Christ in Jesus' Name. Amen!!!

Your house may be so beautiful! As long as it's built with dishonest gain and or proceeds of dishonesty, then it is built with and in wickedness in the Eyes of God! How do you expect God to deal with or see you? God Knows what is behind your wealth; even if hidden from mankind! God is not mocked; a man shall reap whatever he has sown. Father, Help us to value honesty in our daily lives and dealings with others in Jesus' Name. Amen!!!

Who shall ascend up the Hill of the Lord? The qualities of such as qualify to achieve this feat is laid out as above. All your chants of God Loves everybody equally etc. does not change the Word of God! Unless you fulfill the condition for God's Love, you shall continue to lose out on the Love of God. Only those who have the Love of God can ascend unto His Holy Hill! May God Enable us to fit the bill as in to have such a lofty access to the Holy Hill of the Lord God Almighty in Jesus' Name. Amen!!!

What does God require of us? To love the Lord our God and each other; and to act justly, trusting God fully! However, what do we do? We do dishonesty, wickedness with cheating, lying and dishonesty and hating one another instead of loving! The Lord is asking us to come back to Him and do righteously in Jesus' Name. O Lord God, Help us to do love and justice in Jesus' Name; that we might please You in Jesus' Name. Amen!!!

How can the Lord prune us to be even more fruitful when we have dishonesty in us? We cheat ourselves of the Love of God and His Blessings for our sinfulness and generally negative attitudes and approach to life! Why won't we opt to make ourselves ready for the Lord's pruning to be even more fruitful? Our hearts are not right towards God; and this is the reason for ALL of our troubles. Father Lord, Help us! Touch our hearts! Create in us new hearts and renew a righteous spirit within us; so we shall not be castaways in and from Your Presence in Jesus' Name. Amen!!!

267th Day

CORRECTION, LIKE SUFFERING FOR JESUS CHRIST IS GOOD FOR THE BELIEVER! THE LORD CAME WITH A SIGN FROM THE COVENANT-KEEPING GOD! NOBODY ELSE LIKE HIM!!!

Accept correction as part of suffering for the sake of Jesus Christ for your own benefit; because it is good for you! Blessed is the person that God Corrects; for that person will do very well in life and beyond if they accept such chastisement - thus becoming partakers of His Holiness! God, Help us to accept Your Correction and suffering for Your Name's sake in Jesus' Name. Amen!!!

You never leave nor forsake Your Own o Lord; Help us to willingly accept Your chastisement, that it may go well with us; all the days of our lives and beyond in Jesus' Name. Amen!

Let your behaviour be like those who know the Lord and are His children. Set such an example amongst the heathen and pagans such that they will give glory to your God! You are Blessed to have the Holy Spirit Speak deep into your hearts as children of God! We who are His children also share in His Inheritance; including treasures and all, even with Jesus Christ! All creation awaits for the sons of the Living God to be revealed! We are chosen. O Lord, Help us to live up to Your expectations in Jesus' Name. Amen!!!

The sign of the Saviour born into the world is a little baby wrapped up warmly, but lying in a manger! How often before and after has a baby been born in a manger? Think and meditate on this! This message was given to shepherds watching their flocks in a field and not to powerful well-positioned faithful priests or even kings and queens! They were suddenly enveloped with the Lord's Glory too; surrounded by angels! Jesus Christ was not born in a palace but in a manger! Lord, Help us to learn love and humility in this cruel world, for the salvation of our souls and others in Jesus' Name. Amen!!!

God always reveals His Will to His prophets before Acting it out! He is a faithful God, Who Keeps His Covenant/Oath once declared; to those who love Him and keep His Commandments! Make no mistake about it. God does not do this with everybody automatically willy nilly! So, the notion that God Loves everybody and equally and that God's Love is unconditional is very much alien to God Almighty! Otherwise, why would He Require that we obey His Commandments? Hmmm! Be wise! God, Help us to learn Your wisdom for the salvation of our souls and others in Jesus' Name. Amen!!!

268th Day

THE SAVIOUR/MESSIAH IS THE SON OF THE LIVING GOD! HE IS ALL MAN AND ALL GOD! JESUS CHRIST IS THE LORD GOD!!!

Prophecy:

"Who hath ascended up into heaven, or descended? Who hath gathered the wind in his fists? who hath bound the waters in a garment? Who hath established all the ends of the earth? What is His name, and what is His son's name, if thou canst tell?" Proverbs 30:4

There is more than enough evidence in this life that there is nothing impossible for God to do! The above Scripture is so apt and accurately portrays the Lord God our Saviour King, Jesus Christ! The Miracle-Working God! The Lord God Almighty and His Son are one and the same! All you need is to believe, submit to and accept Him. Then you receive the right to sonship and all relevant benefits begin to accrue to you! Lord my Father, Help us to believe in You and remain unshaken in our faith in Jesus' Name. Amen!!!

Fulfillment:

"And Jesus, when he was baptized, went up straightway out of the water: and, lo, the heavens were opened unto him, and he saw the Spirit of God descending like a dove, and lighting upon him: And lo a voice from heaven, saying, This is my beloved Son, in whom I am well pleased." Matthew 3:16-17

The Powerful Sign and Wonders that attended the Life of Jesus Christ on earth have never been the same with any man before or after to date. The ONLY Begotten and Beloved Son of God; Begotten and not created/made! Halleluyah to the King of kings and the Lord of all lords! Jesus Christ is His Name and He is the Lord God Almighty! Give Him Praise somebody! Father, please do not let satan take away our faith in Jesus' Name. Amen!!!

Prophecy:

"I will declare the decree: the Lord hath said unto me, Thou art my Son; this day have I begotten thee." Psalm 2:7

Affirmation of the Father for and unto the Son! The Father is in the Son and vice versa! This can never make sense to the carnal mind which wars against the Spirit Man! The flesh is always at war with the Spirit of God! Do not follow after the flesh; but rather follow after the Holy Spirit and yield to His Power and earnestly desire the same in Jesus' Name. Father Lord God, please fill us increasingly with the Power of Your Holy Spirit; the Power of Your Resurrection in Jesus' Name. Amen!!!

Fulfillment:

"For unto which of the angels said he at any time, Thou art my Son, this day have I begotten thee? And again, I will be to him a Father, and he shall be to me a Son? And again, when he bringeth in the firstbegotten into the world, he saith, And let all the angels of God worship him." Hebrews 1:5-6

There is Power in the Name of Jesus Christ. There is tremendous Power in His Blood! No man existed before nor would there be any after, that would receive such affirmation from the Almighty God in terms of Sonship and Fatherhood! There's nobody like Jesus Christ! The Original Man and God at the same time! Blessed be His Holy Name. Halleluyah! Amen! Father, increase the Grace You have Given to us to believe in and hold firmly onto Jesus Christ and standing firmly in His Holy Name. Amen!!!

This Jesus Christ has been proven to be the Messiah Lord God and King! He is the ONLY ONE that Paid a serious Price with His Life for our salvation! This promise was made by God through the prophets to our forefathers in the faith long ago and came into fruition through Jesus Christ's coming and His Death and Resurrection! All God Asks of us is to believe, honour, fear and love Him; then we get keyed into His Love, Blessings and Life! Father, Help us to engage Jesus Christ in this way forever in Jesus' Name. Amen!!!

Jesus Christ Knew who was going to betray Him! Did He do anything about it to prevent it? No! If you knew who was going to attack or come against you, how would you react? Hmmmm! The difference between man and God! Alas! How Great is our God beyond compare! He Told the disciples that one of them was going to betray him in the presence of that one person and what would happen to that one person! He didn't say He "Loves" everybody did He? Or did Jesus extend His Love to Judas Iscariot? A lady once told me that even though the Lord may send people to hell, He Loves them anyway! Is that justified in the Word of God? Hmmm! We who supposedly believe are amongst the most arrogant alive; we believe and think we can never be wrong, corrected or learn from others! Hmmmm! Is this Christ-like? I leave you to judge. Lord, Help us to humble ourselves in the faith walk in Jesus' Name. Amen!!!

What did Jesus Christ do to warrant this level of ganging up against Him? Or are you in any doubts about the mind-set of man? The Bible says that the heart of man is deceitful and desperately wicked; who can know it? We see this played out in the above Scriptures clearly! However, all things work for the good of them who love the Lord and are Called according to His purposes! The Purpose of Jesus Christ prevailed over the mind-set of conniving evil man! All praise to the Lord God, our Saviour and King in Jesus' Name. Amen!!!

269th Day

FORSAKE THE WORLD; FRIENDSHIP WITH THE WORLD IS ENMITY TOWARDS GOD! GAIN GOD'S FAVOUR INSTEAD!!!

All the strife, hatred, warring and fighting amongst mankind come from worldly-driven lusts that lead to a mixture of negative desires etc.! These in turn lead to death in the final analysis! Despite all of this, mankind is hardly ever satisfied; because they do not ask of God. When they do ask, they receive not, because they ask amiss, so as to satisfy their lusts. In their wisdom, they cannot work out that they are God's enemies; so long as they remain friendly with the world! Hmmmm! Wisen up o man; lest you perish. Father, Give us the Grace to learn and know the Truth; that we might be free in Jesus' Name. Amen!!!

The Lord expects us to be obedient children! We are expected not to conform to the youthful evil desires we had in ignorance, before committing to the Lord Jesus Christ. We ought to emulate the Lord, for He is Holy. We ought to be holy too! Lord, only You Can Help us to live holy lives; please Help us o Lord in Jesus' Name. Amen!!!

All worldliness, including fleshly lusts and boastful pride of life are not from the Father; but rather from and of the world. Know that the world with all its lusts shall surely pass away. When you live in these worldly lusts and crave friendship with the world, you cannot be in the Father's Will; neither can you be doing the Will of the Father. If you want Eternal Life in Christ Jesus, you must forsake the world with all its lusts etc.! Lord, Help us in Jesus' Name to forsake the world and its lusts. Amen!!!

You cannot do what you like with your bodies and claim to be in Jesus Christ. How often do you hear: "it's my body; not yours"! "I'll do what I like." People voice out the focus of their hearts and minds and pursue same in absolute vanity! Do not conform to worldliness; but rather, let God transform you by the Power of His Holy Spirit in Jesus' Name. When God Touches you in this way, you will come to understand and know the Will of God; which is good, pleasing, acceptable and perfect in Christ Jesus. Help us o Lord, to do Your Will in Jesus' Name. Amen!!!

How often have we missed out on God's Favour because we mostly opt for the way of the world? How often worldliness has robbed us of the Will of God and Divine Favour. Especially when we believe the lies that God's Love is unconditional and that God Loves everybody and equally too! These false beliefs harden us to live however we want and feel falsely confident that we're not outside of the "forgiving" God's Will! Hmmmm! God is not mocked; a man shall reap whatsoever he has sown! Lord, Help us to be like Elizabeth and Mary in holy living and in willingly accepting Your Divine Will and Favour for our lives in Jesus' Name. Amen!!!

270th Day

JESUS CHRIST WAS BORN A PROPHET, PRIEST, KING; WITH THE POWER AND MIGHT OF ALMIGHTY GOD! THE JUDGEMENT OF BABYLON THE HARLOT (WORLD) IS SECURE! FEAR GOD!!!

Meditate on the above Scriptural evidence that the Lord Jesus Christ possessed the Powers and Might of the King, Prophet, Priest and all the associated gifts and values as laid out correctly in the Holy Scriptures! The prophetic advent of the LORD Jesus Christ was manifested into reality with great signs and wonders following Him everywhere He went! Jesus Christ went about "Touching" people and their lives with such "Transforming" Powers; and all who even as much as came close to Him or even just touched Him, were "Transformed" likewise! Jesus Christ is the Lord God Almighty! Father Lord God, Help us to believe and hold firmly to our faith in the reality of Jesus Christ as the Lord God Almighty in Jesus' Name. Amen!!!

Jesus Christ is the BRANCH as prophesied much earlier before He Manifested Himself in reality; walking the earth doing wonders! Wherever He went, the prophetic word previously spoken came to pass and was confirmed in the words and actions of those who experienced Him! They called and referred to Him as the Great Prophet, Priest, King that was "to come". Yes, He was crucified, He died and was buried; but He Rose again on the third day and where He is now was and is known to His followers through the Revelation of the Holy Spirit. He is Seated at the Right Hand of the Throne of God in Heaven right now! Amen! Do you believe this or not? Many who claim to be Christians do not even believe that Jesus Christ is the Lord God Almighty! That is the very root and essence of the Christian Faith! Hmmmm! Open our eyes o Lord to see Your Light and Truth in the Gospel of Jesus Christ. Jesus Christ, the Lord God Almighty, Seated on High. Thank You Lord Jesus. Amen!!!

Mary, unto whom the prophetic word came through the angel of the Lord, was as baffled as any other person would be! She was virgin! The Word however came unto her that she would be overshadowed by the Power of the Holy Spirit! She believed. This is the difference that faith makes! Perhaps if she had not believed, the story might be different! However, she believed! Is there anything the Creator of the universe (heavens and earth) cannot do? Why is it so difficult for people to believe the Creator God of all? Hmmmm! Well, faith cannot be enforced. It's a simple matter of believing; a gift received from God. It's one thing to be offered a gift; quite another thing to receive it with gratitude! Mary received the gift and spoke of it in faith, having received it; so it came to be (pass) that she bore the Lord Jesus Christ! This is the Great Mystery of our Faith! However, we believe in Jesus' Name! Help us o Lord to continue to stand strong in our faith in Jesus' Name. Amen!!!

MYSTERY, BABYLON THE GREAT, THE MOTHER OF HARLOTS AND OF THE ABOMINATIONS OF THE EARTH.

When the going seems so good as you embrace and romance the world, spend a little time thinking of the ultimate outcome of that relationship! You must needfully meditate on the above Scriptures which spell out the Judgment of God upon the great beast, Babylon and all those who engaged her in fornication. Remember how beautifully she was dressed and clad in jewelleries etc.; don't however get so carried away with her beauty that you forget who she really is and was in the Scriptural Message! Therefore, is it not better that you disengage from her evil and all its appearances NOW before you get sucked up into her and it becomes too late for you? Repent now whilst you have life; once you're dead, it's all over. Then it will be too late! Father, do not let us be carried away and taken in with the seduction and beauty of the beast in Jesus' Name. Amen!!!

271st Day

JESUS CHRIST GAVE HIMSELF AS A RANSOME FOR ALL MANKIND; BUT SONSHIP COMES ONLY THROUGH FAITH IN HIM!!!

God does nothing without first Revealing to His Mind-set to His prophets! Abraham is the Father of our Faith! So, that makes him a prophet! The Lord Spoke a Word to him and it came to pass! He is our Father in the Faith in Jesus Christ! Wow! How can this ever make sense to anyone except by the Holy Spirit! How can anyone accept Jesus Christ as the Lord God Almighty except by faith and through the Holy Spirit! Stop trying to reason it out with your mind. You mind is incapable of working out who God is! Stop this foolishness. Humble yourself and receive the Gift of Faith! O Lord, Help us to humble ourselves so as not to lose out on Your Gift and Blessing of Faith in Jesus' Name. Amen!!!

We have one who brought the judgment of death on all; and ONE Redeemer, Who Redeemed us from death and purchased our right unto Eternal Life in Jesus Christ! Blessed be His Holy Name. Amen! Help us to appreciate Your Sacrifice and to Live for You in Jesus' Name. Amen!!!

How can the One God be the same one Mediator between man and God? Because God Knew He Alone had the Answer to the problem of mankind, He offered Himself up for us all through Jesus Christ. God Came as and in Christ Jesus to do the needful and succeeded. Many have their egos bruised badly by this glorious feat and can never allow their pride to accept the TRUTH! That's their problem! But for those who accept and obey the Word of God, a reward awaits in Jesus' Name. Amen. Lord, please do not let our faith be in vain in Jesus' Name. Amen!!!

God recognises and rewards faithfulness all the time! God Will subject you to several tests in order to facilitate your promotion in the Faith! Be prepared in and out of season for the testings. The key is not to dwell on the circumstances nor the testings themselves; but rather on the Blessing and or Promise to follow. Keep your focus healthy and right and you are a winner any day; for the battle is the Lord's and the victory is ours in Jesus' Name. Amen! Lord, Help us not to focus on the circumstances, but rather on You, our Great Provider, Rewarder in Jesus' Name. Amen!!!

Faith helped us to leap into the premise of Grace; no longer under the law, but entering by faith into sonship in Christ Jesus through faith in Jesus Christ! In Christ Jesus, we are all one - Abraham's seed and heirs according to the Promise of God! Wow! Lord, Help us to know our place in Christ Jesus and to retain and maintain our place in Jesus' Christ, Amen!!!

When the Holy Spirit Speaks a Word into our hearts, minds, souls and spirits; He Will confirm it through His Word! Mary went to Elizabeth and received confirmation of the Word spoken to her by the angel of God. Double confirmation! One that she's Blessed to bear the Lord and that Elizabeth was also expectant of child! Wow! God is so Good and so true to His Word. Praise His Holy Name. Amen! Help us to believe Your Word and to accept and appreciate confirmation of Your Word to us always in Jesus' Name. Amen!!!

John received the Revelations from the Lord Jesus Christ! This is a sure testament of that fact. Better to believe the Word of God than to doubt it. You're Blessed to believe and if you do not believe, you risk the wrath of God Almighty! I know what choice I have made. I chose to believe and may God Enable us who chose to believe to remain committed and focused on the faith in Jesus' Name to the very end in Jesus' Name. Amen!!!

272nd Day

A CHILD WAS BORN THE MIGHTY GOD; MAKES NO SENSE TO THE UNBELIEVER. BUT TO US, HE IS GOD ALMIGHTY!!!

Many people simply do not believe the Biblical Reality and Truth that Jesus Christ is the Lord God Almighty! They deliberately omit the part of the Scriptures that highlight the Truth and chose the parts of it that is not as clear to prove their unbelief! The above Scripture cannot be clearer! Jesus Christ is the Mighty God, Everlasting Father, Prince of Peace. We have peace only in and through Jesus Christ our Lord God Saviour and King! Give Him praise somebody! Halleluyah! Lord, Help us to learn, know, understand and heed Your Word and Counsel in Jesus' Name. Amen!!!

Only one mediator betweem man and God; only He Can reconcile us with God; only He Qualifies! This is because He IS God who came to mankind supernaturally in the flesh to walk amongst His creation. Jesus Christ is the King of kings and the Lord of lords! Halleluyah! Amen! Lord, Help us to understand and appreciate Your Purpose in life and in our lives in Jesus' Name. Amen!!!

When you have faith in Jesus Christ, you must never let anything beat you down low! You must recall the Word of God in faith; and let your heart rejoice inspite of your problems. You must know and believe that Jesus Christ has delivered victory to you through His Holy Sacrifice. Do you believe? Can you believe? Dare you believe? Hmmmm! Lord, Give us the grace to believe in Jesus' Name. Amen!!!

Jesus Christ came into the world as a human being born as a baby and grew up amongst the people. He Taught in their Temples and Synagogues; yet they were astonished and wondered where He got His Wisdom from - and He Spoke with Power. In fact, they had access to the Word of God but could not make sense of it because their hearts were not right! Father, Give us right hearts to correctly decipher Your Word and share with Power to others in Jesus' Name. Amen!!!

This is how God wants us to be! That we ought to be in togetherness as one Body; comfort each other with the Love of God, such that the mystery of God is revealed and acknowledged amongst us all in Jesus' Name. Amen! The treasurs of wisdom and knowledge are hidden in Jesus Christ and He Gives according to His Will. Father, Give us Your true Treasures of Wisdom and Knowledge; that we might know Christ and the Power of His Resurrection in Jesus' Name. Amen!!!

When you receive the Word of God prophetically, you must have time for meditation and contemplation on the Word; as if watering the seeds sown! Mary spent time with Elizabeth (of like mind in the Word of God). God delivered! God Alone Can Bring such to pass in Jesus' Name. Speak to us o Lord and Bring it to pass in Jesus' Name. Amen!!!

When we claim to come to the Lord, it must be a total commitment! Nothing must be more important than the Lord. Nothing must come before Him in our lives. It must be Jesus Christ first and foremost. Otherwise, we cannot be His disciple! Can you make such a commitment to prioritise the Lord over and above spouses, family, colleagues, co-workers and friends etc.? I have decided to follow Jesus, no turning bye, no turning back! How about you? Lord Jesus, Help us to follow You as a matter of priority over and above all else, to put You first in all things and in everything and every way in Jesus' Name. Amen!!!

273rd Day

JESUS CHRIST IS THE MESSIAH; HE LIVES FOREVERMORE! HE IS GOD INCARNATE! GOD CAME DOWN AS MAN IN THE FLESH!!!

Jesus Christ is the Ancient of Days who sits at the Right Side of the Throne in Heaven! He's the One Who Gave His Life; died, was buried and Rose from the dead three days later. It is He Who Ascended into Heaven and is coming back again soon and very soon! Be prepared in and out of season. You better accept Him as Lord God Saviour and King now, today! Tomorrow may be too late! Heaven and earth are the works of His Hands and both shall pass away; but He, Who is the Word of the Living God, shall remain forever and ever. Amen! Father, Help us to see, hear, learn, know and believe the Truth; so we may be set free in Christ Jesus, Amen!!!

The mystery of the Godship of Jesus Christ was hidden in God Almighty from time immemorial! It has now been revealed in Jesus Christ Himself and through His Apostles! This Gospel Truth has cascaded down from them; even as written in the Word of God prophetically from long ago! Jesus Christ Reigns Supremely over and above all; with all His enemies as His Footstool! He is LORD! Amen! Help us to receive the Truth of the Gospel and propagate the same in Jesus' Name. Amen!!!

Kind David the great psalmist knew Jesus Christ as Lord as much as the doubting Thomas! Why not you? Hmmmm! You better be wise; submit human intellect and embrace the wisdom and knowledge of God Almighty in Jesus Christ! If Jesus was David's son, would David call Him Lord? This is Wisdom from Heaven above. Lord, Help us to accept and embrace the Heavenly Truth and Wisdom in Christ Jesus. Amen!!!

As prophetically spoken and written, Jesus Christ was of the lineage of David born in the flesh into the world! Thus, His earthly parents had to go and register themselves and Him appropriately, to the household and lineage of David! Blessed be the Name of the Lord forever and ever. Amen. Help us o Lord to understand the Truth of Your Word; to accept and embrace the same and to propagate this Truth in Jesus' Name. Amen!!!

When you judge mankind for things the you do yourself, you stand judged too! God is Just! However, God's Judgement is Just and Truth because God is Holy and Pure and True! We shall all be Judged by God Almighty! Will you and or I stand and be proclaimed innocent before the Throne of Mercy? Hmmmm! Take heed! We all better take heed of the Word of the Living God. For all have sinned and fall short of the Glory of the Lord in Christ Jesus! Please Father, count my family and I worthy, like Your saints, whose sins You Will not count against them in Jesus' Name. Amen!!!

274th Day

JESUS CHRIST, SON OF DAVID, SON OF ABRAHAM, SON OF GOD! CANNOT MAKE SENSE TO THE CARNAL MIND!!!

"THE book of the generation of Jesus Christ, the son of David, the son of Abraham." Matthew 1:1

The Alpha is the Omega; the Beginning and the End! He is our God, Jehovah! He is of old; the Ancient of Days! The Mighty God of Israel! He incarnated as the Son of God. Yet, He is the Son of Abraham, of David too! How come? This cannot make sense to the carnal mind! His coming in the flesh had to be through a particular lineage as prophetically spoken and written about from ages past! Hence, the same God is the Son of God, the Son of Abraham and of David through lineages interwoven as ONE! The God of Abraham, Isaac and Jacob (Israel)! Somebody give Him praise! Halleluyah! Help us to humble ourselves to learn, know and appreciate our multi-faceted God in Jesus Christ. Amen!!!

"Of the increase of his government and peace there shall be no end, upon the throne of David, and upon his kingdom, to order it, and to establish it with judgment and with justice from henceforth even for ever. The zeal of the Lord of hosts will perform this." Isaiah 9:7

Whose government and peace does not ever come to an end if not God? Whose government and kingdom with justice can be established for ever if not God? Whose Zeal can bring this to pass except the Zeal of God Almighty? So who is God except the Lord our God and who is the Lord except our God? Even as it says in the Word of God! Be assured that Jesus Christ is the Lord God Saviour King! The Mighty God! Wonderful! Counselor! Prince of Peace and the King of Peace! Hmmmmm! JEHOVAH! You Are The Most High! You Are The Most High God! Father, Help us to know You in Jesus Christ our Lord and Saviour. Amen! Halleluyah!!!

"Behold, the days come, saith the Lord, that I will raise unto David a righteous Branch, and a King shall reign and prosper, and shall execute judgment and justice in the earth. In his days Judah shall be saved, and Israel shall dwell safely: and this is his name whereby he shall be called, THE LORD OUR RIGHTEOUSNESS." Jeremiah 23:5-6

Who is this that the Word of God says the Lord will Raise unto David? He Shall be called Jehovah Rapha! THE LORD OUR RIGHTEOUSNESS! Who else accepts the Lord Jesus Christ? Are you still doubting this? Please do not yield to satanic manipulations! Yield our soul, heart, mind and body only to the Lord God Almighty in Jesus Christ! Only Jesus Christ Can SAVE! No other person or power can save! Jesus is the ONLY Name that is above all other names! We are fully assured in the Word of God of this. No shaking at all! Father, Help us to value the name of Jesus Christ and to yield only to His Holy Spirit in Jesus' Name. Amen!!!

We have a purpose in life that is sure and unlike any other; to be ambassadors for Jesus Christ! Are you ready and willing? If you are, then the whole world should know it! You cannot hide and claim to be an ambassador for Jesus Christ! Your role is to beseech others in God's Name to be reconciled to God through Jesus Christ. He who was sinless was made to become sin for all mankind; that all might become the righteousness of God in Jesus Christ! Hmmmm! What love! Help us Lord to appreciate Your Love and to respond to this Love as is appropriate in Christ Jesus. Amen!!!

(3) "Blessed are the poor in spirit, For theirs is the kingdom of heaven. Matthew 5:3

Poverty has different levels and degrees and is of different types! So, to say poverty is poverty may not be correct at all! The poor in spirit referred to in the above simple Scripture is of a different kind! It's of a kind that hungers and thirsts (a type of poverty) for the righteousness of God. Blessed are those who hunger and thirst for the righteousness of God; for they shall be filled in Jesus' Name. Amen. O Father, Help us to hunger and thirst for Your Righteousness in Jesus' Name; and Fill us o Lord in Jesus' Name. Amen and Amen!!!

275th Day

I WILL CALL UPON THE LORD! MY HELPER! HE'S WORTHY OF MY PRAISE, LOVE AND ALL!!!

The Lord God Almighty has always got my back! No matter what comes my way; especially troubles, distress and the likes, my hope, faith, trust, my all is in the Name of the Lord my God Saviour and King! He Will never fail me; rather, He Will alwas Deliver me! He is my fortress, my rock, my salvation! He's my redeemer; the One Who Revives me! My God is the Chief Revivalist of my course and my ministry in Jesus Christ! He Will Perfect all that concerns me! He is ever faithful, merciful and ever sure. Father, we are the work of Your Hands; please do not forsake nor leave us in Jesus' Name. Amen!!!

Those of you who are Godly must love the Lord! He Takes Good Care of His godly ones anyway and appreciates and responds to their love! Be bold and courageous in the Lord; and be assured that He Will Recompense you for your good works in Him and do likewise to the prideful and wicked. He is Able, abundantly Able to deliver and to save all who trust in Him! He is Able to continue and finish every good work that He Began in His godly ones in Jesus' Name. Lord, Help us to love You and never stop hoping, trusting and having faith in You in Jesus' Name. Amen!!!

A thousand years in the Eyes of my Lord is as yesterday; just one day, just as one night watch. Teachus to number our days o Lord; that we may apply our hearts unto wisdom! All Power and Authority belongs to You o Lord; as with all life! From everlasting to everlasting You Are God Eternally! Even before the creation, You Are! You Give life and take it away when You are good and ready! We do not own our own lives! We are as if on loan to ourselves from Almighty God! Into Your Hands dear God, I commit my family, our lives, our everything in Jesus' Name. Amen!!!

Jesus Christ is coming back again; soon and very soon! You better be prepared in and out of season so you are not caught unaware! In face, we shall all be caught unaware; as nobody knows when He's coming back. He Will come at an hour we are not expecting! Hmmmm! We all better be prepared. Lord, please have mercy on my family and I when You come back in Jesus' Name. Amen!!!

276th Day

JEALOUSY AND COVETING DO NOT PLEASE GOD! BE CONTENTED WITH GODLINESS AND BE BLESSED!!!

Do not look at circumstances to focus on what your friends, enemies, contemporaries etc. are doing; using that as a yardstick to judge yourself and then begin to have the unhealthy drive to have what they have too! If you do, you will be caught out in the web of the wicked, which will greatly displease the Lord and cause you to be an abomination to the Lord! Father, Help us to keep our focus on You; to provide all our needs supernaturally and not get caught out in the web spun by satan in Jesus' Name. Amen!!!

Neither shall you covet your neighbor's wife; and you shall not desire your neighbor's house, his field, or his manservant, or his maidservant, his ox, or his ass, or anything that is your neighbor's. Deuteronomy 5:21 RSV

Stop your "ojukokoro" (Yoruba; meaning, staying your eyes on what is not yours)! If you are not contented with what you have, you will be enticed into stealing, coveting and or jealousy; which all lead to dishonesty and all sorts of evil, wicked schemes to possess whatever your neighbour has by hook or crook! Would God be pleased when you sin against your neighbour in this way? No! Father, please Help us to keep our minds and hearts unpolluted with unhealthy desires which destroy our spirits in Jesus' Name. Amen!!!

God's Word above is very clear - unlike what many say - that God loves the man but hates the sin; which I have never read in the Holy Bible! The devious and violent are detestable, an abomination to the Lord. The Lord hates them. He does NOT love them. The Lord however loves the upright and relates intimately with them! If you're wicked, violent and evil and keep believing that God loves you, you are living in error! Repent and do right so you can enjoy the Love of God which is not unconditional! Father, Help us to correctly divide the Word of God and apply the same to our lives in Jesus' Name. Amen!!!

Owing people debt without settling such is displeasing to God. This is considered a sin against your fellow human beings. In case you take this very lightly. Let your eyes be opened now by the Spirit of the God of Israel! The Laws and Commandments of God are guides to humanity so as not to sin against one another. Love pleases God because love does no harm to it's neighbour! Therefore, owe no man no debt except the debt to love! Love covers a multitude of sins! Love your neighbour as yourself; you can please and satisfy God in this loving! Father, please Grant us to love sincerely from the depths of our hearts and souls; so as to please You in Jesus' Name. Amen!!!

The Gospel of Light in Jesus Christ is the Good News of great joy; and it's for all humanity! God has factored every human being potentially into the love relationship based on faith in Jesus Christ! That is the condition! You have to believe in Jesus Christ as Lord God Saviour and King! When the angel of the Lord appeared to the shepherds, they believed his message! God, when You Speak to us or Send us a Message, Help us to believe and not doubt in Jesus' Name. Amen!!!

God is the ORIGINAL MAN! God is a Spirit! Therefore man is spirit! Those who accept God and humble themselves worship and relate with God in spirit and in truth! We do not dwell on circumstances; neither do we know any man any longer by the flesh, but rather by the spirit! Let us draw near to God; so God draws near to us in return! You can sing "Nearer my God to Thee" all you want! It is conditional upon you drawing near to Him and not automatic! Father Lord God, Help us to draw near to You; for nobody can draw near to You unless You Draw them - in Jesus' Name. Amen!!!

277th Day

STILL LOOKING FOR YOUR PURPOSE IN LIFE? LOOK NO FURTHER! HEAR THE WORD OF GOD, OBEY AND LEARN!!!

I hear so many people stressing and in great distress; they're busy looking for what their purpose in this world/life is? As for me, in Christ Jesus, I found my purpose and not only am I fulfilled, I am fully satisfied! If you will search for Jesus Christ; seek after Him and eventually find Him, you will find your purpose in life! He's not far from us though; but who is willing to seek after Him. This you can only do by faith; because you may not see Him physically, but He Will often Reveal Himself to you if you are sincere and in faith! Then, we shall live in Him! For, in Him we live, move and have our being! Thank You Lord Jesus! Lord, Reveal Yourself to us increasingly in Jesus' Name. Amen!!!

This cannot be clearer! Many have money and wealth but no faith; absolutely meaningless! Many even desire to please God and begin to do good deeds etc.! No way! You cannot buy God's Love or buy yourself into pleasing God! God is a rewarder of those that diligently seek Him; and although you may not see Him physically, you stand a chance to find Him when you believe that He IS in existence! Lord, Help us to believe not just that You Exist; but in seeking for You, to find You in Jesus' Name. Amen!!!

Where can anyone hide from the Lord? Be wise and humble yourselves! God is Omnipresent! There is nowhere that He is not! He is present wherever you may think to hide yourself. His Eyes See everywhere and all things. He Does not miss anything! If you are so Blessed that He Chooses to look away from your sin and not count them against you; then you are fortunate! However, if He chooses to take His Eyes off you, you are in serious trouble! Father, please do not take away Your Eyes from us and please be pleased not to count our sins against us, in Jesus' Name. Amen!!!

Faith indeed comes by hearing; hearing by the Word of the Lord God Almighty! Hearing without faith yields no profit spiritually; but hearing mixed with faith is profitable to the hearer. God stirs the heart unto faith; but you must be willing! By faith you can enter into the Sabbath Rest of God! God makes the impossible possible for those who are full with faith! Father God, Help us to be full with faith in Jesus' Name. Amen!!!

278th Day

MY GOD SAID HE WOULD GIVE US A NEW SONG! I RECEIVE MINE IN JESUS' NAME! AMEN! HALLELUYAH!!!

A promise from the Lord God Almighty to whomsoever would believe and receive it now, today, in this season, on this day, week, month, year, at this time! I receive in Jesus' Name for my family and I in Jesus' Name. Amen! Do something new in our lives, something new in our lives, something wonderful in our lives, today! We shall glorify You o Lord! Because You o Lord Have Made and Given daily portions and provisions to us in due season, even till today, Lord, we shall declare Your praise in Jesus' Name. Amen! On behalf of my family o Lord, I celebrate You and declare Your praise and faithfulness in Jesus' Name. Please Lord, accept my gratitude in Jesus' Name; because I know it's not automatic! Amen and Amen!!!

Put a fresh new song in our spirits, hearts and mouths o Lord; that we might praise You continuously for Your Faithfulness, Mercies, Love with manifold Blessings in Jesus' Name. Amen! Like the heavenly hosts that appeared with the angel of God, Grant unto us a spirit, heart, mouth of praise and thanksgiving unto You for Your Favour that rests upon us in Jesus' Name. Amen!!!

Help us o Lord to apply Your Wisdom in obeying Your Word in Jesus' Name. When we enter into Your Rest, we must not stop doing good deeds because we are in the Sabbath Rest! For You Made certain to tell us that You are the Lord of the Sabbath; and that the Sabbath is made for the people and not the people for the Sabbath. Therefore, when we do good on the Sabbath, we are not sinning! Help us to understand Your Word and apply Your Word in our daily living o Lord, in Jesus' Name. Amen!!!

279th Day

IF GOD IS FOR US WHO CAN BE AGAINST US APPLIES ONLY WHEN WE ARE TRULY FOR GOD AND NOT OTHERWISE!!!

Did the Word of God say that everybody will automatically live in safety and be at ease without fear of harm? No! What does it say? Whoever listens to God! Are you listening to God? Are we? We can bind and cast out etc.; it all amounts to nothing, unless we listen to God and obey His Word! His Love was never designed to be unconditional. All through the Scriptures, this Truth rings out; but many are not listening! Be wise; and stop believing in lies! Father God, Help us not to believe in lies; but rather to listen to and hear You and obey Your Voice in Jesus' Name. Amen!!!

God's Promise unto the house of Israel! Who are they? They are those who trust, hope in the Name of the Lord and honour fear and obey Him; living in holiness and righteousness! This promise is not for all and sundry, willy nilly at all! Hearken unto the Word of the Living God and enjoy the Blessings thereof! Father, Help us to dwell in Your Secret Place; so we may abide under Your Shadow in Jesus' Name. Amen!!!

Who is your Light and Salvation? Who is the Strength of your life? If you submit your life to the Lord our God to be your mainstay and sustenance, He'll take good care of you in every way possible; for His is a Faithful God in every way! Through all the changing scenes of life, the Lord'll be there for you! I have made Him my fortress, my everything; therefore, I am secured in every way! Father, please continue to be our all in all and everything from now unto all eternity in Jesus' Name. Amen!!!

When the shepherds heard the Good News! They believed. As a show of their faith, they went to verify! After that, they went and spread the Good News all over! Have you heard the Good News? What are you doing with what you have heard? If you believe the Good News, you cannot sit on it! Go, tell it on the mountains, over the hills and everywhere! Go, tell it on the mountains, that Jesus Christ is Lord! Help us o Lord, to spread the Gospel of Jesus Christ as You desire for us to do in Jesus' Name. Amen!!!

The lying words also include: God's Love is unconditional. God Loves everybody. God loves us all equally etc.! Rather, strive to do the Will of God and enter into His Love and Blessings! This is not as in trying to earn His Love and Blessings! No! Just in obeying His Word; so as to please Him - because, He is a rewarder of all who diligently seek Him! In seeking Him, you do His bidding to please Him! Be wise folks! We only live once! Get it right for Eternity; otherwise, lose out eternally! Lord, please Help us to get it right with You in Jesus' Name. Amen!!!

280th Day

TO FOLLOW GOD'S WAY IS NOT AT ALL EASY; BUT IF YOU CAN FOLLOW, YOU WILL BE VERY BLESSED IN JESUS' NAME!!!

Meditate on the above Scripture verses very carefully and be diligent to obey what God is Saying in His Word; and your life will never be the same again! Love my enemies? Wow! O Lord my God; that is a very difficult one! But I know that with You, nothing shall be impossible! Please show my household and I and all who trust and hope in You, the way to love our enemies; in Jesus' Name. Amen! This is profound teaching o Lord! If we can get this right, our hearts will surely be truly transformed as will our thinking in life! This is a life changing Word of God! Love your enemies! Wow! Help us o Lord in Jesus' Name. Amen!!!

In the beginning was the Word and the Word was with God and the Word was God; and the Word BECAME Flesh! Very simply, God became flesh and in Christ Jesus! That is the bane of the Christian Faith! The very bone of contention against the Christian Faith is the fact that Jesus Christ is both the Son of the Living God and God Himself and He is the Holy Spirit of God, Sent to all believers! We have received the Truth of the Gospel of Jesus Christ! O Lord, anoint us fully and effectively with Your Holy Spirit to Empower us to take this Gospel everywhere in Jesus' Name. Amen!!!

281st Day

WHO IS ON THE LORD'S SIDE? SUCH WILL BE DIVINELY PROTECTED AND DEFENDED AGAINST ENEMY FORCES!!!

When you choose to be on the Lord's Side, the Lord has certain expectations of you! This relationship is not one based on unconditional love or any such thing! God expects you to follow through with His Commandments and His Love! When you comply, then God Will Deliver to you His Promises! This does not mean God cannot or will not choose to act according to His Will at any time. However, it is wrong to assume, presume or expect that God's Love is unconditional and as such you don't have any obligations owed to God. The Bible says, unto whom much is given, much is expected after all! When you are on the Lord's Side, He offers to you Divine Protection and no weapon formed against you shall prosper! This is the heritage of the servants of God; and their vindication is from Him! All of this is so that we can serve Him without fear; in holiness and righteousness. It's not for a joke or for nothing's sake! O Lord, Help us to be and remain on Your Side in Jesus' Name. Amen!!!

God saved you by his special favour when you believed. And you can't take credit for this; it is a gift from God. Salvation is not a reward for the good things we have done, so none of us can boast about it. For we are God's masterpiece. He has created us anew in Christ Jesus, so that we can do the good things he planned for us long ago. Ephesians 2:8-10 NLT

For those of us who have accepted the Lord Jesus Christ as Lord God Saviour and King, it is by His Special Divine Favour that we are so saved! This is not about being "good" as many claim to be; nothing to boast about in your being "good" by your own standard! How does God see you is the most important! In being saved, we are God's masterpieces! He Created us anew in Jesus Christ for a purpose: to do the good things He preplanned for us to do long ago! So, let no one dwell on not being sure of their purpose in life. In fulfilling this Divine Purpose, your life takes the turn God Wants for you in particular. Lord, Help us to accept Your salvation and submit to You in Jesus' Name. Amen!!!

When you are comfortable and at home with your body, it proves absence from the Lord; true faith is to rather be absent from the body and present with the Lord! Our purpose is to strive and labour to please God; so to be accepted by Him! For, one day, we shall all be Judged by the Lord! Lord, please prepare us appropriately with Your discipline so that we shall not fail on Judgement Day in Jesus' Name. Amen!!!

The Lord warns us to beware of hypocrisy! When we present ourselves as what we're not and do things we privately and publicly ask others not to do! God Sees everything and we shall be judged for all! Anything hidden is only temporarily so; because in due season, all shall be revealed and nothing shall be hidden! Please HolyFather, Help us to do good and right in Jesus' Name. Amen!!!

282nd Day

BE WISE AND HUMBLE IN WALKING THE FAITH IN JESUS CHRIST! IT IS EXPEDIENT FOR YOU TO BE EFFECTIVE!!!

Some people exist to deceive others; so be very careful not to be so gullible to whatever people say or do! Investigate to be sure that the truth is established! Deceivers abound; just as liars and hypocrites! Also, you have the arrogant and prideful; who are wise and clever in their own eyes. Do not be one nor be like them. Father, Protect us from such in Jesus' Name. Amen!!!

It is wisdom not foolishness to hide yourself away from evil; rather than think that by confronting evil head on, you are being wise and Godly! Even at war, the wise ones know when to battle and when to retreat! Humility and the fear of the Lord is great gain; just like godliness with contentment - and by them both God Bestows riches, honour and life in Jesus' Name. Amen! Guard your soul against perversions of any type whatsoever; then you will avoid thorns and snares in your paths. Father, Help us to fear You and be humble; so to avoid diverse predicaments in life in Jesus' Name. Amen!!!

When trying to help someone else out of sin or trouble, guard your spirit lest you be tempted. Bear each other's burdens and not "look out for number one" as peddled in the world! Christ connotes and advocates for oneness and unity of purpose. Love and help one another! Father, Help us not to think of ourselves as some big deal and to be completely humble so as not to deceive ourselves in Jesus' Name. Amen!!!

Men and women love to commend and recommend each other to boost their mutual egos! Hmmm! What counts is not that at all; but rather, who God commends and or recommends! Did man call you or commend and recommend you or is your call and commendation or recommendation from the Lord God Almighty! Hmmmm! Who recognises the one Called and Commended or Recommended by God Almighty in today's world? Father, Help us to desire and trust only in Your Call, Commendation and or Recommendation in Jesus' Name. Amen!!!

473

Whomsoever disdains correction hates himself; but the one that yields to instruction and correction gets wiser and learns more. Fear God; for that is where the Wisdom of God begins. Pride begets a fall; even as humility begets honour! Lord, Help us to be humble and fear God; so that we may learn the Wisdom of God and gain honour in Jesus' Name. Amen!!!

The Holy Communion is not about ceremonial rites at all; it's about sharing food and dring in godliness, righteousness, holiness and in love, with brethren of like minds in Jesus Christ's Holy Name! Jesus Led us by example right in the above Scriptures! Let us come together in love and purity of hearts within ourselves and towards each other and break bread and drink the cup together in unity and in love in Jesus' Name. Amen! Help us to do this increasingly o Lord, in Jesus' Name. Amen!!!

This is where the words holy ghost came from! When Jesus Christ was crucified, of course, it was very public; so when people suddenly saw Him Walking on water, they thought they had seen his ghost. They knew what ghosts were! They knew that ghosts were sightings of dead people as if alive! Jesus assured them that He was the one and not a ghost! Peter desired to go to Him on the water too and Jesus Called him; but he feared and began to sink. He cried out and Jesus Saved him and said to him "o ye of little faith"! So we must never doubt nor fear anything or anyone but God alone! Clearly, also, there is no such thing as holy ghost; but rather Holy Spirit! Jesus Christ Rose from the dead and is alive not a ghost! How can His Spirit then be a ghost! Error of errors! Lord, help us to humble ourselves to yield to the Holy Spirit and not to see Your Holy Spirit as a ghost anymore in Jesus' Name. Amen!!!

283rd Day

DOUBT IT ALL YOU WANT! JESUS CHRIST IS COMING BACK AGAIN! BETTER SAFE THAN SORRY! BE PREPARED!!!

We see these manifest in the life of John the Baptist in the New Testament many many years later! He lived out these prophetic words in the Holy Scriptures! Every Word God Has Spoken comes to pass without fail! Jesus Christ Himself Spoke of His Coming back and I believe the Word of the Living God! He IS coming back again! Better be safe than sorry. Prepare your heart, mind, body, soul and spirit! When He Comes back, there will be no more opportunity to repent of sin, evil and wickedness. It will be Judgement Time! Lord, Help us to be prepared; Help prepare us for Your Second Coming in Jesus' Name. Amen!!!

Jesus Christ confirms in the above Scripture that Elijah indeed came first and they did to him whatever they wished. Let us recall how John the Baptist died? He was beheaded as if for fun to please the daughter of a king who asked for what her mother wanted because the servant of God preached against her unfaithfulness! Hmmm! There is a God; the Judge of all things. His Name is Jesus! He was treated with utmost contempt but triumphed at last! He Lives forever and ever as LORD! Help us o Lord to appreciate Your Word and receive Your Counsel in Jesus' Name. Amen!!!

Jesus predicted that He would be left all alone by the disciples! Peter affirmed his loyalty! Jesus told him otherwise. Hmmmm! The Word of the Lord came to pass eventually! He is the Lord! We must be careful not to be flippant nor arrogant in our hearts! We ought to be quick to hear and slow to speak. Meditate carefully on the Word of God; don't just react to it. Consider the Word of God carefully before responding, reacting to and or acting on it! Father, Help us to take Your Word seriously and not receive it in a haste in Jesus' Name. Amen!!!

God set apart a day of rest! It is pleasing to God when we obey Him! So therefore let us enter into His Rest and do good continuously in Jesus' Name. Are you resting? Are you observing the Sabbath? Are you in His Rest? With man this may be impossible; but with God all things are possible! Lord, Help us to enter into Your Rest in Jesus' Name. Amen!!!

284th Day

MAKE NO MISTAKES ABOUT IT; JESUS CHRIST IS COMING BACK AGAIN SOON AND VERY SOON! BE PREPARED OR BE SORRY!!!

You know scoffers by their words; they always question and ridicule the word of God. Don't bother wasting your time or life with them! They are lustful and will do anything to justify their way of life. Often they know the Word of God but wilfully ignore it for their own convenience to do as they wish! But one day, Judgement is coming upon the whole earth/world. Heaven and earth will pass away; but the Word of God shall remain Eternally! As per timing, human timing is not the same as God's Timing. In your eyes, God may appear not quick enough for you; however, consider wisely that God's Timing is perfect in Jesus Christ! God appears slow to act because He's Waiting for humans to make relevant changes according to His Word; but sadly, we often don't till it's too late! Lord, Help us not to be scoffers and to avoid associating or fellowshipping with them in Jesus' Name. Amen!!!

As a servant or child of God, you must do your best to fulfill your Calling and or Ministry with a gentle spirit. Especially with the opposition (and there will be plenty); perhaps it will please God in His infinite mercies to "Touch" their hearts and open them up to the knowledge of the Truth by repentance and humility, having been taken captive to do the devil's will previously. God be praised forever and ever. Amen! Father, Help us to be completely humble and gentle with the Help of Your Holy Spirit in Jesus' Name. Amen!!!

There will be times in your life when you feel like Jesus did here! Do not despair because even friends will desert you just like family will too! But don't despair; trust in the Name of the Lord Jesus Christ. He Will See you through! Don't live your life in sin because your stressings will be in vain and not like this of our Lord Jesus Christ! Father, Help us to trust in You in times of crisis when our souls are troubled and we are sorrowful, in Jesus' Name. Amen!!!

285th Day

DEUTRONOMY 25 IS AS REAL THEN AS IT IS NOW AND FOREVER; BLESSINGS FOR OBEDIENCE, CURSES FOR DISOBEDIENCE! THE WORD OF GOD IS UNCHANGEABLE!!!

Many wittingly or unwittingly believe in lies and the words of false prophets! That God's Love is unconditional was NEVER spoken by God Almighty! Those are the words of depraved men and women how want to impress their hearers with niceties and kind words! Speaking these words in the Name of the Lord is pure heresy and sinful because they mislead many! All over the Holy Scriptures, God Gives Instructions and urges obedience, followed by Blessings! This has been from the beginning and will never change. It's God's Law and Ordinance. It's the way God Has Ordered the world and life to function! Blessings for obedience and curses for disobedience!

Hearing and or reading are the easy bits; doing and obeying constitute the "big deal" the "real deal"! The Key to God's Love and Blessings is in obeying and doing the Word that is heard! If you truly love the Lord God Almighty, you will have no problem obeying Him! The evidence of love for God is in obedience! Then the Love is activated in Blessings! Please God, Help us to understand Your Word and the workings of Your Holy Spirit and Heart; so we may obey Your Word and have access to Your Love and Blessings in Jesus' Name. Amen!!!

Anyone that listens to and does (obeys) the Voice and Will of the Father, the Lord and the Holy Spirit is the Lord's family member! Do you claim to belong to the Lord? What is the evidence proving this in your life? The Lord is mine and I am His is very easy for even satan to say because he is the master of deceit, falsehood and lies! You may say anything you like and many may be deceived. However, you cannot deceive God Almighty in Jesus' Name. Lord, please Help us to be hearers and doers of Your Word and Will in Jesus' Name. Amen!!!

There will be times in our lives when we'll be as Jesus was here! Even many times! We're in need of and looking for support from human beings. This is natural; but we mustn't be surprised that we find that everyone deserts us at such times! They're only being human. That's why our trust must be wholly and fully in God Almighty in Jesus' Christ our Lord God Saviour and King! We must not stop watching and praying; because satan gets a field day when we lose faith - evidenced by giving up on praying and watching in the Name of the Lord! Father, Help us to watch and pray so we will not fall into temptation in Jesus' Name. Amen!!!

Just meditate on the Word of God above to see how God trusted and blessed man with such glorious responsibilities for His Creation as a firstborn with His firstfruits! Great Love manifesting in great responsibility! What did man do? Was he faithful to the charge God Gave him? If not, why not? God Blessed man to increase and multiply; what more could man ask or pray for in life? Man however fell to the wiles of woman. What has changed today? Hmmmm! O Lord God Almighty, please save us from ourselves in Jesus' Name. Help us to Love You absolutely and follow Your Ways; that we may be truly Blessed in Your Divine Love in Jesus' Name. Amen!!!

286th Day

PLEASE THE LORD AND SET YOUR CONSCIENCE FREE TO SERVE AND PRAISE HIM FOR LIFE AND ETERNITY!!!

How can we free our hearts, minds and consciences from condemnation? Only by obeying the Lord's Commandments and doing what is pleasing unto Him. His Command is primarily to Love the Lord our God wholly, believe in the Name of Jesus Christ His Son and Love one another! Why is this so difficult for us human beings? It's because of our love and preference for sin which is sweet to our fleshly souls! Please Lord, Help us to die to our fleshly desires and to embrace Your Truth and Light in Jesus' Name. Amen!!!

We must bear in mind that we shall all be Judged and as such seek to please God the Lord our Saviou and King so we can have His Favour on the Day of Judgement! May God Help us to do what is right and pleasing to Him; for all have sinned and fallen short of His Glory in Jesus' Name. Amen!!!

Many pray for God's approval! Do you know what it takes for God to approve you? You must endure unjust pains and much suffering! This is the very core and essence of the Calling of God upon the life of a person! We must follow the example of Jesus Christ and suffer like and for Him in Jesus' Name. Father, please Help us to accept the truth of Your Word and to accept and endure suffering for Your Name's sake in Jesus' Name. Amen!!!

Many times you will pray and it would appear that your prayer is not answered just like that of Jesus Christ! Do not despair! It's because of the Higher Calling of God Who Sees and Knows and Has Ordained everything! Lord, Give us the grace to accept Your Calling and all that comes with it in Jesus' Name. Amen!!!

This time was predicted in prophesy and such a time is now upon us. Father, please protect and defend us against any untoward foulness that might want to attack out spirits, minds, souls, hearts, bodies and all in Jesus' Name. Keep us in Your Love o Lord I prya in Jesus' Name. Amen!!!

Father, Help us to Love like You want us to in Jesus' Name. Amen! Teach us Your Love in Jesus' Name. Amen!!!

287th Day

THE PROPHETIC WORD OF GOD IS SPOKEN AND SHALL COME TO PASS! JESUS CHRIST IS COMING BACK AGAIN! FAITH IS RECEIVED BY GRACE! JESUS LIVES THROUGH ME! AMEN!!

A time is coming when the Glory of the Lord will be feared, honoured and respected again in the land! A time is yet coming upon the earth when the Lord God of all life will take His rightful place in Jesus' Name. Father, let Your Will be done on earth as it is in Heaven and in our lives in Jesus' Name. Amen!!!

The message of Elijah is so very clear in the above Scriptures! Lord Help us to heed the Word You Sent us through Your servant Elijah and to obey in Jesus' Name. Amen! Prepare us o Lord for Your Second Coming because we have no power nor strength of our own in ourselves to make preparation successfully! Help us o Lord so we do not lose out on that Day in Jesus' Name. Amen!!!

The Message of Jesus Christ is a Transformational Message! It is such that we ought to be changed in a way so as to be like Jesus Christ! To submit to Christlikeness is to embrace this transformational change message! Father, Help us to be more like You day after day in Jesus' Name. Amen!!!

288th Day

I AM AND YOU CAN BE REDEEMED ONLY BY JESUS CHRIST THE ONE GOD SAVIOUR REDEEMER KING SACRIFICED ONCE FOR ALL!!!

Jesus Christ is God who came in the human flesh to save mankind from their sins through forgiveness of sins by faith (believing) in Him. Thereby, Jesus Christ is the One Who Justifies anyone as the law cannot do! I have decided to follow Jesus Christ; for me there's no turning back nor bye. Help all who have made and will make this choice o Lord to stand firm to the very end in Jesus' Name. Amen!!!

You live once and die only once; then you must face the Judgement of God Almighty! So, mind how you live your life; because your every move is noted by the Almighty God! The Sacrifice made by Jesus Christ at his first coming was made once for all mankind (not animals)! He's coming back again a second time for the purpose of salvation without reference to sin because a decision would already have been made in His Judgement! Then He Will Save those who eagerly await Him! Father God, please count us worthy to be amongst those You Will Save in Jesus' Name. Amen!!!

Jesus Christ Commissioned all believers to take the Gospel they believe(d) all over the earth starting from Jerusalem. We must let others know that there is forgiveness of sins available to all who choose to turn to Jesus Christ for salvation of their souls! Lord, please Help us to fulfill Your Commission to the best of our ability in Jesus' Name. Amen. We cannot do it by ourselves o Lord; we need You!!!

Unto the Lord be the Glory, great things He Has Done; unto the Lord be the Glory, great things He Has Done (2ce)! Great things He Has Done, greater things He Will Do; unto the Lord be the Glory, great things He Has Done (repeat)! In You O Lord I put my full trust my Father God Saviour Lord and King! Lead me on this Your Journey; Teach me Your Ways! Do not count my sins against me o Lord; let me be so Blessed for Your Goodness' sake in Jesus' Name. I pray! Remember o Lord, all Your children likewise o Lord in Jesus' Name. Amen!!!

O Lord, we look to You for vengeance upon our enemies! We have suffered and continue to suffer in the hands of the oppressor! Remember us kindly o Lord in Jesus' Name. Amen! Remember Your children kindly o Lord; and Help us in Jesus' Name. Amen!!!

289th Day

REFLECT AND MEDITATE ON THE LOVE OF GOD FOR YOU IN JESUS' NAME! DON'T BETRAY OR ABUSE HIS LOVE! LOVE!!!

My mother often said to me from my childhood that "eni ta ba fe la n'beru". Meaning, it is the one we love that we fear (not as in the negative fear, but rather that we fear to hurt or that we fear to see us in any compromising situation)! If we truly love Jesus Christ, we must remember always that He first loved us; and as such we must strive to always obey and please Him in all that we think, speak or do! Help us o Lord to love You in Jesus' Name. Amen!!!

Jesus Christ is very clear in His Word that the proof of our love for Him is in our obedience to His Word! When we prove our love for Him in this way, He said we shall be loved by the Father and Himself and He shall Reveal Himself to us! In fact, He said in the Word of God in the New Testament, that He and the Father will come and make their home with us! O Lord, please come and make our homes Your resting place in Jesus' Name. Amen!!!

We who love the Lord truly absolutely need His Love, Eternal Comfort, Good Hope, Grace, Strength, Mercy and all His Goodness in our lives and families. Lord, may we find this Divine Favour with You in Jesus' Name. Amen!!!

For the Father himself loves you dearly because you love me and believe that I came from God. John 14:27 NLT

I keep telling people that the Lord Told me that His Love, the Love of God is not unconditional! The above Scriptures all point to the fact that God Reveals His Love and Himself to you when you love Him and prove your love in obedience to His Word! God doesn't just bandy His Love about willy nilly. God's Love is very focused although readily available! Please do not take the ready availability of God's Love for chear or for granted! Please Father, Give us understanding and wisdom to recognise the value of Your Love and not to take Your Love for cheap or for granted in Jesus' Name. Amen!!!

Judas Iscariot betrayed the Love of Jesus Christ; he took His Love for cheap and for granted in betraying Him to His enemies! But the Word of God came true for Jesus Christ; as all things worked for His Good because He IS Love and Called according to the purposes of God Almighty! With an act of "love", Judas gave Jesus Christ away; and he paid an eternal price. Father, forgive us our trespasses and do not let us live our lives in vain in Jesus' Name. Amen!!!

Marriage is an institution approved and designed by God for His Purposes; and He fashioned it after His Word and only likens the relationship He Wants with His Church with marriage! God's design for marriage is that a man and a woman come together; the woman as his helper. A lack of respect and or understanding for this holy ordinance is the root of much discomfort and pain in humanity today! Father, please Help us to appreciate, value and respect Your holy ordinance of marriage in life in Jesus' Name. Amen!!!

290th Day

TO GROW IN GRACE WE MUST BE CONSISTENT IN GOODNESS, MERCY, LOVE, LOVING WITH INTEGRITY WITH GOD'S HELP!!!

We ought always to thank God for you, brothers, and rightly so, because your faith is growing more and more, and the love every one of you has for each other is increasing. to Thessalonians 1:3 NIV

Be always grateful when you find people of faith to fellowship with and spend quality time with. By their quality of faith living, God Causes them to increase in every way even as He Protects, Defends and Blesses them increasingly even with the greatest gift of all, Love in Jesus' Name. Father, so Bless us in this way in Jesus Name and Keep us abiding in You throug Jesus Christ our Lord. Amen!!!

As a believer we must never give up; but rather keep striving for the best choice of all - towards the mark for the prize of the high calling of God in Jesus Christ! We must maintain this mindset to the very end and for those who still do not understand these things, may God Reveal them unto you in Jesus' Name. Amen. Father, please Enable us to walk with faitn, hope, love, with integrity and standing firmly in Jesus Christ. Amen!!!

In doing good, the believer must pursue and strive for righteous holy living rigorously and hold onto the goodness of God with integrity and love as an urgent priority in Jesus' Name. Amen! Then the Lord Shall Cause increase to come upon us in every way through Jesus Christ our Lord God Saviour and King. Father, Help us to stand firmly in the Faith in Jesus' Name. Amen!!!

The Lord is the Greatest and Highest Authority in Heaven and on earth; yet He Takes congnisance of the lowly and does not despise His creation especially man! So, why don't we choose to emulate God; rather we emulate the pride of man and despise one another and even the Great Almighty God Who Possesses life and death in His Hands! Only Jesus Christ Can Save! Father, Help us to humble ourselves and accept Your full and maximum Authority as the best way for us in Jesus' Name. Amen!!!

Vain is the help of man as in this case; but the believer's reliance must be upon the Help of God Almighty! Some things are meant to be; no matter how hard you try, nothing moves. So, you must learn to let go and let God and all will be well. Trust God that all things work for the good of those who love the Lord and are Called according to His Purposes! Lord, Give us discernment to recognise Your Will in Jesus' Name. Amen!!!

The contents of the Book of Revelations in the Holy Scriptures is real and true unto the Lord. It makes no sense to the carnal mind and man; but to the faithful, it is very significant for the faith in Jesus Christ! It is prophetic and discernible only by revelation through the Holy Spirit in Jesus' Name. Amen. Lord, Help us not to add to nor take away from Your Word; so not to fall under Your wrath - but rather to obey Your Word so as to be Blessed and Loved by You to the very end in Jesus' Name. Amen!!!

291st Day

LOVE IS PATIENT! DO NOT BE WEARY IN DOING GOOD! TAKE ADVERSITY POSITIVELY! YOUR LABOUR SHALL NOT BE IN VAIN!!!

Patience is the very first virtue in love. God is love and very patient indeed; slow to anger and abounding in love! In anything in life, like the farmer, we must be very patient; especially when we encounter a situation where we can be angry. Anger never leads to anything positive especially if managed badly and not kept in control! Lord, Teach us to be patient as You are in Jesus' Name. Amen!!!

When God Lays it on your heart to do good, keep doing good and don't give up nor get tired. Continue to do good as far as it is within your power to all people; especially people who belong to the family of believers and God Will Bless and Reward you in Jesus' Name. Father, Help us to do good and be increasingly like You in Jesus' Name. Amen!!!

Tribulations are not necessarily bad for us. They help us to learn and gain perseverance. That helps to hone our character, which in turn increases our hope! So, it's all goodness and from God Almighty. Knowing this, we ought to not worry so much at all. The Bible urges that we should not worry but trust God. But being human, we tend to worry so much. Learning, knowing and understanding the Word of God gives us a solid foundation of trust on which we can build with love in Jesus' Name. Father, Help us to see adversity in a positive light and brace us up for any challenges life may throw in our way in Jesus' Name. Amen!!!

Every other thing that we do is meaningless; vanity upon vanity! Only whatever we do in the Name of the Lord is never useless and matters in this life and in the next! Spend your time wisely; because your time is your life! You get only one life and live just once. It is appointed once to live and once to die; after that, judgement! Father, Help us to make the best and the most of the life that You Have Given us in Jesus' Name. Amen!!!

The hypocrisy and deviousness of the human nature, with the deceitfulness and desperate wickedness is revealed fully in the action of the captors of Jesus Christ. They came with swords and clubs to arrest an innocent man who had been among them for a long time and they didn't lay a finger on him. However, it was all part of God's Divine Plan. Father, Help us to be wise in all situations and to take whatever comes our way as You would have us take things in Jesus' Name. Amen!!!

Please do not expect everybody you preach or speak the Word of God to give you audience, to be kindly or; to understand and appreciate you or what you deliver to them! To many of them, your message is as foolishness because they are of the perishing folks. However to those who shall be saved and are being saved it is the Power of God! Remember your message is that of the Cross of Jesus Christ and not just a mere message of yours! God however uses the foolish things of the world to confound the intelligence of the wise and their wisdom! The wisdom of the world did not bless the world with the knowledge of God; however, it pleased God through what the world sees as foolishness of the Gospel of Jesus Christ, to save those who believe the message. Father, Help us to believe the Word of God and never lose our faith in Jesus' Name. Amen!!!

292nd Day

I CANNOT SPEAK OR WRITE ENOUGH ABOUT LOVE AND LOVING GOD AND LOVING ONE ANOTHER! LOVE MUST BE SINCERE!!!

How can you claim to be in the light but still hate your brethren? Love is light. When you love your brethren, you prove that you are in the light. However, hatred is synonymous with darkness. When you hate your brethren, you are in darkness! We need God in Christ Jesus to help us love one another. Father, Bless us with Your Love o Lord in Jesus' Name. Amen!!!

The best Teacher on the subject of Love is God Almighty! His Name is Jesus Christ! You can learn from men and women who have been Taught by God; but the best Teacher of all is the One Who is LOVE Himself! Father, Give us, Teach us, Bless us with Love, as You would have us love in Jesus' Name. Amen!!!

When you are in Jesus Christ, this must show in your life in every way and in everything you touch and wherever you go! Forgiveness is a big part of love. We must learn to forgive. Forgiveness is mutually beneficial. If you cannot forgive, then you are really very unwell and will run into trouble! However in forgiving one another, you show true love. Please do not hesitate to say you are sorry when you wrong your brethren. Sometimes you say sorry even when you are right for love's sake. My wife is the queen of that kind of love. This makes me to never want to hurt her. A woman who strives always to be very humble, respectful, positively inclined and supportive of me in every way possible for her. It's very hard not to love such a woman and even harder to hurt her. I pray that someone reading this will learn a thing or two. Jesus my Lord! O God, please Help us to show love for one another because love is not by mouth but by action; in Jesus' Name. Amen!!!

Oh so we are to make allowance for each other's faults? How can we do that except by loving one another! There is no othe way to make room for each other except in our hearts; so that when we hurt each other, we should not close our hearts to one another! Hmmmm! Also to unite by the Holy Spirit with the bond of peace requires Love. Only love can bind us together in unity of the Holy Spirit! Wow! We are ONE body, same SPIRIT and Called to the same glorious future by this same God! Glory to the Lord Most High in Jesus' Name. Father God, please Help us to know who we are in Christ Jesus and to act accordingly towards one another in Jesus' Name. Amen!!!

The one Jesus is supposed to have trusted the most also deserted Him. That's human. Put your trust only in God; in Jesus' Christ! In deserting him, he followed to see the outcome of the arrest. But remember he told Jesus that even if everybody else deserted Him, he would die for Jesus Christ. Hmmm. Man is full of mouth and found wanting when it's time for action. Father, Help us to trust You and be prepared to walk the Faith alone just with You; for with You, we are never alone in Jesus' Name. Amen!!!

We all judge but don't like to be judged. But God is telling us all the time that we shall be judged by the same measure we use to judge others! Deal with your own issues first; before looking to see and trying to deal with the issues of others! Then you will see clearly to help another person! Love your neighbour as yourself. If you don't love yourself, how can you love your neighbour? Yet the Bible says that the man of God shall be a judge of all things but be subject to no man's judgement. The Word of God takes God's Wisdom and the Revelation of the Holy Sprit to decipher! Father, Help us! Give us discernment by Your Holy Spirit to understand Your Word and to judge only according to Your Love and direction in Jesus' Name. Amen!!!

293rd Day

WHEN YOU TRUST IN THE LORD, HE MAKES ALL GRACE ABOUND UNTO YOU AND MEETS ALL YOUR NEEDS!!!

Do you trust in the Lord really and truly? Do you believe that He Will Do what He Promises to do? When God Says He Will Supply all our needs, we need to believe this. How many of us claim to trust Him but live in anxiety and fear daily. Do we really trust Him? When you want to jump into your bed at night, do you fear that the bed might crash to the ground? That's faith! You believe in your bed more than you believe in God! Father, Help us to trust in You because only You can give us true faith in Jesus' Name. Amen!!!

In meeting our needs, God Gives us Grace; and so we may abound unto every good work in Jesus Christ! He is the Giver of all gifts and He Gives unto whomsoever He Wills; especially to the poor. He is a righteous God; and His righteousness endures forevermore! If you need your coasts enlarged, it is to Him that you must go! When God Makes you rich, it is not for you to hoard, it is so you may be generous to people who will show gratitude to God for your generosity! This is how to live in Jesus Christ; and not the looking out only for number one that is so prevalent today! Father God, please Help us to get our priorities right in Jesus' Name. Amen!!!

Go and tell the whole world that the Kingdom of Heaven is at hand. The Lord Will go with you by the Power of His Holy Spirit as you do so; and the sick will be healed, the lepers cleansed, the dead raised and the demons cast out! This ability cost you nothing and you are to deliver freely accordingly! Father, Help us please to do Your Will and please Back us up with the Power of Your Holy Spirit in Jesus' Name. Amen!!!

There was a decision taken to look for false evidence with which to nail our Lord Jesus Christ; any wonder that the same thing happens to us today? However when we face such things, what do we do? We tend to panic and become anxious! No need to stress yourself; just trust in the Name of the Lord Jesus Christ who went through worse at the hands of evil men! God

Will Deliver us in Jesus' Name. The enemies' testimony will not tally and will be conflicting in Jesus' Name. Help Deliver us o Lord from the wiles of the enemy in Jesus' Name. Amen!!!

Be careful how you engage people and what you engage in because the Lord Jesus Christ is going around by His Holy Spirit and you may not be aware. Remember the Word of God that told us that whatsoever you do unto one of my brothers, that you do unto me! Be careful how you entertain strangers because you might be entertaining the Lord Jesus Christ without knowing so. Jesus my King, Help me my Father to be discerning of Your Holy Spirit whenever present and whether present or not that I may not sin against You in Jesus' Name. Amen! Pray this over your life and family in Jesus' Name. Amen!!!

294th Day

WHEN YOU KNOW THE LORD AND ARE TRULY IN HIS LOVE, NOTHING CAN SEPARATE YOU FROM HIS LOVE IN CHRIST JESUS!!!

Can anything separate you from the love of Jesus Christ? Is there anything you cannot give up or do for the sake of Jesus Christ? Jesus Christ gave up HIs Life for you on the Cross at Calvary even though you were conceived, born and bred in sin! He didn't even think about it or bat an eyelid! He just did it! How do you want to react to the Love of Jesus Christ in your life today? Please think and meditate on this folks! Lord, Help us to appreciate Your Love and Sacrifice for humanity in Jesus' Name. Amen!!!

No matter what comes my way, I'll live for Jesus day after day, come what may; His Holy Spirit, I will obey, I'll live for Jesus, day after day! Help us o Lord, to live for You, no matter what comes our way, good or bad in Jesus' Name. Amen. You are more than Able! We love and appreciate You fully o Lord in Jesus' Name. Amen!!!

Godliness with contentment is great gain! The Lord is my Teacher and He has taught me how to cope in whatever circumstances I find myself under; whether in abundance or in lack. Therefore, I can do anything through Jesus Christ who Gives me Strength! Thank You Lord Jesus. Halleluyah, Amen! Father, Help me to live each day one day at a time according to Your Will in Jesus' Name. Amen!!!

God's Love for humanity is so real, pure and so dynamic! However this love will not work for you unless you believe! The only condition is that you believe and obey His Word to get the best of His Love and be Blessed by and in Him! He Alone can save us from all evil. We are reconciled with God only through the death of Jesus Christ on the Cross and His Resurrection! We shall be saved from eternal damnation and punishment only by faith in Jesus Christ. Help us o Lord to believe in Jesus Christ and His Holy Sacrifice in Jesus' Name. Amen!!!

You cannot love God and know His Love and go around hating people! If you are capable of hatred, then you don't know God's Love! We are to love one another deeply and sincerely from the heart. No hatred whatsoever is allowed for one unto another. Lord, please keep us away from hatred of any kind whatsoever in Jesus' Name. Amen!!!

295th Day

BE WISE! WORK HARD EARN YOUR KEEP AS A BELIEVER! TO GET REWARDED FOR AND ENJOY YOUR HARD WORK IS A GIFT FROM GOD!!!

Basically God is Just and wants everyone to earn their pay; also to work for their food. Idleness leads only to many temptations to sin and mischief making. Busybodying and gossip mongering go together. God wants all to live honourably in Christ Jesus. Father, Help us to work and earn our pay and food; to live honourably amongst all men in Jesus' Name. Amen!!!

The way of the slothful man is as an hedge of thorns: but the way of the righteous is made plain. Proverbs 15:19 KJV

When you live an idle lazy life, your life becomes a misery and a disaster; your way becomes like a hedge of thorns! However, not so for the righteous; for the righteous do what is right according to the Word of God, even shared above. Help us to live the holy and righteous life approved for believers by God in Jesus' Name. Amen!!!

When you eat and enjoy your food and drink; enjoy and reap the fruits of your labour - this is a Blessing from God Almighty. God Gives wealth and riches to whomsoever He Desires. If you have that good fortune and He Enables you to enjoy it all, then you are truly Blessed. Father, please Bless us and Enable us to enjoy Your Blessings in our lifes o Lord in Jesus' Name. Amen!!!

Ants are God's creation too! They have no ruler or leader to direct their affairs; yet are most organised and achieve great feats simply by co-operating with each other! Is that not the power of love and caring for one another? If only we can learn from those little despised creatures, how Blessed we would be. Lord, Give us wisdom as You Endowed the ants so we may collaborate like them and have great success in Jesus' Name. Amen!!!

God Created all things for our sakes! Why? That we may appreciate and give Him thanks always. The Bible says to give thanks in all circumstances; not just when things are good but also when they're not good! No matter how hard things are for us; even though we may perish on the outside, inside, we are renewed continuously! Be assured of this: that our afflictions are all momentary; achieving for us a glory which is eternal. We often focus on things that we see; forgetting that they are temporal. It is the things that we do not see that last forever! Do not focus on circumstances; rather, give room, make room for the things that are unseen. Focus on the unseen. The spirit is most powerful as everything is controlled and driven by the spirit! Father, Help us to be wise and to understand the driving force of life, the Holy Spirit of God and to submit ourselves and lives to be so guided in Jesus' Name. Amen!!!

This simple paragraph of Scripture captures the essence of the believer's faith in Jesus Christ; proving the Lordship and Godhead of Christ Jesus beyond any doubts for those who will listen and be saved. Meditate on the Word of God always; for it is very profitable so to do! Jesus Christ is the Lord God Almighty! Believing in Him and in His Sacrifice changes and transforms lives and leads the believer right unto Eternal Life and Eternity; Jesus Christ is Eternal Life!!!

296th Day

WE ASSUME THAT LONG LIFE IS AUTOMATIC DESPITE ALL THE EVIDENCE AROUND US! WHO REALLY CARES TO TAKE THE WORD OF GOD SERIOUSLY! CHOOSE LIFE!!!

God gave us commandments from His infinite wisdom for our own good; but we always think that we know better than God. Just like when children rebel against parents; thinking and sometimes saying that their parents' counsel is archaic and believing that the parents don't know what is best for their children. Hmmmm! Be very careful folks! God is Love truly; but He is also an All-Consuming Fire! Father, Help us not to sin against You in Jesus' Name. Amen!!!

God made a promise to the children of Israel! He is reminding them in the Scripture above. What does God ask in return? To fear God and obey His Commandments. People always say that God's Love is unconditional. This is so far from the truth of God and His Word. Otherwise God would not go on and on about fearing Him and obeying His Commandments in His Word! To whom much is given, much is desired is part of God's Word too! Father, Teach us Your Ways and Give us a heart that is willing to obey and please You in Jesus' Name. Amen!!!

Some even say to you that God is your father and you don't need to fear God! What rubbish! The Word of God tells us to fear God and some smart intellectual tells you otherwise and you believe him or her over God and His Word? That is disrespectful in itself and punishable by God! Hmmm! O Father, we are so foolish; Help us to receive Your Wisdom for life in Jesus' Name. Amen!!!

There is none holy as the Lord! Who is like the Lord for us who believe? No one! You raise us from youth until we're old and grey, just for Your Purposes in Christ Jesus. To seek Your Face and to declare Your Wonders to our generation and the next generation; such that they do likewise and Your Renown moves with the Power of Your Holy Spirit through the generations forever and ever. Amen. Father, Help us to do Your Bidding in Jesus' Name. Amen!!!

Our Lord Jesus Christ was charged under oath to confirm His Identity like a common criminal. He took it all for our sakes; that we might be reconciled to God Almighty! Jesus did; but was He believed? That very confirmation was used against Him; and for that reason He had to die. They thought they were doing right; however, they didn't know that they were acting out God's already written script! He was brutalised maximally and subsequently sentenced to death; the worst possible death reserved for the worst of criminals. Yes, this is what Jesus Christ went through for you and for me and indeed for all humanity! Yet, how many of us accept Him? How many of us obey His Word? Hmmm! Forgive us o Lord; for we have sinned against You. Help our unbelief and sinfulness. Help us to be more like You day after day till we are perfect in Jesus Name. Amen!!!

The world teaches us that faith is "seeing is believing"! Would we listen to the world or to God? Judge yourself; and see who you really believe! Faith is being sure of what we hope for and certain of what we have not seen! Faith is the substance of things hoped for, the evidence of things unseen! Faith is the substand and evidence of what you hope for but have not seen. It is certainly NOT "seeing is believing"! Let God be true and all else liars. Our God is TRUTH! Jesus Christ is the Way the Truth and the Life! Glory Halleluyah!!!

297th Day

LOVE GOD; LIVE LIFE; LOVE LIFE! LIVE GODLY WITH GODLY LOVE FOR ONE ANOTHER DOING NO HARM TO ANYONE!!!

Apart from God's express Command to Love the Lord our God with all our hearts, might, minds and souls; we are to love our neighbours as ourselves! We are basically to harm no one because love does no harm to its neighbour! Now going onto marriage; the only institution God likens His relationship with mankind to as in the above Scripture! Marriage is a profound mystery; a man leaves his parents and unites with his wife as one flesh! Who does that? Whoever gets that right will have peace in marriage. The man and the woman must get this right! Unite as one flesh! The key is the "unite" bit! The man must love his wife and the wife must respect her husband. This came up whilst discussing Christ and the Church! Father, Help us to recognise the value and importance of obeying Your Ordinances in marriage and in our relationship with You in Jesus' Name. Amen!!!

This is part of the valuable roles of the older women in the Church. Where are these women today? Will the true godly women, the mothers in Israel stand up please? Who teaches these things today? In not teaching these things, we subscribe to the Word of God being blasphemed! Father, Help us; Give us role models - men and women who love and value the Lord and the Word of the Lord to teach to the younger generations in Jesus' Name. Amen!!!

To be able to enjoy the woman you love all the days of your fleeting life on earth is a gift and a blessing from the Lord God Almighty! Make the most of it; or strive to make this happen in your life as a man. Likewise, the women ought to make this concept their goal in life too. This is the true value of love. Marriage works with the right principles according to the Word of the Living God; all knowing, all Wise, all Present, all Powerful, all Kind, He Alone is God and Knows how to do the best thing for us! Father, Help us to apply the principles of Your Word in our daily lives; in marriage and all our ways in Jesus' Name. Amen!!!

Submission in marriage is not an easy thing for any wife to do; it's a choice wives must make. If you make the right choice according to the Word of the Living God as described above, you will reap a just reward for your obedience in Jesus Christ! If men would truly learn to apply the principles of love in marriage, the wheels of that marriage will be truly well oiled and love will flow if both the man and woman embrace the principles guiding love according to the Word of God! Father, Help us to love one another in marriage and in our daily lives in Jesus' Name. Amen!!!

The weight of unfaithfulness and betrayal is much to carry for anyone. God hates for us to break faith with one another; especially in marriage, but also in daily living! Peter assured Jesus Christ of his faithfulness to the very end no matter what; however, he failed very badly, didn't he? We all must and should look inwards! Are we faithful? Remember, love does no harm to its neighbour! Breaking faith is harming one another when we do so! Father, Help us not to break faith but rather keep the Faith with You and with each other in Jesus' Name. Amen!!!

We are to find ways to stir up love and good works in each other and fan love to flame; even as we meet up with each other and have sweet fellowship. Even in resolving our differences; we must strive to do so peacefully! Rather, what do we do? We often just keep on stirring up dissension and causing disaffection amongst our brethren! We seem to love evil far more than we love good! May God Help us! Sin has practically become our master! Lord, Help us to obey Your Word and forsake sin, lies, falsehood and all evil and wickedness; rather to embrace LOVE in Jesus' Name. Amen!!!

298th Day

IN LIVING AND LOVING PATIENCE, PESEVERANCE, ENDURANCE ARE VERY CRITICAL VIRTUES TO HAVE IN JESUS' NAME. AMEN!!!

Such things are happening even today; that cause many to turn away from the Faith, betray, hate each other etc.! Deceivers deceiving, false prophets teaching and prophesying lies to many people! Wickedness increasing daily; the love of many growing cold and waning. The believer must stand firm to the very end in order to be saved. Only those who stand firm to the end shall be saved! Lord, Help us not to fall into temptation and be taken in by sin and wickedness; Help us to stand firm for the Truth and in the Faith to the very end so we are Saved in Jesus' Name. Amen!!!

When you face tribulations and temptations, you don't have to be saddened, rejoice! These allow your faith to be tried, in order that you may develop patience; which works perfection into you when allowed to perfect its work until you reach maturity fully and wanting for nothing. Only Jesus Christ can bring this about; but we must have faith and be prepared to go with Him all the way, no matter what we face. Father, Help us to see adversity and temptation as opportunities for our faith to develop and work us into perfection in Jesus' Name. Amen!!!

Do not allow your confidence in the Lord Jesus Christ to weaken or be taken or stolen away from you by the forces of darkness! Even after living right for Jesus Christ, patience is required; as a farmer waits until the harvest after planting. There is a waiting time before the reward comes. During this waiting time is when many fall away discouraged and others ridicule the Lord and question the reality of God etc.! Do not fall victim likewise! The Lord is coming back again and His Reward with Him. Be patient to gain the prize and not fall away unto perdition. Father, please Save us in Jesus' Name. Do not allow us to fall away in Jesus' Name. Amen!!!

Who are those who put Jesus Christ to death? Is it not the chief priests and the elders of the people? His own people? Of course, it took betrayal by

Judas Iscariot; who after the act, was convicted. He returned the money he took for the betrayal and confessed that he had betrayed innocent blood. But, it was too late; they told him that was all his responsibility and they washed their hands off in their own minds and way! Convicted, Judas went on to hang himself! Justice served seemingly. But was that the end? Where is Judas today? Heaven or hell? Hmmmm! Be careful when you betray one another for the risk of hell fire is very high for all traitors and betrayers! Father, Help us not to break faith with one another; once faith is established, help us to see it right through to the end - even faith with our Lord Jesus Christ in Jesus' Name. Amen!!!

The greatest enemy of our lives is often our egos and selves, fueling our pride and arrogance! We think of ourselves better than our neighbours and strive always to be better than our neighbours. In so doing, we forsake God and end up not living our own lives according to our own destinies because we want to be like and better than others, rather than strive to be who God Wants us to be in Him! This works against the principles of love and brotherhood; and affects the recognition and usage of our giftings in the Lord. We are created individuals and thrive when we are able to live in harmony with our brethren; serving each other with God's Love driving us! We ought to focus on our individual calling and how to effectively administer that calling to the benefit of all our brethren at all times. Father, please Help us to be the best that we can be especially for the benefit of our brethren rather than to their detriment in Jesus' Name. Amen!!!

299th Day

SALVATION, STRENGTH, GOODNESS ALL COME FROM THE LORD WHO ALONE IS ABLE TO BLESS MANKIND IN JESUS' NAME!!!

This is faith! Although I see the goodness of the Lord everyday in the land of the living, I believe that there's much more to come in Jesus' Name. Therefore, I will wait for the Lord to Deliver for me. I will be strong, take heart and wait upon the Lord for the manifestation of His Blessings and Promises for and upon my life and family in Jesus' Name. Amen! Lord, Grant unto us the Grace to wait upon You rather than the world in Jesus' Name. Amen!!!

The Lord can and will sometimes punish and or chastise us for wrongdoings because no one is perfect. But, because He Loves His children, He chastises us. However, He relents and does not punish us forever! God doesn't grieve us willingly or for the fun of it; He's a good and merciful God! Father, please correct and or chastise us; but for Your Name's sake and with Your Mercy and Grace in Jesus' Name. Amen!!!

The Lord is my refuge and in my family and home, He is our refuge! Father I have no other Strength besides You in times of trouble! Help, save and deliver me from the wicked and evil ones! Lord my Father, Help us to keep You as our refuge forever in Jesus' Name. Amen!!!

You cry out to the Lord and He Delivers you every time; so why do you keep going back for more trouble in the troubled seas? Why do you remain in the world and dance to its tunes and follow its ways and keep coming back to the Lord to be saved? You are so steeped in rebellion; change your ways for your own and goodness' sake. Father, Help us keep our hearts loyal to You and Your Words in Jesus' Name. Amen!!!

So, clearly the chief priests knew that the money they paid Judas was blood money! Hmmmm! This world and this life! Folks, not all money is clean money. If you earn clean money, praise God; otherwise, you're in for some big time trouble as you add blood and dirty money to your account! Unclean money corrupts all your money and you cannot do much good with it ultimately! This is why the chief priests bought a field with the money for burying foreigners and called it the Field of Blood to date! Father, Help us to earn clean good money with which we can do good for our families, ourselves and others in Jesus' Name. Amen!!!

Loud and clear; no mincing words! You shall not steal! Sadly, stealing has associated behaviours bordering on dishonesty, lying etc. and sometimes progresses into armed or other forms of robbery and even murder! If only we would obey the Word of God, how much better our lives would be. Father, Help us to take Your Word seriously to obey in Jesus' Name. Amen!!!

300th Day

IT'S OK IF YOU FEEL A LACK OF CONFIDENCE SOMETIMES!
I RECOMMEND THAT YOU TRUST JESUS CHRIST FOR YOUR
CONFIDENCE! I FOUND THAT I'M BETTER OFF WITH JESUS!!!

Confidence is about faith, hope and love! When you love the Lord truly, you will trust Him with your life and every aspect of it! So, why worry about anything? Whether what to eat, drink, wear etc. The God Who takes care of the birds that do not sow and reap; just like He takes care of the ants who have no leader, is He not Able to take care of your every need? Will your worry make anything happen for you positively? So, from today, live a healthy, worry-free life in Jesus' Name. Amen! Father, Help us to live with confidence only in You and to live worry-free in Jesus' Name. Amen!!!

Let not thine heart envy sinners: but be thou in the fear of the LORD all the day long. For surely there is an end; and thine expectation shall not be cut off. Proverbs 23:17,18 KJV

Do not focus any of your attention on sinners and the gain they appear to always accumulate! Continue to live and be encouraged in Jesus Christ and with the Fear of the Lord. Surely the Lord who is the Alpha and Omega will bring you to an expected end and your hope and expectation will never be cut off in Jesus' Name. Amen! Father, Help us not to envy sinners nor want to be like them in Jesus' Name. Amen!!!

We all love to be acclaimed and for this reason many sell their souls to the devil for peanuts! If you truly value your life, you would avoid friendliness with the world because it makes you an enemy of God! I'd rather be on God's side than be against God! You would think that's common sense; but how people disregard this fact tells you that common sense is never common at all! God is very jealous of the spirit He Gavve us to dwell in us that gives us life! Stay on the Lord's side for your own good. Just my little humble advice; you don't have to take it. After all you are a big man or woman with a full mind of your own. Your choice! Father, Help us to choose to be Your friend than being friends with the world in Jesus' Name. Amen!!!

Help us o Lord to number our days and to take cognisance of how fleeting life is really! To You o Lord, a lifetime is no more than a mere moment, just a breath! We struggle for the "good" things in life that we cannot take to the grave where we're ending up. We fight, hate and kill for these futile things without a thought about how fleeting life is. Father, Grant us wisdom to take a proper account of life and to live it according to Your Word in order to maximise our potential in fulfilling our destinies, living for You and You alone in Jesus' Name. Amen!!!

When queried, Jesus gave answers according to His convictions but no more. He never once tried to defend Himself or talk His way out of the crimes they accused Him of committing. How very different than mankind! We would lie through our teeth even under oath (often taken in the Name of the Lord)! O Lord, please forgive us for we are unclean and worthless of Your Love, Mercy and Grace. O Father, change us in Jesus' Name. Amen!!!

When the Lord has Given you a charge, be faithful to it! There is a reward for all who diligently seek Him! God Sees all that you do and don't do! Don't think you will get away with eye service! God is a God of integrity and everybody's work shall be tested! If you serve, serve as you are serving the Lord Jesus Christ. Likewise, do everything you do with the same approach! May God Help us all to sincerely and diligently serve the Lord our God and seek His Holy Face in Jesus' Name. For in this, there is great reward. Amen!!!

301st Day

CHILDREN MUST NOT BE LEFT TO THEIR OWN DEVICES AS PREACHED BASICALLY BY THE WEST! CHILDREN NEED GUIDANCE AND TRAINING ARIGHT!!!

In the instructive Word of God, we are encouraged to teach the Word of God to our children in normal settings of daily living always. The Word of God ought to be passed on from one generation to the next unfailingly; for the wellbeing of the whole family progressively into the next generation! Father, Help us to value Your Wisdom and pass on Your Word to our generation and the next one; and on and on in Jesus' Name. Amen!!!

God Speaks His Heart and Mind and Plans to His prophets; so they in turn can pass it on to their generation and others to come! Abraham was clearly thus a prophet of prophets; a prophet to prophets! He was entrusted with the Word of God; for God Knew that he would do the right thing to pass on the Word of God to his family after him progressively and thus the Word of God would come alive over his life as Spoken by the Lord God Almighty! O Father, Help us; that we might gain Your trust likewise in Jesus' Name. Amen!!!

Teach and correct your children; for only then will they delight your soul and gain a good vision of the Lord and learn to be restrained and keep the laws of God. That's called home training right from my childhood to date. Children with sound and good home training turn out well in the end. Teach a child the way he should go and when he grows up he will not depart from it is what the Word of God teaches! Father God, Help us to do right by our children; for we as parents have a responsibility to You and to these children in Jesus' Name. Amen!!!

Do we really love the Lord our God with all our hearts, souls and minds? Does the Lord have that kind of special place in our hearts? Judge yourself as I am doing all the time on this matter. This is very crucial for your salvation and mine. If you do not love the Lord this way, how will you know even to love yourself, let alone your neighbour? Can you make a full commitment to the Lord God Almighty? Does not God deserve this commitment from us? If He Does, do we give Him His dues? Hmmm! O Lord my Father, please Help us; we cannot do this on our own. We need Your Holy Spirit! Help us to Love you as You desire and our neighbours too in Jesus' Name. Amen!!!

302nd Day

THERE ARE WATCHMEN CHOSEN AND RAISED BY GOD ALMIGHTY AND THERE IS THE GREAT WATCHMAN OF ALL!!!

If and when you allow the Great Watchman of all, the Lord God Almighty in Jesus Christ to be your Watchman, to Watch over you and yours, it shall surely and truly be well with you! The above Scripture will then apply to your life and family; you shall live in and have peace and rest in Christ Jesus. Amen! Father, let this be our portion, for we put our hope and trust fully in You, in Jesus' Name. Amen!!!

When you make the Lord your Refuge, you must follow up with righteous and holy living in obedience to the Word of the Living God! Then the Eyes and Face of the Lord shall be opened unto you and be over you; and you shall come to no harm, especially if you follow after the good and righteousness of God in Jesus' Name. Amen. Father, please let Your Eyes and Ears be open onto and over us in Jesus' Name. Amen!!!

I repeat, when you make the Lord your Refuge and Habitation, you shall dwell in the secret place of the Most High and abide under the shadows of the Almighty. Then you shall proclaim that the Lord is your Refuge and your Fortress, your God in whom you shall forever trust! Our God will then Give His Angels charge over you and yours; and no evil nor scourge shall befall you nor come near your tent in Jesus' Name. Amen! Father, Help us to make You our Refuge and Fortress in Jesus' Name. Amen!!!

Even though the governor had the choice to release a prisoner, such a one must be chosen by the people! Although the governor has the power to propose the one to be released to them, it's up to the people to decide at the end of the day. That is the politics of the time based on the popular culture! The governor knew the truth that Jesus Christ was stitched up; but he had to go along with the wishes of the people. They chose Barabbas over Jesus Christ for release and Jesus' fate was sealed; to the Cross He was headed! Do not expect the world to be on your side in any matter in life on earth; put your hope and trust in God and know that it shall be well with you and all things shall work out for your good in Jesus' Name. Amen! Father, Help us to trust and hope in You to the very end in crisis or not in life in Jesus' Name. Amen!!!

The Church has always faced persecution. Even Saul was consenting to the death of Stephen I believe as above. Persecution will always arise out of this wicked world against the Church of the Living God; but let no one think that the apparent success of anyone in the persecution, killing, maiming, bullying etc. and making the lives of Christians a misery is overlooked by our God. God Will never let the blood of Christians spilled especially needlessly, go unpunished. The Lord will AVENGE the blood of every Christian spilled in Jesus' Name. Father, Help us to be strong in the face of evil meted out against us in Jesus' Name. Amen!!!

303rd Day

THE LOVE OF MONEY IS THE ROOT OF ALL EVIL! NEVER MAKE MONEY OR WEALTH YOUR FOCUS LEST YOU MISS YOUR WAY!!!

The irony of life is such that those who are rich often live as though they are not; and it's often those that are not rich that live and pretend as though they are! Hmmmm! What a life! Father, Help us to judge correctly in all situations and at all times in Jesus' Name. Amen!!!

When you fear God, you learn to be satisfied with whatever you have; if a lot, you strive to fear God all the same - if little, you fear God all the same! You learn that it's better to have little and fear God than to have much without the fear of God. Better to eat a vegetarian dinner with love, than a feast full of meats with hatred! Lord, Help us to be wise in all that we do in Jesus' Name. Amen!!!

A man with an evil eye hastens after wealth and does not know that want will come upon him. Proverbs 28:22 NASB

Those who hasten after wealth are often laden with evil in their eyes and souls and it's very easy for them to sell their souls to the devil! They most often end up in poverty because God Has no Hand in their affairs. But the one who trusts and hopes in God will be fully satisfied and the Blessings of God makes one rich without adding sorrows to it! Help us o Lord to wait upon You for our Blessings in Jesus' Name. Amen!!!

The impact of a good wife is felt and evident only if she's listened to, heard and obeyed! Pilates wife warned him not to have anything to do with innocent Jesus Christ. However, he did not listen. He listened instead to the wishes of the crowds at the end of the day! What did they ask for? Crucify Him they cried in unison with mob action! So therefore, Pilate's hands were also soiled with the Blood of Jesus Christ! Father, Help us to be wise and to listen to Godly wisdom when we are Blessed to have this all the time in Jesus' Name. Amen!!!

(18) Where there is no revelation, the people cast off restraint; But happy is he who keeps the law. Proverbs 29:18 NKJV

Where the fear of the Lord is absent there can be no revelation or vision and so the people fail to restrain themselves and do as they wish to their own peril! Some bring up their children to do their own will and fail to discipline the children. The children end up very badly behaved and get into trouble all the time. Lord, Teach us to be wise in the way we live and bring up our children in Jesus' Name. Amen!!!

304th Day

FAITH MEANS TRUSTING IN GOD IN JESUS CHRIST THAT HE IS WITH YOU IN ALL WAYS AND NO NEED FOR FEAR ANYMORE!!!

Some trust in their horses, chariots and great wealth; but we trust in the Name of the Lord our God! Because we hope, believe and trust that God is with us; all shall and is well with us in Jesus' Name. Amen. Therefore, He who Gave us His Son for our sakes will not fail to Give us all things and meet our every need in Christ Jesus. Amen. Father, give us faith to be as little children, who are of immense value to You in Jesus' Name. Amen!!!

Surely goodness and mercy shall follow me all the days of my life: and I will dwell in the house of the LORD for ever. Psalm 23:6 KJV

All things work out for the good of those who love the Lord and are Called according to His Purposes! Therefore, believers must KNOW that goodness and mercy shall follow us all the days of our lives and we must dwell in the House of the Lord forever and ever in Jesus' Name. Amen! Father, Grant us the Grace and Your Mercy that will enable us to enjoy this Your Promise as our portion with our families in Jesus' Name. Amen!!!

Lord Help us who believe in You to be strong in faith to know that You are forever on our side because You are not a part-time God! Our God who shattered the teeth and smote all our enemies' cheeks is more than ABLE to Save us and Deliver us in Christ Jesus! Amen! Help our faith o Lord in Jesus' Name. Amen! You NEVER fail us o Lord; we fail You all the time. Forgive us o Lord, in Jesus' Name. we pray, Amen!!!

The knowledge that God is with me and forever on my side changes all the game plans! If God be for me and for us who can be against me and or us? As this is the case, shall I look to man for help? O no no no! I will look to and trust the Lord and have my confidence in Him than in mankind! For this reason I shall always look in triumph upon my enemies and all my haters in Jesus' Name. Amen! Thank You Lord for all You have done and continue to do for my family and I and all those who put their hope and trust in You! Help us to stand strong in faith in You o Lord in Jesus' Name. Amen!!!

Once you get your hands bloodied especially with the innocent's blood, no amount of washing can cleanse you! Except you repent in the Name of the Lord Jesus Christ ALONE, you are finished! So when God Gives you power and you use it in the spilling of innocent blood or oppression of innocent people, they have a God who Fights their cause all the time and all your actions are against GOD Almighty and will not go scot free! You will get your dues in due season in Jesus' Name. Is not the Blood of Jesus Christ perpetually upon "them and their children"? Hmmmm! God Alone Knows and Can Do all things! Father, Help us not to soil our hands with the blood of the innocent nor get involved in the oppression of the innocent in Jesus' Name. Amen!!!

Let us meditate upon this particular Scripture as above; for many remain unsure and questioning the Lord Jesus Christ as the Lord God of hosts! Look at the words and let them speak into your spirit. Then be sure to listen with your inner ears to hear what the Word of the Lord is saying expressly! You will find that the Lord Jesus Christ is the Lord God Almighty; who came in human flesh to humanity. I am fully satisfied that this is the case. May God Help us to understand His Word in Jesus' Name. Amen!!!

305th Day

WE ALL HAVE CHOICES; HOWEVER, PURSUE HOLINESS, RIGHTEOUSNESS AND PURITY BY THE GRACE OF GOD!!!

No one is born perfect except Jesus Christ. All have sinned and fallen short of the Glory of the Lord! So therefore, we lived in the world and acted accordingly. Thank God for Jesus Christ who came to set us free from sin and show us the way to righteousness through forgiveness of sins and the gift of the Holy Spirit to Enable us to live a holy life in Jesus Christ! This is by Grace not according to any man's works at all! For this we remain eternally grateful! Father, Help us to appreciate Your Grace that Saved us in Jesus' Name. Amen!!!

It's by the Grace of God that anyone can hear the message of the Cross and change their ways and lives! The turnaround to the Christlike living is by Grace only in Jesus' Name. Salvation is in the Name of JESUS CHRIST alone! We are to forsake worldliness and embrace holiness and righteousness in Jesus' Name. Amen. Father, Help us not to deceive ourselves; but rather to receive Grace from You to do right in Jesus' Name. Amen!!!

When you belong to Jesus Christ, you must crucify the flesh with its worldly passions, desires and ungodliness! We must live and walk by the Spirit of Jesus Christ as evidence of our Salvation. We cannot continue as we were and claim salvation! Father, please Help us to live and walk by Your Holy Spirit always in You in Jesus' Name. Amen!!!

Jesus Christ was subjected to unbelievable intimidation, harassment, brutalisation for no just cause. He took it all even though He Had POWER to free Himself! So, whatever you face in life, you do not ever need to be desperate, fearful or act weird or depressed. Hand everything over to Jesus Christ, the Author and Finisher of our Faith! He was mocked too! What are you going through that is like what Jesus went through? Have you been made to sweat as blood? You can hope, trust and keep faith in Jesus' Christ; He Will surely DELIVER you. Jesus NEVER lets down His own! Father, Help us to put our full hope, trust and faith in Jesus' Name. Amen!!!

It is clear in the Word of God in the Book of John, Chapter 3, verse 16 to 18, if you care to read carefully! Salvation is offered to all and sundry through the dynamic and Supreme Love of God. Better to accept and receive it; if not, you will pay an eternal price, period! You stand condemned automatically for opting against receiving the free Salvation offered in the Name of Jesus Christ! Reward for choosing aright and eternal damnation for choosing otherwise. Don't let anyone deceive you folks! This is God we are dealing with and not a man that can be bribed! God is not corrupt; He is Holy! Father, Help us to take the right decision and make the right choice to receive Salvation in the Name of Jesus Christ. Amen!!!

306th Day

BE THANKFUL TO GOD INSTEAD OF MURMURING AND COMPLAINING! GOD DETESTS THAT! CHECK THE SCRIPTURES!!!

Let your hearts be moved by God unto thanksgiving willingly and not because anybody pressured you! Remember that even in the New Testament, the gift is acceptable if the willingness is there! Your thanksgiving or offering is not automatically acceptable; especially if given for the wrong reasons. God does not appreciate thanksgiving for its own sake. God Knows your heart! Righteousness and holy living in the fear of God moves the heart to give willingly, generously, joyfully and never grudgingly or for the wrong reasons! Beware! Father, Stir up our hearts with Your Love to show appreciation with the right spirit, motives and emotions in Jesus' Name. Amen!!!

Whatever we do on earth we must strive to do in the Name of the Lord and to His Glory in Christ Jesus! God Created all things and we can enjoy His Creation and not reject such as long as we give thanks to God in receiving and enjoying them in Jesus' Name. However, remember that all things are permissible; but not all things are beneficial. So, you must be wise at all times to ensure that you are in the Lord's Will for the sake of your salvation! Father, Help us to the point where everything we do is done to please You; and for your Name's sake and to Your Glory in Jesus' Name. Amen!!!

There is always a reason to give thanks to God. We must look for reasons! The Bible says to give thanks to God in all situations! Some of us claim to see nothing good in our fatherland and hence even vex when others give thanks to God on Independence Day! Yet, many of those claim to be believers! Hypocrisy! Disobedience! God is good and His Mercies endure forevermore! God does nothing without giving room for thanksgiving. Find reason to thank God so He Will be pleased with you! Father, give us a thankful heart in Jesus' Name!!!

Adaniloro fi agbara koni! Meaning: the one who makes you suffer teaches you strength and endurance! In punishing you sometimes the enemy blesses you unknowingly! Can you imagine this man who was "forced" to "help" Jesus Christ to carry the cross? What a blessing! Wow! Can you see him in Heaven with the King of kings right now? I can! Lord, Help me (us) to be blessed via the actions of my enemies in Jesus' Name. Amen!!!

Complaining and grumbling are not pleasing to God especially if habitual and for no just cause; or especially against God's ordinances or against the servant and or anointed of God! Be very careful! God punished the children of Israel relentlessly for such! Be wise to obey the Word of the Lord and His servant! Father, Help us not to abuse nor insult or disobey the Word of the Lord or HIs servant in Jesus' Name. Amen! Keep us from grumbling and complaining habitually o Lord in Jesus' Name. Amen!!!

Is it not better to face the responsibility God Placed upon your shoulders rather than complaining, grumbling or not being satisfied with your portion? I believe that it is safer to be on the Lord's side; especially in not grumbling or complaining against the Lord's Will, His Word or His Anointed. It is unwise to try to usurp another's role and responsibility! Face your own squarely! Paddle your own canoe! Lord, Help us to mind our own business in Jesus' Name. Amen!!!

307th Day

JESUS CHRIST CAME TO SERVE! IF IN HIM YOU MUST STRIVE TO BE CHRIST-LIKE; NOT MOTIVATED BY FOOD OR GREED!!!

Most people in life desire to be great. However, what is greatness? Who would disagree that the best way of life is the godly kind of life? Even if you find it difficult, will it not be folly to disagree that it's the best way of life? The godly standard of life is to be the last if you desire to be the first; to be the servant if you desire to be the greatest! Basically, whoever wants to be first must be the slave of all else; this is being Christ-like - for He came to serve and not to be served, giving His life as a ransom for all. Amen! Halleluyah! If people truly know what it is to be the first, best, leader, would people still want it so much? Hmmmm! Father, Grant us the humility to learn the truth and apply it to our lives every day in Jesus' Name. Amen!!!

Do you see a man wise in his own eyes? There is more hope for a fool than for him. Proverbs 26:12 NASB

To be wise in your own eyes is the height of pride and arrogance! It is a big time folly. So many people suffer this kind of myopia sadly! They think, speak and act "wise in their own eyes"! Such people believe that they know best about almost everything and hardly ever take on board the views of other people! They must have a say, their say on all issues and they tend to be very forceful and aggressive in pushing their views and ideas over and down everybody else's throat! Wow, what a way to be and what a life! Father, please Give us wisdom to think, speak and act in humility in Jesus' Name. Amen!!!

Jesus Christ Knew that He IS God but acted with and in utmost humility; servant-like, even unto a most gruesome death, for the salvation of humankind! What an exemplary life! Father, Help us to be Christ-like; for it takes God to Help anyone to live like Jesus Christ in this evil, cruel, wicked world that we are in! Please Help us o Lord in Jesus' Name. Amen!!!

Prophecy fulfilled in Jesus Christ's crucifixion! The manner of His death most humiliating! For God to come down in the flesh to be amongst us and die for us in such a manner is the utmost love shown to humanity ever! No love can compare with the Love of God for humanity! This should not ever be compared with human love at all; nor spoken of nor taken for granted as the much spoken of "unconditional love"! There is a condition! You must believe this God and His Sacrifice to put yourself in any position to benefit from the LOVE! Those who refuse to believe stand condemned already! If the love was absolutely without condition, no one would be condemned for not believing. God is not man; although the "original Man"! His ways and thoughts are far Higher. Father, Help us to understand, appreciate, accept and believe Your Love and Sacrifice in Jesus' Name. Amen!!!

God Will always take care of your needs if you believe and trust in Him! Your focus in life must not be your needs; but rather, the Word of God! What is more important to you? Your life and needs or the Word of God in and for your life? Your answer to this question would go a long way to determining the shape of your life! Your destiny is very much tied to this question and your answer to it whether you are aware of this or not! May God Give us the wisdom to understand the question, give the right answer and submit our lives accordingly in Jesus' Name. Amen!!!

308th Day

THE KINGDOM OF GOD AND HIS RIGHTEOUSNESS PROVIDE KEYS TO EVERY NEED BEING MET IN CHRIST JESUS! SEEK AFTER THESE AND IT SHALL BE WELL WITH YOU ALWAYS!!!

It pays to seek and to praise the Lord from a pure and sincere heart! It's an abomination unto God to take His name on your lips when you live in evil and wickedness; that's like making a mockery of His Name! Keep your tongue and lips from evil, lies and falsehood! Seek the Lord and live! Father, Help us; that we might seek You and keep away from evil, lies, falsehood and wickedness in Jesus' Name. Amen!!!

It pays to be good; it's like a man who finds a wife, finding a good thing and obtaining favour from the Lord God Almighty! Goodness in mankind is rewarded by God. Wickedness shall never be established! Never! Righteousness and goodness shall however be rooted and unmovable and unshakeable! Father, Help us to be good and to walk in holiness and righteousness in Jesus' Name. Amen!!!

The Bible says to be anxious over nothing; but in all things to bring our petitions and prayers to Him! So, why worry? We worry because we're disobedient to the Word of God! God looks after many things He Created that cannot even fend for themselves and they never lack! So, how much more shall He Provide for our every need in Christ Jesus if we would only trust Him! We worry about every and anything; yesterday, today, tomorrow and all! God Tells us not to worry but to trust in Him! Father, Help us to trust in You fully and absolutely and not worry about the cares of this life in Jesus' Name. Amen!!!

Jesus Christ was taunted, mocked, insulted, abused etc. He took it all, bearing up with all the pain and anguish (physical, mental, psychological etc.)! After all He said He IS the Son of the Living God! He shouldn't be in this position! That is the thinking of mankind; very different than the thinking of God! They didn't know that it was all part of God's Plan as

523

Revealed in the Holy Word of the Living God! What Love! The purpose of Jesus Christ is REVEALED! Father, Help us not to make a mockery of the Lord our God in disobeying His Word and bringing His Name into disrepute in Jesus' Name. Amen!!!

Jesus revealed to His disciples what was to happen and they didn't understand. Even Peter, a senior aide and an apostle rebuked Him sternly; telling Him it was impossible for His prophecy about Himself to come true. Jesus Spoke a very stern word to him; telling him to get behind Him and calling him satan - after the things of man rather than of God! Wow! How do you think Peter must have felt? O! So, Jesus Christ was not always loving and very kindly disposed by human standards? Wow! So, watch how you judge; and be very careful! Father, Help us to appreciate, receive and act on the Truth; no matter how hard it is for us to take; Help us o Lord in Jesus' Name. Amen!!!

309th Day

PRIDE, ARROGANCE, BOASTFULNESS ETC. GO BEFORE A FALL! LEAVE ALL THAT OUR OF YOUR LIFE!!!

Exalting one's self almost certainly leads to a fall; why do it? If we risk God's fury being unleashed upon us in His wrath with attending punishment as listed above, why don't we live a more careful life pleasing God than otherwise? If we know that the reward for being prideful is as unto wickedness, we ought to strive to be more on the Lord's side in my view! Father, Help us to take/make the right decisions when we are able to choose how to think, speak and act in Jesus' Name. Amen!!!

Humans are very full of self-praise and "friends" love to praise each other and heap accolades upon each other and organise special gifts, awards etc. for each other! Listen to the Word of God! Let another praise you, a stranger and not your own lips (nor your friends I can infer from the Word of God above)! The Wisdom of God is very different than the wisdom of man! Father, Help us not to wanton in self-praise nor praise from friends but to wait upon the Lord for praise from strangers and other people who have no vested interest in us or in praising us in Jesus' Name. Amen!!!

If you glory, let it not be in yourself or in man; but rather in the Lord God Almighty! Yourself and friends' commendations are meaningless and does not make you truly "approved"! The true approval comes from the Lord Commending you! Be wise and stop fooling yourself! It's so easy and very convenient to make a fool of one's self! Father, Help us to wisen up and think clearly not to glory in any other but You in Jesus' Name. Amen!!!

Human beings make plans; man proposes and God disposes! The future is all in God's Hands; no matter how much we plan, it's the Will of the Lord that shall prevail! Who controls your life? You may flex your muscles all you want; but try as you may, your life does not belong to you, neither is it really controlled by you! We ought always all to defer to the Will of God in all things. Father, Help us to remember that our lives and times do not belong to us; but rather, that You are in full control and have the whole world in Your Hands in Jesus' Name. Amen!!!

Huge signs and wonders manifested when Jesus Christ was crucified! Darkness came over the land in broad daylight! Terror gripped all who were present to witness this event and many affirmed that surely He IS the Son of the Living God! Still He was given wine vinegar off a sponge! With a loud cry, He gave up His Spirit! O Holy Father, truly and surely, You are the King of all kings and the Lord of all lords. Thank You for Your Supreme Sacrifice in Jesus' Name. Help us to accept and submit to You in Jesus' Name. Amen!!!

The Word of God is POWER! Powerful beyond measure is the Word of the Living God! Jesus Spoke the Word and Power Flowed! He Told the cripple to rise up take up his mat and walk and he obeyed Him right away and was healed completely! O Lord, please speak a Word into my life right now. Speak a Word into our lives right now in Jesus' Name. Let Your Will be done unto us in Jesus' Name. Amen!!!

310th Day

WHO IS THE LORD GOD TO YOU IN YOUR LIFE? FOR ME HE'S MY SAVIOUR, REDEEMER, PROTECTOR, DELIVERER, LIGHT, LIFE, MY ALL, MY EVERYTHING IN JESUS' NAME. AMEN!!!

Advice for all mankind in general as above is to keep sound wisdom and discretion which is of course godly! Only then will you walk secure and not stumble nor fall. You will not fear nor lose confidence. The Lord Will be your confidence and your feet shall not be ensnared! Who wants these things to be true for them and their portion? To be eligible for these blessings you must ask for, receive and apply Godly wisdom and discretion with discerning in your daily life. Father, Help us to receive wisdom, discretion and the right kind of discernment from You in Jesus' Name. Amen!!!

Is the Lord Your God? If yes, then you are in line for great favours when you obey His Word and take heed of His Counsels in Jesus' Name. Amen! He Will Protect you from all disasters in life; whether famine, destruction, floods, fire, rain, snow, sunshine, whatever will hurt you or your family, you shall be protected from in Jesus' Name. Amen! Even the scourge of the tongue (which no other power in heaven and or earth can deliver from) you shall be delivered from in Jesus' Name. Amen! Wow! Father thank You for Your Favour and Blessings which I receive by Grace in Jesus' Name for myself and family. Amen!!!

Father, we receive Your Light into our lives; even as You o Lord fill our hearts with the greatest joy than anything life can bring us. Because of Your Love and Favour, we are able to sleep and lie down in peace; You alone keep us safe o Lord! Our hope and trust in You must never fail o Father of all lights in Jesus' Name. Amen! There is nobody else like You o Lord! Thank You Father Lord God for Your Divinity, Grace, Mercy, Favour and all You do for us in Jesus' Name. Amen!!!

Great signs from Heaven above at the crucifixion of Jesus Christ! Apart from the fact that day suddenly turned into night, the temple curtain tore right from the top to bottom suddenly. Dead bodies were raised! Glory

Halleluyah! What great signs of the Son of the Living God who Himself is God Almighty! Do you believe this? If you do, you are Blessed! I believe! O yes Lord; I believe! What a Mighty God we have! What a Great God we serve! Thank You Lord Jesus for Your Power and Might! Halleluyah! Glory!!!

When God Blesses you as a servant of God, He Will Exalt you and Glorify Himself in you and your experience! He Will make manifest His Love and support for you and your ministry! He Will Reveal Himself in your daily experience! Samuel is a great example of the true servant of the Living God! God Caused a rarity of the Word of God and Revelation of the same in the time of Samuel. So, Samuel's ministry shone for all to see with distinction! Father, let my family and ministry shine for You in Jesus' Name. Amen!!!

311th Day

GOD SPEAKS TO US ALL THE TIME, TELLING US HE'S ON OUR SIDE; BUT WE MUST FOLLOW AND OBEY HIM SINCERELY!!!

Whoever listens to me will live in safety and be at ease, without fear of harm. Proverbs 1:33 NIV

Who is prepared to listen to God's Voice and obey His Instructions and Ordinances? Those are the ones that will enjoy and live in the peace of God and in safety, Protected by Him and without fear of any harm. Are you ready? Father, Help us; touch our hearts so we are attuned to Your Ways and Word, to obey in Jesus' Name. Amen!!!

When the Lord is determined to Work on a case; be it of a human being or a nation, He Will Remove their shame and all threats against them. God is Able to Establish such a people, such that they will not suffer even famine or any such thing; and nations shall be Blessed through them and not insult them anymore. God does this so they will know that He is indeed with them. This is the lot of the House of Israel according to the Promises of God. Who is the House of Israel today, except those who believe in the Name of the Lord Jesus Christ? Glory Halleluyah! Father, please consider us worthy to be counted amongst those on Your Side in Jesus' Name to be so Favoured in Jesus' Name. Amen!!!

When I am fully submitted to the Lord God Almighty, He becomes my Light; a Lamp unto my feet and a Light into my paths! Then I need fear no evil. My enemies shall all stumble and fall at my feet in the Name of the Lord! My heart shall not fear even the soundings of war or enemies because the Lord IS my confidence! Father, please be our confidence and Grant that our hearts are deeply rooted in You to trust You to the very end in Jesus' Name. Amen!!!

When the signs and wonders were manifested at the Crucifixion of Jesus Christ, they were terrified to believe that He IS the Son of God. There were both men and women there who witnessed these events recounted in the Holy Word of God! Some of the women cared for His needs; the

Lord Granted them to be able to do this. Remember Joseph of Arimathea who was commanded to help carry His Cross. Imagine how Blessed they would be who helped the Lord on His way to the Cross! O Lord, receive, accept and use us for Your Glory in Jesus' Name. Amen!!!

312th Day

NEVER GIVE UP HOPE BECAUSE SOMEDAY YOU WILL BE FREE INDEED! STRIVE TO KNOW THE TRUTH AND BE FREE!!!

When you are scattered among the heathen, God Knows you will suffer; He however assures you that one day you will be free and return to your homeland and be Blessed! God Knows the plans He Has for you; to give you hope, prosper you and give you peace! God Will Cause you to walk with and in Him. He Will "Touch" your heart to be flesh and not stone! God Will surely Bless you! So, do not lose or give up hope! Continue to trust. hope and have faith in God; be expectant of your freedom. It's coming; and soon you will thank God that you are free at last, free at last, free at last! Father, we wait upon You to set us free in Jesus' Name. Amen!!!

True freedom is a departure from the past and embracing the new in everything! This freedom comes only in Jesus Christ; the Way, Truth and Life! The Bible says "and you shall know the Truth and the Truth shall set you free"! Since Jesus Christ is the Truth, only Jesus Can Save and set anyone free! God reconciles us to Himself through Jesus Christ; and we likewise have a responsibility to help reconcile others to Him in Jesus' Name. Father, Help us to be true ambassadors of You to reconcile others to You in Jesus' Name. Amen!!!

You are not free when you are hemmed in by sin. To be truly free, you must give up sin! Listen to and take in the above Word of God and let the Word permeate your whole being! Do not present your members to sin as instruments to be used for evil. Rather, present your members as instruments to be used for righteousness unto God! Father, Help us to act as people under Your Grace and no longer under the law! Help us to keep out of evil and live holy righteous lives in Jesus' Name. Amen!!!

The Word of God is very valuable! You will benefit immensely if you value it. But no one can force anyone else to value the Word of God! It's the Word of God that can make any man complete as a servant of God and well equipped for ministry! Father, equip us in Jesus' Name with Your Word. Amen!!!

313th Day

JESUS CHRIST WAS BRUTALISED FOR OUR SINS: HE TOOK IT ALL OUT OF LOVE FOR US; WE OWE HIM OUR VERY LIVES AND LOVE! WILL YOU DARE TO LOVE JESUS CHRIST?!!

The reason for the death of Jesus Christ and all of His Sufferings is so that sin is done away with in our lives and that rightesousness might replace sinfulness in our lives! For the sake of our salvation, joy, peace, wellbeing and love, Jesus Christ suffered in the utmost sense! By faith in His sufferings, we are able to receive healing and blessings already RECEIVED on our behalf even before we believed! In our disobedience, pride, arrogance, ill-will, we have all strayed from God's Ways and it pleased the LORD to lay on Jesus Christ all of our iniquities! Wow! What love! Father, Help us to do our own bit in loving Jesus Christ and obeying His Commands as evidence of our love for Him in Jesus' Name. Amen!!!

We have grace and peace from and in Jesus' Holy Name; because He gave His all for the sake of our deliverance and redemption from sin and this evil world. This being the original Will of the Father; to whom be Glory forever and ever in Jesus' Name. Amen! Help us o Lord, to receive these gifts willingly by first accepting that of faith to believe and to live in obedience to Your Holy Word in Jesus' Name. Amen!!!

Wow! What a God we serve. He Knows the end from the beginning and makes His Plans accordingly in a way that is inexplicable to any man really! Was it not in God's Supreme Plan for the rich man, Joseph of Arimathea to go and ask for the Body of our Lord Jesus Christ? His purpose was to ensure the Body of Jesus Christ was laid in a tomb fit for a king! He was born in a manger but buried like a king! What an irony even in holiness! What a Mighty God we serve. O Glory Halleluyah! Amen! Father, Help us, Use us for Your Glory in Jesus' Name. Amen!!!

The way the Kingdom of God works defies human understanding or logic. God's Thoughts and Ways are higher than man's by far! All sorts of people are accepted into the Kingdom of Heaven; not just your average and or holy people! The worst offenders could be saved by Grace and come into the Kingdom of Heaven, just like the holiest of people! All come together to share in the same inheritance in Jesus Christ by His Special Grace, Mercy, Favour and through His Divine Love! Father, please count us worthy for this Kingdom. Prepare us o Lord in Jesus' Name for Your Kingdom. Amen!!!

314th Day

COME INTO JESUS CHRIST; WALK IN HIS LIGHT; SO YOU WON'T FULFILL THE DESIRES OF THE FLESH AND BE DONE WITH SIN!!!

Whatever you sow you shall reap! You cannot sow tomato seeds and reap corn! If you sow the seeds of sin, you shall reap destruction; but if you sow to please the Holy Spirit in righteousness and holiness, you shall reap Eternal Life which is Christ Jesus! If God Lays it upon your heart to do good, do not stop; for in due season you shall reap a bountiful harvest of goodness and mercy if you do not give up. If you give up, how will you reap? Father, Help us to sow according to Your Heart, to please You; so we may reap according to Your Harvest of righteousness and Eternal Life in Jesus' Name. Amen!!!

Many hide under the love of God to continue in sin! Do not judge me do not judge me they cry and continue in sin! Jesus sets free yes in love; but He Does not want us to continue in sin as in going back to our vomit! When we make a commitment to Jesus Christ, Light comes into our lives and we never walk in darkness again! Give us Your Light o Lord; Keep us abiding in You, so we do not walk in darkness in Jesus' Name. Amen!!!

Before we came into Jesus Christ, we were in darkness! But now that we are in Christ Jesus, we are in the Light of God! Therefore we came from being darkness to being light in Jesus' Name! We must continue to walk as children of the Light; that way we shall bear much fruit of the Holy Spirit - which is in all goodness, righteousness and truth! O Lord, Help us to forsake darkness and the treasures it promises to enter and stay in the Light of God in Jesus' Name. Amen!!!

Those who crucified Jesus Christ tried to pre-empt His Rise on the third day in absolute vain! No one can block whatever God is determined to DO! No one! No power! No force! God Will Frustrate every scheme and plan of the enemy against the Will of God in any situation and for any lives! God is GREAT beyond measure! Who can stop Him! Whom God Blesses, no man can curse! However, as the wicked plans for evil or against the righteous; so the Lord Plans against them to frustrate their efforts! Father, frustrate every evil plan against my family, myself and all Your children in Jesus' Name. Amen!!!

It cannot go well with the lazy man; he's like the wicked who are like chaff in the wind before the Lord! His vineyard is overgrown with thorns, nettles etc. Poverty awaits him. But it shall go well with the man who works and toils hard to earn his living; his vineyard is plush with crops and fruits and all manners of goodies abound in his vineyard. His lot is like that of the righteous and shall have plenty even when there's famine in the land! Lord, apportion our lot with the righteous and not the wicked in Jesus' Name. Amen!!!

315th Day

DO YOU KNOW THAT IN CHRIST JESUS YOU HAVE POWER OVER YOUR ENEMIES? IF YOU BELIEVE THEN ACT LIKE YOU DO!!!

The help of man is futile in times of trouble folks! Have you never been disappointed by people you were relying on in times of trouble? Most human beings have a story of disappointment to tell of this nature and magnitude! Only God is reliable in times of trouble; indeed at all times! He is Able to Send mankind to help us too no doubt; but a God-Send is always different in every way than ordinary mankind helping out in times of trouble! Only God is Able to crush our enemies for us effectively; we may not have the ability on our own nor in our own strength! Father, Help us to trust You and not put our hope vainly in mankind in Jesus' Name. Amen!!!

Whenever you are facing a challenge or battle against the enemy, if you will trust in the Lord, no need for you to panic, fear nor tremble! God Goes ahead of you to take the victory by knocking off your enemies and save you! Father, we trust in You; Save us in Jesus' Name. Amen!!!

When trouble comes, I have a Father who will hide me in His Tabernacle/ Pavilion; in His secret place shall He hide my family, myself and all His children! He Will set us up on high; above our enemies round about us. For this reason, we shall offer Him sacrifices of praise, thanksgiving, joy etc. in song, dancing, with musical instruments and a great shouting! He alone delivers and sets free! Father, let us always have a place in Your House and in Your Heart in Jesus' Name. Amen!!!

When the Lord Jesus Christ was to be Raised from the dead, there was a great and mighty earthquake that opened up graves of the righteous who had died and they arose with the Lord and all went back to their homes! The women who had gone to take care of the Lord's body were amazed at what they witnessed in the form of an angel of the Lord who even spoke to them! They were thus terrified; shaken and became as dead men! O Lord our God, how Great You Are! Thank You Lord for Your Supreme Sacrifice and for interceding for us and setting us free in Jesus' Name. Amen!!!

When the Holy Spirit Came, His Purpose was to lead us who believe into all truth and righteousness! He is from the Father and is the Father and the Son and communicates what He Hears. His nature is very prophetic; telling us of the future as well as other things! Only those who submit themselves to be led of the Holy Spirit are sons of the Living God! Father, Help us to submit to the Leading of Your Holy Spirit in Jesus' Name. Amen!!!

316th Day

THE JOY OF THE LORD IS THE STRENGTH OF THE BELIEVER RIGHTEOUS HOLY ONES! OUR GOD HAS DONE GREAT THINGS!!!

Those ransomed, redeemed by the Lord Jesus Christ would return with gratitude and great joy, to Zion, the City of our God. They will be Crowned with everlasting joy. They will be exceedingly glad, joyful and overtaken by gladness and joy! For them there shall be no more sorrow, tears, sighing, hissing etc. Father, Give us a heart of gratitude in Jesus' Name. Amen!!!

Those that have the joy of the Lord in their lives will know the joyful sound from the Lord! The Light of the Almighty God shall surround them and they shall walk in the Light of the Lord! They shall have joy all day and night. Everlasting joy that is unending shall be theirs and they shall be exalted in the righteousness of God Almighty! O Lord, I want this joy so much; give us this joy that only You can give in Jesus' Name. Amen!!!

Because the Lord has taken away my nakedness and shame and clothed me with His garment of salvation and wrapped me with His robe of righteousness, just like a bride made beautiful. I shall rejoice in Jesus' Name. As God Breathes on the earth and a garden to bring forth whatever is sown therein, so the Lord God Almighty will cause His righteousness and praise to spring up before all the nations. This is the Word of God and it shall come to pass in Jesus' Name. Amen. Use me, use us o Lord to achieve Your Purposes on earth in Jesus' Name. Amen!!!

Notice how quickly sadness can turn to joy when the Lord is involved! I pray in the Holy Name of Jesus that as you are reading this inspirational book, the Lord Will Cause you to be led into experiences that will cause you great joy that no man can take away in Jesus' Name! Jesus Christ Arose from the dead. He has gone before us into Galilee where we shall see Him! Father in the Name of Jesus Christ of Nazareth, Lead us into our Galilee right now in Jesus' Name. Go before us and Guide us into our place of Galilee in Jesus' Name. Amen!!!

The thoughts of sin is sin is what the Lord is saying to us in this Scripture! Whatever will lead you astray, you must let go from your life! Father, Help us to let go of anything that will take us away from Your Ways and Paths; that we may not fall o Lord in Jesus' Name. Amen! Help us to think, speak and act rightly in the Name of the Lord in Jesus' Name. Amen!!!

317th Day

OUR GOD IS FAITHFUL, MERCIFUL AND TRUE! TO BE FAITHFUL IS TO BE GODLY! SO ARE YOU FAITHFUL, TRUSTWORTHY?!!

God understands Faithfulness for He is the epitome of Faithfulness! Mostly, we are the ones unfaithful to God! If we are faithful to God, He Will Keep Faith with us; however, God is not obliged to Keep Faith with unfaithful people! Yet, I can testify that God is always Good to me despite my shortcomings in my relationship with Him. This is not to say that His Love is unconditional; but rather, that His Mercy is Great. He definitely has expectations of us. Indeed, unto whom much is Given, much is desired/expected! When God Promises, He NEVER fails. Lord, Help us to be faithful to You in Jesus' Name. Amen!!!

Does God lie? Does God shift like shadows? I say not; because He's not like the sons of men to lie, repent! Yet, God is the Greatest Dynamic in existence! He IS and acts in any way that suits His Purposes at any point in time. He can blow hot or cold; say no or yes; bless or curse; He Knows and can do all things. For with God nothing shall be impossible! God is Faithful to His Words and Promises! Of course, He reserves the right to change His Mind at any time on any issues! He is God Almighty! Father, Bless us in Jesus' Name; and please do not change Your Mind on this in Jesus' Name. Amen!!!

We who are in Christ Jesus have died with Him and so will live with Him unto Eternity; but we must live as He did and be like Him in our daily walk. This is very difficult for our flesh but that is why we must kill the flesh and die to the flesh daily. May God Help us in Jesus' Name. Amen! Endurance is very central and key to walking the Faith in Christ Jesus. He endured much and to be like Him increasingly, we must likewise endure much! So, as we endure, we shall also reign with Him in the Heavenly Places! To deny Him is pure evil and He Will likewise deny us. If we refuse to keep the faith, He cannot deny Himself and must remain Faithful. He is the Lord God Almighty! Jesus is Lord and King! Halleluyah! Amen! Glory! Father, Help us; Walk with us Father, to see us through to Eternity in Jesus' Name. Amen!!!

This Promise and Blessing is for those who love, fear and follow the Lord God Almighty faithfully! You are more than a conqueror because you put your faith, hope and trust in Jesus Christ! God Will be with you as long as you obey His Commandments and you don't turn away. You will succeed in all your undertakings. Be bold and courageous; do not fear anything except the Lord your God! You are delivered in Jesus' Name. Amen! Father, Help us to stand firm in obedience to Your Word and not give in to fear in Jesus' Name. Amen!!!

The women's sadness turned into great joyfulness; as they ran to share the Good News with the Lord's disciples. They believed what they had heard. Perhaps because of their faith, Jesus Christ appeared to them immediately, suddenly! They worshipped Him fearfully. He Told them not to fear and to go and share the Good News with His "brothers" - Jesus considered the disciples as His "brother" and "friends"! Father, Help us to believe You and be rooted in our Faith in You in Jesus' Name. Amen!!!

He's coming back again! My Lord is coming back again. He went away and promised He's coming back again! I believe Him! When He Comes back again, the dead in Him shall rise first! So, as the time did come when the dead heard His Voice and lived; so will it be again at the Second Coming in Jesus' Name. Amen! Father, please Prepare us for the Second Coming of Jesus Christ; that we may be ready in Jesus' Name. Amen!!!

318th Day

WHO IS LIKE OUR GOD? LOVING, MERCIFUL, FAITHFUL, TRUE! NOBODY ELSE LIKE HIM! PUT YOUR TRUST IN JESUS CHRIST!!!

Akiirisoore; Asoorekiri (The One Who goes round doing good; The One Who Does Good round about)! When Jesus Christ Speaks a Word, He Brings it to pass always! When He Plans a thing, He Does it! His Call reaches out to whomsoever shall listen; including the wicked and evil willing to hear Him and repent! He is a Restorer of broken walls. His "products" include salvation and righteousness; for all who willingly submit and receive! Jesus Christ forces no one to accept Him. Your faith will speak a good word for you into the Ears of Jesus Christ and you will be recompensed accordingly! He will not delay to save you; why do you delay coming to Him? Obey the Voice of the Spirit and come to Jesus Christ right now. Father, open up our eyes; that we may come running to You and be saved in Jesus' Name. Amen!!!

The Word of God is very consistent and constant! He does not shift like shadows! The promises of God are Yes and Amen in Christ Jesus! To stand firm in Jesus Christ is Given only by God through Jesus Christ; so let no man boast! What have we received or what do we have that we were not Given? So, thanksgiving is always due unto the Lord our God, with praises always in Jesus' Name. Amen! Father, Help us to appreciate You and to willingly come to You in Jesus' Name. Amen!!!

O Lord, there is not one without sin! But as You Know all things Father, You Know that I love You and love Your Word and Instructions. I believe that Your Word is Truth from the beginning unto Eternity. Your Judgments are secure, fair and endure forever in Jesus' Name. Amen! Father, do good unto us who trust in You; that the world may know that we are Yours in Jesus' Name. Amen!!!

The Greatest Dynamic ever is the Lord God Almighty. His Name is Jesus Christ our Lord God and Saviour! He works in different ways yet remains essentially the same forever and ever! He is the Lord! Blessed be His Holy Name. Halleluyah! Amen!! Thank You Jesus!!!

Many there are, like Israel, who are zealous for God but not according to the true knowledge of God. They do not know about the Righteousness of God; but rather work hard at establishing a righteousness of their own contrary to the Word of the Living God! Better to give up your own pride, integrity etc.; submit to and embrace the Wisdom of God! Therein lies your salvation! Father, Help us to drop our worldliness, pride, all that keeps us away from You; and submit to Your Ways and be saved in Jesus' Name Amen!!!

319th Day

GOD IS FAITHFUL AND JUST; PATIENT WITH MANKIND; YET HIS DAY OF JUDGMENT IS COMING! BE PREPARED! HE IS HOLY!!!

The LORD is a refuge for the oppressed, a stronghold in times of trouble. Those who know your name will trust in you, for you, LORD, have never forsaken those who seek you. Psalm 9:9,10 NIV

Are you feeling oppressed or in trouble? Do you know the Name of the Lord? If not, if you need Help, you can choose to come to know the Name of the Lord so that He Can be your Refuge and Stronghold! When you know His Name, you will trust in Him; knowing that He never forsakes those who trust in Him! O Father, Help us to Know Your Name; that we may have You as our Refuge and Stronghold and never be forsaken in Jesus' Name. Amen!!!

Please Father, Help us come to a place where we would have Your full confidence in our imperfections that You will not utterly take Your lovingkindness from us nor allow Your faithfulness to fail over us in Jesus' Name. We trust that when You Speak a Word over our lives, like Your Covenant with us, You will never break either in Jesus' Name. Amen. Father, Grant that we are Divinely Blessed by You to receive the very best of You always all our lives in Jesus' Name. Amen!!!

We tend to forget that God's Ways and Thoughts are not like ours! How many times we think God is too slow to fulfil some promise or the other according to our thinking and ways! Many have questioned the second coming of the Lord Jesus Christ and concluded that since so many years have passed by since many have been talking about this "elusive" second coming, perhaps no such thing will happen! Hmmmm! Be very careful what you believe! A time is coming when Heaven and earth shall pass away but the Word of God shall remain. Judgment Day is coming fast for real! The Word of God ALWAYS comes to pass! Be prepared in and out of season! Father, Help us to be prepared in Jesus' Name. Amen!!!

Lord, my soul and my flesh thirst and long for You respectively in this dry and thirsty land! I want to see Your Power and Glory as You Have Revealed Yourself to me in Your Holy Sanctuary! I have seen the Lord's Goodness, Mercy and Compassion. Halleluyah! Praise the Lord! Your Love is better than life. O Lord You Have been so good to me. You Are Excellent in my life every day! I will Bless Your Holy Name as long as there is life in my body. I will lift up my hands, voice, soul, my all to worship You in Jesus' Name. Amen! Father, Grant me the Grace, Inspiration and Wisdom to show forth Your Praise in this generation in Jesus' Name. Amen!!!

Justification by Christ Jesus is not by the works of any man but by faith in Jesus Christ Himself! No flesh shall be justified by the works of the law; but rather by faith in Jesus Christ! It is futile to seek justification in any other way; especially by man in a way according to favouritism! Only Jesus Christ CAN Save! Father, be Thou Magnified in my life and experience in Jesus' Name. We look unto You for our justification in Jesus' Name. Amen!!!

320th Day

THE STEADFAST LOVE OF OUR LORD NEVER CEASES; HIS MERCIES NEVER COME TO AN END! THEY ARE RENEWED EVERY MORNING; GREAT IS HIS FAITHFULNESS!!!

O Lord Spare my life and that of my family because of Your steadfast love. I will never stop testifying to Your Goodness, Mercy and Love unto my family and I! Your Word is Eternal; fixed in the Heavens forever firmly. You established the earth and it stands firm unto the very end. You are faithful unto all generations. You alone are God! Father, You alone are able to spare our lives; we look up to You o Lord our Father to do this in Jesus' Name. Amen!!! O Almighty God who came in the flesh of Jesus Christ to us as God! Blessed be Your Glorious Name. Halleluyah! Amen!! Thank You Lord Jesus!!!

God who led us into triumphant walk with our Lord Jesus Christ Blessed us with every good and spiritual gift; even as we eagerly await the second coming of our Lord Jesus Christ! It is God's Will to ensure that we are blameless on the Day of the Lord at the Judgment! We however, do have a responsibility to keep holiness and righteousness as a standard for us to follow! May God Help us to follow and meet up with God's Standard of holiness and righteousness in Jesus' Name. Amen!!!

On the day of our Galilee, may we not be found wanting and may we have faith to receive every Blessing due to us in Jesus' Name. Amen! Jesus Christ had told the disciples to go up to Galilee where they would meet with Him after rising from the dead. They went; some with faith and other without faith! Those with faith worshipped Him and believed Him. Some however doubted Him! Hmmmm! May we keep faith to the very end in Jesus' Name. Amen!!!

The Word of God ALWAYS comes to pass! The true servant of God will and must suffer in the Name of the Lord! That is the cost of the faith! No point praying against suffering; but rather pray for strength! Just look at the story of Stephen, Paul, Peter etc. and the Lord Jesus Christ Himself! If you truly want to follow Jesus Christ and you do not want suffering, but only enjoyment and blessings, then you cannot be for real! Follow Jesus Christ has its costs. Likewise, His Love is fully conditional! Father, Help us to follow You and brave up all the odds in Jesus' Name. Amen!!!

THE DAILY SWORD – DIVIDING THE WORD OF GOD ACCURATELY

321st Day

FEAR AND OBEY THE LORD AND YOU SHALL LIVE! THE CHOICES YOU HAVE ARE LIFE OR DEATH! CHOOSE LIFE!!!

Tell out my soul the Greatness of the Lord! When you come to know the Lord Jesus Christ as your Lord God and Saviour! You must never forget His Goodness to you nor forget His benefits! You must watch your life very closely; judging yourself and making sure that you remain steadfastly committed to His Cause in your day to day living! You owe it to the Lord God Almighty to share all of this with your children so they can pass it onto the next generation and hence the heritage of the Lord may endure forever and ever in your lineage! The fear of the Lord you must learn and pass on to the next generation! Then it shall be well with you and you shall have life everlasting! Father, Help us to learn to fear You and pass it on to our children onto the next generation in Jesus' Name! Amen!!!

When you learn the fear of the Lord and act always upon it, you must share the same with your brethren and all who live within your cities so that nobody goes against the Lord. Only then will you be saved from the potential wrath of the Lord upon the land! The sinner will not go unpunished! God does not condone sin. He may not act immediately; but don't think you will get away with sin. Sin is very dangerous to life! Father, Help us not to sin against You o Lord; it is very difficult for us, but nothing is impossible for You o Lord in Jesus' Name. Amen!!!

The Lord's Commandments are beautiful, pure, holy, righteous and good for the heart, soul, mind, spirit and even body of mankind! The Word of God is a Lamp unto our feet and a Light into our paths! We are ideally supposed to desire the Word more than all the wealth in the world because all of that is left when we leave this wicked world. But it's the Word of God that propels us unto the next plane where the choices are between Heaven and hell! What we do with the Word of God determines where we spend Eternity! Father, Help us to choose wisely; and to choose Life and Eternity over anything else in Jesus' Name. Amen!!!

What man in the history of life has ever made such a statement as this? Anyone that could make this statement cannot be an ordinary man! For a man to possess all Authority in Heaven and on earth, that is a privilege only God Has. This Man must be God in Man; Man God God Man! Jesus Christ is the Lord God Almighty who came to mankind in the flesh of man! JESUS IS LORD! Father, Help us to understand the Godhead of Jesus Christ in Jesus' Name we pray. Amen!!!

The prophetic Word Spoken by the Lord Jesus Christ over Peter came to pass from the Biblical records made available to us through the holy writings as Inspired by the Holy Spirit! When He Speaks a Word, He Brings it to pass. Father, Speak Your Word into and over our lives today in Jesus' Name. Amen!!!

322nd Day

WHEN YOU LIVE IN THE FEAR OF THE LORD, THERE IS GREAT BENEFIT TO YOU AND YOURS! JUST DO IT AND TESTIFY!!!

If you want to enjoy a time of peace as described above, just try, strive to live in the fear of the Lord; then you will taste, see and testify that the Lord is Good and His Mercies endure forevermore! You will receive Supernatural Strengthening and Encouragement from the Holy Spirit; your coasts shall be enlarged supernaturally even as you continue to live in the fear of the Lord God Almighty! Father, please Help us to live in the fear of the Lord; for it is not easy in today's world. We need Your Help o Lord, in Jesus' Name. Amen!!!

Your body is not your own as a believer! You hear lots of people saying things like: leave me alone, it's my body etc.! But, is your body really yours? The Bible tells us that our body is the Temple of the Living God! We cannot therefore do whatever we like with our bodies! We must keep our bodies holy and pleasing to God as living Temples, living sacrifices offered unto the Lord! We are no longer to conform to the pattern of worldly living; but rather be transformed by the renewing of our minds by the Holy Spirit of God. When we live right, we are then able to test and approve the Will of God which is Good, Pleasing and Perfect! Father, Help us to offer our bodies unto You as sacrifices that will please You in Jesus' Name. Amen!!!

When you are in Jesus Christ, there is a pattern of behaviour that is associated with Jesus Christ that you are to adopt! You are to put aside all evil, malicious, deceitful, hypocritical, envious, slanderous and like behaviour. You are to crave for pure spiritual milk of the Word of the Lord; by which you will grow as per salvation, as long as you have tasted the kindness and love of God in Christ Jesus. Father, please Help us to adopt holy and godly behaviour according to the Faith we accepted in Jesus Christ our Lord. Amen!!!

We have a commission from the Lord Jesus Christ; if we truly are in Him! We are to go and make disciples of all nations; baptising them all in the Name of the Father, Son and Holy Spirit! We are to share with them the Goodness of the Lord that we have received ourselves! He Promised to be with us in so doing and I believe Him. Do you? Will you? Father, Help us to obey Your Word to go out and make disciples of all nations in Jesus' Name. Amen!!!

323rd Day

THE KINGDOM OF GOD IS NOT ABOUT MUNDANE CARES OF LIFE; RATHER IT'S ABOUT PLEASING GOD THROUGH RIGHTEOUSNESS PEACE AND JOY IN THE HOLY SPIRIT!!!

Many people cannot see beyond their noses as far as religion is concerned. Some even see religion as evil. They talk about Jesus Christ as if He has nothing to do with religion. The Bible does not support the demonising of religion. They say some people are religious but not Christian. They say Christianity is not a religion. This is very unbiblical! Religion is real and the Christian faith is a religion. You are religious if you practice it as appropriate; not like the Pharisees and Sadducees! The Kingdom of God is not about the mundane things of this world; but rather to strive to please God in righteousness, peace and joy in the Holy Spirit! Father, Help us to understand Your Kingdom and the principles guiding the Kingdom; and Help us to live by those principles in Jesus' Name. Amen!!!

Children are to look after widows that are their parents as a part of their duty to God Almighty. It's good to pay back our parents who have been faithful to us with good; to take care of such parents is a duty owed to God and to those parents! Father, Help us to honour and take care of our parents; especially when they have become widows in Jesus' Name. Amen!!!

The Kingdom of God must be guided by Love! Love consists in all knowledge and judgment; to approve excellence in sincerity without blemish until the Day of our Lord Jesus Christ! If you apply the Kingdom principles daily, you shall be filled with the fruits of righteousness in Jesus Christ unto the Glory of God! Lord, Bless us with Your Love and to live guided by Your Kingdom principles in Jesus' Name. Amen!!!

There is a potential for hypocrisy in practically every human being! We accuse other people of things that we are guilty of ourselves. We love to leave the mole in our own eyes and "help" remove the log from other people's eyes! Hypocrisy is punishable by God; yet whilst we wish for others to be punished by God for things that we ourselves are guilty of, we are self-condemned already! God is not unjust. God Will not punish others for things you do as well and leave you? However, God is just and He Says in His Word that He Will Show Mercy to whomsoever He chooses and destroy whomsoever He chooses! Father Lord, Have Mercy on us that we may forsake hypocrisy and not be judgmental! If we judge, Teach us to judge correctly in Jesus' Name. Amen!!!

We ought to take cognisance of our Great Commission from the Lord to preach the Word of God to all the nations of the earth; baptising all in the Name of God the Father, Son and Holy Spirit! We have an assurance from God that He Will be with us in so doing till the very end of time. So, know that for reality, our labour in the Lord is never in vain. Father, You Have Spoken Your Word unto us; please bring it to pass in Jesus' Name. Amen!!!

All have sinned and fallen short of the Glory of the Lord. None of us is clean; no not one! We thank God for Christ Jesus and all He Did for us to save us and set us free from the laws of sin and death; to embrace the law of Love and Life. Help us o Lord to embrace Life and reject death in Jesus' Name. Amen!!!

324th Day

ALWAYS LOOK UNTO JESUS WHO IS ABLE TO ESTABLISH, KEEP YOU FROM ALL EVIL and ROOT YOU IN JESUS CHRIST!!!

The hope of every believer is for and in the Return of Jesus Christ as in the second Coming! Please Lord Help me that You Might Find me worthy of Your second Coming and that I might find Favour with You in Jesus' Name. Amen!!!

The Lord's Got me in His Holy Mighty Right Hand; satan and his cohorts cannot snatch me! God the Father, Son and Holy Spirit is Greater than all and Possesses all Power and will not let anything/anyone snatch me in Jesus' Name. Amen!!!

The Faithful Lord Jesus Christ is the ONE who Has Established me; He Will Keep me from all evil and He Commissioned me and Empowered me to fulfill my destiny in Him. Thank You Jesus! Halleluyah! Amen!!!

This is a Word of Comfort and Victory for somebody (at least for me)! Comfort from Jesus Christ comes with Peace and Forgiveness of sins you know?! Bible says Blessed is the man whose sins the Lord Does not count against him! Oh my Lord/Word/God! I claim it in Jesus' Name! Even with Double Blessings despite my filthiness! Oh Lord my God I thank You! The Way of the Lord was prepared as prophesied long ago; made straight; and the Glory of the Lord Has been REVEALED for all flesh to see - the coming of our Lord God Almighty in the flesh in Jesus Christ our Lord/God/Saviour/King! Halleluyah! Amen! Thank You Jesus!!!

When you're Called into Jesus Christ is when you accepted Him into your life as personal Lord/God/Saviour; then you're Called into fellowship with Jesus Christ! No shaking! All gifts of the Holy Spirit are available unto you by faith if you dare to believe and activate! If you don't activate you don't know do you? God then commends/confirms me (and you?) according to His Will and Choosing!!!

Wow! What a role model! He is for me and mine; as for me and my household, we will worship/follow the Lord God Almighty! His yoke is good enough for us as well as His incredible humility - a great model for us to learn from. O Lord, please Help me to live for you in Jesus' Name I pray. Amen!!!

Who wants to be a prisoner today? Even for the Lord? Everyone is crying out for freedom forgetting that only knowing the TRUTH can set us free! Our walk in Faith must be in humility, peaceable, longsuffering; and we must bear with each other in the faith in love and working for the unity of the Spirit in the bond of Peace!!!

Come and see oooo! Come and see! Come and see what the Lord Has Done!!!

325th Day

YOU REAP WHATEVER YOU SOW; SOW TO PLEASE THE
SPIRIT and NOT THE SINFUL NATURE and REAP ETERNAL
LIFE and NOT DESTRUCTION!!!

You deceive yourself when you think you can short circuit God's Power
Flow or short exchange God! There are laws of life that when you break
them you must face consequences! If you think God Loves you regardless
of what you do that's your problem but know that you may be very wrong.
God is Love; yes! But God is also the All-consuming Fire! If you're saying
that even though God Consumes somebody or they go to hell and God
Loves them still, that's your problem! You can believe whatever you like!
I will rather strive to please the Holy Spirit and keep doing good so I can
reap Eternal Life!

Jesus is Merciful oh yes! But don't think that He condones sin! He Knows
the value of Mercy on a person because He Said somewhere that He who is
forgiven much loves much but he who is forgiven little loves little! He Knew
that forgiving that woman who He'd just prevented from being stoned to
death would be valuable to her as her very life so He Told her He didn't
condemn her but to go and "sin no more"! That is a powerful message and
would encourage the woman to refrain from sin in the future!!!

Before I came to the Lord I was darkness through and through but now
am in Jesus Christ I am light! I must walk as a child of LIGHT and the
fruits of the Holy Spirit must be evident in my life/ways in goodness,
righteousness and truth! My life cannot remain as it was; I must change!
I cannot say God Loves me just the way I am and claim to accept Him
yet remain the same. Then I deceive myself and am causing Him to be
Crucified all over again!!!

Sometimes when it's unsafe as believers, it is God's Will for us to run for
dear life and not turn the other cheek and give our lives up to the evil
ones for nothing! Hence Paul and Silas were sent away by night into safety
in Berea. Despite the lack of general safety preaching the Word, they
continued diligently. The Bereans didn't just hear the Word; they searched

the Holy Scriptures to confirm that what they heard was the truth. We must do likewise. May God Help us to do our best to search out the Truth and receive our freedom through the truth!!!

Come and see oooo! Come and see! Come and see what the Lord Has Done!!!

326th Day

JESUS CHRIST SUFFERED GREATLY; SO THAT WE MIGHT BE FREE (FROM SIN and ALL INFIRMITIES) INDEED!!!

Because of my transgressions, iniquities, sins and for the sake of my peace, Jesus Christ was brutalised very badly. I am healed by His wounds so that His sufferings were not in vain but profitable unto me. He bore the same for all humanity; but to benefit from This Grace/Love you must believe otherwise you stand condemned because you have not believed the only Son of the Living God who came from God to set us free and who Himself is the exact representation of God and His Wisdom and Power! Jesus Christ is the Lord God Almighty! Glory! Halleluyah!!!

You can receive Grace and Peace from God, our Father and Jesus Christ and Lord who Sacrificed Himself that we might be delivered from this present evil world, the Will of God, the Father! Give Him Glory for it is His due in making atonement for our sins in such a spectacular way. A Holy God coming in human flesh form to save us and show us the Way, reconciling us to Himself! Wow! What a Saviour!!!

Jesus Christ personally bore our sins/infirmities in His Body on the Cross so we can die unto sin and live unto righteousness. We are healed and delivered fully by the evidence of His sufferings (His stripes and wounds)! We'd all strayed like sheep away from the Shepherd but through His Sacrifice, we have returned to the Shepherd/Guardian of our souls in Jesus' Name. Amen!!!

The blessing of Grace/Mercy can be given through a servant of Jesus Christ, Anointed to serve Him by God's Will even according to the holy life that is in Jesus Christ to whomsoever the Lord God Chooses! May I receive Your Blessings likewise o Lord directly from You and from Your servants here on earth in Jesus' Name. Amen!!!

We need the Holy Spirit to live for Jesus Christ because He is the Enabler! He comes to dwell in our body which is God's temple even though made of clay; hence, we have the Treasure (Holy Spirit) in earthen vessels so that the excellent Power is of God and not of ourselves. No matter how much pressure, pain, suffering etc. we come under, we are never destroyed/hopeless; bur rather remain hopeful and are made even stronger by the Power above all powers in the Name of Jesus that is above all names. Amen! Halleluyah!! Thank You Jesus!!!

327th Day

YOU STILL DOUBT THAT JESUS IS THE LORD GOD ALMIGHTY? THE GREAT GOD OUR SAVIOUR JESUS CHRIST IS THE LORD!!!

When all around is dark and hope dimmed and deemed lost; I will lift up my eyes unto the hills from whence cometh my Help. I will look up focus on Jesus Christ, my Blessed Hope, Saviour; the Great God and I know that He Will LIGHT up my situation/life. Amen! Halleluyah!!!

Only by submission to the Will of Jesus Christ, my Lord/Saviour, can I grow in His Grace and Knowledge of Him; because through submission of my will in total unto His Divine Will for my life, I become One with Him. Halleluyah! Amen! Thank You Jesus for Your Love for me!!!

This is the heritage of the Lord's Anointed! Because the Lord Called and Anointed me, I know that He Will Enlarge my coast and Empower me to conquer all and be more than a conqueror because I put my hope/trust in His Holy Name! I know that He is the Rock of my salvation, my Father, God and King in Jesus' Name. Amen!!!

When you trust/hope in the Living God, the Saviour of all mankind, especially of those that believe, you will labour and suffer reproach like Jesus Christ did and like I do! It is good to remind oneself of this truth; it will help lighten the load and ease the pain - because it is very painful. Persecution is very very painful. Jesus suffered tremendous pain on the Cross and He never promised that following Him would be as a bed of roses at all!!!

Servant of God, mind your own business (that to/for which reason you were Called)! Godless chatter and the opposing ideas of what is falsely called knowledge is very attractive and commonplace; remember that for this reason and in professing same, many have wandered from the Faith. Do not get involved in this. Avoid such at all costs because it is not profitable unto you! !!

Verily my forefathers served other gods; yet God was Merciful to Call/Choose me and take me away from the comforts of my homeland and bring me to a foreign land and He Has Promised to multiply me and give me hope beyond my imagination! He who promised is Faithful and He Will Bring it to pass in Jesus' Name. I fully trust in Him and so shall it be in Jesus' Name. My God is a Covenant-keeping God! When He Promises, He Brings it to pass! Amen!!!

328th Day

THE LORD JESUS CHRIST IS OUR RIGHTEOUSNESS and PEACE!!!

The Lord assures us who believe/trust in Him that He is a Covenant Keeping God who Will Fulfill His Promises to His servant David, the king! God Will Raise a Righteous Branch called THE Lord, our Righteousness. Surely, this is Jesus Christ that came in due season as prophesied. I believe in Jesus Christ and in His Prophetic coming to the earth to Save sinners and reconcile mankind to God. I believe and know that He is the Lord God Almighty!!!

There's a difference between the wicked and the non-wicked (d good)! Which of the two would pay attention to the Lord's Commands? Of course the good! If your desire is to be good in the Name of the Lord Jesus Christ and you pay attention to His Commands to heed and to obey, your peace would be like a river; and your righteousness like the waves of the sea. But for the wicked, there is NO peace. That's the difference!!!

Jesus Christ came into the earth; born of a woman and fulfilling all of the Words prophesied about Him according to the above words! He is indeed our Peace; the Prince of Peace!!!

Jesus Christ was crucified ignobly on the cross as He became sin for all and at the same time the propitiation for sin for all for all time - that we may enter into the righteousness of God Almighty through Him. Accordingly, in no other name is there salvation, Jesus Christ is the Lord of all!!!

Command the believers according to the Word of God to live a godly life and be rich in good deeds, generous, willing to share, unselfish... thereby laying for themselves a firm foundation for the coming age... only then can we take hold of true LIFE in Jesus Christ!!!

God Will Punish the wicked! Some say God Loves us unconditionally no matter what we do! If this were true, there would be no need then for anyone to be punished, wicked or not! But I read differently in the

Word of God that God hates the wicked and the violent and I deduce rightly from this that God cannot love everybody equally nor is His Love unconditional! YOU may believe whatever you like or be wise to believe what is true and be Saved in the end! May God Open our eyes unto the Truth of His Word; for only Jesus Christ Can Save us! Only the Truth can set us free; but we must know the Truth to be free!!!

329th Day

IF IN JESUS CHRIST, THEN WALK IN THE LIGHT! ALL WHO FELLOWSHIP WITH HIM MUST WALK IN HIS LIGHT!!!

How glorious it must have been for the disciples and all who encountered Jesus Christ "live" on earth? What a great privilege! But then did they all see it as such? But according to Hebrews 11, to walk by faith is even more glorious! Jesus Told the doubting Thomas that he had proof that He was Crucified and Rose again, but Blessed are those who believed without proof! Walk by faith in Jesus' Light so darkness does not overtake you as a believer! Remember that satan waits around prowling, wanting to devour! YOU can only be sons of Light when/if you walk in the Light. JESUS is the LIGHT!!!

There is nobody who is absolutely ignorant of their walk in darkness in my view; when you're living in sin, you know through universal ideologies/means! If you have fellowship with Jesus Christ, you do not walk in darkness! If you walk in the light, you have fellowship with other believers and the Blood of Jesus purifies all from all sin. If you however claim to have no sin, the truth is not in you! So, you activate the Cleansing Blood of Jesus in having fellowship with other believers!!!

Those who walk in the light of day are unlikely to stumble because the light enables them to see; unlike those who walk at night who stumble because the light is not in them and it's dark! As a believer, you have the advantage of walking in the light of God because you belong to the LIGHT!!!

If you're blessed to be wealthy in this world, do not be prideful/arrogant or put your hope in your wealth because you're wealthy today, tomorrow you may not be. Wealth is so unpredictable/uncertain. Rather, hope in God in Jesus Christ who accordingto His Riches in Heaven makes all provisions for us to enjoy all things through Jesus Christ our Lord! Trusting/hoping/faith in your wealth is equivalent to self-deceit and would lead you astray because riches are fleeting like your human beauty!!!

The law with relevant sacrifices it demands cannot perfect the man! If the law could achieve perfection for the man, there would not be a need to offer such sacrifices continuously; for there would be no more consciousness of sins once the man is purified! THE blood of bulls/goats cannot take away sins; so the need to offer atonement continuously. However, Jesus Christ came to shed His holy unblemished Blood as a once for all Sacrifice and this is effective not just for the forgiveness of sins but also for reconciling us with the Lord God Almighty in Jesus Christ!!!

330th Day

WHEN YOU DELIGHT YOURSELF IN THE LORD GOD
ALMIGHTY, YOU WILL PRAY TO HIM and HE WILL ANSWER
and BLESS YOU!!!

When you submit to God and have your peace in Him, receive His
Instruction and begin to obey Him, then you will prosper! Return to God
and He Will Restore you! Let His Words take root and rule your heart, cast
away and refrain from wickedness; let your wealth be cast off and replace
it and let God Be your wealth by so doing even as you reject your wealth
as God is more important for you, He Will be your wealth!!!

If you allow God's Word to abide in you and you in Him you set yourself up
for the Blessing of God so when you pray to Him for anything according to
His Will, He Will Do it for you! In so doing, God's Glory is Revealed and
Enables youto bear much fruits that will last, evidencing your discipleship!!!

If you who are mortal, sinners know how to give good gifts to your children;
does not God our Father therefore Know how to give good gifts to those who
have faith and ask Him? God is a Rewarder of those who diligently seek Him!!!

There's a Command from God to flee from sin and worldly/fleshly lusts
(youthful or not); but rather focus on and pursue righteousness, godliness,
faith, love, endurance, gentleness and peace rigorously! Fight the good
fight of faith and take hold of Eternal Life to which every believer is called
when we make the decisionto follow Jesus Christ in the presence of many
witnesses! This God who lives in unapproachable Light, who no one has/
can see except the one who is from Him and Knows Him because He is
HIM, JESUS CHRIST our Lord!!!

God Said it is not good for man to be alone; for that reason He Created
woman! Two are better than one because they have a better reward for
their labour! When one falls the other helps pick the one up unlike when
one is alone! It's warmer for both when to lie together! It's more difficultto

overcome/overpower two than one when attacked! Two stand up together against opposition better than one person! When three or more co-operate together, how much more glorious and effective! Please let us all learn from this great lesson!!!

331st Day

PRIDE IS DEFINITELY NOT A FRUIT OF RIGHTEOUSNESS! IT IS WHAT BROUGHT SATAN DOWN FROM GLORY! AVOID IT!!!

Unleash the fury of your wrath, look at every proud man and bring him low, look at every proud man and humble him, crush the wicked where they stand. Bury them all in the dust together; shroud their faces in the grave. Job 40:11-13 NIV

Job's words only attest to the reward due to the wicked! Pride is as a necklace for the wicked and like the proverbial "necklace" in jungle justice will serve as fuel for the destruction of the wicked and will "help" bring down the prideful/arrogant!!!

Nobody knows tomorrow except God; and no man is God except He who IS both Man and God, Jesus Christ! So, mortal man, better stop boasting about tomorrow and give up on self-praise; because you do not know what tomorrow holds in store and when others praise you, it's more authentic/real/true! Be wise!!!

If you must boast at all, let it be in the Lord God Almighty; that you know Him and even as you testify of Him! YOU can commend yourself all you want; it means nothing to God! It is he who the Lord God Himself Commends that He Approves! Mankind love to approve/commend one another and applaud accordingly! Who matters to God the most is the one the Lord Himself commends, recommends... approves! Again, be wise and stop following after the foolishness of mankind!!!

We who believe are like strangers in this world; for we've been Called forth out of darkness into His Marvelous Light and He Has Saved us from this darkness and we must rejoice in His Power and Might! We're a royal priesthood, holy nation, chosen generation, peculiar, strange etc. So, no need to keep wondering why we're different; nor wishing/wanting to be like everybody else which is a very common statement believers make! Flee from fleshly/worldly lusts that war against our souls and deal so uprightly even amongst the ungodly such that even as they speak evil of you, when they observe your righteous ways, they will praise our God on that Day!!!

The anointing of God is not ever automatically transferable! It's not impossible either for such a transfer to occur! However, it happens by faith; and faith is sincere, truthful, honest and pure... childlike for it to please God! When the Anointing of Jesus Christ (God) shows up, life/health/power flows through any vessel as chosen and anointed by God Almighty in Jesus Christ!!!

332nd Day

GOD'S LOVE! "IF"! IF YOU LOVE ME, YOU WILL OBEY MY COMMANDS! GOD'S LOVE IS VERY CONDITIONAL; IT'S NOT CHEAPENED EVEN BY MAN'S MANIPULATIONS!!!

Before God's Blessings/Love is declared/assured/proclaimed/offered, there's a condition attached to be fulfilled all through the Holy Scriptures! Don't let anyone deceive you with hollow, self-gratifying carnal teachings! Follow the Holy Spirit! God's Love/Blessings are conditional - all the time!!!

The washing of His disciples' feet by Jesus Christ was very symbolic act of humility and servitude in leadership! How many of today's leaders and would-be leaders are willing to emulate this set godly holy standard? Look around you and see what you have? it's no wonder everything everywhere appears upside down! May God Help us to humble ourselves and obey His Word - this world would be a better place if we do!!!

We are all as trees in the Eyes of the Lord; and whether we like it or not (want to or not), we're bearing fruits all the time on a daily basis! But God Gave us the abilityto check ourselves! ARE we in the Faith? What fruits are we bearing (good/bad)? Many of us are calling upon the Name of the Lord; but does that guarantee a place in the Kingdom of Heaven? From This Scripture, clearly not! May God Help me to be and stay on His Side in every sense/way so asto get the prize of faithfulness on that day in Jesus' Name. Amen!!!

Look around and see if these perilous days are not yet here; and if you find they're here in your judgment, then is This not the time to cry out unto the Lord God Almighty for Help? Draw near to God and He Will Draw near to you! O Jesus! Please help my unbelief and infirmity! Make me whole to serve You faithfully to the very end in Jesus' Name. Amen!!!

Have you known Him? Do you know Him? Do you wish/wantto know Him? If you wantto know Jesus Christ, then submit your will/life unto Him today and give Him Control over your everything/life! Then you will receive the Word of the Living God and He Will Make you strong! THE world is very sinful but very attractive to all! Butto overcome the wicked one (satan) you must not love the world because that's his territory! If you love the world or the things in it, then the love of the Father is not in you! After all what is in the world? Lust (of the eyes, flesh; the pride of life etc.) is not of the Father but of the world! Take heed! Help me Jesus not to love the world and all that it holds; rather to forsake the world and embrace You and Your Ways totally in Jesus' Name. Amen!!!

333rd Day

THE FEAR OF GOD LEADS TO DOING GOOD and OPENS UP THE HEART OF GOD TO A PERSON +VELY; FEAR GOD and OBEY HIS COMMANDS!!!

In my book "The Flaming Sword" by Folayan Osekita, God Opens up This topic of the fear of God. Please get a copy; you will be blessed! YOU have to love God to fear Him; and to fear God you must be drawn to Him! When you fear God you must do His Will and that includes keeping your tongue/lips from evil/lies and guarding your heart likewise! When you're so drawn to God by faith working through love with fear and trembling, God Blesses you in every way!!!

It is the fear of God that makes a man want to be good! No human being with a human heart which the Bible says is deceptive and desperately wicked, can be good of himself! It is the fear of God that drives a good man rooted in love for God! THE root of such a man shall not be moved; but wickedness shall not cause the wicked to be established!!!

Worry is not for the believer! Does not God Know your every need? Is God not able to meet all your needs? Then do you trust Him to? Faith trusts God absolutely (no compromise at all). YOU cannot be ordinary when God Calls you into an extraordinary faith! YOU cannot keep wanting to be like normal men/women when you're in Jesus Christ! Faith in Christ must change you such that just looking at you people will be able to tell that you're not of the world! So, if you claim to be in Jesus Christ and you're still worldly (even in your outlook/appearance), something ain't right! God Knows your every need; do not worry!!!

May God Help Teach us who believe to fight the good fight of faith! It is not a normal fight! We use different weapons for This fight (capable of wrecking destruction on the kingdom of darkness); not for fighting each other as brethren! Eternal Life is in us when we obey the Word of God proving that we love the Lord truly! Jesus Said so!!!

God Will not now just Send Prophets from Heaven! God Will raise and or choose His Oracles/Prophets from amongst mankind! That was what humans asked of Him and He Granted because of a great fear of and for God! Then God puts His Words in the mouth of such prophets and such speak the Words of God to the people! Oh Lord please Grant us to have discerning spirits to distinguish between true and false prophets that we be not led astray in Jesus' Name I pray with thanksgiving. Amen!!!

334th Day

IN CHRIST JESUS WE MUST HAVE AN ATTITUDE OF SERVITUDE and FLEE FROM ALL EVIL and ITS APPEARANCE! HELP ME LORD!!!

We all want to be greater than our neighbour! We would rather pursue that objective than love our neighbour as ourselves! Be truthful to yourself and ask God for a Touch on your heart for change. Repent and obey the Word of God before it's too late! Nobody wants to be rich for the sake of it or just for meeting needs. We all wantto "show" the world how "successful" we are and how much better than our neighbours we are. What a futility! Jesus Christ preached LOVE and love is an action in faith and through service in humility! Can we embrace Jesus truly? Really? Hmmm! Your choice; my choice! May God Help us all in Jesus' Name. God alone Knows those who are truly serving/worshiping Him!!!

How many of us think we're wise? This Scripture is talking to you; please don't deceive yourself! YOU know your heart and what you're thinking in it! YOU know how you believe you're wiser than everybody else and expect all else to listen to/bow to your every whim and caprice! Repent! Otherwise, there's more hope for a fool than for you! !!

Most of us love positions of leadership; but for the wrong reasons! We love such for show and to be respected and have favours! However, in Jesus Christ it's supposed to be for service in humility. THE more you desire to lead, the more you wantto serve; not to be in positions of authority so that you'd be served (which is the way we love it)! We love to be big men/women for show! Believer! Beware! Satan is on the prowl; he'll have you if you let him!!!

Man/woman of God; flee from all evil, unrighteousness and all the ungodliness in the world. Do not be a friend of the world! Go in pursuit of fruits of the Holy Spirit: righteousness, godliness, faith, hope, humility, endurance, perseverance and most of all LOVE! This is profitable for bearing good fruits that will last and for spiritual growth!!!

The disciples did not believe really! Jesus did not condemn them outright; He understood and forgave their unbelief! Jesus Revealed Himself to them supernaturally, powerfully! They thought he was a ghost! Then He Told them He was not a ghost as they could see he had flesh and bones which ghosts do not have! I still don't understand how people can refer to the Holy Spirit as holy ghost! THE Holy Spirit of the Living God can never be a ghost because a ghost is not alive; whereas the Holy Spirit is ALIVE! Amen!!!

335th Day

JESUS: FRIEND/GOD/ALL IN ALL - IN WHOM WE'RE SAFE, SECURE and ALL NEEDS MET! HEARS OUR CRIES OF DISTRESS and HELPS!!!

Who is the Saviour unto whom all mankind come for all their needs? Who can come close to Him unless He Draws them? Who quenches hunger/thirst even without food? Who forgives sins and takes away even the guilt? In whom do we find satisfaction in the goodness of His House/Temple? His Name is Higher than any other name; His Name is JESUS/Lord! Halleluyah! Amen! Thank You Jesus!!!

Hear o ye wicked! God is so far from you and will recompense you according to all your evil machinations and you end up in hell fire! Repent today and come to Jesus, the Author/Finisher of the believers' faith!!!

There's only one God and one mediator between man and God to whom we can choose to call and He Will Hear us through our faith and save us! YOU can reach Him anytime of the day and you don't have to book an appointment to see/speak to Him! JESUS!!!

For all of us who want to get rich! A word from the Lord! Who will heed though? THE love of money is the root of all evil! Some have shipwrecked their faith by wandering from the truth/faith, piercing themselves with diverse griefs because of their love/eagerness for money! THE drive to get rich has led many into a fall into temptation and trapped in many foolish/harmful desires leading into ruin and destruction! Think about it! YOU probably know such people in your life and communities! Please God! Keep the love of money away from our lives in Jesus' Name. Amen!!!

Be careful what you ask God for otherwise you might just get it! All things are permissible but not all things are beneficial! Not all prayer answered is good for us! Please God Help us not to be given into greed/avarice but rather to be godly and content with fear and trembling work out our salvation in Jesus' Name. Amen!!!

336th Day

HAVE FAITH IN THE CREATOR! COMBINE THAT WITH WISDOM and DISCRETION (SELF DISCIPLINE) and LOVE! THEN YOU WILL BE SAFE and SECURE IN JESUS' NAME IN ALL WAYS!!! VERY PROFITABLE!!!

Keep sound wisdom and discretion, so they will be life to your soul

If you have Godly wisdom and show discretion you will not take God nor His Word for granted and will not go against His Word. Hence, you will avoid the diverse pitfalls of life and stones that cause people to stumble and fall and perish! YOU will be safe, secure and saved in Jesus' Name!!!

When your truly in the Lord and walking in His Light your paths will always be lit up and not dark nor darkened! YOU will also be spared from calamities of the world that consume others. YOU will dwell in safety even where others live in fear and insecurity, God Will Keep you protected and safe in Jesus' Name. Amen!!!

God is Light! When God Shines His Light on a man's face, his life is transformed with joy! Do you know that Joy Transforms? With Light comes Love, Joy, Peace and other fruits of the Holy Spirit because the Holy Spirit is the Light of God and is Love and even comes with Wisdom because His is God!!! Light brings security/safety o Glory Halleluyah! Thank You Jesus!!!

If only we all take heed of this Word of God! We chase after material/ wealth so much that we forget that one day we'll die and take nothing with us! Hardly is anyone Godly today let alone contented! Hmmm! May God Have Mercy on us to Grant us His LOVE with wisdom and keep our hearts from straying away from Him in Jesus' Name. Amen!!!

Hmmm! Poverty in the midst of plenty! May God Give us revelation into why those who have will be given even more whilst those who do not have even the little they have will be taken from them and given to those who have! Hmmmm! ARE God's Ways like ours? No! Teach me o Heavenly Father! I want to learn Your Ways in Jesus' Name. Amen!!!

337th Day

GIVE THANKS IN ALL SITUATIONS; THAT WAY, YOU CAN REJOICE ALWAYS - FOR THANKSGIVING IF A JOYFUL ACTIVITY!!!

Go, eat your food with gladness, and drink your wine with a joyful heart, for it is now that God favours what you do. Always be clothed in white, and always anoint your head with oil. Ecclesiastes 9:7,8 NIV

Rejoice always and give thanks in every situation! Eat your meals with a thankful/joyful heart; bearing in mind that you're enjoying God's Grace. Clothe yourself in purity and always refresh yourself with the Holy Spirit and annoint your head with oil always and it shall be well with you in Jesus' Name. Amen!!!

Make joyful noises unto the Lord our God with thanksgiving! Such will hopeful go up to God as an offering, an aroma that pleases the Lord greatly! May the words of my mouth and the meditations in my heart be acceptable in Your sight O Lord both now and forevermore. Amen!!!

Stop worrying or being anxious about anything in life! Pray about everything! With a thankful heart, present your requests humbly to God; and God Almighty Will Guard your hearts/minds in Jesus Christ with the Peace of God!!!

today, many do not agree to the sound instruction of our Lord Jesus Christ and to godly Teaching! Such peddle false doctrines too! All of these are borne out of pride/conceit and ignorance with a lack of understanding! Such thrive on satanic wiles/wickedness and believe that godliness is a profitable "business"!!!

Basically, unto whom much is given, much is expected! THE person who receives forgiveness for a little loves little but the one forgiven for much loves much! THE deeper the forgiveness, the deeper the love! Do not judge a book by its cover! This woman was probably being judged for apparent immorality and the disciples wondered about Jesus Christ along those same lines! Hmmmmm! What a life! May God Have Mercy on me in Jesus' Name I pray, Amen!!!

338th Day

JESUS CHRIST OFFERS FORGIVENESS OF SINS; FORSAKE WORLDLY/FLESHLY LUSTS and PURSUE PURITY VIA THE POWER OF THE HOLY SPIRIT!!!

We all who are Saved once lived in sin; gratifying the cravings and following the desires of the sinful nature. We were objects of God's Wrath. But God's Love offered us a way out through Salvation (faith in Jesus Christ through believing His Holy Sacrifice); thus made alive in Christ Jesus and Saved by His Grace and seated with Him in Heavenly realms. Oh! What a Salvation/Saviour!!!

It is through the Grace of God in Salvation that we're Taught to deny ourselves and do away with ungodliness and worldly lusts; to live sinless, sober, godly lives, even in this present evil, ungodly world of violence and sinfulness! Oh! Thank You Jesus for such an opportunity!!!

It is ONLY by living in the Spirit (Holy Spirit) that we can walk in the Holy Spirit; because we belong to Christ Jesus and thus have crucified the fleshly passions/desires! Oh God! Please Help us in Jesus' Name! I desire to do Your Will O Lord; but I realise that I cannot do it on my own! I NEED You every breath I take O Lord! Please Help me in Jesus' Name. Amen!!!

We who believe must strive to enter into the Kingdom of God through the narrow gates (which alone lead therein)! Many will come on the Day of Judgment and lay claims that should grant them access but shall be firmly denied because they have not lived their lives in a manner worthy of the Lord. Hence, the Lord Will not acknowledge having known them. Their names are not in the Book of Life! O God! Please let not my faith be in vain in Jesus' Name. Please count me worthy to partake with others who find Your Favour at Your Dinner Table in the Time of Relevance in Jesus' Name. Amen!!!

In life, we are constantly sowing seeds whether we're aware or not! It is very important to remember that not all the seeds we sow will bear fruit! Not all a farmer's seeds do. Some will fall by the wayside and the birds of the air will devour them! Some will fall on the mountains with very little soil and will be scorched by the Sun; and some will fall amongst the thorns and be choked to death and not allowed to grow! However, there will be some that will fall on fertile ground and grow and thrive unto a bountiful harvest! Lord, please Help Guide our sowing that we bear much fruit that will last in Jesus' Holy Name. Amen!!!

339th Day

JESUS CHRIST WAS MANIFESTED FOR A REASON; LOVE DEFINED!!!

Jesus Christ was manifested/came to destroy the works of the devil! When you're born again, the Holy Spirit (Seed of Jesus Christ) is in you and with His Help Only can sin be kept at bay away from you. As many as are Led by the Holy Spirit of the Living God, such are the sons of the Living God!!!

Love is defined as God Loving us so much as to Send His Son, an atoning Sacrifice for our sins (through His death on the Cross)! Such an atonement/ Sacrifice is love! Greater love has no man than for one to lay down his life for his friends! God Gave His Life for us for a reason; that we might live through Him - first accepting His Love and Sacrifice through believing/ faith in Him and in This Sacrifice!!!

Love demonstrated through the death of Jesus Christ (Holy Sacrifice) for us whilst we were still sinners (undeserving)! So, when we have accepted This Sacrifice and believe/have faith in Him, justified by His shed Blood, we shall be Saved from the wrath of God! If while we were enemies of God we were reconciled through the death of Jesus Christ, surely we shall be saved by the Life of Jesus Christ after being reconciled!!!

The Kingdom of Heaven is so valuable that a person ought to do everything possible to get in! No matter how rough, narrow or tough the gates/ pathway is to This Kingdom! Hence the man that found a treasure and hid it in a field and then sells all he has to buy that field because he knows the value of the treasure - much more than all he had! If we truly value the Kingdom of God, we would value the righteousness that comes with it and would in like manner seek after that Kingdom and Righteousness knowing that all things shall be added unto us once we have that in Jesus' Name!!!

340th Day

WHEN YOU'RE IN JESUS CHRIST, YOU HAVE SUPERNATURAL PROTECTION FROM ALL EVIL and YOU'RE SAFE/SECURE! DO YOU BELIEVE THIS? FAITH!!!

When we walk with the Lord in the Light of His Love, what a glory He'll Shed on our way! Whist we do His Good Will, He'll Abide with us still, as with all who will trust and obey! There's always a condition to God's Love/Blessings whether you a mere mortal admit/agree to This or not is irrelevant! THE Lord Has Spoken! By the way, can anyone show me in the Holy Scriptures where God ever said He Loves everybody; loves all equally; or that His Love is unconditional? Mankind love to make up stories like artists at work and peddle the same as God's Spoken/Revealed Words! Beware, lest you believe in vain!!!

In today's world, wickedness is on the increase! God Knows that there will always be some under the yoke of slavery and He Makes Provision for how they are to live even in Jesus Christ as believers! Therefore, believers will not always be free! Why then do we despise one another as believers; mocking those who are enslaved and suffering all manners of injustice? Even our so called leaders teach as if none amongst us must be impoverished etc.! Please Help us o Lord!!!

You want to learn some lessons in faith? Then read the above with your whole heart; meditate on the words and let them sink into your soul fully! Faith is not seeing is believing at all; contraryto what is peddled and taught by the world and science! Faith is being sure of what we hope for; and certain of what we have not seen! Period! No more no less! I hope in meditating on these words, faith's fire is lit up in your spirit, heart, mind, soul, being and fueled with the Power/Spirit of the Lord Jesus Christ from now unto Eternity. Amen in Jesus' Name. Amen!!!

341st Day

IRONIES OF LIFE; THE RICH FEIGN POVERTY WHILST THE POOR FEIGN WEALTHINESS! RICHES ATTRACT WOES; THE POVERTY IS NOT THREATENED! YET MOST WANT TO BE WEALTHY!!!

The rich often pretend not to be whilst the poor make out like they're not! Hoodlums often target and threaten the rich whereas the poor hear no threats! Still, most people drive themselves almost crazy to be wealthy! Even at the expense of godliness many go readily astray just for the sake of riches!!!

It's more profitable to have the fear of the Lord in one's life with little material possessions etc. than have great treasure with sorrow and troubles with it! It's more profitableto have and eat very little but have Love than eat fat expensive food with hatred! Hmmm! THE Wisdom of God is truly Supreme!!!

People purchase/have the evil eye for the sake of making loads of money and material possessions not knowing that in the end they will lack! Be wise and follow after the path of godliness with contentment which is great gain!!!

The laying on of hands has become increasingly popular! The believers of old used it sparingly with God's Wisdom! Through the laying on of hands foul spirits are transferred and many have been polluted and gotten in trouble! The good/evil that people do go before them with consequent/attendant results!!!

This is what life is like for the man of peace/righteousness who lives holy! The enemy is on his case often! However, the believer must trust and hope in the Lord God Almighty (JESUS CHRIST) alone! He's a rock and His Name a Strong Tower to which the righteous run and are saved! The enemy will surely be consumed. Believer, have This confidence and don't let it shake/wane! A person may become stupendously wealthy and in the way of the world with that comes much power! However, be assured of this: All Power, Mercy, Wisdom, Authority belongs unto the Lord our God and He Rewards each one according to his/her work! Grant us who trust/hope/believe in You in Your Name LOVE O Lord; for LOVE has all our needs within in Jesus' Name. Amen!!!

342nd Day

BEWARE THE LAST DAYS! LOSS OF FAITH WILL CAUSE LOVE TO WAX COLD IN MANY; STANDING FIRM WITH PATIENT ENDURANCE WILL LEAD TO PERFECTION IN JESUS' NAME!!!

Don't get caught in the web of satanic wiles/wickedness that will cause many to lose faith and begin to hate each other! False prophets will arise and deceive many; wickedness will increase and the love of many will wax cold. Be bold and courageous; stand firm to the very end and you will be saved. May God Protect us from such a time that is unavoidable; so we can stand firm to the end and be saved in Jesus' Name. Amen!!!

It's a foregone conclusion that every believer will fall into temptation! We are to count it all joy! Who can do this except the Grace of God is upon them? Therefore, we need to pray ceaselessly; and particularly for the Holy Spirit, the Power behind our faith working through love! Temptations allow our faith to be tried/tested and teach us patience/endurance, which leads us on the road to perfection in faith!!!

God Gives confidence to the believer; do not cast yours away! The believer needs confidence with patience so that after doing the Will of God, we wait for the promise to be fulfilled! It doesn't necessarily come automatically! Like the farmer plants his crops and waits patiently for harvest time, so we must learnto wait upon the Lord! Jesus is definitely coming back again; and we must wait patiently with faith! The just shall live by faith and must not turn back for that will displease God and we must strive alwaysto please the Lord. Without faith no one can please the Lord!!!

Regarding inheritance; there's the Word of God laid down/out that mankind may follow. However, who really cares today for the Word of God? When we deliberate and enact laws prohibiting God's Word from being learnt in our educational and other institutions in the societies of the world. Laws enacted based on the Word of God are being repealed and replaced with commonsensical laws which enable the permeation of evil in all areas of our daily living with attendant consequences evident to all! The Judge Stands at the door!!!

The Word of God is not just to be learnt/mastered; but applied to daily living impartially and not applied with favouritism! Who is listening today? Almost everything we do is riddled with favouritism, bribery and corruption including positions of responsibility and authority in our congregations/fellowships!!! Hmmm! Jesus is Coming! Will He find faith on the earth when He returns? What will He meet in your hands? Please Help us O Lord so we do not live our lives given to us through the Holy Sacrifice in vain! Amen!!!

343rd Day

DO NOT WORRY WHEN EVILDOERS/SINNERS/WORLDLY PEOPLE PROSPER - IT NEVER LASTS; FEAR GOD and OBEY HIS COMMANDMENTS; IT WILL GO WELL WITH YOU!!!

Stop worrying like pagans do; they have no faith! YOU who have faith ought not to think like they do! Does your worrying profit you in any way at all? Can you add an hour to your life by worrying? If anything, worrying shortens your dear life; so why worry? Life is above food and the body above clothes. Trust God, Who Alone Can Provide for you!!!

Do not envy apparent success in the ungodly; much sorrow is attached to their success and it never lasts! It's the Blessings of God that prospers a person without adding sorrows! The hope and expectation of the believer is secure and never cut off in the long run (at the end)!!!

Some befriend the world just for the sake of success in this world not knowing that they become enemies of God in the process! God is very jealous for His Spirit which is in us and He Doesn't want us to befriend the world so we don't get polluted like them! Don't do it; resist the devil and temptation to do so and he will flee from you and you will be free from such befriending of the world!!!

Don't simply believe/entertain an accusation against an elder unless established by two or three witnesses; and those who sin or are found guilty are to be publicly dealt with so others may learn from their example how not to live/behave! Who cares about this today eh? May God Help us all in Jesus' Name. Amen!!!

God found fit that man ought not to be alone; hence, God Made woman for him as a helper! Do not change God's Ways; in the end it leads you astray and into eternal damnation! God Gave a natural order! Change this at your own peril! No one can force you to live a godly life; but you pay for your choices!!!

344th Day

IF YOU HAVE FAITH AND ACT IN FAITH DOING GOOD YOU WILL SEE THE GOODNESS OF THE LORD; OTHERWISE, HIS WRATH AWAITS YOU!!!

To have this confidence is not a small thing at all! It's easier said by mouth than for real! However, if said by faith, the Lord is Merciful to bring it to pass! Learn to wait upon the Lord because it pays to do so in the long run; for whatever He promises, He brings to pass. With the Lord, your secure if you trust/believe in Him!!!

When the Lord punishes a person/people, He Gives room for repentance and forgives; i.e. He relents. God does not punish forever as long as the lesson He's teaching you has been learnt! It is not in His nature to cause man grief; however, man leaves God no choice because of disobedience and lack of fear/love for God and His Word!!!

Salvation is of the Lord and He delivers the righteous from calamities, the wicked etc. because they put their trust in Him. God Helps the faithful holy ones and delivers them from all afflictions always! Just believe Him and trust Him!!!

It is written that the elders who direct the affairs of the church well (especially preachers/teachers) are worthy of double honour! Do not frustrate their efforts; make sure they're well looked after and their needs met! Only Jesus Christ the Great Provider is ABLE to Provide in this way; but He Works through people!!!

Laziness and slothfulness does not pay; period. Work and Pray; watch and pray so that you will not fall under temptation!!!

345th Day

LEARN GODLINESS AND TEACH THE SAME TO YOUR CHILDREN; PASS THE LEARNING ON FROM GENERATION TO GENERATION!!!

Make the Word of God come alive in your lives as a way of life and ensure that you pass the same onto your children so they can do likewise with theirs! That is with God really wants for us to do!!!

When God Blesses you, He lets you know about it! But can God entrust His Word to you as He did with Abraham? Everyone sings Abraham's blessings are mine! ARE you faithful like him? Will/Can you be? Because there is a condition for the blessing to cometo pass! It's not automatic and definitely not unconditional! Quit deceiving yourself!!!

Do not leave your children in wrongdoing which you know about without correcting them; otherwise, you're destroying your own lineage! How can your generation endure when you condone wrongdoing and ungodliness? Set a vision clearly for your familyto follow and let this vision be engrained in your children so they follow through with it! Let the laws of God be entrenched in your family psyche so it will be well with you and with your children after you and so they can do likewise!!!

No matter what happens; no matter how clever man is and how much man deviates from the laws of God and distorts the same, God's Word will prevail! Only God Speaks and it comesto pass! Who can bring anything to pass without God's approval? Even if a leaf falls from a tree, it is with God's Knowledge and approval! Whether a seed grows and leadsto a harvest or dies with no fruits, God Knows all! Fear God; and obey His Commandments! This is good for your life!!!

Living righteously has its drawbacks! The human mind-set wants to be loved, approved, appreciated and acknowledged! It doesn't work that way for those truly in the Lord in reality! Very scarcely will anyone give up their life for a righteous man; although for a good man, perhaps someone might venture/dare to die! Hmmmm! Whilst we were sinners, Jesus Christ Gave His Life for us; so even much more having been reconciled to God, we shall be saved by His Life. This is our hope of Eternal Life even in Christ Jesus. Amen!!!

346th Day

THE MEEK ARE KNOWN TO THE WORLD AS FOOLS/IDIOTS/ MUGUS; BUT THE BIBLE SAYS THEY ARE BLESSED! SO, I'D RATHER BE MEEK THEN!!!

Why do you think God chose the meek to inherit the earth and not the arrogant, prideful, powerful, etc.? It's because humility begets much Grace and promotion usually follows! Humble yourself in the Sight of the Lord and He Will Lift you up!!!

God looks to Teach sinners the Way as well as the sheep (humble) not the goats! Choose your preference now! I choose humility! I choose to be a sheep! I choose to be a fool/idiot for Jesus Christ's sake! My reward awaits; I will be Guided Divinely because the steps of the righteous are ordered by the Lord!!!

God is a God of the humble/meek, poor, impoverished, widows, orphans etc. He Favours them and doesn't let them suffer in vain! O Lord God I thank You that You're not like mortal man! Help me to get to increase my joy in You and to rejoice in You my Holy One of Israel; in Jesus' Name I pray!!!

Abram was Called out of his comfort zone! ARE you ready/prepared to leave your comfort zone? If you're not, you're wasting your time! Abram did not become Abraham until he had accepted the Call! Sarai his wife did not become Sarah until her husband accepted the Call! Abram didn't know where he was going; yet, he trusted God and took off! Wonderful! The rest is history! Is God's Word confirmed or not? He is Faithful! Just put your trust in him like a little child! Remember when you get there, build an altar to the Lord Who Called you! Make a mark in His Name! Do something in the Name of the Lord Jesus Christ! I'd leave an indelible mark in Jesus' Name! Help me Lord Jesus to do so effectively!!!

347th Day

KEEPING THE COMMANDMENTS OF GOD CAN/WILL PROLONG YOUR LIFE; FOCUS ON SPIRITUAL, MORE THAN PHYSICAL EXERCISE!!!

The Bible says physical exercise profits a little bit; but spiritual exercise profits in ALL ways! Which do you think wisdom will go for? YOU choose! Everywhere these days, there's a craze for physical exercise! Why? People want sexy bodies and to look good! Hmmm! No wonder there's less and less value placed on spiritual exercise which profits for ALL things! The heart of man is deceitful and desperately wicked who can know it? Man's mind-set is warped! We love sin! THE Scriptures are very clear; we choose to ignore rather than follow!!!

The Word of God keeps on reassuring us in terms of the benefits of trusting and putting our faith in God alone and obeying His Commandments! We ignore this to our own peril; and often cry out to Him when trouble comes. Yet, even after saving us time and time again, we return to our vomit and expect to be saved again!!!

Is there still fear for/of God in man's heart today? Do we ever take God's Word seriously? If you fear God, will you do what you're doing right now? THE fear of God is not of mouth alone when your sober; it's a daily living thing! Often we learn and know about Him; but I wonder if we truly have knowledge of the Holy One, because if we truly do, we would fear Him and live by His Word in obedience - evidence of our love for Him!!!

Take care of your family as God Gives you the Grace! That's what Christianity is about! Living and loving one another! How can you say the love of God is in you when you can't even take care of members of your own family or those in need in your own family? Hmmm! God is not mocked; a man will reap whatsoever he has sown!!!

This outlines the unique Calling of Saul (Paul) by Jesus Christ Himself after He had been Taken up into the Heavens! Evidence that He is Alive and not dead! Ignore and or despise the teachings of Apostle Paul at your own peril! Fear God! Obey His Commandments! If Jesus Christ could touch Saul's heart and change his name to Paul and use Him for His Glory, He Will and Can do the same with your life! Will you let Him? I have decided to follow Jesus; no turning by, no turning back!!!

348th Day

WORK! DO NOT BE IDLE! SATAN FINDS WORK FOR IDLE HANDS! DON'T GET INTO HIS TRAP! FREE YOURSELF FROM SATANIC WILES RELATING TO SLOTHFULNESS!!!

This is good ethics to hold and to imbibe and teach to children and young people especially today! God Willing such will bear good fruit and reduce the explosion of criminal activities all over the world! Settle down and earn the bread you eat! Work and Eat (work and jeba meaning work and eat "eba" - a soccer game we used to play when I was small)!!!

The lot of the lazy slothful man is a full of thorns; whilst the way of the righteous is made plain! YOU cannot be righteous if your lazy and or slothful! Serving God is not about making easy lazy money! It's about serving God!!!

Eat, drink and enjoy yourself in the labour you toil for in your life; this is your reward, God's Gift to you because many toil and cannot even enjoy the fruits of their labour at all! Many rich and wealthy people have little or no joy in their lives and they die miserable deaths! Be thankful when God Favours you and make the very best of your lot!!!

The ways of mankind are known to God very clearly! Younger widows are counseled to marry and have children and manage their homes so as not to give the enemy the opportunity for slander or profanity of God's Name/Word! Is anyone listening?!!

To grow in Jesus Christ you must lay aside all negativity and all evil including unforgiveness and bitterness! Then, as small babies, DESIRE the pure milk of the Word of God. Crave the Word earnestly and faithfully and prayerfully and God Will Answer your prayers in Jesus' Name!!!

349th Day

NOTHING WILL SEPARATE ME FROM THE LOVE OF JESUS CHRIST! NOTHING! NOTHING! NOTHING!!! I WILL NEVER GIVE UP!!!

I'll live for Jesus day after day; I'll live for Jesus then come what may! Thy Holy Spirit, I will obey; I'll live for Jesus day after day! Nothing will take this joy away from me; I will not give this in exchange for anything in this wicked world! I am sold out to Jesus Christ for life! Thank You Jesus Christ for having me! Help me to love You as I should to the very very end. Amen!!!

No matter what I face in this wicked evil world, I will not fear nor allow fear to overcome or overrun me! I have God's Discipline for Comfort at all times through His Word and His Perfect Love which drives out all fear! Please Jesus let Your Perfect Love Continue to flow into and through me in Jesus' Holy Name. Amen!!!

I can and will under any circumstances without ever getting so frustrated that I don't want to live! With the Help of God Almighty in Jesus Christ, I am more than a conqueror so therefore, nothing shall overwhelm me that is negative! I know prosperity and lack and am able to live in both according to His Will and Help! I will be overwhelmed with the Love, Grace, Mercy and Compassion of God Who Gives me Strength!!!

There is a test before promotion and or reward! God's Love is not automatic nor is it unconditional! The believer must learn the Way of Faith to walk in the Light of Jesus Christ! Do we think any believer will have his/her name in the Book of Life without testing? Why do we think the Bible says if you're standing, then stand firm so you do not fall! If anyone thinks they cannot ever fall; they have believed a lie and a great big humpty dumpty type of fall awaits them! Be very careful!!!

God is not only after your heart! Your body is His temple! Make it holy, a living sacrifice! Make it acceptable to God; your reasonable service to God!

Don't conform to the dictates of this world because it's easy and attractive; but allow your mind to be renewed by the Power of the Holy Spirit and the Love of God! Then, you will be able to prove what is right and acceptable; the perfect Will of God!!!

350th Day

LOVE, MARRY AND LOVE SOME MORE; IT'S A REWARD FROM GOD! WHEN WE LOVE, NO NEED FOR DIVORCE BECAUSE GOD HATES THAT!!!

This is the ordinance for marriage! If the to are truly one, less problems; if love is fully activated, no need for divorce! Husbands, love your wives; wives respect your husband! Submit to him as unto the Lord! Be like Sarah who humbled herself, honoured her husband and called him Master! How many women want to give such honour to their husband in this women's lib ridden world of today? God is clear!!!

Older women must behave themselves and be a good example to the younger women and teach them what is right and godly! How many women hold these values today? Search your soul! Are you in the faith? If you've strayed from these godly values, return for your own good before it's too late! The Word of God is blasphemed because of you!!!

When you marry a woman (or vice-versa), "enjoy" life with her and love her all your life! There are consequences for straying from time immemorial! YOU can never cheat on nature/life! God is not mocked; a man will reap whatever he has sown (applicable to all)!!!

Preach/teach the truth; spread it all around so that no one is without excuse for misdemeanors! Provide for your nuclear family and extend a helping hand even to relatives because this is godly! I didn't write the Word of God! Otherwise, you deny the faith and you're worse than an unbeliever! The unbelievers sometimes obey God's Word far more than the believers! Hmmm!!!

Believers! We're to hate evil and love good! Strive all you can to establish justice whenever it is within your power to do so! for This reason, perhaps the Lord Will Show Mercy to the rest of us kept alive by His Grace!!!

351st Day

GOD OPPOSES THE PROUD and GIVES GRACE TO THE HUMBLE; HE LIFTS THEM UP WHO LOWER THEMSELVES BEFORE HIM!!!

Humility begets much grace and is Rewarded by God abundantly! YOU may correct your brethren based on love; anything else outside of this is malicious and unacceptable in Christ Jesus! If you must judge, do so correctly and in love so as to edify not destroy!!!

God misses nothing! Be encouraged! Do not fret when evil doers prosper! Surely, they cannot endure! Be bold, strong and courageous and know that the Lord Will Vindicate the just and the wicked will never go unpunished! God abhors covetousness!!!

To be upright you must avoid evil and guard your way/life! YOU can't do anything you like in Jesus Christ! YOU must strive to do the Will of God! Better opt for lowliness of spirit than share spoil with the arrogant! Beware!!!

Anger and hot temperament do not bear good fruit! Avoid both at all costs! Opt instead for humility! YOU may be taken for a fool just like Jesus Christ; but your better off than giving vent to anger in a hot temper! Lowliness of spirit exalts; pride only brings one down - so what's the point?!

Different types of widows and suffering - one is sincere and calls/looks to God absolutely for help; the other is insincere and worldly in disposition - desirous and pleasure seeking! God Sees all!!!

Clear evidence of God'sPeace Love and Mercy! God always offers "another chance"; i.e. God always gives people a chance to repent and change their ways and embrace His Ways before Judgment is visited! However, take This for weakness at your own peril!!! Hmmm! Amen! Glory! Halleluyah!!!

352nd Day

ETERNAL LIFE: BY FAITH THROUGH KNOWLEDGE OF AND HOPE IN JESUS CHRIST - GOD'S PROMISE MADE BEFORE TIME BEGAN - VERY SECURE!!!

Faith without works is dead! Faith requires knowledge! How can you have faith in the ONE that you do not know about? Knowledge is as fuel to faith. Hence, faith comes through hearing the Word of God! Hearing can be through listening, reading and or simply observing; the point is that you need knowledge (however you can get it) to know/learn about the Lord Jesus Christ, Who Himself is the Eternal Life!!!

Jesus Christ KNOWS who His Sheep are! YOU can pretend all you want knowing fully well that it would only lead you to hell! YOU can use all the fetish you like to get "power" to "help" your so called ministry all you want! I see no point whatsoever since it leads to hell fire! But those that truly follow the Lord are known to Him and no one can take them away or even lead them astray!!! Oh thank You JESUS for You Alone Can Keep me safely in your Holy Grasp/Reach/Hands!!!

There is a reason for God saying do not give up doing good; for when you persevere in so doing, your heading for glory, honour, immortality, Eternal Life! But for the disobedient, selfishly ambitious, who don't obey the truth, head for wrath and indignation of God! for these, there awaits tribulation/ distress for their evil doing! However, for those who persevere in doing good, there awaits glory, honour and peace! No peace for the wicked and no partiality with God. He Cannot be bribed!!!

God's Love for mankind is made manifest in His Holy Sacrifice; but to enter into His Eternal Life, you have the duty to believe so not to perish but live forever! Otherwise, you stand condemned. Let no one teach you otherwise; they're only deceiving you!!! God's Love is NEVER unconditional! The condition is to believe and obey the Word of God and then the reward!!!

Humble yourself! That's the only way God Will Lift you up! Resist the devil and he will flee from you! Know that when suffering for and in the faith, God is Building in you perfection; to establish, strengthen and settle you down in the faith! Put all your cares, faith, hope and all in Him!!! Jesus Christ is a Mighty God and very very Faithful!!!

353rd Day

SEEK GOD'S KINGDOM AND HIS RIGHTEOUSNESS AS PRIORITY; THEN ALL OTHER THINGS WILL BE ADDED UNTO YOU!!!

We worry too much in our lives and chase after the same things pagans chase after! Aren't we missing something vital? Aren't we doing something wrong? We worry so much even about the morrow! If only we can utilise the Word of God favourably for our own good! How much better off we would be!!!

God always leaves His Mark! When His Hand is in it, you just KNOW about it! He is very mindful of His Covenant with the faithful and the obedient; those who fear Him and live according to His Word and Instructions never go without and they're always Blessed/Rewarded!!!

If you make God proud to call you His people by obeying Him and doing His Will, you will never be put to shame! This is the heritage of those that fear the Lord and do His Bidding; not for all and sundry willy nilly! The Lord is Good and His Mercies endure forevermore! Come to Him faithfully and obediently and experience His Wonders unceasingly!!!

Believer! Do not fear persecution; just keep praying and if you will remain faithful even unto death, you will receive the crown of life, a worthy prize!!! Lord Help me to remain faithful in the face of all that life throws at me in Jesus' Name till the very end!!!

354th Day

LORD PLEASE HELP ME TO INCREASE IN LOVE - IN KNOWLEDGE AND DEPTH OF INSIGHT!!!

Love Enables the believer to discern with his best and be pure and blameless and filled with the fruits of righteousness that comes through Jesus Christ to God's Peace Praise and Glory; unto the Day of Christ Jesus! As you increase in love, you will increase in the gift of discernment!!!

God's Peace and Love is not automatic! Believers have a part to play! The only thing that matters is faith that works through love. Faith is the foundation upon which love is built! We must increase in the attributes of love; some of which are laid out as above! As these abound in the believer, barrenness or unfruitfulness in the knowledge of our Lord Jesus Christ disappear!!!

Why would the path of the righteous shine increasingly brighter till the fullness of the day like the light of dawn? It's because they increase in love; and love is light! Lord, Help me to increase in LOVE through Jesus Christ our Lord. Amen!!!

God's Peace Wisdom is Supreme! In discharging the Christian duty in Jesus Christ, applying Godly Wisdom is essential as above. Humankind have a duty in the Lord to love one another! This includes daily responsibilities to family members and the society at large!!!

Be aware that deceivers will come in these last days and some will even say they are the Christ! Do not be taken in by them! Be very diligent to search the Scriptures and seek the Help of the Holy Spirit to help you understand the Word of God and obey!!!

355th Day

PRAY CEASELESSLY and FOR HELP OF THE HOLY SPIRIT TO DO SO and PERSEVERE NO MATTER WHAT YOU FACE!!!

Don't dull with the devil; smarten up in Jesus' Name! Never give up praying! Don't look at or dwell upon circumstances; like feeling, they deceive and take your mind off the right target or focus! Be vigilant; be alert! Watch and pray; especially for the saints of God!!!

Are you weak, tired, weary, heavy laden? Finding it hard even to pray? YOU need the intervention of the Holy Spirit! To gain access to the Holy Spirit, first, you got to submit your life to the Giver of the Holy Spirit! His Name is Higher than any other name; His Name is Jesus and He is the Lord! Accept/receive Him into your life immediately without delay!!!

Who shall ascend unto the Mountain of the Lord? The Lord Has Spoken! Is anyone listening? Do you want joy in the Lord's House of prayer for all nations? Then be holy even as the Lord is Holy; and be perfect even as the Lord is Perfect!!!

How do you treat people older/younger than you (male/female)? There's a Standard in the Love of God for all to follow! This is not about common sense, it's about discipline in Love! Show people a modicum of decency and respect even as you respect your own self! Remember! Love your neighbour as yourself!!!

Come, enter into the Sabbath rest of God! Forsake wickedness! There's no peace for the wicked say the Lord! Resting from working is very important; but there's a rest that is superior! The peace of God that surpasseth all human understanding! Still, the believer must keep the Lord's Sabbath!!!

356th Day

BE PRACTICAL and TRUTHFUL WITH/IN LOVE!!!

Enikeni ti'wo ba nipa lati se iranlowo fun o ohun na l'enikeji re toju re! Whosoever your able to assist is your neighbour; take care of them! Loving your neighbour is practical and not just about your next door neighbour - could be anybody; so be sensitive!!!!

When you choose good over evil, you're bound to have enemies! Some preach that as a believer, you shouldn't have enemies! Did Jesus have any enemies? Take a cue of living faith from your answer to that question! Always remember that the Lord is our Helper as believers!!!

When you strive to live a holy and blameless life, be fully aware that it comes at a price; although the benefits far outweigh the costs! YOU will be persecuted! Wisdom does not vent all feelings; nor does love - show restraint; be wise! To be prone to vent all feelings in the name of being godly and truthful is hypocrisy and foolish!!!

Mind your faith and the execution of it and be true and diligent in terms/matters of such nature for all to see! Then you will save both yourself and your hearers! Some say faith is very personal; between you and God! Is that what God Says? Watch and pray so you will not be overrun by temptation!!!

There are wily foxes out there as always! Be matured to avoid being taken captive by them as little children are prone to be! have you never heard the phrase: "catch them young?" Study the Holy Bible; it is the Word of the Living God!!!

357th Day

GOD LEADS BELIEVERS ALWAYS IN TRIUMPH; WE ARE THE AROMA OF JESUS CHRIST! WE MUST DEVOTE/COMMIT TO LETTING HIS LIGHT SHINE THROUGH US EVERYWHERE!!!

Believers always have victory because God Fights their battles! Let the Beauty of Jesus be seen in me! All His Wondrous Compassion and Purity! Let the Spirit Divine all my nature refine till the Beauty of Jesus be seen in me!!!

God Inhabits the praises of His people! God Loves sacrifices of praise coming from a pure clean heart! Strive for holiness always for this pleases God through faith!!!

Mankind tend to underestimate the depth of the riches of God's Wisdom/ Knowledge! Who can search out His Judgments or trace out His Paths? Who can know His Mind to counsel Him? No comparison at all with God! Mankind! Submit! Humble yourself! Forget your pride! Bow to the Living God!!!

This is what believers ought to dwell upon! If only we would obey the Holy Scriptures! What a difference the Word of God would make in our lives!!!

The Sun shall shine no more! The moon shall turn to blood and the Lord shall appear in the midst of sinners! What a terrible Day it shall be; the Day of the Lord! and yes; it is surely fast approaching!!! JESUS CHRIST IS COMING!!!

358th Day

WHAT/WHERE IS YOUR MINDSET? ABOVE/BELOW? GODLY COUNSEL: SET YOUR MIND ON THINGS ABOVE!!!

It is no longer I that lives but Christ that lives in and through me! When I received Jesus Christ, I also died as He did so in Him I can live as He Lives. Jesus Christ is my life and when He is Revealed in Glory, my hope is that I will be also in Jesus' Name!!!

When we are in Christ, we ought no longer to be selfish; but to take an interest in one another's welfare genuinely! In so doing, we're looking out for the interests of Jesus Christ!!!

Contrary to common teachings, believers are to be like unto Christ in suffering the flesh as opposed to giving in to sin! We ought to arm ourselves with the Mind-set of Jesus Christ and live the rest of our lives not in fleshly lusts but for the Will of God! Can not God Help us in This regard? Yes, He Can!!!

Learn the truth of the Gospel and don't think your too young and don't give in to those who might despise your youthfulness! Teach/Preach the true Gospel based on the one Standard laid down for us in and through Christ Jesus!!!

Don't waste your time on useless unprofitable things; but rather on things from Above - pure, noble, true, just, lovely, good, excellent, virtuous, praiseworthy, of good report - dwell/meditate on such things and you will bode well and be even more Blessed!!!

359th Day

TRUSTWORTHY AND FAITHFUL IS HE WHO PROMISED NOT TO LEAVE/FORSAKE AND TO BLESS THOSE WHO LOVE AND OBEY HIS COMMANDMENTS!!!

Let us not shake (no shaking) in our faith/resolve to follow Jesus Christ as Lord, God and Saviour and in encouraging others through faith that works through love unto doing likewise!!!

As long as we remain faithful and love Him unto the end; even according to our calling for His purposes, God Works for our good! Without fear/favour; with God for us, who can stand against us successfully? No shaking!!!

Jesu ngbala Jesu nwosan ara ore e wa town oyin momo! Jesus Saves Jesus Heals folk friends come and taste beautiful honey! When Jesus Does His "thing" some think its magic impure untrue impossible! Apostle Peter here assures all listening of the authenticity of the miracle performed in the Name of the same Jesus that they crucified! Only Jesus can Save! Salvation is in no other name! Jesus Christ is the Lord of all, God Almighty!!!

The Lord is Holy and although very loving and compassionate, He Does punish sin. He is all Powerful, Knowing, Present, Compassionate/Kind but also all Consuming fire!!!

360th Day

BE VERY PATIENT AND DON'T STOP DOING GOOD EVEN IN THE FACE OF BLATANT INGRATITUDE AND PERSECUTION!!!

Do not be like those unbelievers who say there's no God/Heaven or that Jesus is not coming back again! Better be prepared in and out of season and wait very patiently; even as a farmer waits patiently for the harvest of crops planted!!!

You will meet with negativity whenever you're engaged in doing good! Don't give up! Make the most of every opportunity to do good; especially to members of the believers' family!!!

Trials and tribulation are not necessarily bad for you! The potentials are listed above! Pray for strength when going through such and God Will Send you Help because He is Faithful!!!

If you hate your brother you don't have Eternal life; you're a murderer! Hate never bears good fruits!!!

361st Day

ARE YOU GROWING SPIRITUALLY OR STATIC; CHECK YOURSELF! ARE YOU STILL IN THE FAITH? HMMMM!!!

Many keep going through the motions of their perception of the Christian Faith and remain static and if truth be told, uncomfortable; but they keep on with the same old routine! Check yourself! ARE you still in the faith? Many have derailed without knowing it and are following after teachings taught by demons and not what the forefathers in the faith left for us! Remember, the only thing that matters is faith that works through LOVE!!!

Forget/forsake what is past and move on towards the higher calling of God in Christ Jesus! This must be the mind-set of the believer who follows after perfection in Jesus Christ! If you're not yet there, God Will Help you; continue striving, prayerfully! Whatever you do, keep moving in Christ Jesus; do not be static! Watch and Pray!!!

There's godly reward for diligence in righteousness for the believer! The Lord Will Cause such a person to wax stronger and stronger in the faith in Jesus Christ! Lord, this is what I desire in my heart/soul/mind; Help me Lord to follow you faithfully in LOVE!!!

The believer's labour/strive is to keep hope alive in the Living God, Saviour of all men, especially of those who believe! Faith is a choice! Each man/woman has the choice to believe; and for your choice there is a price to pay and a just reward - read John 3 to gain a deeper understanding of this and take it very seriously!!!

Following the mindless butchering of a British Soldier a couple of days ago, This Scripture is very apt! Many are likewise being slaughtered by some of a particular faith (so they claim) relentlessly! These are unreasonable and wicked men and they have no faith at all! We all must remember this and continue to pray that we do not fall victims! As for the unfortunate ones who I believe will find Favour with God Almighty in Heaven, I pray for the repose of their souls and comfort for their loved ones. May God Bless us all in Jesus' Name. Amen!!!

362nd Day

LOVE IS LIGHT! LIVE IN LIGHT! LOVING INVESTS LIGHT AND THE PROFIT IS INCREASED LOVE/LIGHT! LOVE ONE ANOTHER!!!

Do you hate your brother? Repent or risk hell fire! It's a lot easier to love than to hate trust me! When you love your love gives light to the object of your love in their lives and your light increases inside of you too. The more love you give the more love you get from the SOURCE (Jesus Christ our Lord and God)!!!

Have you submitted to God to receive the Teaching on Love and how to Love? If you want to learn about Love in this way, you must submit your live to God in Jesus' Christ. Only Jesus Christ Teaches you how to love because Love Comes from Him and He is LOVE!!! Jesus Christ is the LOVE/LIGHT of all the earth! Satan NEVER does LOVE anyone! Satan only deceives with lust and fake love to draw you. Resist satan and he will flee! YOU must RESIST satan for him to flee from you!!!

These are some of the attributes of love; i.e. manifestations of love - how to show love to others (yourself first in this case because if you can't love yourself you can't love anybody)!!!

Stop wasting your life on irrelevant issues that yield nothing but sinfulness and godlessness; rather train yourself to be godly! Yes, godliness is not something you're born with! It is learned through rigorous training; refusing to pamper your ego; disciplining your self/your life! Spiritual exercise is prayerfully disciplining yourself, your body, your life in following after the Ways of God rigorously!!! It is a sacrificial thing to do and can be painful; however, it is very joyful and fruitful both for now and the life to come!!!

This is the origin of man! Forget all the nonsense science tries to teach you as well as the rubbish coming from the anti-Christ spirit-led teachings of the haters of anything Godly/Christly!!!

363rd Day

OBEDIENCE IS EVIDENCE OF LOVE FOR GOD (JESUS CHRIST) AND VERY PROFITALBE (YOU GET GOD'S, JESUS' LOVE, REVELATION OF JESUS AND MUCH MORE!!!

The summary of God's Commandments is to LOVE; first God and then your neighbor as yourself! However, make no mistake about it; God's Love Came to us first before ours towards Him! Our love for God is not by mouth (confession) alone at all; it's got to be proved by our obedience to His Word (not just by hearing but doing)!!!

This prayer is very specific and focused, directed at the faithful believer I'm sure! For God to comfort and strengthen our hearts in every good work/word! Hmmm! So, I imagine that God will not do likewise for our every bad work/word (sin)!!!

Is it not worth studying the "things" Paul the Apostle referred to above? I say yes! I want to be a good minister of Jesus Christ and show that I've been brought up in the truths of the faith and good teaching that I have followed! I do not want to run my race in vain as many are bound to do when care is not taken in walking This faith! May God Help us all in Jesus' Name! The Word of God is not a joke at all!!!

The Day of the Lord is Coming like a thief in the night! It will not be a pleasant day at all; so, be very careful and prepared in and out of season! Jesus Christ is Coming back to judge this sinful world! If you're caught off guard napping you're finished, history! May God Help us to be ready for that day in Jesus' Name. Amen!!!

364th Day

ARE YOU REDEEMED? DO YOU WANT TO BE REDEEMED? ONLY JESUS CHRIST CAN SAVE/REDEEM; COME RUNNING; COME NOW!!!

Prophetically spoken was the word and it came to pass that Jesus Came and indeed is Savior Lord, King! Halleluiah! Amen! Glory!!!

Make no mistakes about it; Jesus Came with forgiveness of sins and justification by faith in Him from things the law of Moses could not justify one from. This Jesus is different o! I want Him. I want Jesus!!!

Man has only one life and after death to face judgment; regardless of whatever anyone else says, God's Word is Supreme (tried and tested)! He's Coming back again. Get ready in Jesus' Name!!!

Who keeps This word today eh? We prefer demonic teachings that allow us to do whatever we please; This is to our shame and our own peril! Be wise! Trust in the Word of the Living God!!!

Who is clean? Let him who has no sin cast the first stone! Hmmm! Only the fear of God can remedy our situation. Yet, humans don't want to hear it seems! Arise o servants of the Living God; do the Lord's bidding in Jesus' Name!!!

365th Day

JESUS CHRIST IS COMING BACK AGAIN WHETHER THE WORLD LIKES/BELIEVES IT OR NOT; JESUS CHRIST IS COMING BACK!!!

All Heavens declare the Glory of the Risen, Living Lord, God! Who can compare with the Beauty of the Lord? Forever He Will be the Lamb upon the Throne! I'll gladly bow my knees and worship You O Lord! His Awe will come upon all! The fear of God will descend on all! Everyone will behold His Glory including those who pierced Him and those who forced a crown of thorns on His Head!!!

All the ends of the world shall remember and turn unto the LORD: and all the kindred of the nations shall worship before thee.

Every knee shall bow and every tongue confess that Jesus Christ is the Lord God Almighty to God's Glory! The Kingdom, Power and Glory are His! OGA PATAPATA (Supreme Head)! He is the GOVERNOR! JESUS CHRIST is the true ONE and ONLY OGA AT THE (VERY) TOP!!!

Prophetically, the advent of Jesus Christ was proclaimed from of old and it came to pass! Good Lord! The Word of God is REAL and LIVE! Jesus Christ came, He was crucified, died, buried. He Rose again and now He Lives forevermore! Glory! Halleluiah!! Thank You Jesus for Your Holy Sacrifice that I may live!!! I stand in awe of You!!!

Are we not now in those later days? Once again as before and as always the Word of God that never fails is unfolding right before our very eyes and yet many deny the obvious! Is there not a faith movement that forbids people from marrying and abstaining from various foods? Hmmm! I will never doubt the Supremacy of the Word of God! God Exalted His Word even above His Name!!!

366th Day

If we are justified at all, it is by faith; then the peace of God comes upon us ONLY through our Lord Jesus Christ. Through Him we have access by faith into the Grace wherein we stand, rejoicing in our hope of God's Glory! Christ in me the hope and expectation of Glory! Oh Glory! Halleluiah!! Thank You Jesus for saving me!!!

ABRIDGEMENT

Pleasing god provokes his love/blessings; the love and blessing of god is not unconditional; do not be deceived!!!

Dear friends, if our hearts do not condemn us, we have confidence before God and receive from him anything we ask, because we obey his commands and do what pleases him. When we do God's Will and please Him, even our hearts will not be under condemnation; nor will our hearts condemn us! The goal of our faith is love. This is the ultimate Command building upon loving the Lord our God with all our hearts/minds/strengths in Jesus' Name!!!

Our ambitions as believers must be how to please our Commanding Officer (Jesus Christ) and the Field Marshall of the Armies of God in Heaven! The Alpha and Omega! Judge of all the earth; before whom we shall/must all appear for judgment! He Will Judge justly!!!

Self-commendation/approval does not confirm approval by any means and essentially means absolutely nothing to God! But who God Commends is he/she that stands approved by God Almighty! YOU stand in good stead not running away or fighting for yourself when suffering unjustly; rather when you endure, mindful of God! This is our Calling in following after Jesus Christ's example!!!

Love is holy and love loves the enemy too! Doing good to those who hate you and showing them love provokes God's Love and Blessings increasingly! Believers must put this to practice as much as it's within your power so to do! This moves you on towards perfection. Be ye perfect even as your Father in Heaven is perfect; likewise, be ye holy as He Is Holy! Very difficult! However, with God all things are possible!!!

Jesus power; super power! Jesus power super power!!! Faith that works through love is all that matters!!!

The Power of Jesus Christ and in His Word is here exemplified as well as the simple (but great) faith of the centurion! Read this, meditate prayerfully on it in Jesus' Name and listen for the Voice of the Holy Spirit... He Will Minister to your heart in Jesus' Name! If we have faith as small as a mustard seed, we shall say to this mountain be removed into the sea and it will obey is what the Bible says! Also, that if we cannot believe as a little child, there's no place for us in the Kingdom of Heaven! Is anybody listening? Also, those who belong to the Kingdom; some of them will be removed and replaced with people from the outside! May that not be my portion in Jesus' Name. Amen!!! Me I just prayed for myself; to each his/her own; up to you now o!!!

Faithful reliable deliverer of the children of israel!!! Come on! Why wait! Be grafted in! Come on board!!!

Are you in need, afflicted, weak, oppressed, suffering injustices etc.? There is a God Who Delivered Israel from all their woes Reaching out to you right now! Will you come to Him? Will you submit to Him? Forsake your old ways of sin and worldliness and come... He Will Deliver you even from death, in Jesus' Name! Come right now; come running!!!

Jesus said if you love Him you will obey His Commands and then He and the Father will come and make their home with you! Also, the Bible says they that trust in the Lord shall be as mount Zion that cannot be shaken but stands firm forever! God chose Zion! When you choose to show love to God proven by your obedience to His Word you become as mount Zion and will become His habitation! What a Great God we have!!! What are you waiting for? I have a great heritage by following Jesus!!!

If you say you're in Jesus Christ; born again, sold unto Him, then you must forsake your love of/for the world and seek after a new focus i.e. things above! YOU must put to death by submission to the Holy Spirit earthly passions and sinful ways which are idolatry! Give them up now! Tomorrow may just be too late!!!

THE LIGHT EXPOSES THE TRUTH - Satan hates to be exposed is why when evil happens the perpetrator goes to great lengths to scare the victim into not telling using same old strategies... "I will kill" you if you tell anybody... this is where the Spirit of Counsel is most important in dealing with life's issues... many evils meted out to us are kept in the dark secret recesses of our hearts!

Hmmm... with grievous consequences. Victims or people suffering from all sorts of secret need to open up and speak up... choose a trustworthy Godly vessel to make confessions to as today the days are evil. I've counseled with many people and know that lots of people are suffering needlessly!! Get help now!! Don't be ashamed or afraid or shy... I'm available (at least I volunteer to help) and I know that The Spirit of the Sovereign Lord is upon me as well as the Spirit of Counsel!!! Shalom!!!

Some useful information about the author, prophet and evangelist folayan osekita and his ministry, windows of heaven revival outreach (international)!!!

Tune in to Windows Of Heaven Radio HYPERLINK "http://www.windowsofheaven.caster.fm" www.windowsofheaven.caster.fm; just click on the white hand sign to vote for it, then like it, rate it & be Blessed by it & spread it all around! It's a life-changing experience!

Visit our Facebook page https://www.facebook.com/windowsofheaven outreach and "like" it

Kindly visit our tweeter account on: https://tweeter.com/osekita

Kindly visit/register on our website; leave prayer requests, testimonies, comments etc. & join/make use of our forum 4 all ur needs.

http://www.windowsofheaven.co.uk/

https://www.facebook.com/photo.php?fbid=10150665719244856&amp%3Bamp%3Bset=a.70720329855.76457.723369855&amp%3Bamp%3Btype=1&amp%3Bamp%3Btheater&amp%3Bamp%3Bnotif_t=photo_comment Twitter handle: @osekita

Help spread the word around all over! HYPERLINK "http://www.folayanosekita.com" www.folayanosekita.com Dare to be different! Go for the book: "The Flaming Sword" by Folayan Osekita - http://bookstore.trafford.com/Products/SKU- 000136919/The-Flaming-Sword.aspx …; http://www.amazon.co.uk/Flaming-Sword-Folayan-…/…/1426933665 …; http://www.scribd.com/doc/32311314/The-Flaming-Sword … get a copy!!!